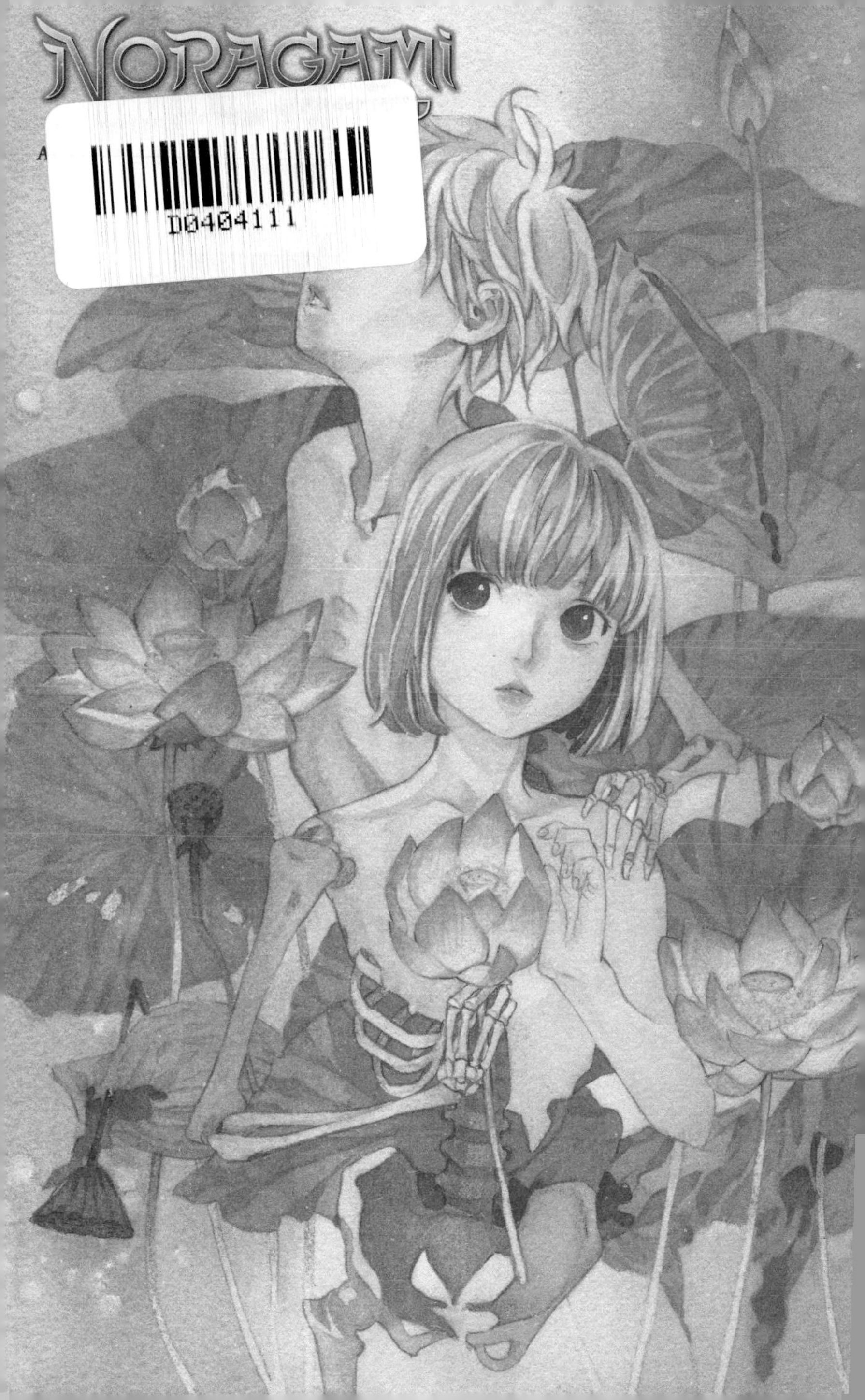
NORAGAMI

characters

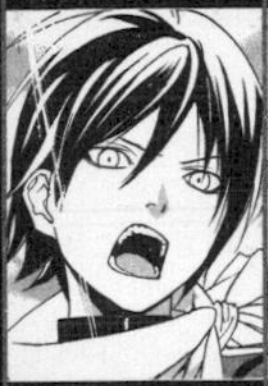

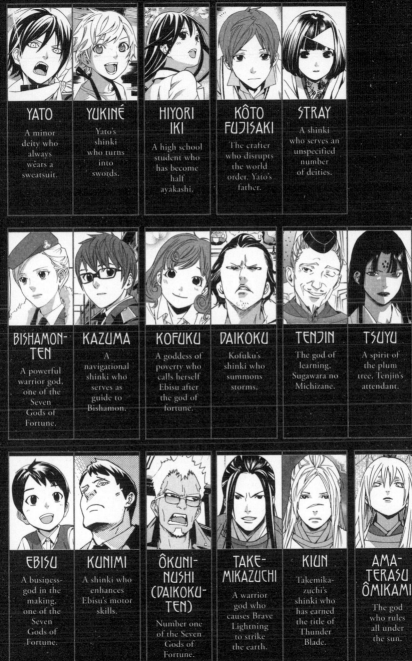

YATO

A minor deity who always wears a sweatsuit.

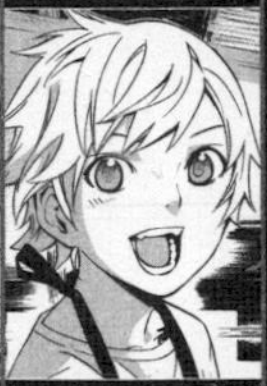

YUKINÉ

Yato's shinki who turns into swords.

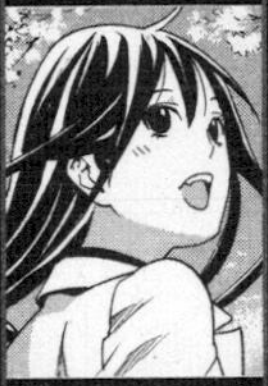

HIYORI IKI

A high school student who has become half ayakashi.

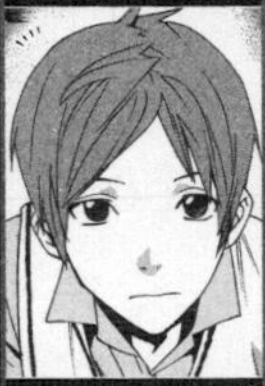

KÔTO FUJISAKI

The crafter who disrupts the world order. Yato's father.

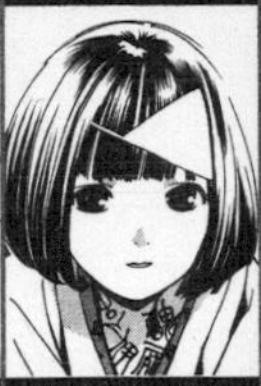

STRAY

A shinki who serves an unspecified number of deities.

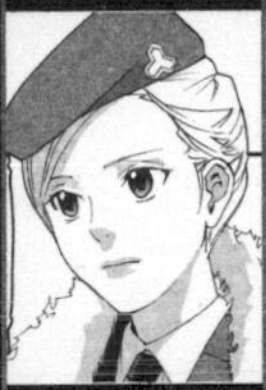

BISHAMON-TEN

A powerful warrior god, one of the Seven Gods of Fortune.

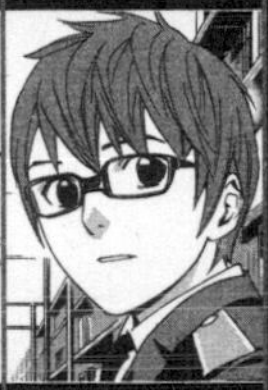

KAZUMA

A navigational shinki who serves as guide to Bishamon.

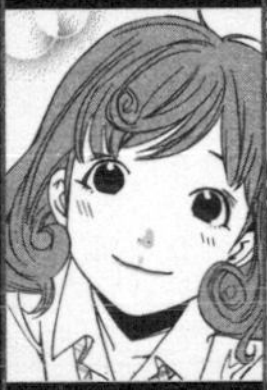

KOFUKU

A goddess of poverty who calls herself Ebisu after the god of fortune.

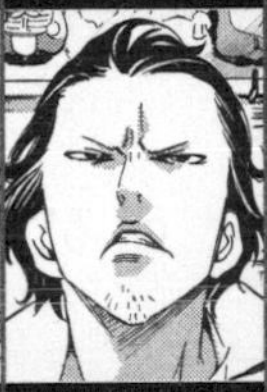

DAIKOKU

Kofuku's shinki who summons storms.

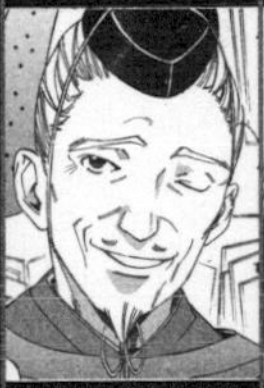

TENJIN

The god of learning, Sugawara no Michizane.

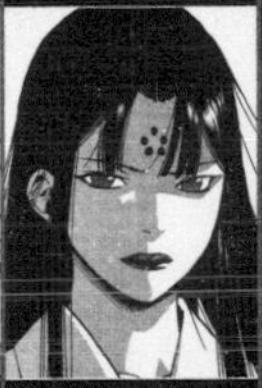

TSUYU

A spirit of the plum tree, Tenjin's attendant.

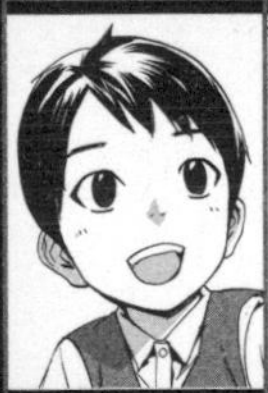

EBISU

A business-god in the making, one of the Seven Gods of Fortune.

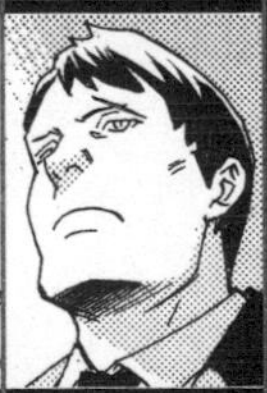

KUNIMI

A shinki who enhances Ebisu's motor skills.

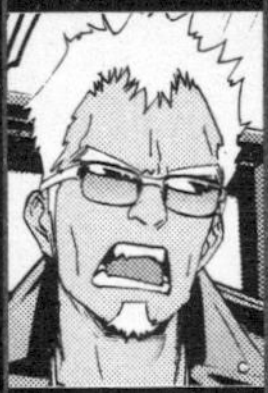

ÔKUNI-NUSHI (DAIKOKU-TEN)

Number one of the Seven Gods of Fortune.

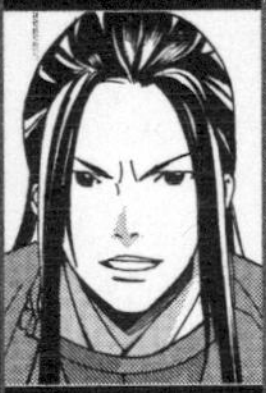

TAKE-MIKAZUCHI

A warrior god who causes Brave Lightning to strike the earth.

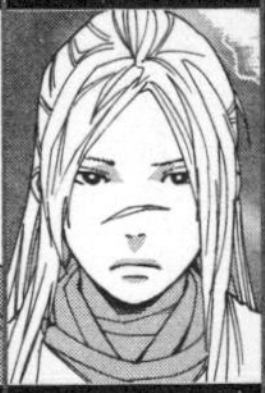

KIUN

Takemika-zuchi's shinki who has earned the title of Thunder Blade.

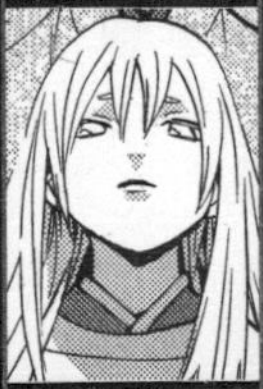

AMA-TERASU ÔMIKAMI

The god who rules all under the sun.

野

[illegible]

[illegible]

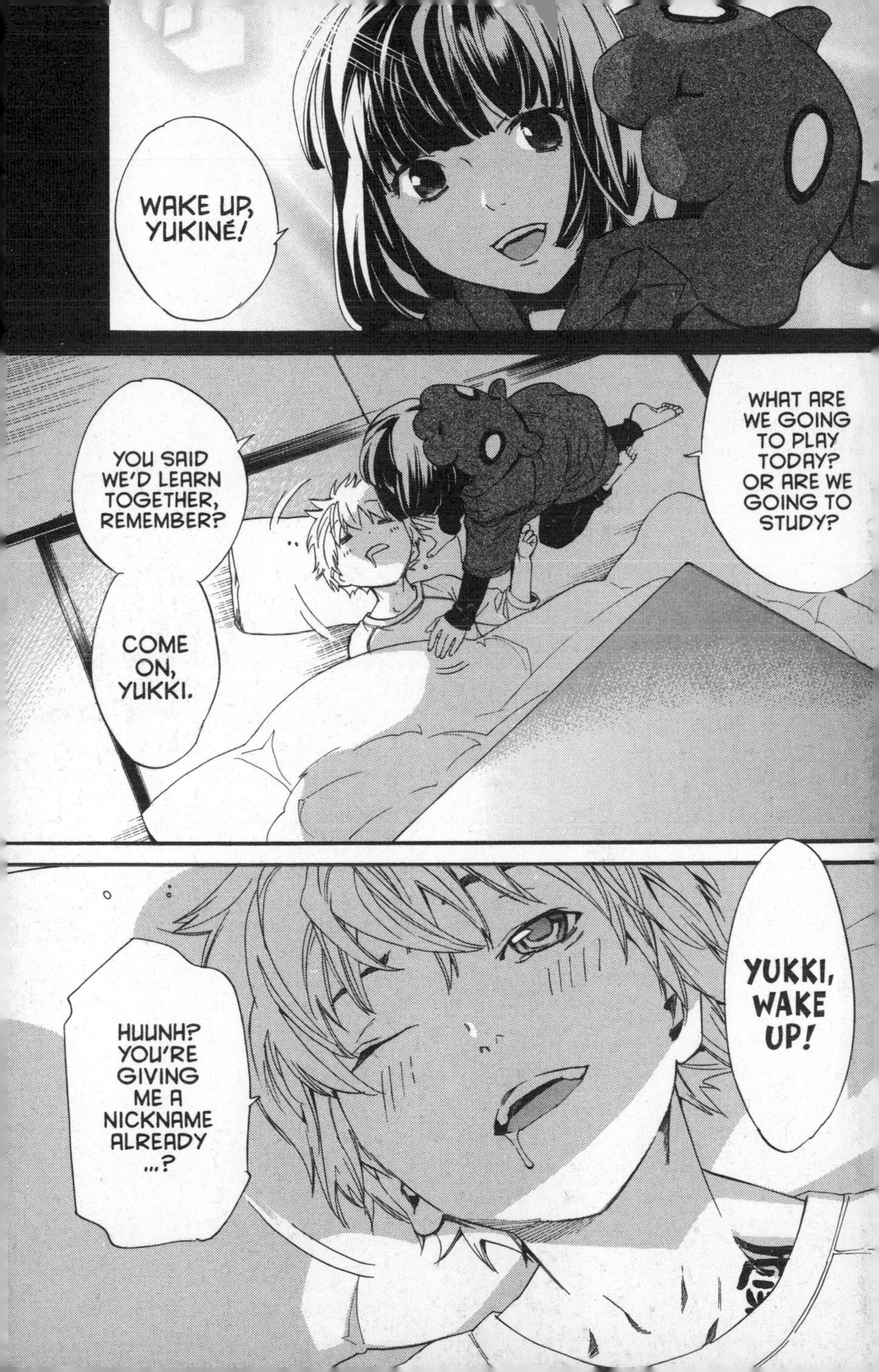
WAKE UP, YUKINÉ!
WHAT ARE WE GOING TO PLAY TODAY? OR ARE WE GOING TO STUDY?
YOU SAID WE'D LEARN TOGETHER, REMEMBER?
COME ON, YUKKI.
YUKKI, WAKE UP!
HUUNH? YOU'RE GIVING ME A NICKNAME ALREADY ...?

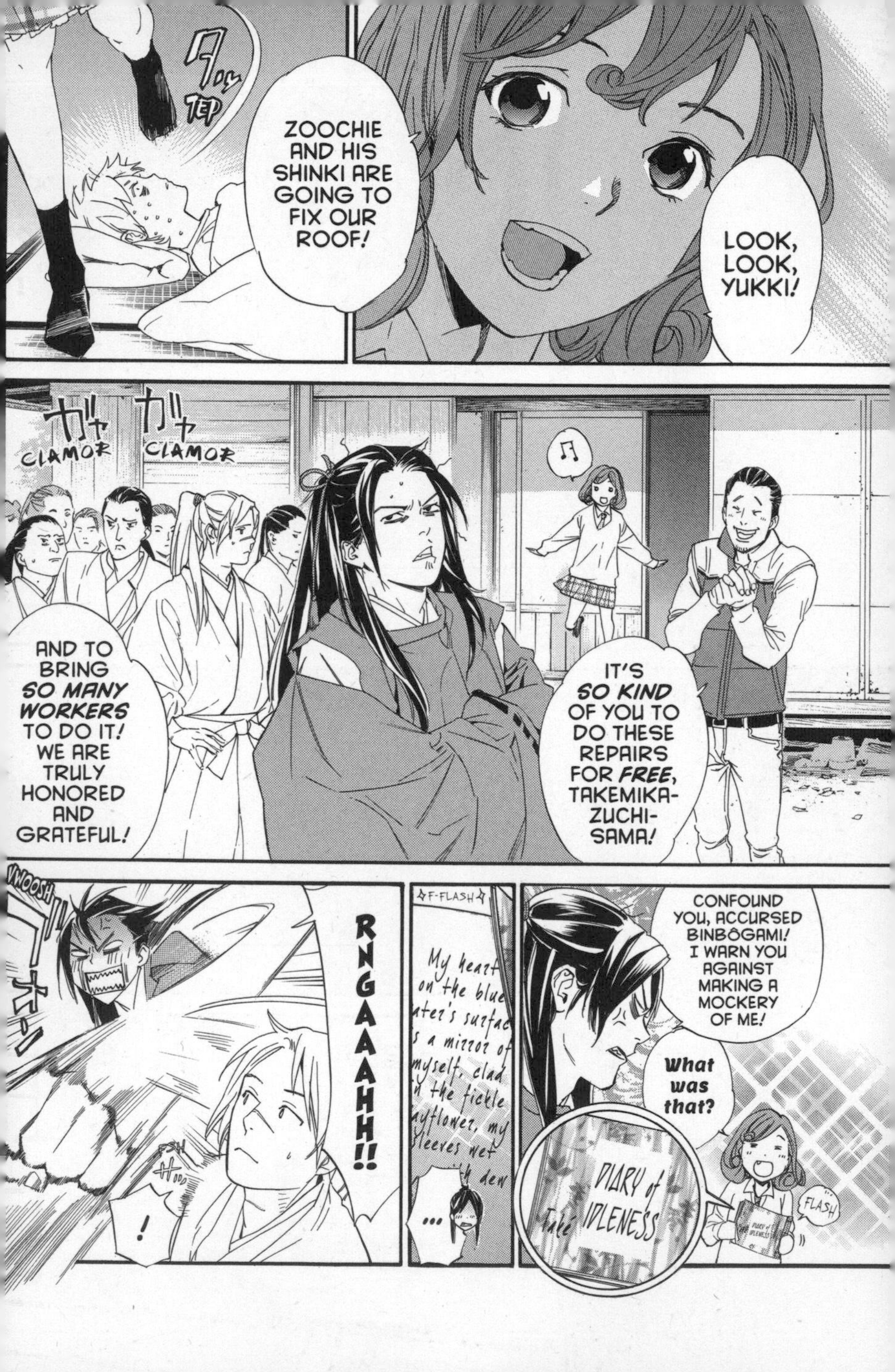
LOOK, LOOK, YUKKI!
ZOOCHIE AND HIS SHINKI ARE GOING TO FIX OUR ROOF!
TEP
♫
IT'S **SO KIND** OF YOU TO DO THESE REPAIRS FOR ***FREE***, TAKEMIKAZUCHI-SAMA!
AND TO BRING ***SO MANY WORKERS*** TO DO IT! WE ARE TRULY HONORED AND GRATEFUL!
CLAMOR CLAMOR
CONFOUND YOU, ACCURSED BINBÔGAMI! I WARN YOU AGAINST MAKING A MOCKERY OF ME!
What was that?
DIARY of IDLENESS
FLASH
F-FLASH
My heart on the blue ater's surfac s a mirror of myself, clad n the fickle ayflower, my sleeves wet dew
...
RNGAAAAHH!!
VWOOSH
!

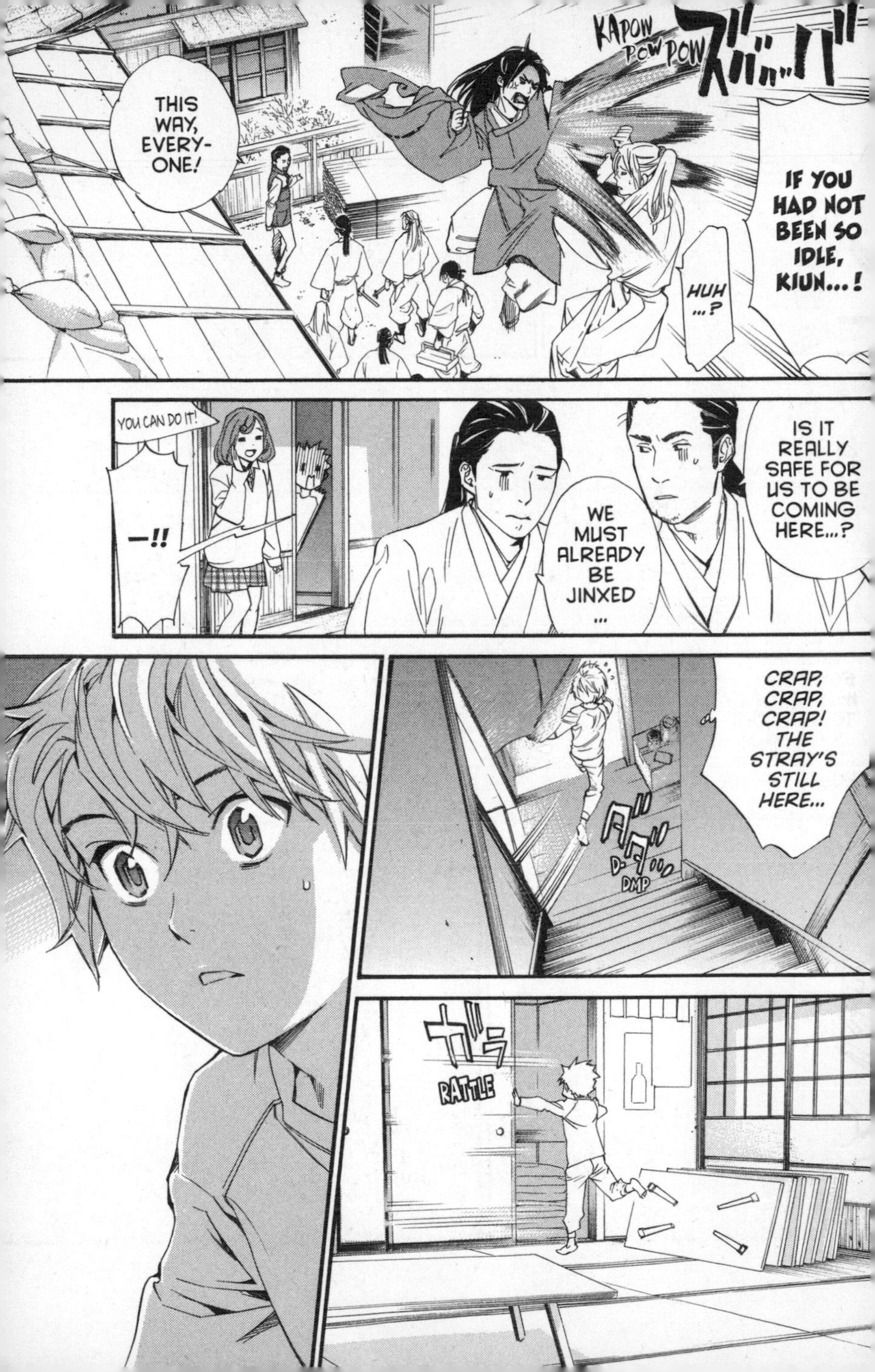
KAPOW POW POW
IF YOU HAD NOT BEEN SO IDLE, KIUN...!
HUH ...?
THIS WAY, EVERY-ONE!
IS IT REALLY SAFE FOR US TO BE COMING HERE...?
WE MUST ALREADY BE JINXED ...
YOU CAN DO IT!
—!!
CRAP, CRAP, CRAP! THE STRAY'S STILL HERE...
D-DMP
RATTLE

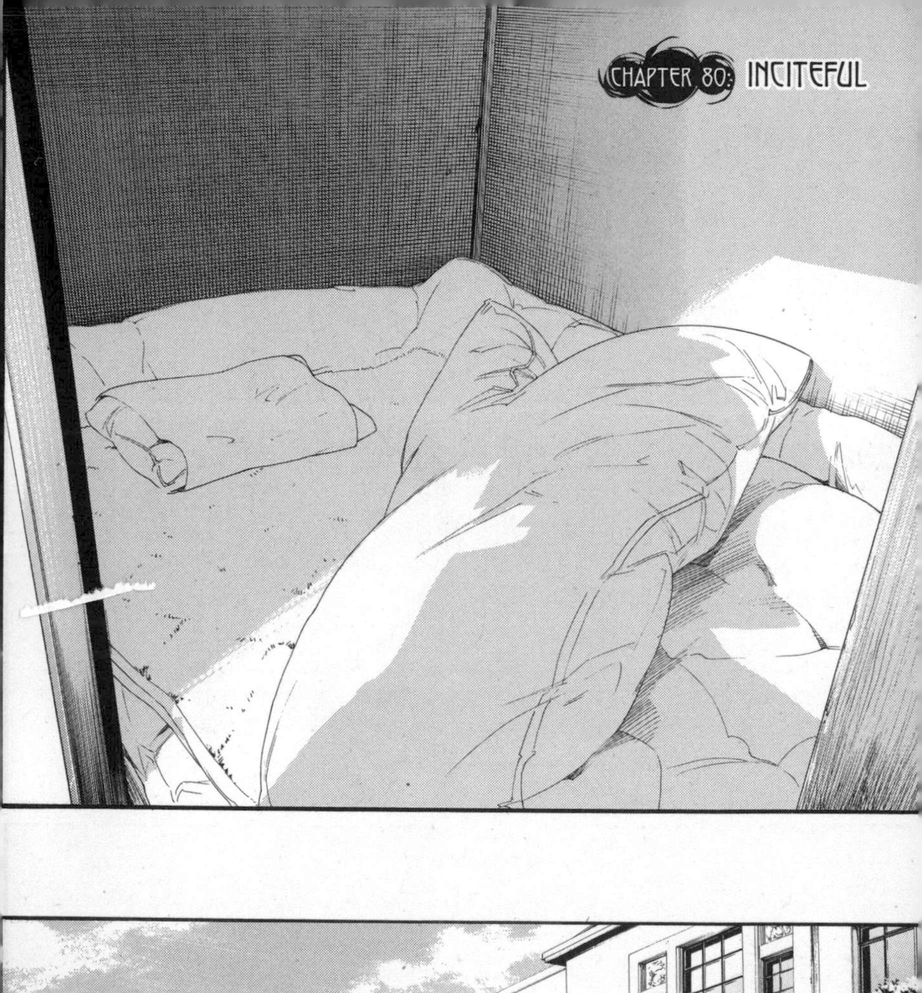
CHAPTER 80: INCITEFUL

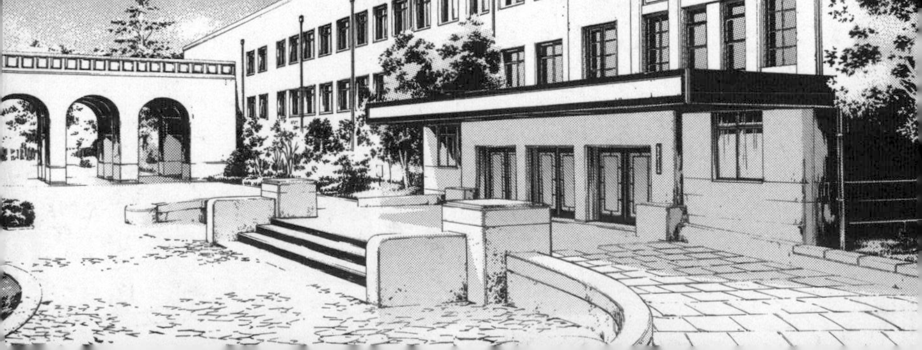

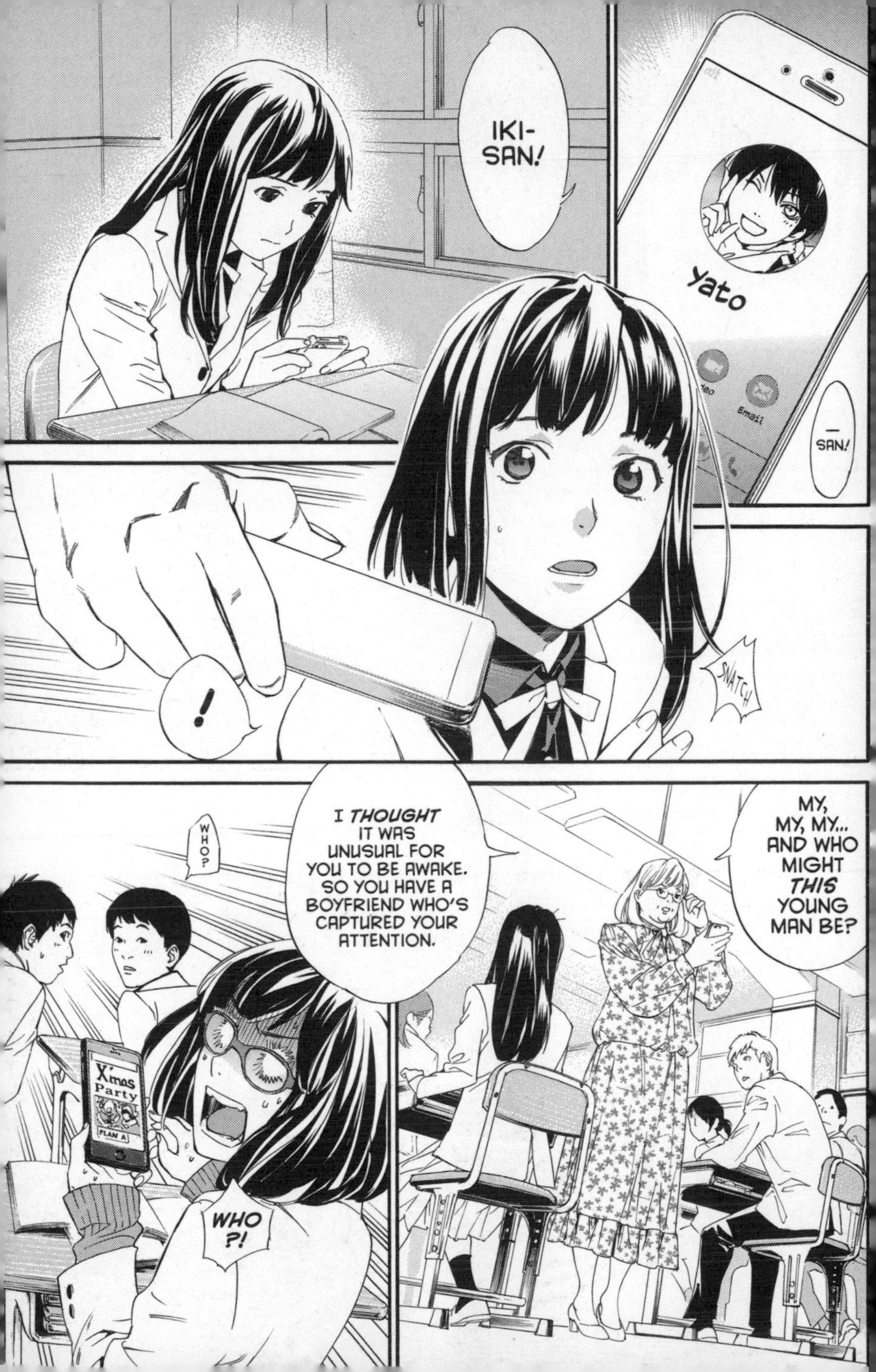
Yato
Email
—SAN!
IKI-SAN!
SNATCH
!
MY, MY, MY... AND WHO MIGHT *THIS* YOUNG MAN BE?
I *THOUGHT* IT WAS UNUSUAL FOR YOU TO BE AWAKE. SO YOU HAVE A BOYFRIEND WHO'S CAPTURED YOUR ATTENTION.
WHO?
X'mas Party
PLAN A
WHO?!

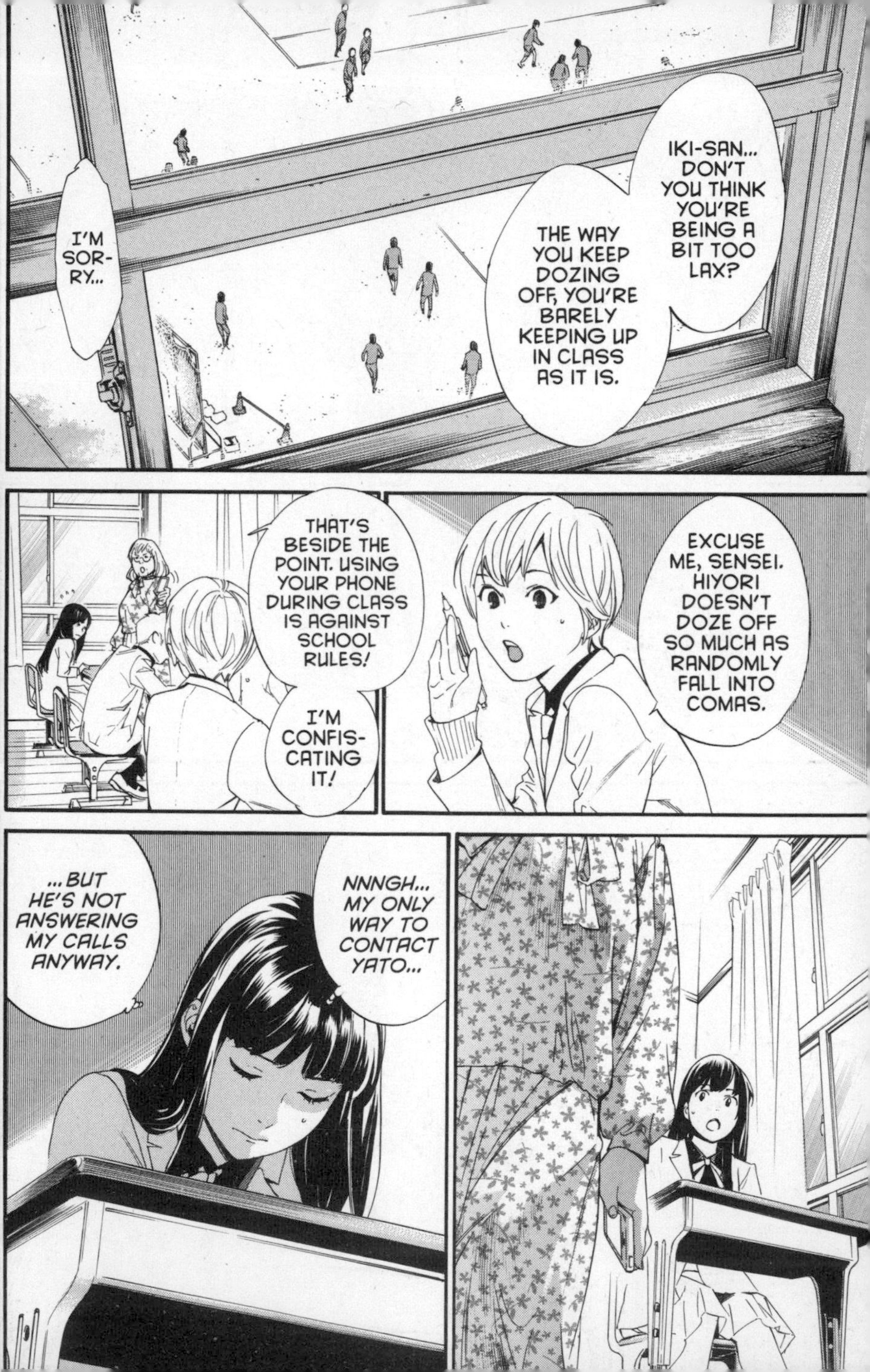
IKI-SAN... DON'T YOU THINK YOU'RE BEING A BIT TOO LAX?
THE WAY YOU KEEP DOZING OFF, YOU'RE BARELY KEEPING UP IN CLASS AS IT IS.
I'M SOR-RY...
EXCUSE ME, SENSEI. HIYORI DOESN'T DOZE OFF SO MUCH AS RANDOMLY FALL INTO COMAS.
THAT'S BESIDE THE POINT. USING YOUR PHONE DURING CLASS IS AGAINST SCHOOL RULES!
I'M CONFIS-CATING IT!
NNNGH... MY ONLY WAY TO CONTACT YATO...
...BUT HE'S NOT ANSWERING MY CALLS ANYWAY.

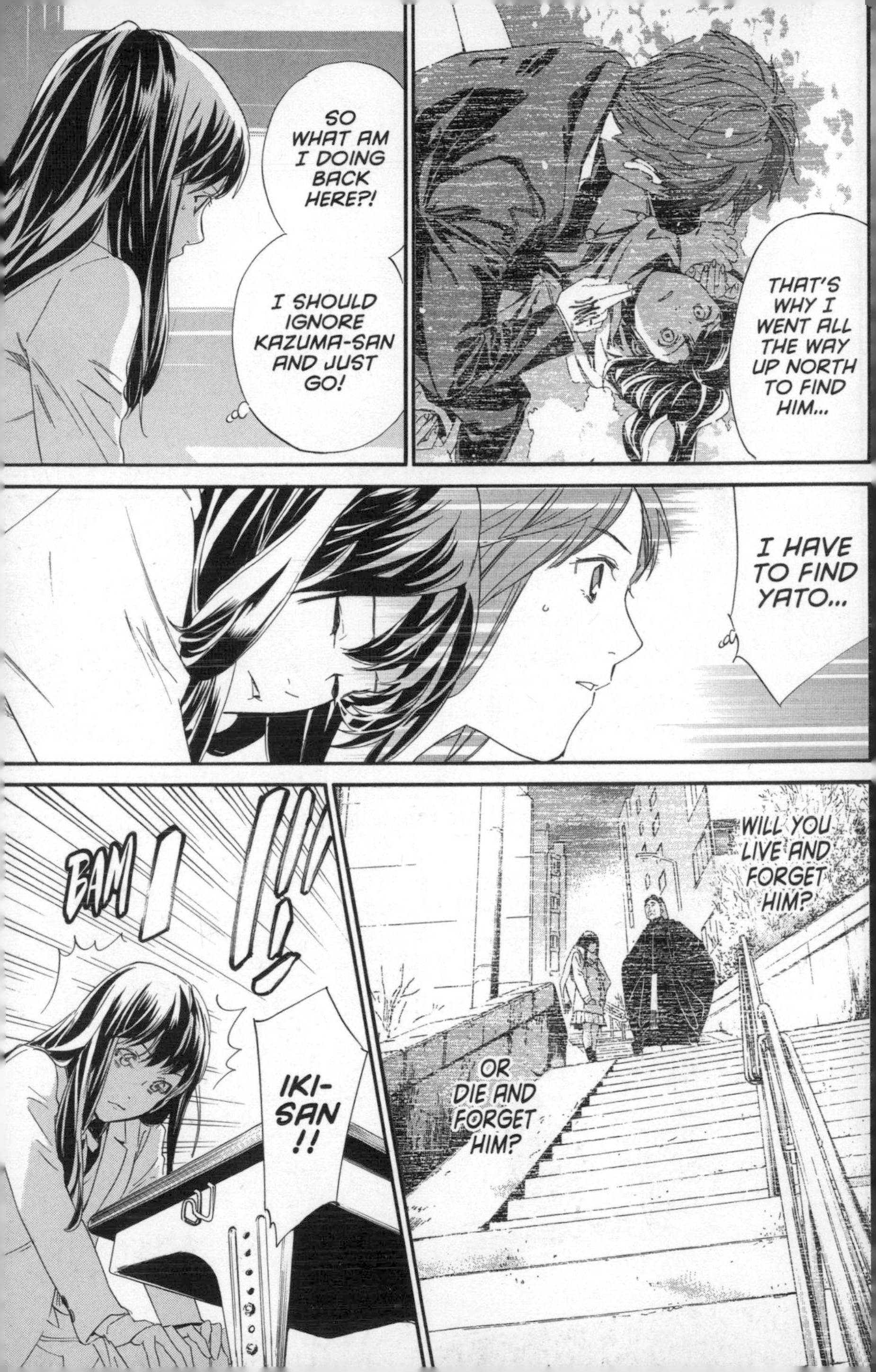
THAT'S WHY I WENT ALL THE WAY UP NORTH TO FIND HIM...
SO WHAT AM I DOING BACK HERE?!
I SHOULD IGNORE KAZUMA-SAN AND JUST GO!
I HAVE TO FIND YATO...
WILL YOU LIVE AND FORGET HIM?
OR DIE AND FORGET HIM?
BAM
!!
IKI-SAN!!

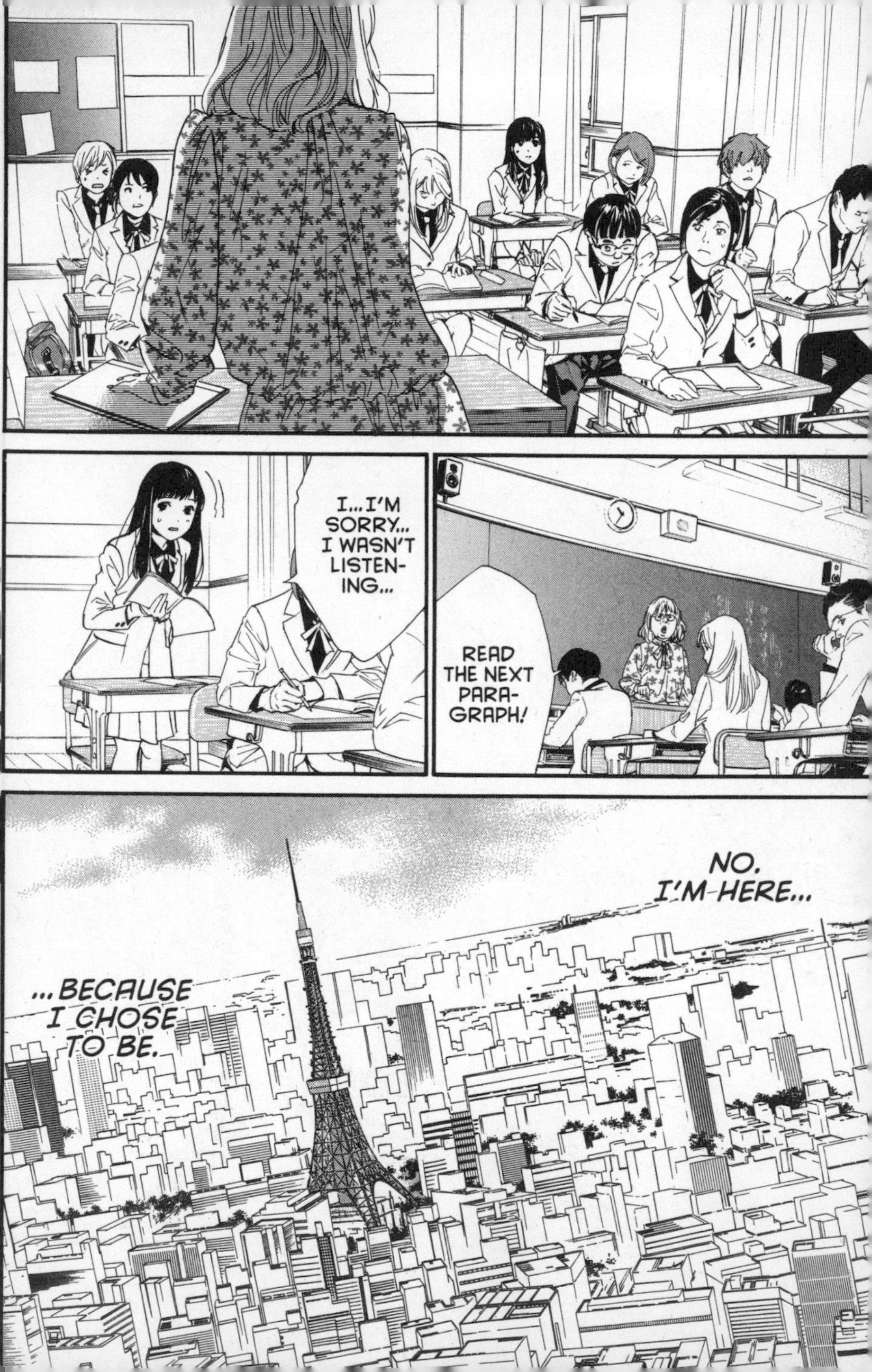
READ THE NEXT PARA-GRAPH!
I...I'M SORRY... I WASN'T LISTEN-ING...
NO. I'M HERE...
...BECAUSE I CHOSE TO BE.

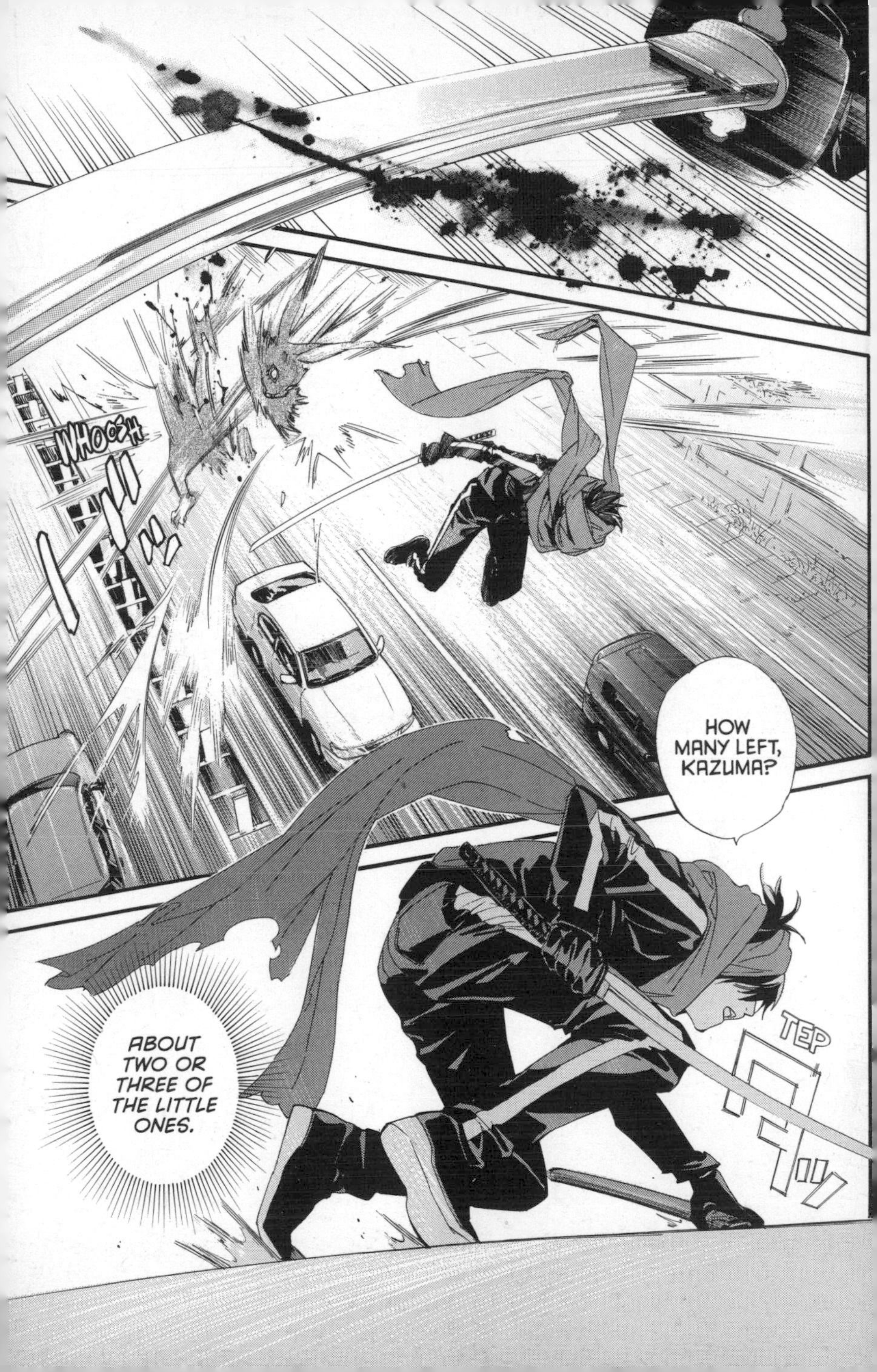
WHOOSH
HOW MANY LEFT, KAZUMA?
TEP
ABOUT TWO OR THREE OF THE LITTLE ONES.

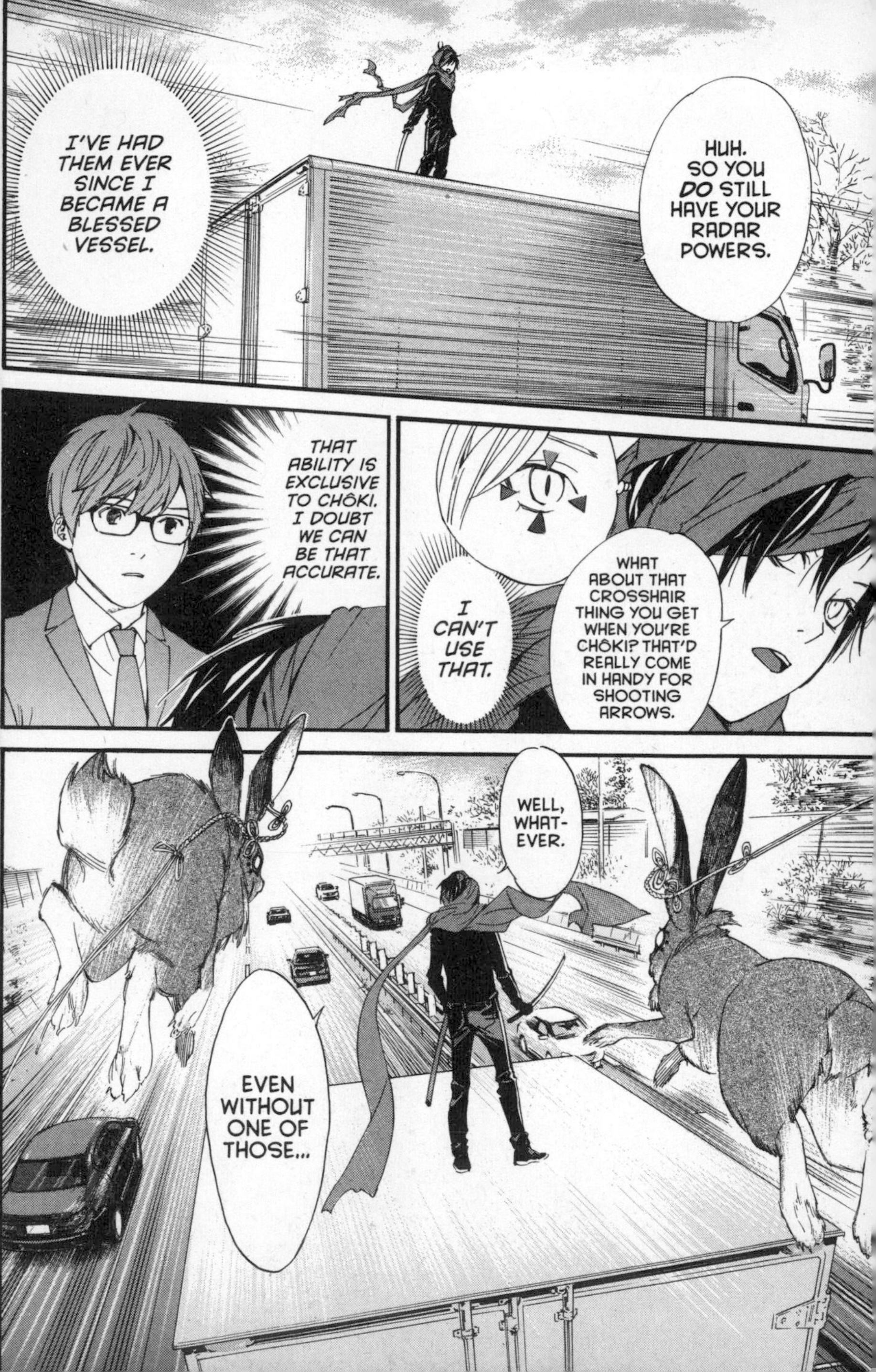
HUH. SO YOU DO STILL HAVE YOUR RADAR POWERS.
I'VE HAD THEM EVER SINCE I BECAME A BLESSED VESSEL.
WHAT ABOUT THAT CROSSHAIR THING YOU GET WHEN YOU'RE CHÔKI? THAT'D REALLY COME IN HANDY FOR SHOOTING ARROWS.
I CAN'T USE THAT.
THAT ABILITY IS EXCLUSIVE TO CHÔKI. I DOUBT WE CAN BE THAT ACCURATE.
WELL, WHAT-EVER.
EVEN WITHOUT ONE OF THOSE...

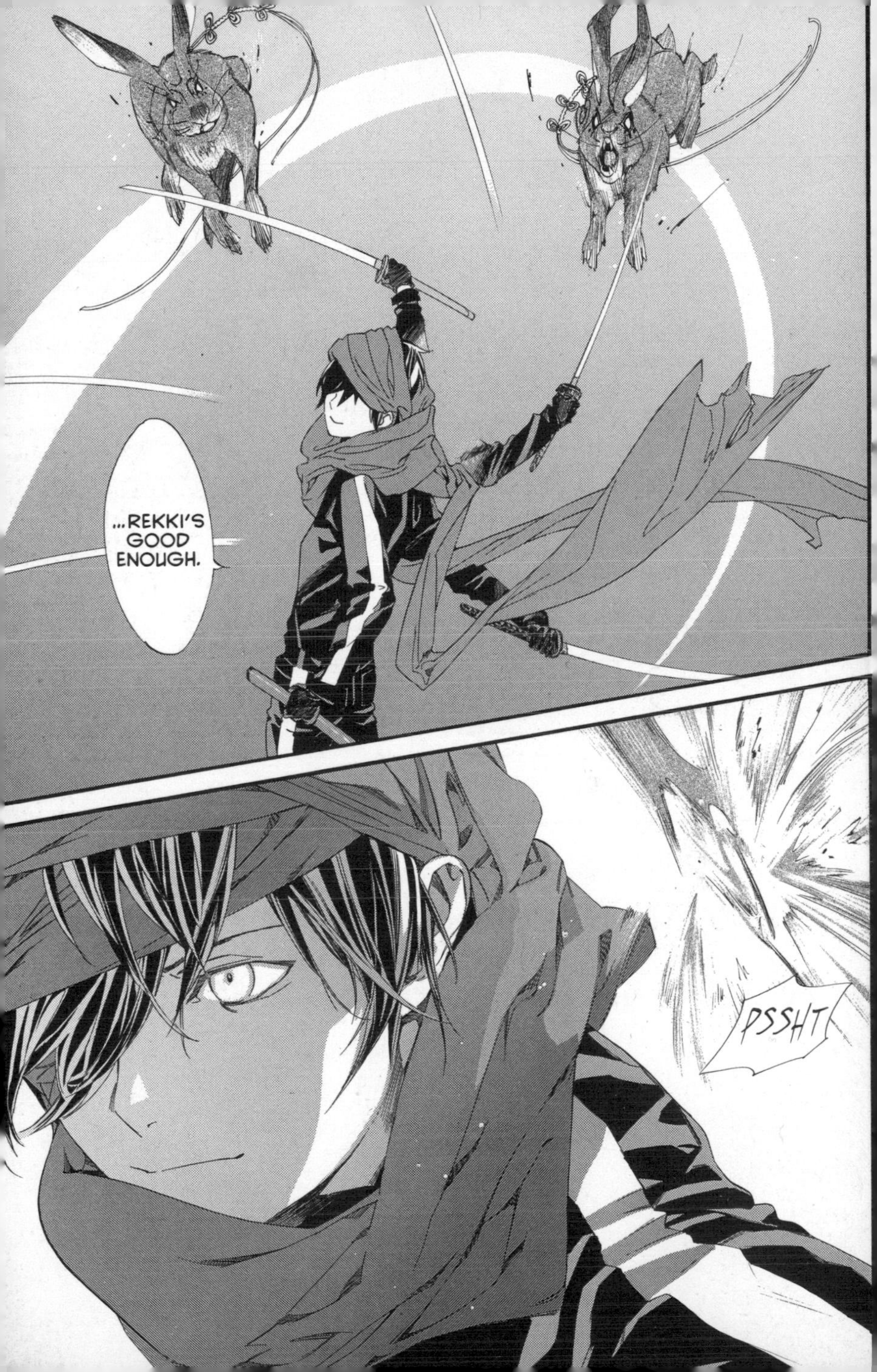
...REKKI'S GOOD ENOUGH.
PSSHT

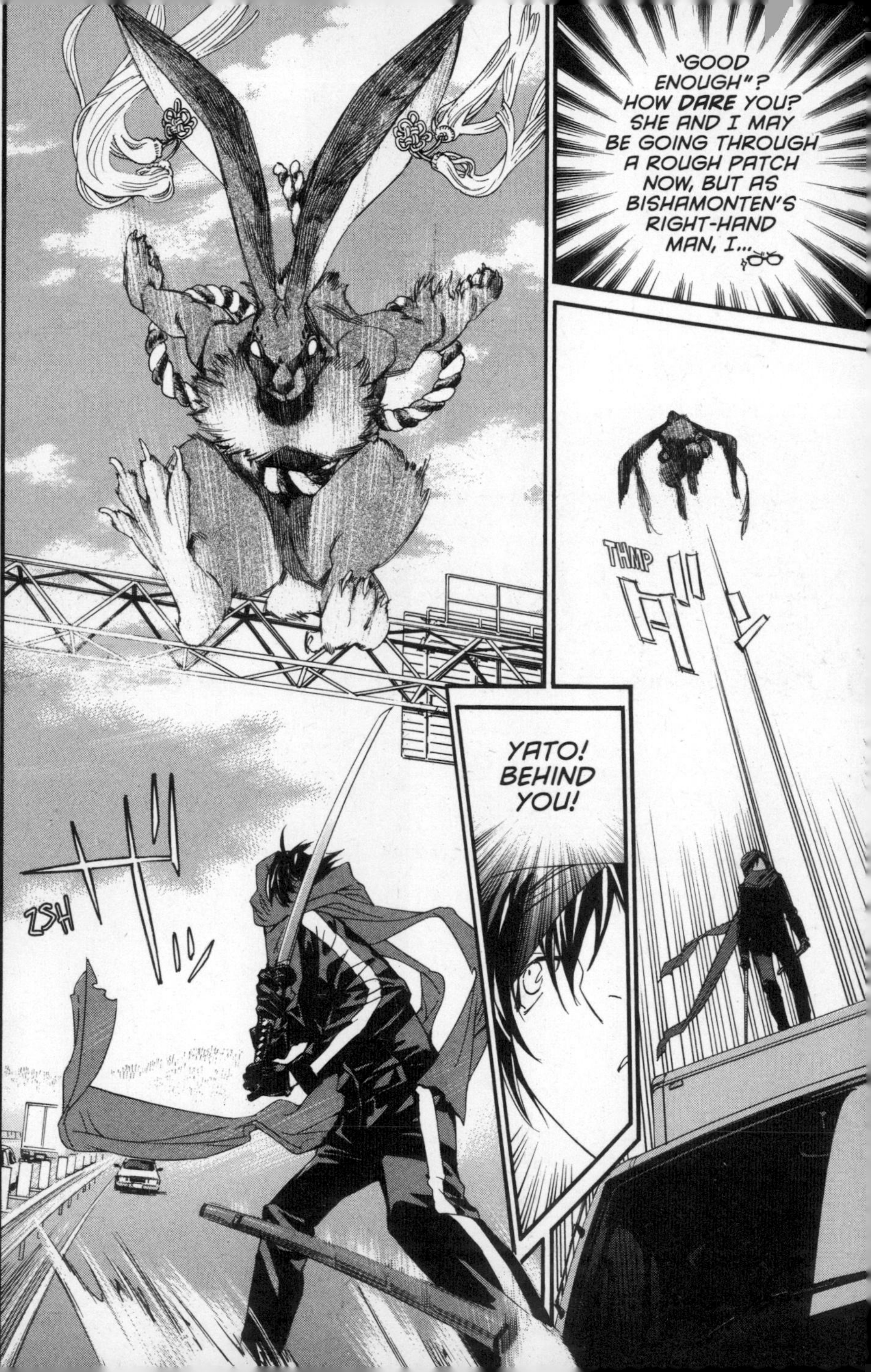
"GOOD ENOUGH"? HOW DARE YOU? SHE AND I MAY BE GOING THROUGH A ROUGH PATCH NOW, BUT AS BISHAMONTEN'S RIGHT-HAND MAN, I...
THMP
YATO! BEHIND YOU!
ZSH

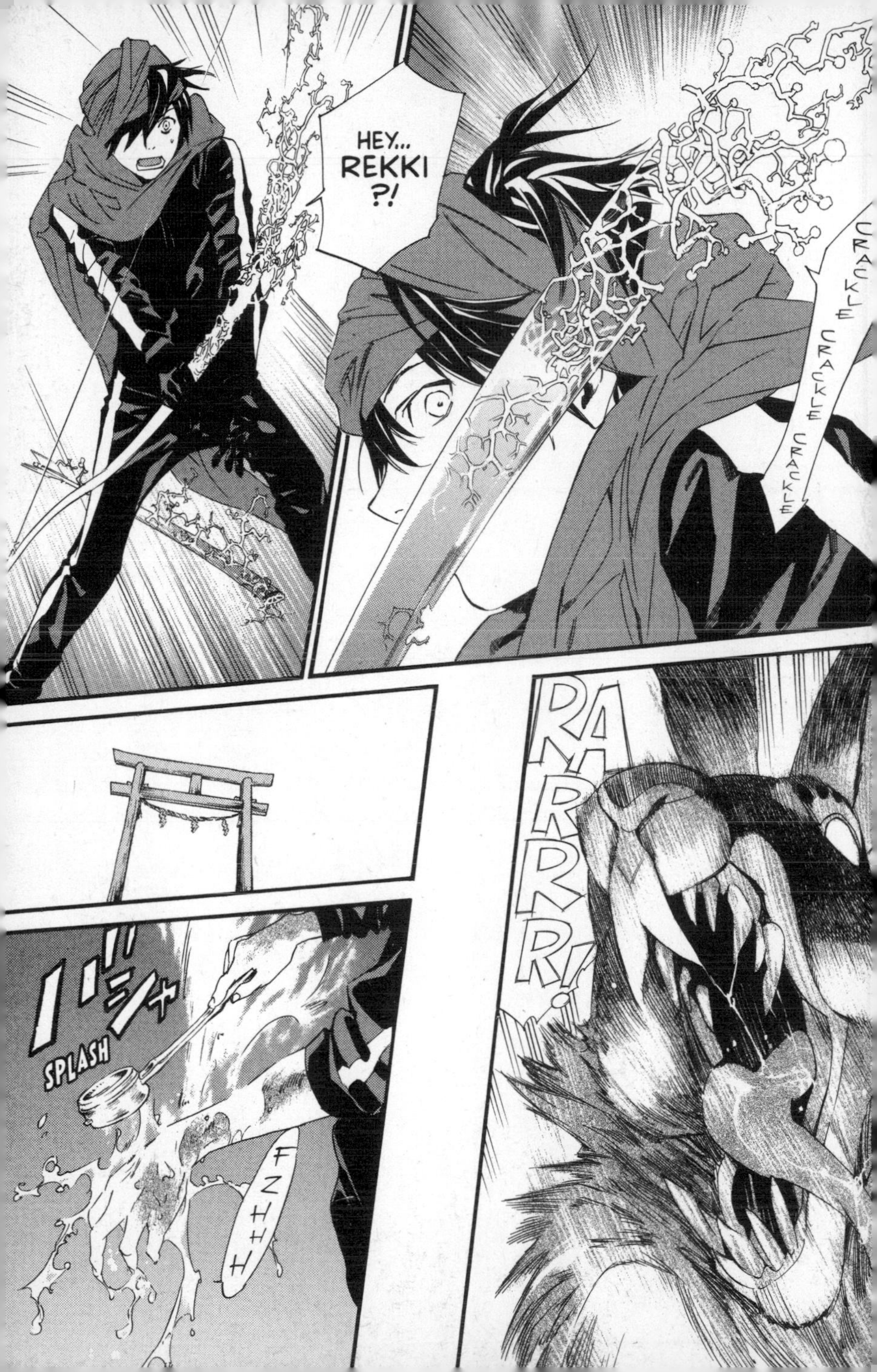
CRACKLE CRACKLE CRACKLE CRACKLE
HEY... REKKI ?!
RARRRR!
SPLASH
FZHHH

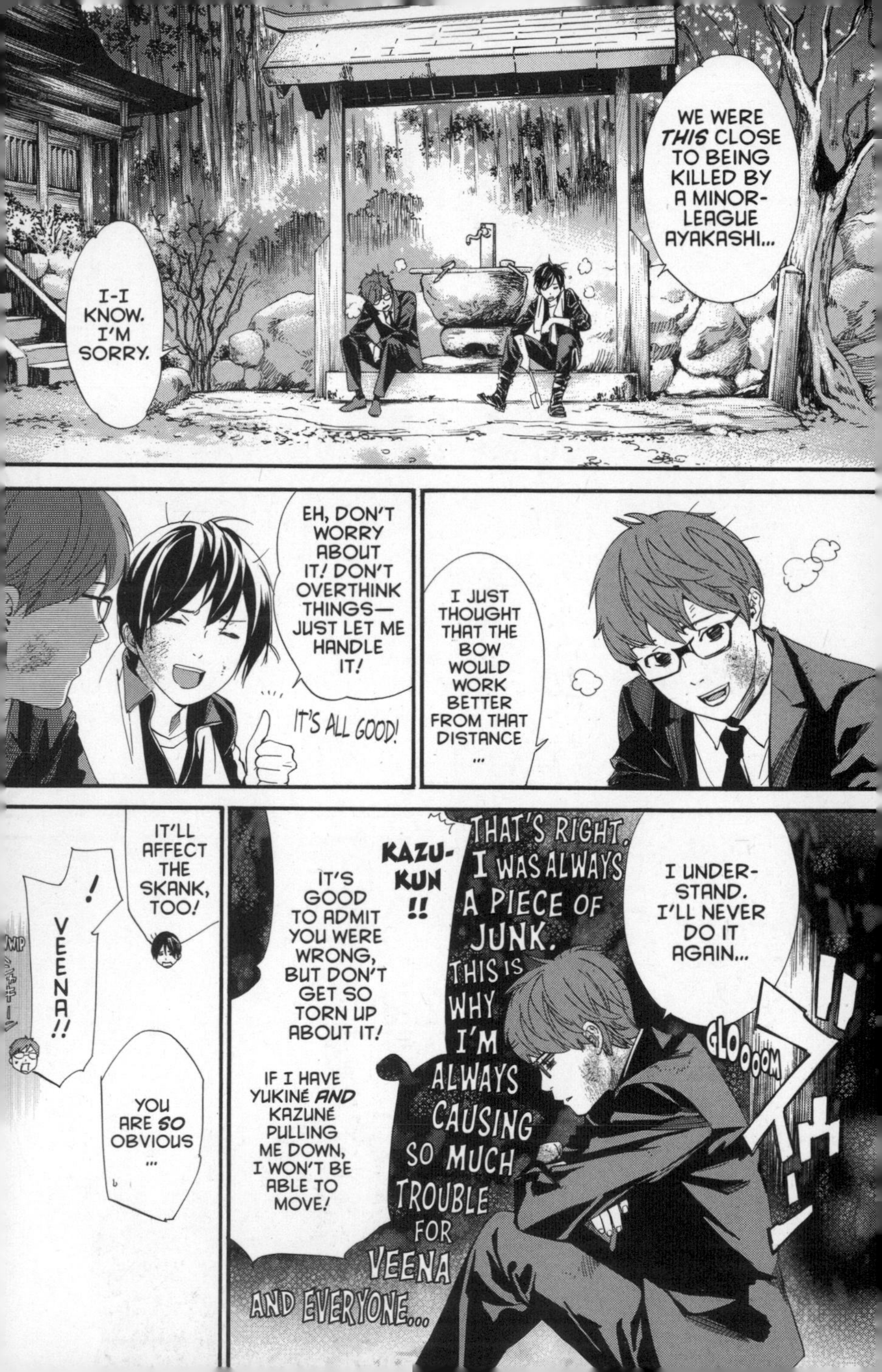

WE WERE *THIS* CLOSE TO BEING KILLED BY A MINOR-LEAGUE AYAKASHI...
I-I KNOW. I'M SORRY.
I JUST THOUGHT THAT THE BOW WOULD WORK BETTER FROM THAT DISTANCE...
EH, DON'T WORRY ABOUT IT! DON'T OVERTHINK THINGS—JUST LET ME HANDLE IT!
IT'S ALL GOOD!
I UNDER-STAND. I'LL NEVER DO IT AGAIN...
GLOOOOM
THAT'S RIGHT. I WAS ALWAYS A PIECE OF JUNK. THIS IS WHY I'M ALWAYS CAUSING SO MUCH TROUBLE FOR VEENA AND EVERYONE...
KAZU-KUN!!
IT'S GOOD TO ADMIT YOU WERE WRONG, BUT DON'T GET SO TORN UP ABOUT IT!
IF I HAVE YUKINÉ *AND* KAZUNÉ PULLING ME DOWN, I WON'T BE ABLE TO MOVE!
IT'LL AFFECT THE SKANK, TOO!
!
VEENA!!
YOU ARE *SO* OBVIOUS...

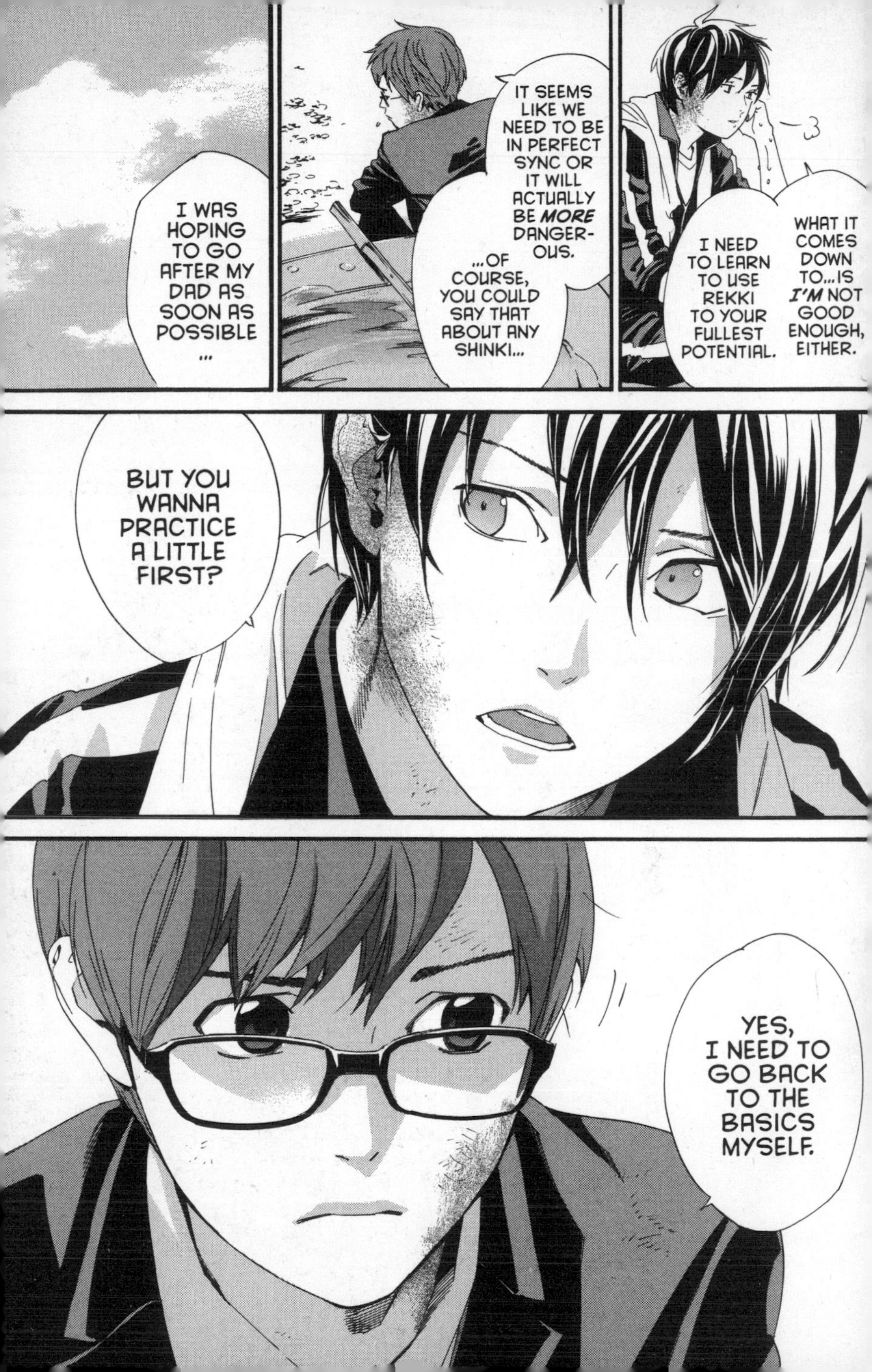
WHAT IT COMES DOWN TO...IS *I'M* NOT GOOD ENOUGH, EITHER.
I NEED TO LEARN TO USE REKKI TO YOUR FULLEST POTENTIAL.
IT SEEMS LIKE WE NEED TO BE IN PERFECT SYNC OR IT WILL ACTUALLY BE *MORE* DANGER-OUS.
...OF COURSE, YOU COULD SAY THAT ABOUT ANY SHINKI...
I WAS HOPING TO GO AFTER MY DAD AS SOON AS POSSIBLE...
BUT YOU WANNA PRACTICE A LITTLE FIRST?
YES, I NEED TO GO BACK TO THE BASICS MYSELF.

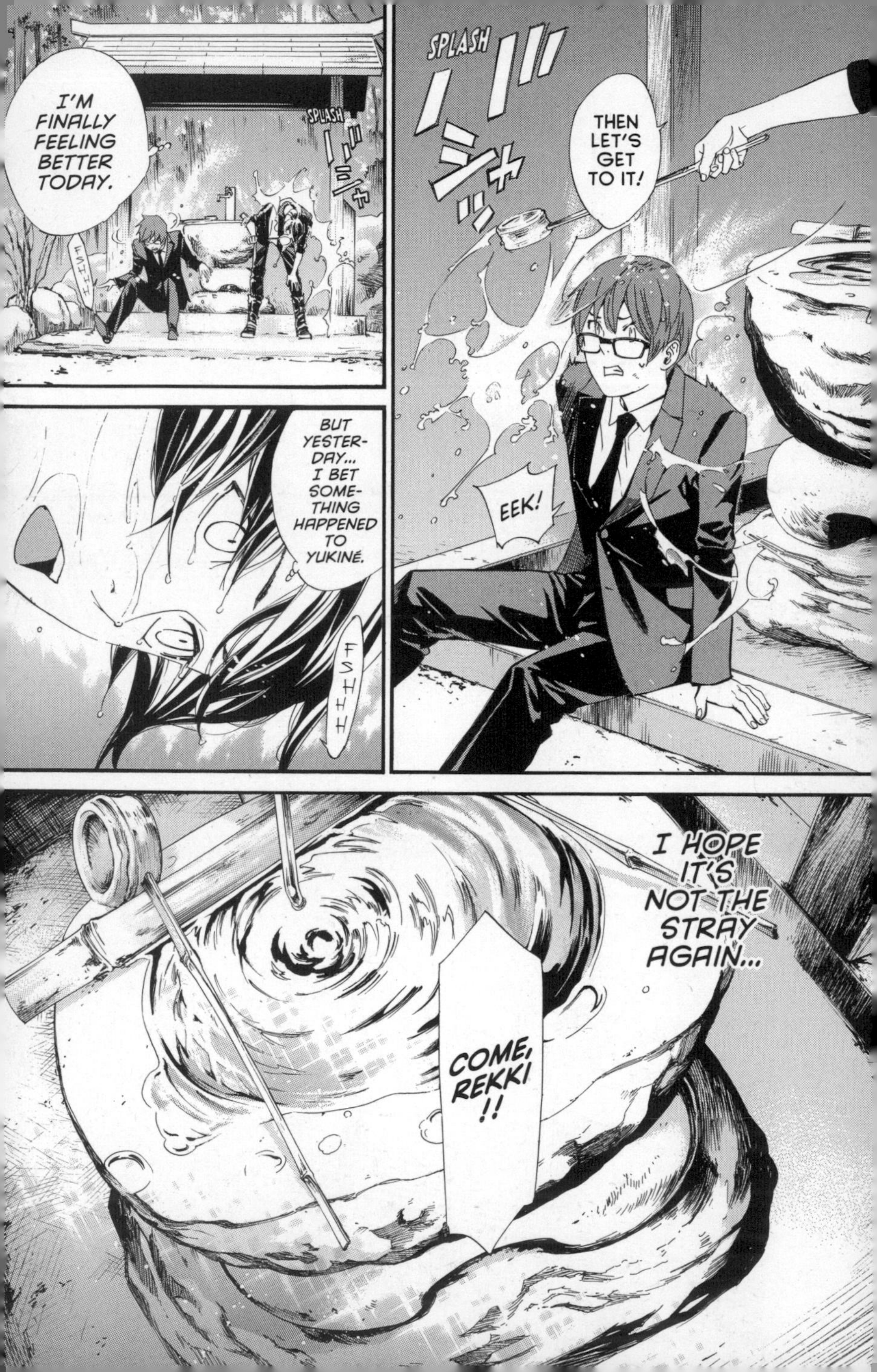

SPLASH
THEN LET'S GET TO IT!
EEK!
I'M FINALLY FEELING BETTER TODAY.
SPLASH
FSHHH
BUT YESTERDAY... I BET SOMETHING HAPPENED TO YUKINÉ.
FSHHH
I HOPE IT'S NOT THE STRAY AGAIN...
COME, REKKI!!

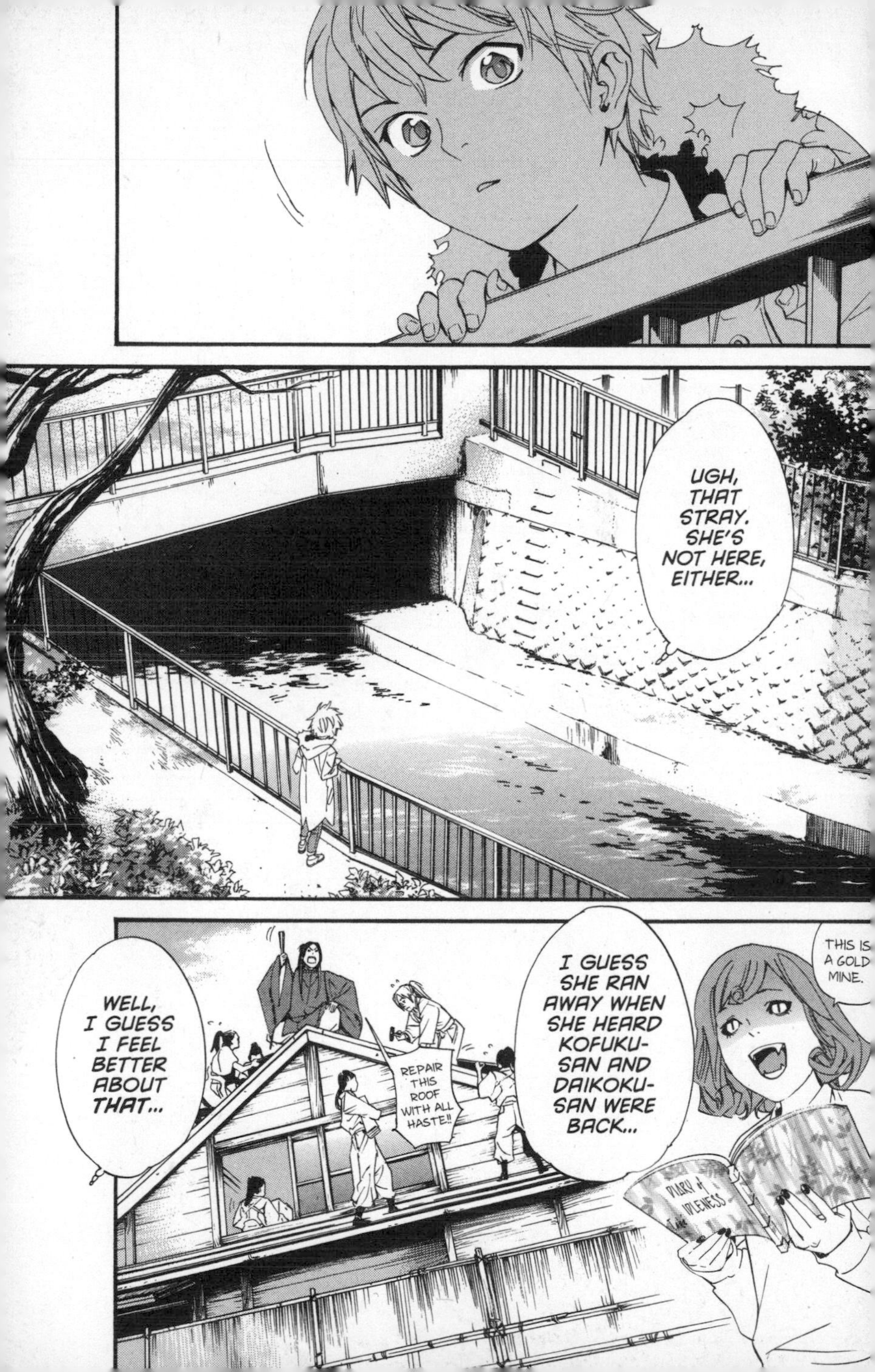
UGH, THAT STRAY. SHE'S NOT HERE, EITHER...
THIS IS A GOLD MINE.
I GUESS SHE RAN AWAY WHEN SHE HEARD KOFUKU-SAN AND DAIKOKU-SAN WERE BACK...
DIARY of IDLENESS
REPAIR THIS ROOF WITH ALL HASTE!!
WELL, I GUESS I FEEL BETTER ABOUT THAT...

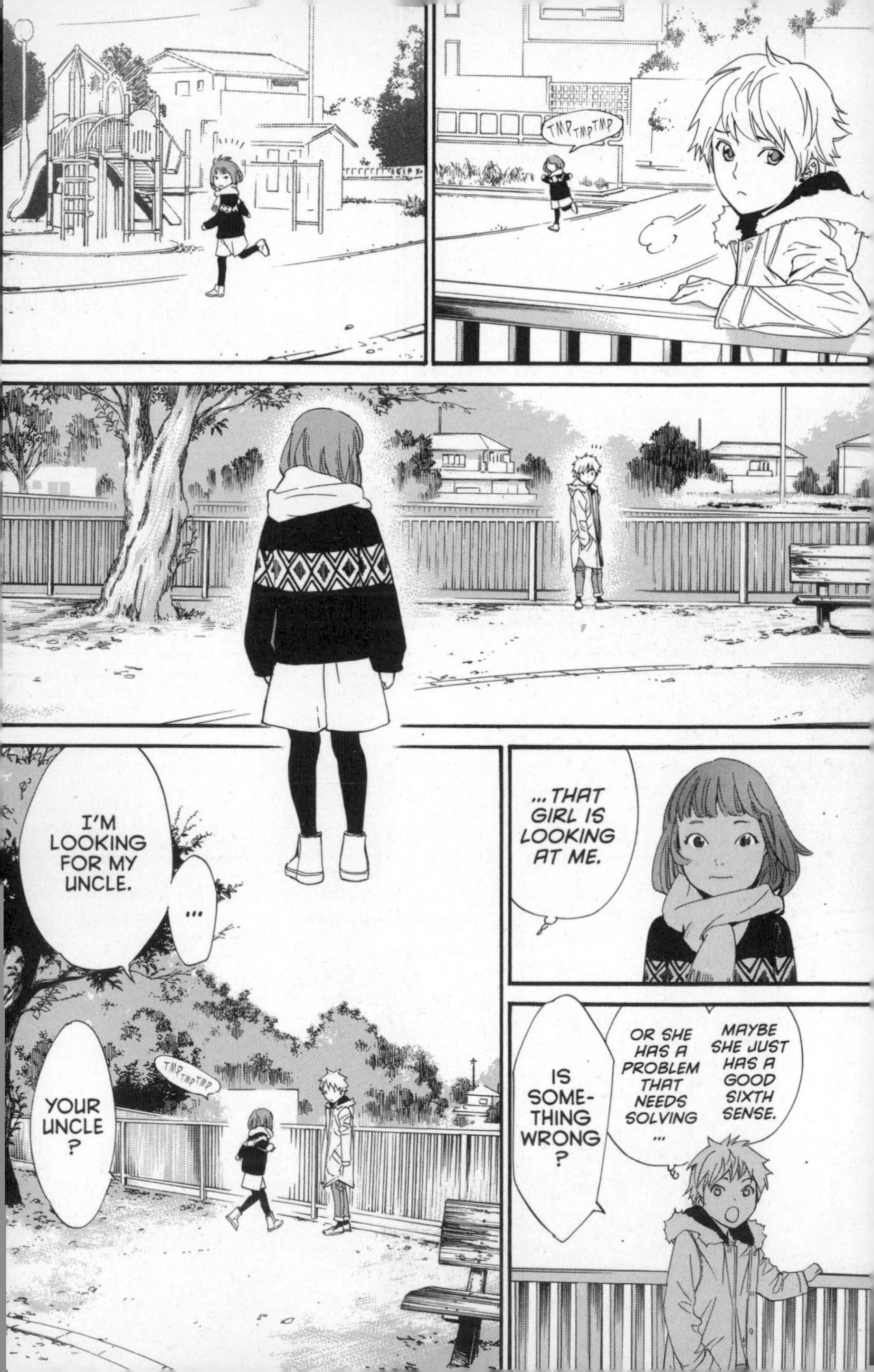
TMP TMP TMP
...THAT GIRL IS LOOKING AT ME.
MAYBE SHE JUST HAS A GOOD SIXTH SENSE.
OR SHE HAS A PROBLEM THAT NEEDS SOLVING ...
IS SOME-THING WRONG?
I'M LOOKING FOR MY UNCLE.
...
YOUR UNCLE?
TMP TMP TMP

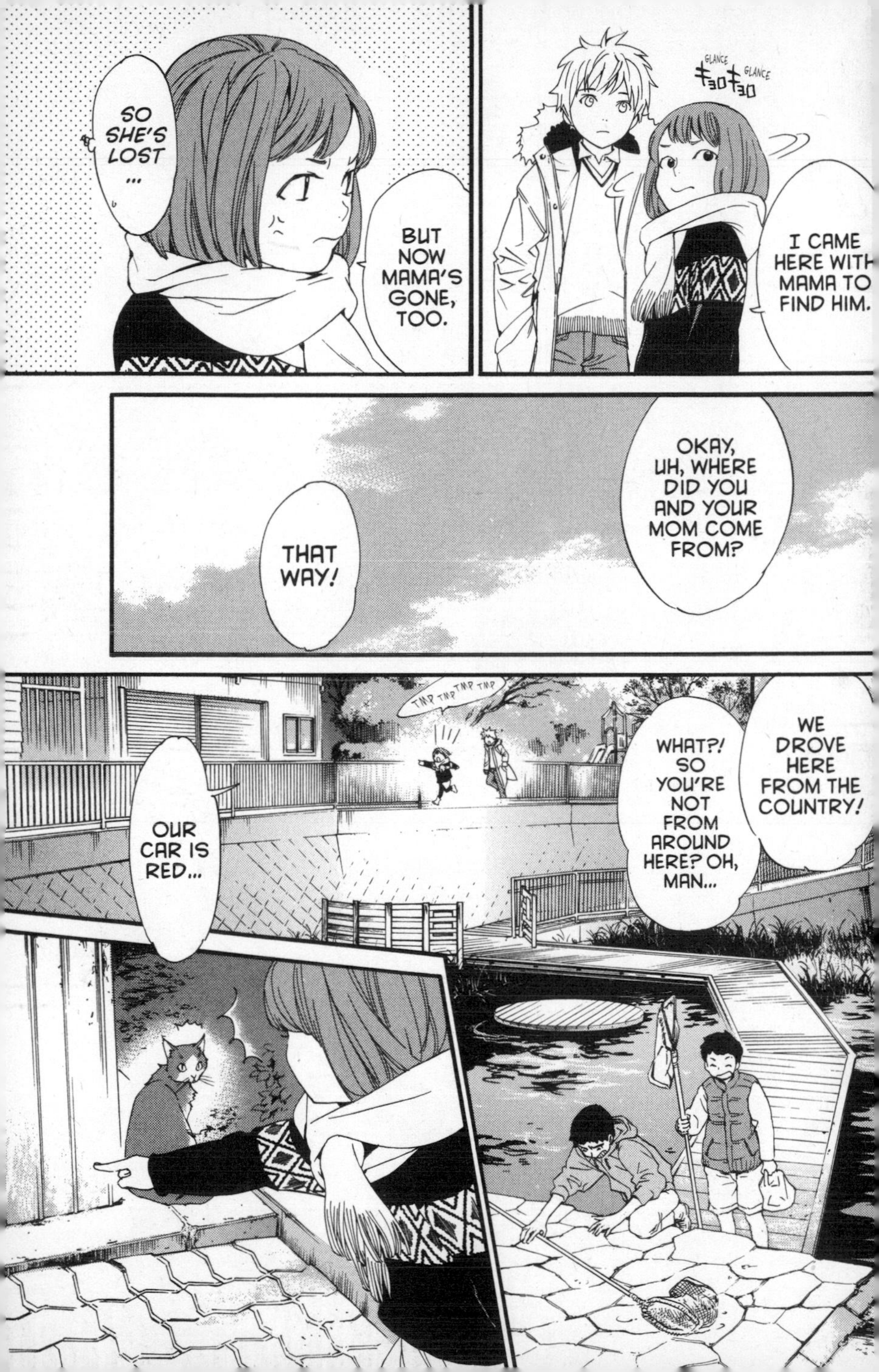
キョロキョロ
GLANCE GLANCE
I CAME HERE WITH MAMA TO FIND HIM.
BUT NOW MAMA'S GONE, TOO.
SO SHE'S LOST ...
OKAY, UH, WHERE DID YOU AND YOUR MOM COME FROM?
THAT WAY!
WE DROVE HERE FROM THE COUNTRY!
WHAT?! SO YOU'RE NOT FROM AROUND HERE? OH, MAN...
TMP TMP TMP TMP
OUR CAR IS RED...

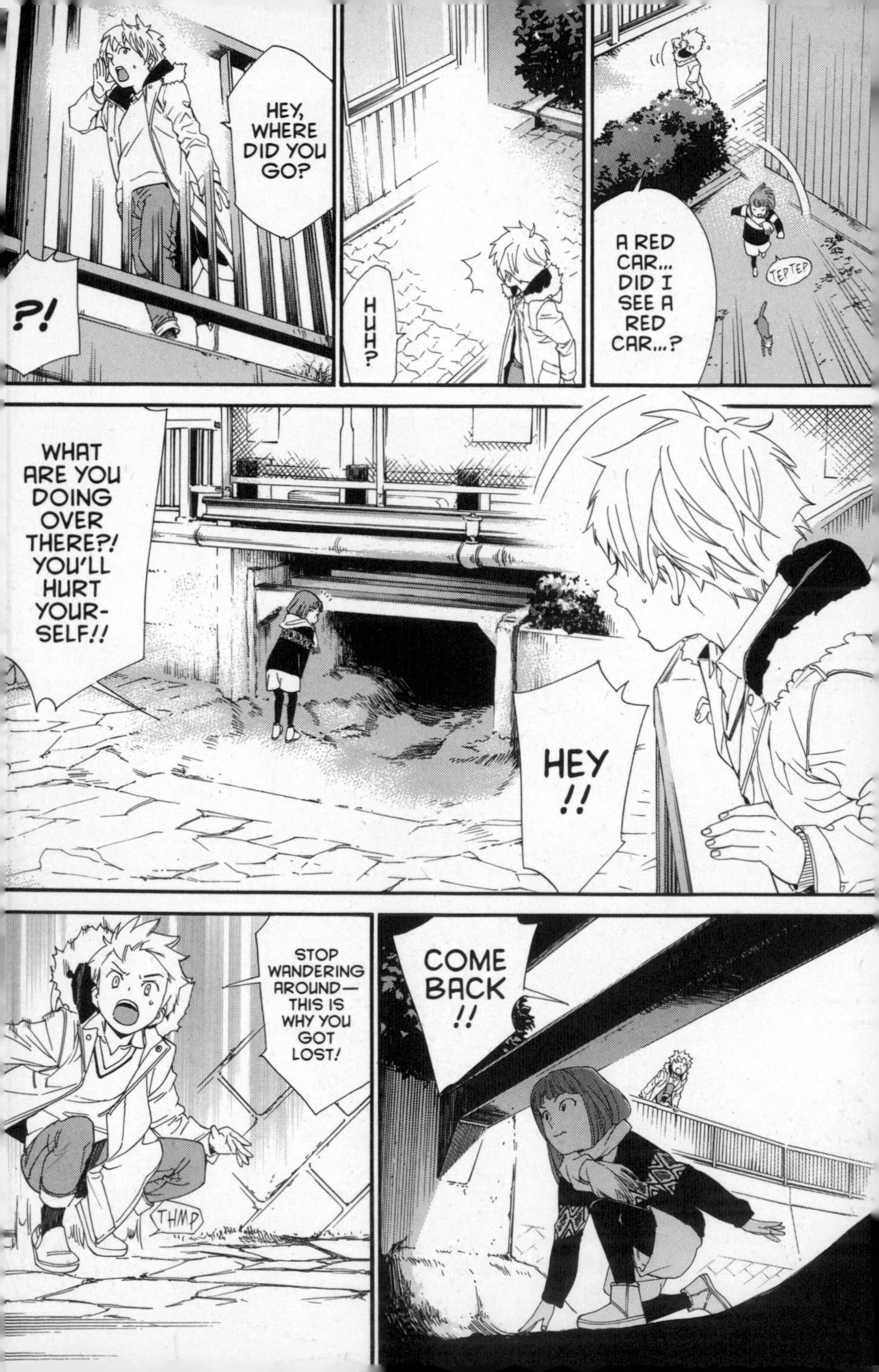
A RED CAR... DID I SEE A RED CAR...?
TEPTEP
HUH?
HEY, WHERE DID YOU GO?
?!
HEY!!
WHAT ARE YOU DOING OVER THERE?! YOU'LL HURT YOURSELF!!
COME BACK!!
STOP WANDERING AROUND—THIS IS WHY YOU GOT LOST!
THMP

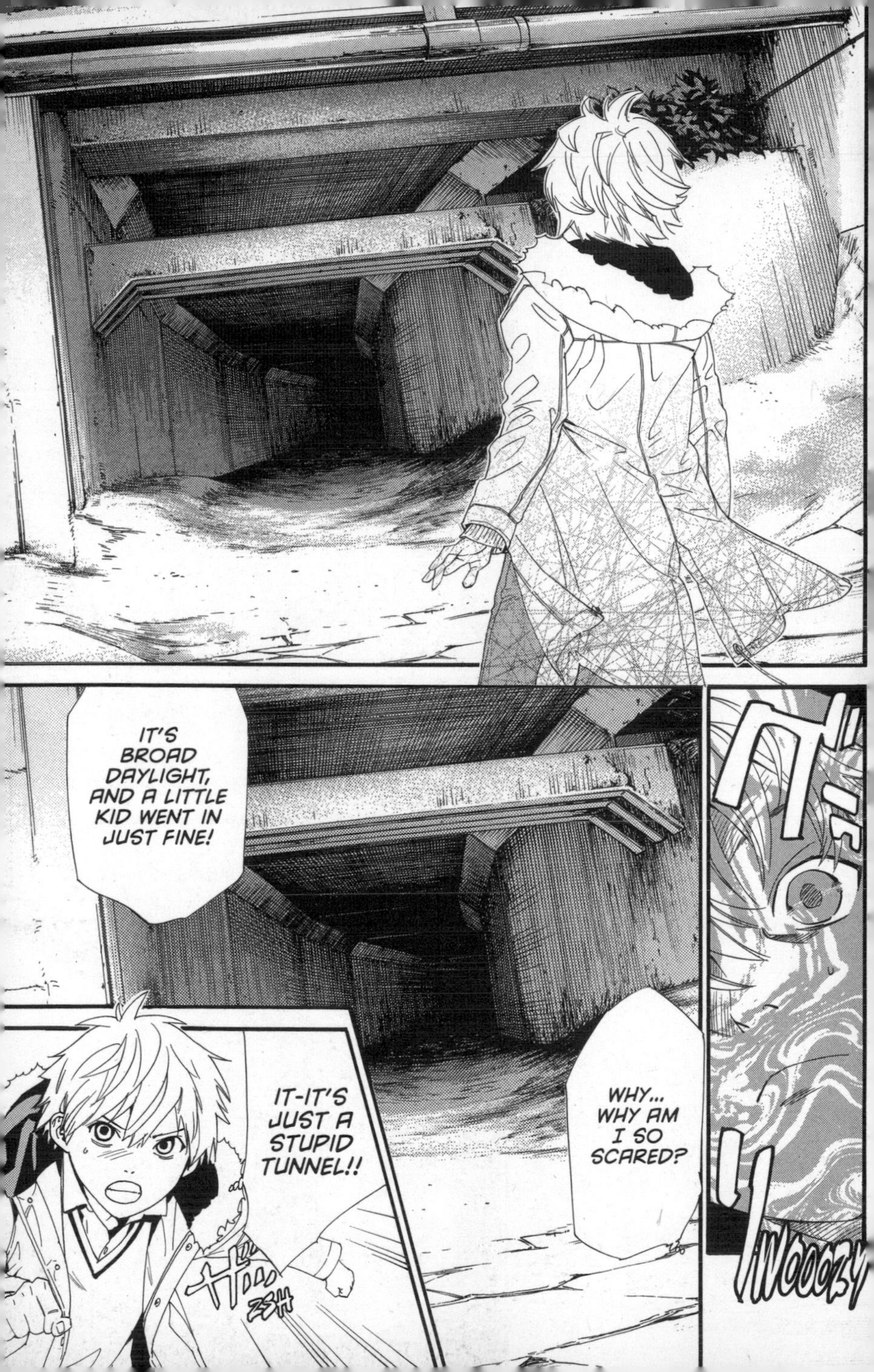
WOOOZY
IT'S BROAD DAYLIGHT, AND A LITTLE KID WENT IN JUST FINE!
WHY... WHY AM I SO SCARED?
IT-IT'S JUST A STUPID TUNNEL!!
ZSH

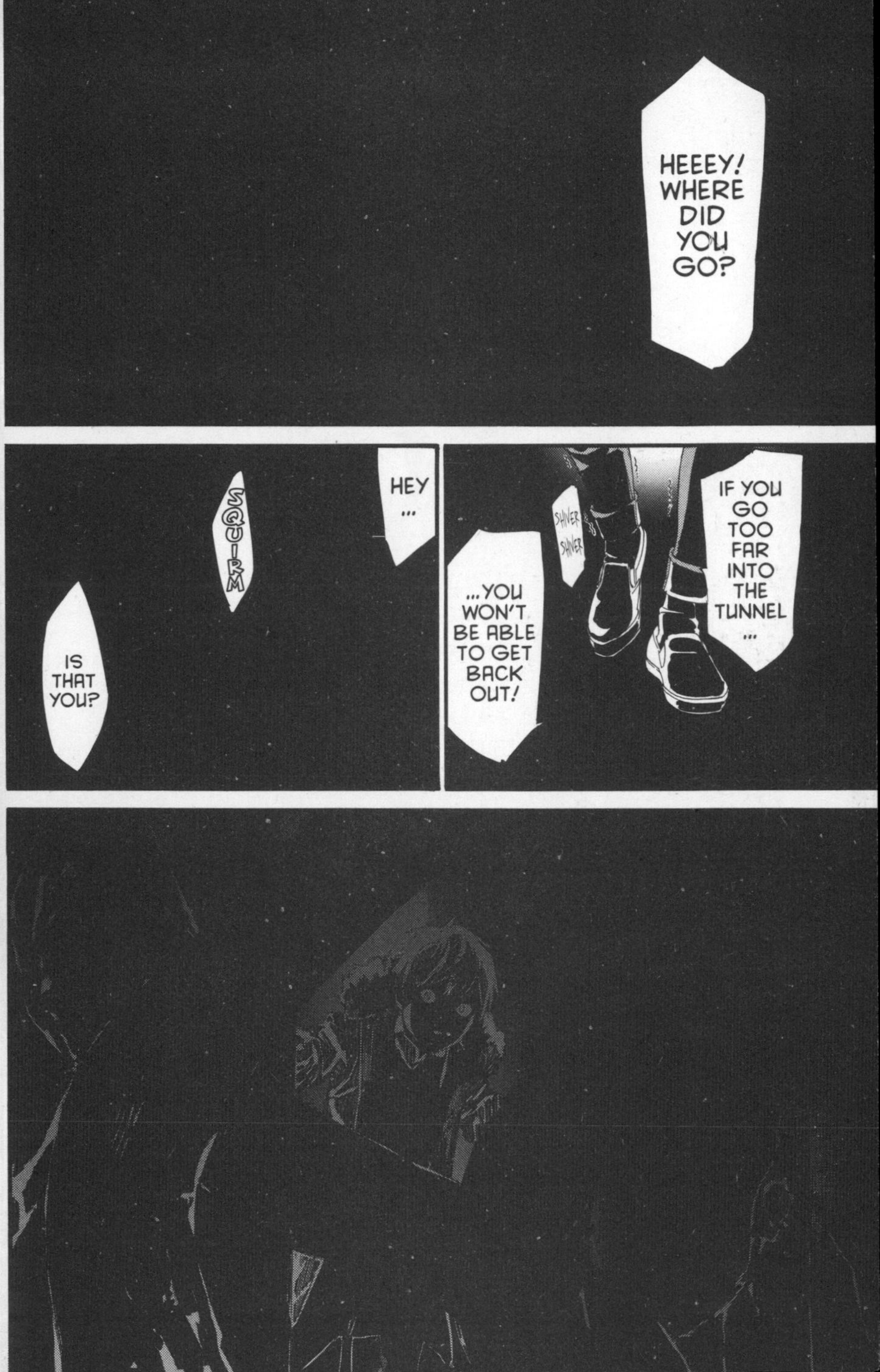
HEEEY! WHERE DID YOU GO?
IF YOU GO TOO FAR INTO THE TUNNEL ...
...YOU WON'T BE ABLE TO GET BACK OUT!
SHIVER SHIVER
HEY ...
SQUIRM
IS THAT YOU?

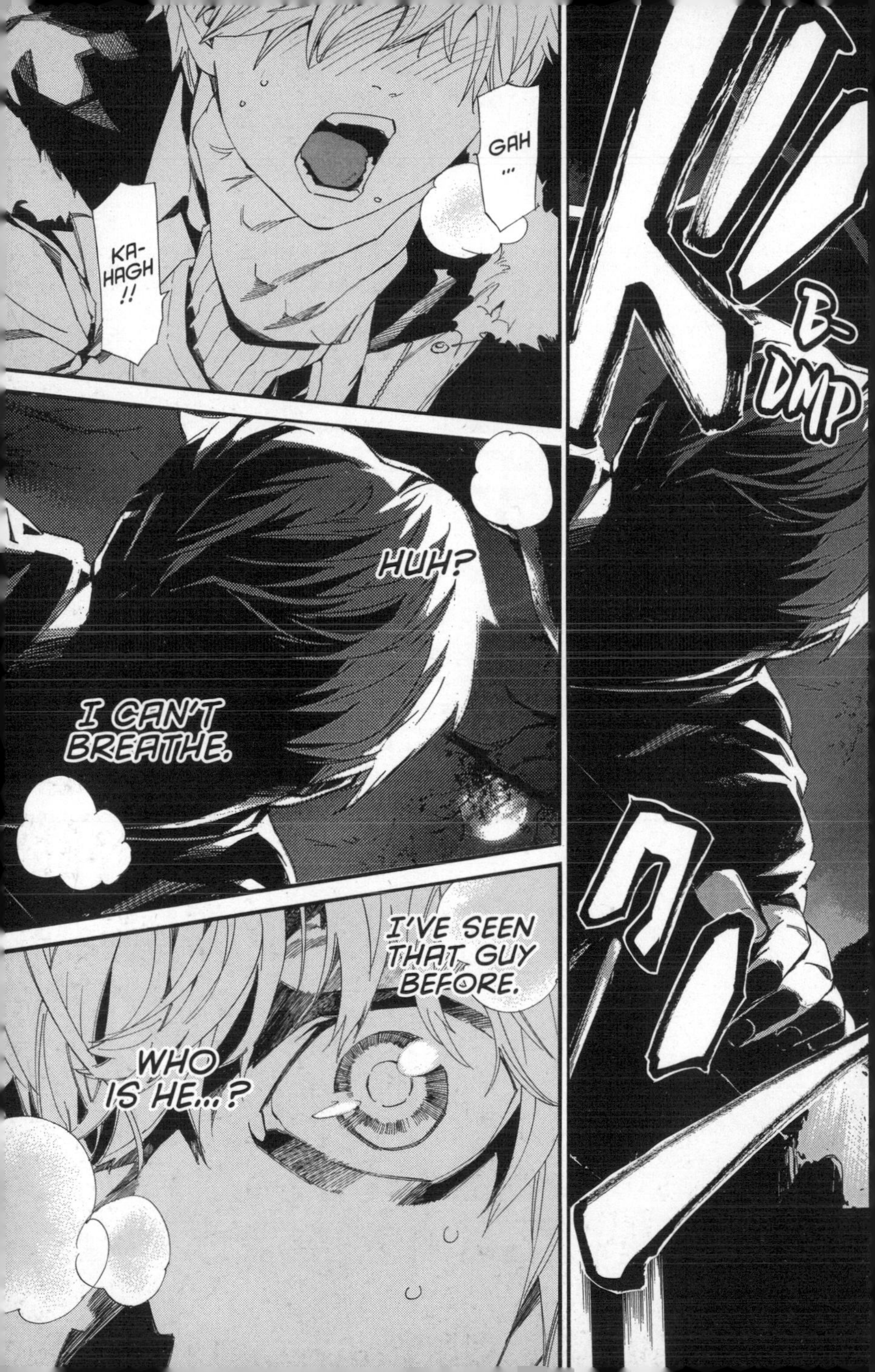
B-DMP
GAH ...
KA-HAGH !!
HUH?
I CAN'T BREATHE.
I'VE SEEN THAT GUY BEFORE.
WHO IS HE...?

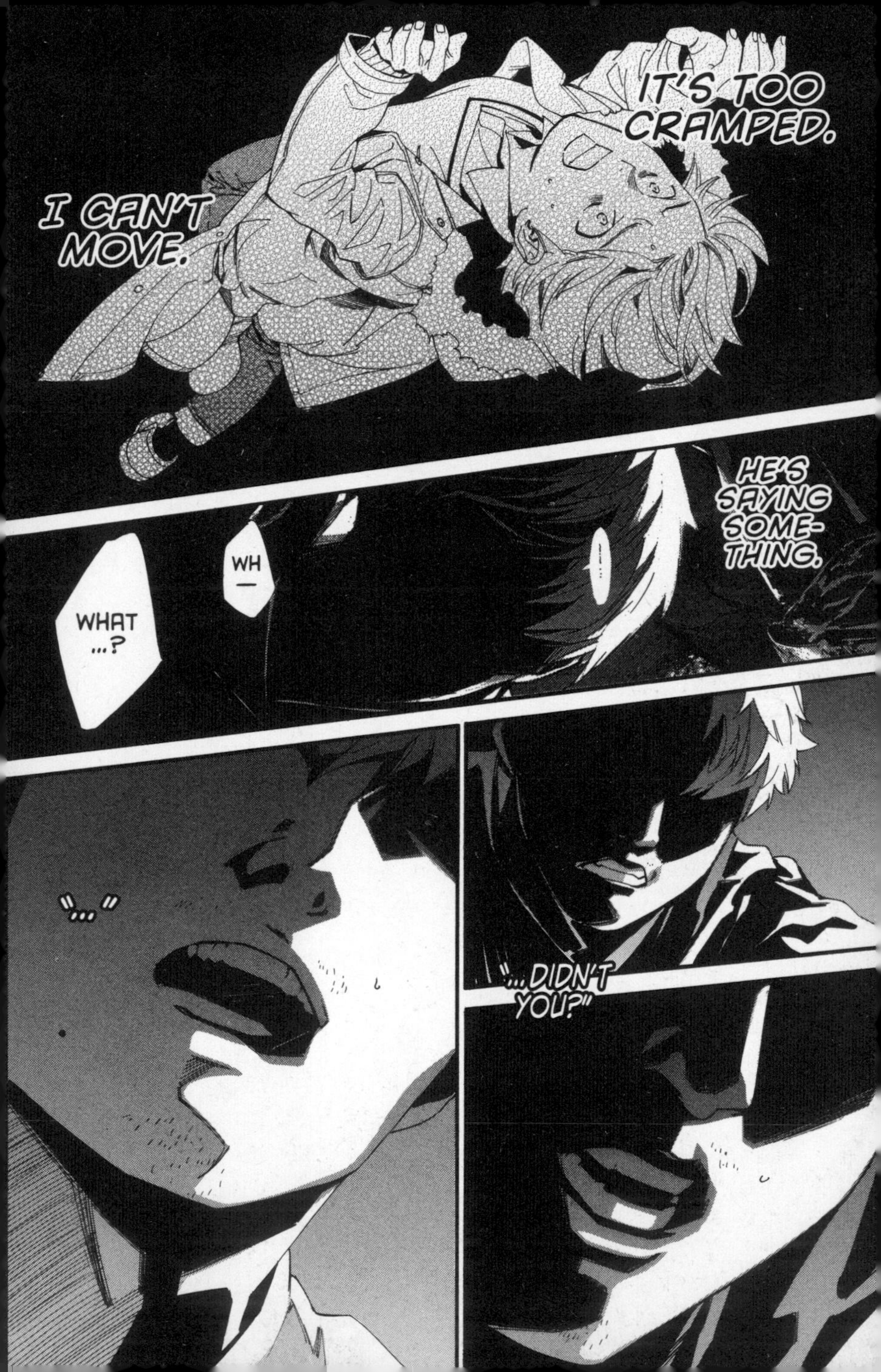
IT'S TOO CRAMPED.
I CAN'T MOVE.
HE'S SAYING SOME-THING.
WH—
WHAT ...?
"...DIDN'T YOU?"
"..."

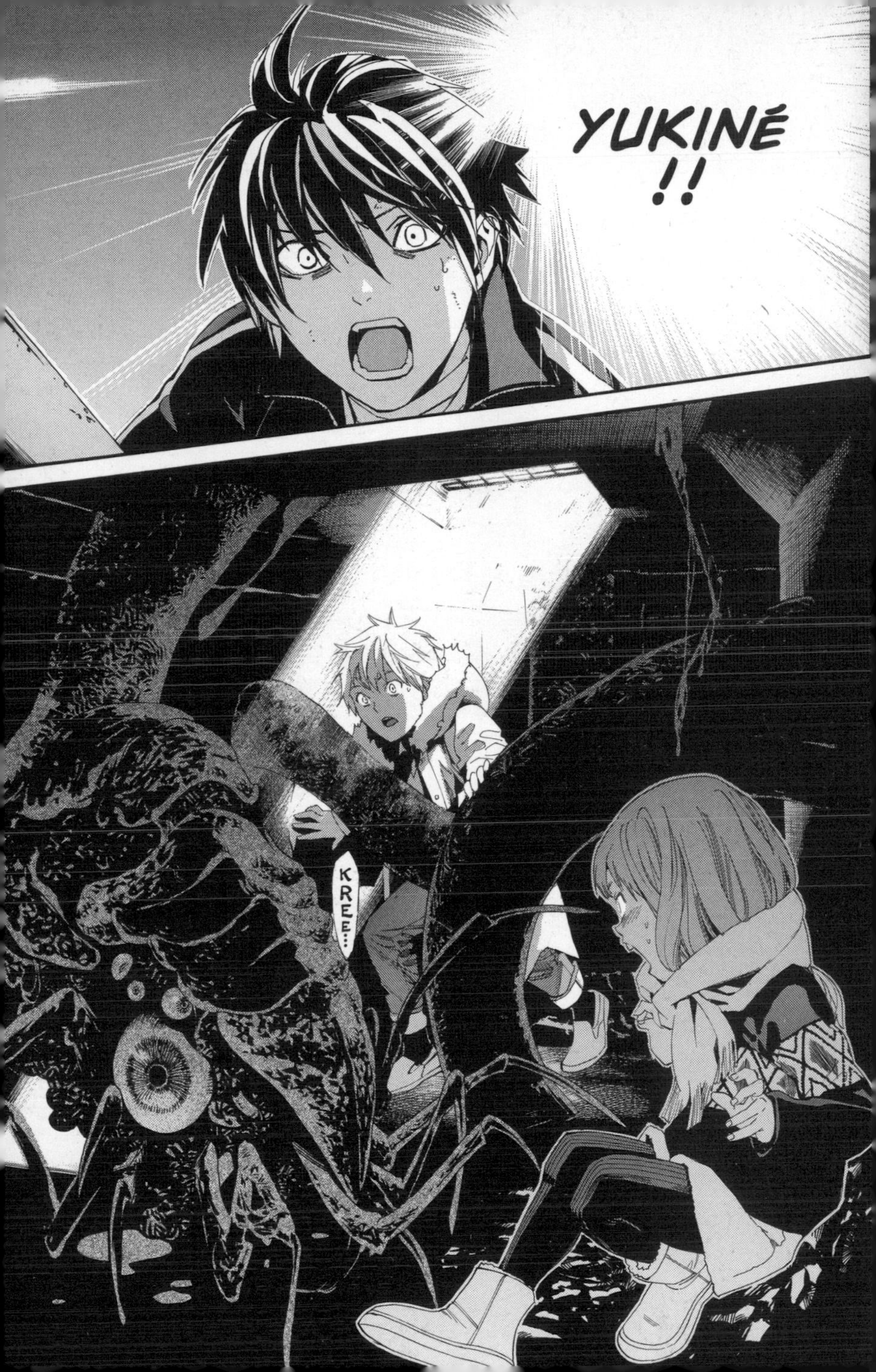
YUKINÉ !!
KREE...

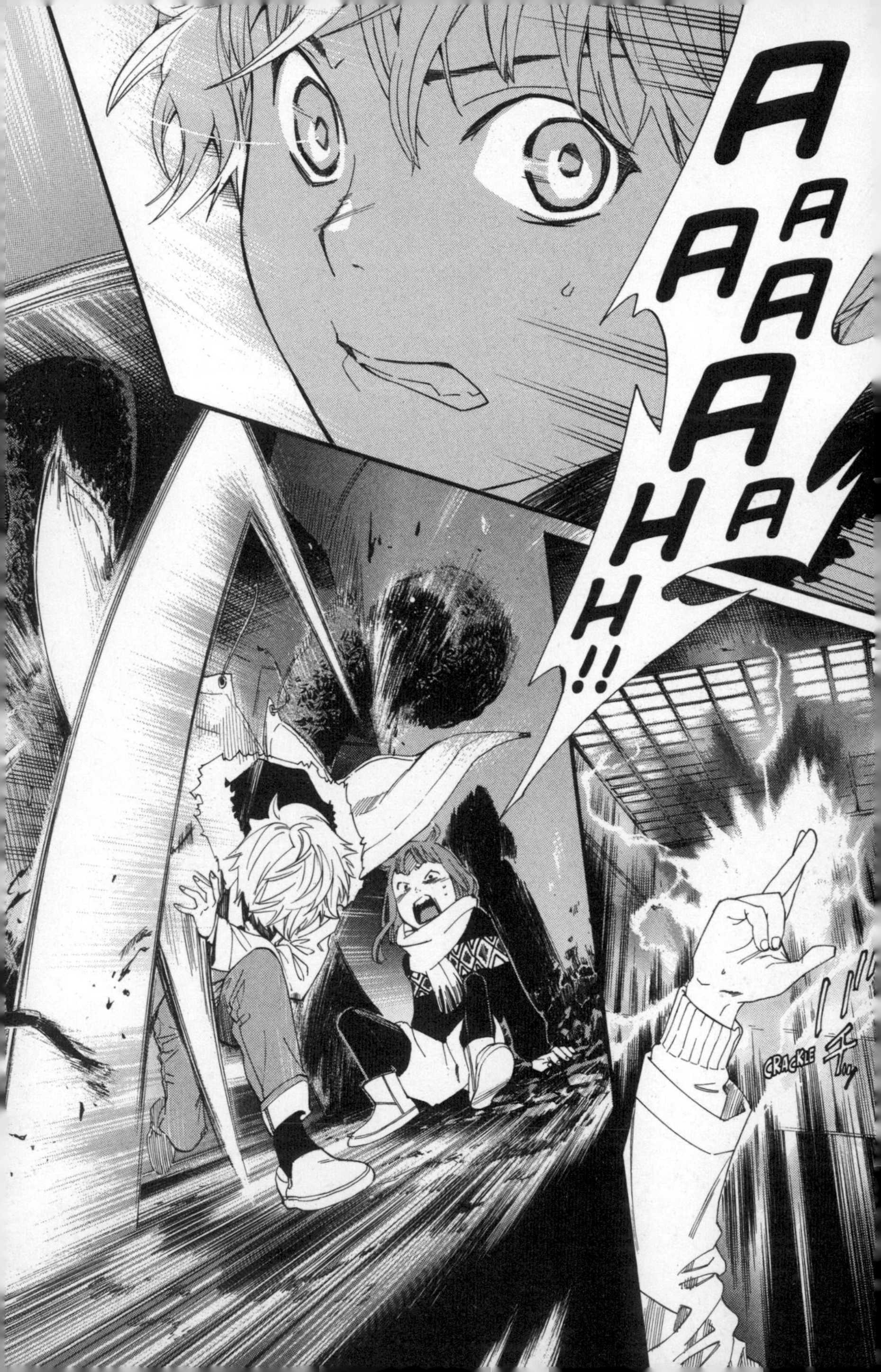

AAAAAAAHHH!!
CRACKLE

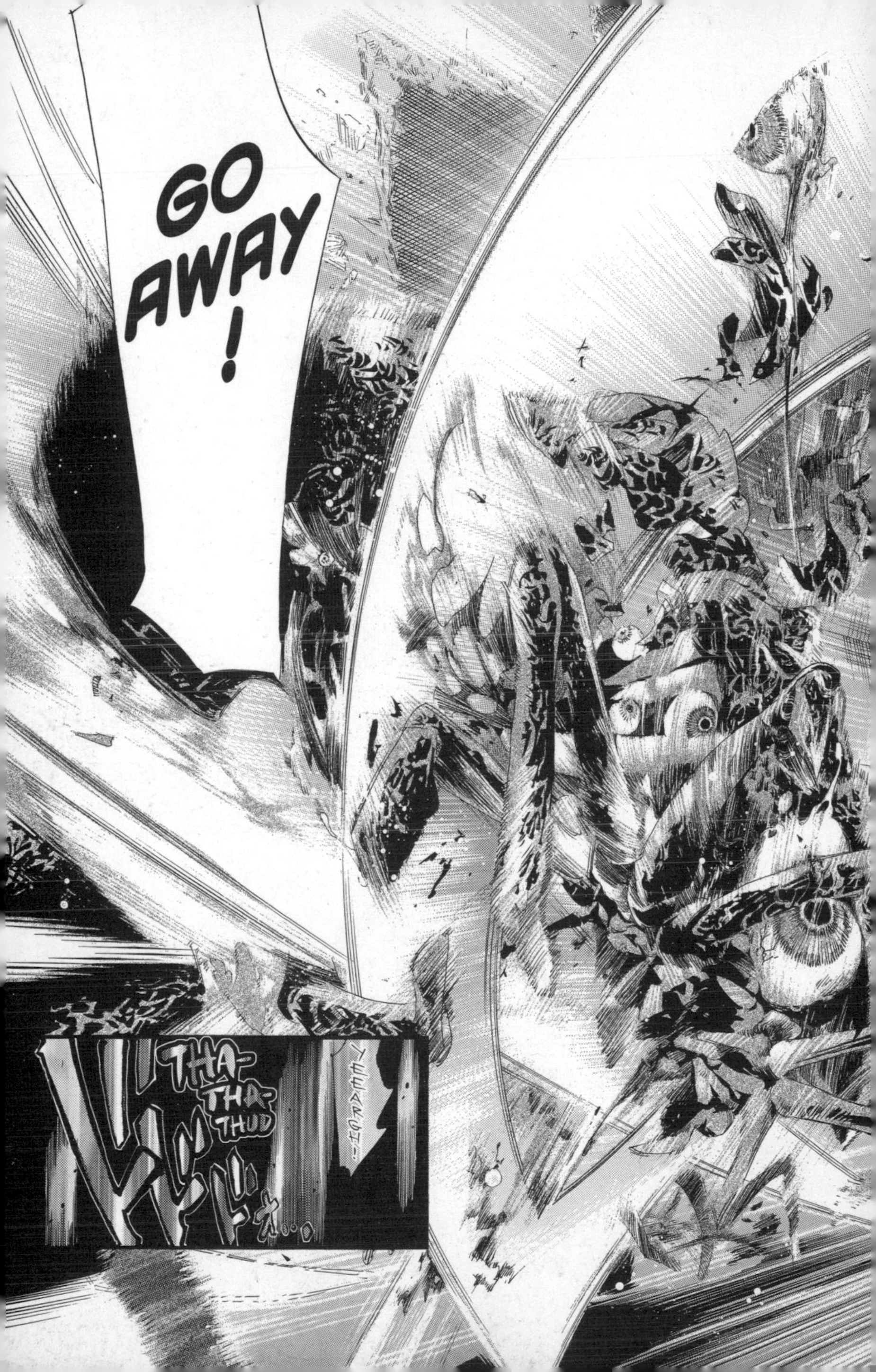
GO AWAY!
YEEARGH!
THA-THA-THUD

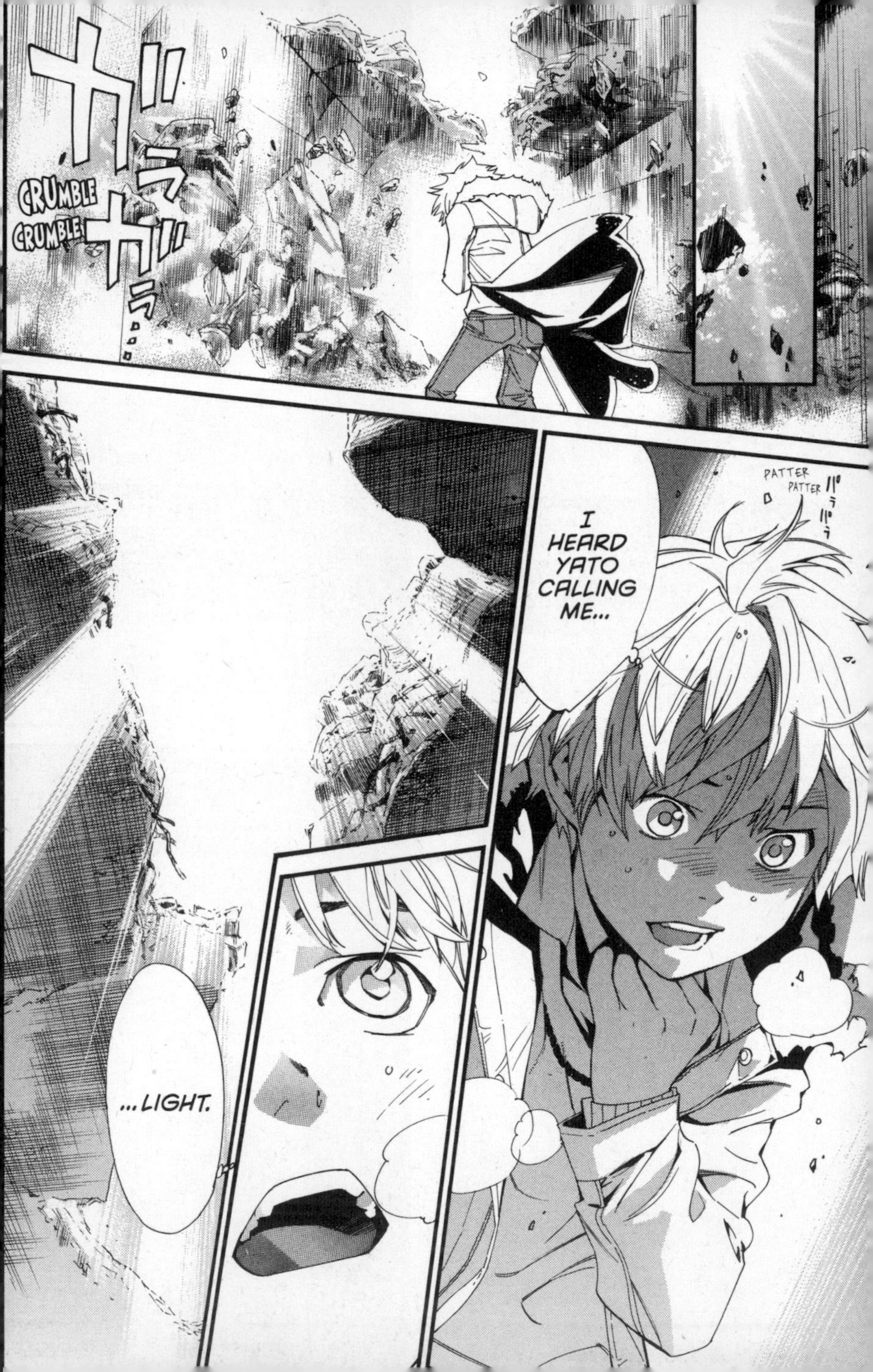
ガラガラ
CRUMBLE CRUMBLE
パラパラ
PATTER PATTER
I HEARD YATO CALLING ME...
...LIGHT.

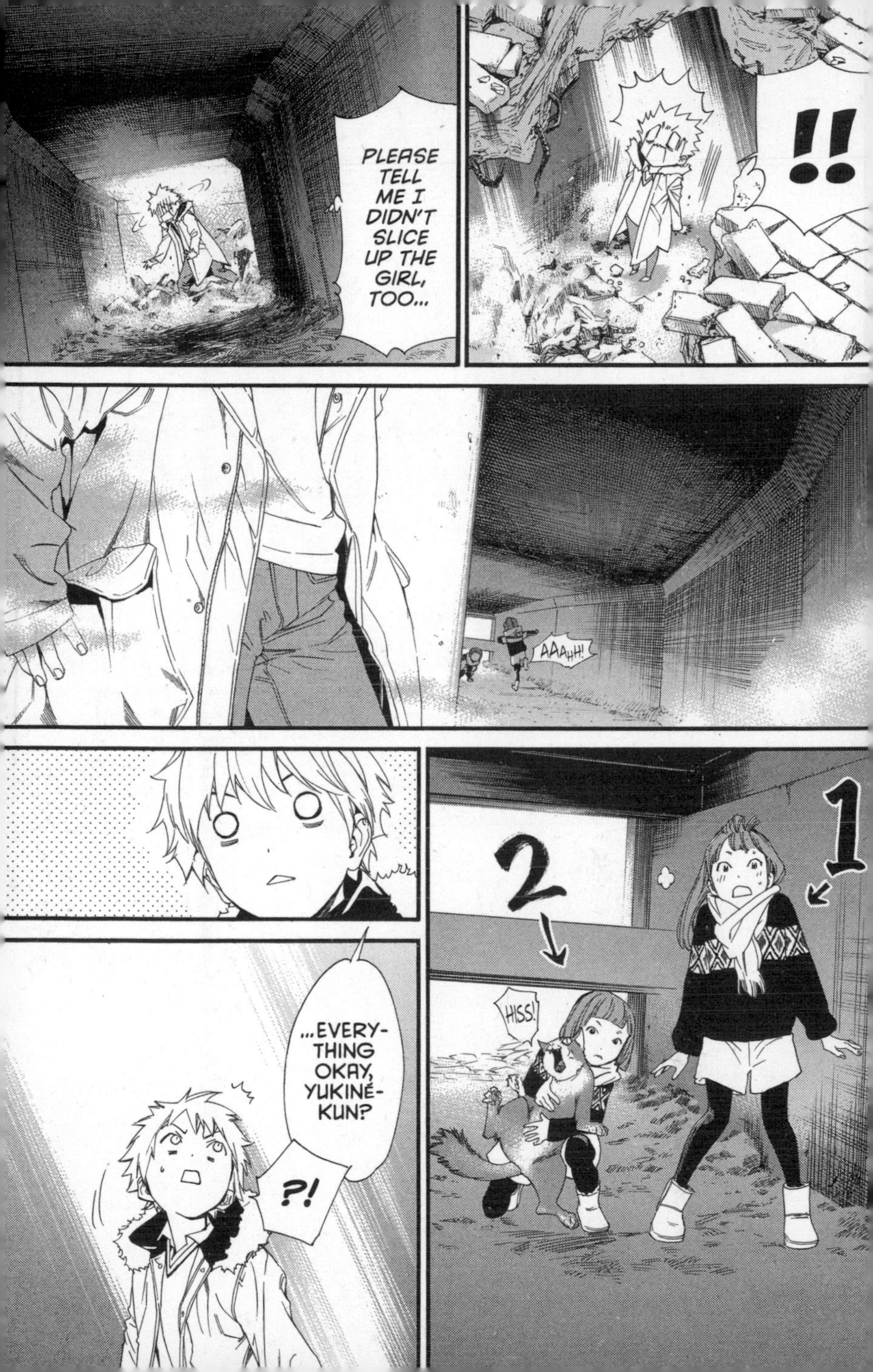
!!
PLEASE TELL ME I DIDN'T SLICE UP THE GIRL, TOO...
AAAHH!
1
2
HISS!
...EVERY-THING OKAY, YUKINÉ-KUN?
?!

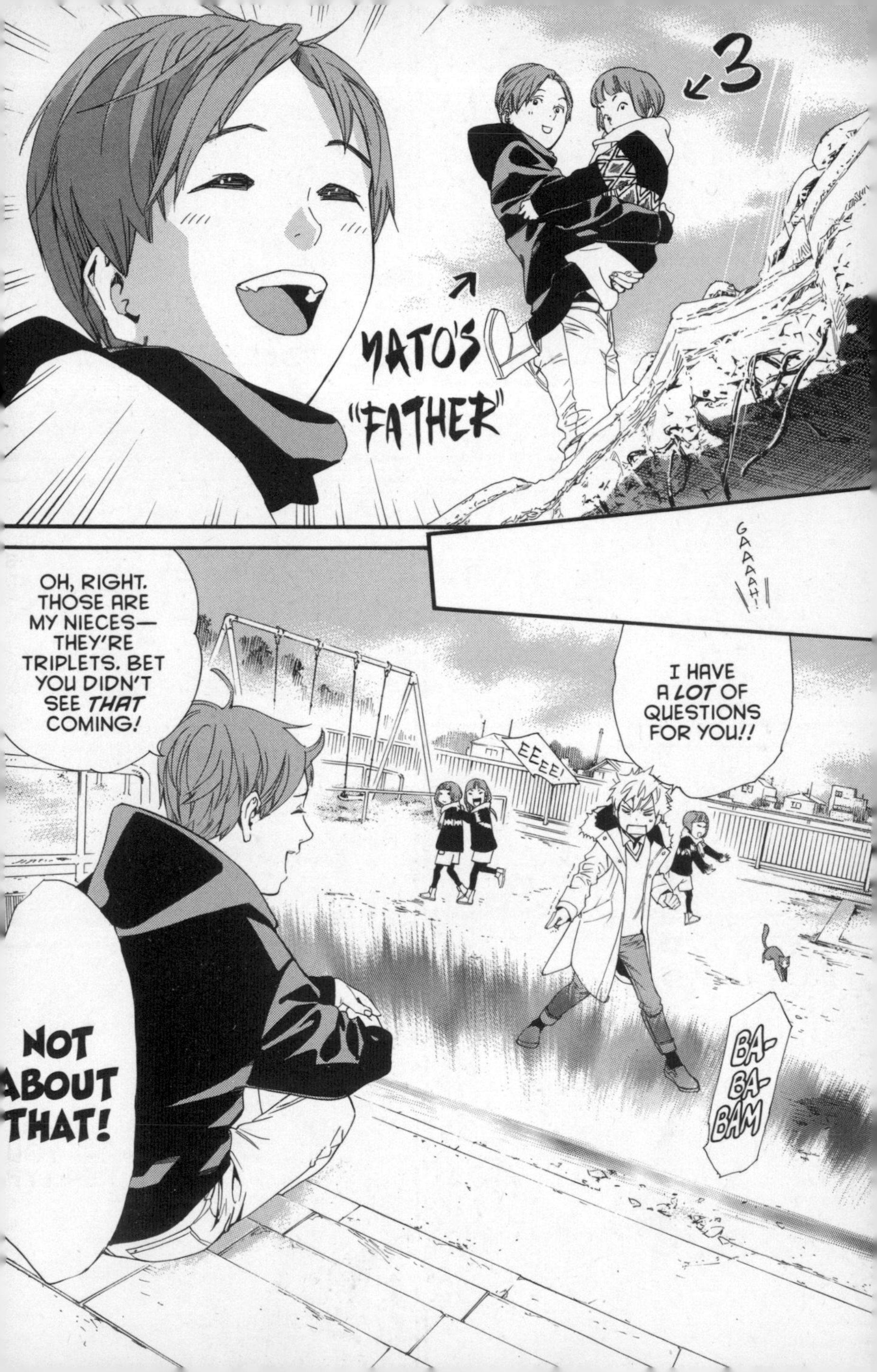
3
YATO'S "FATHER"
GAAAAH!
I HAVE A *LOT* OF QUESTIONS FOR YOU!!
EEEE!
BA-BA-BAM
OH, RIGHT. THOSE ARE MY NIECES—THEY'RE TRIPLETS. BET YOU DIDN'T SEE *THAT* COMING!
NOT ABOUT THAT!

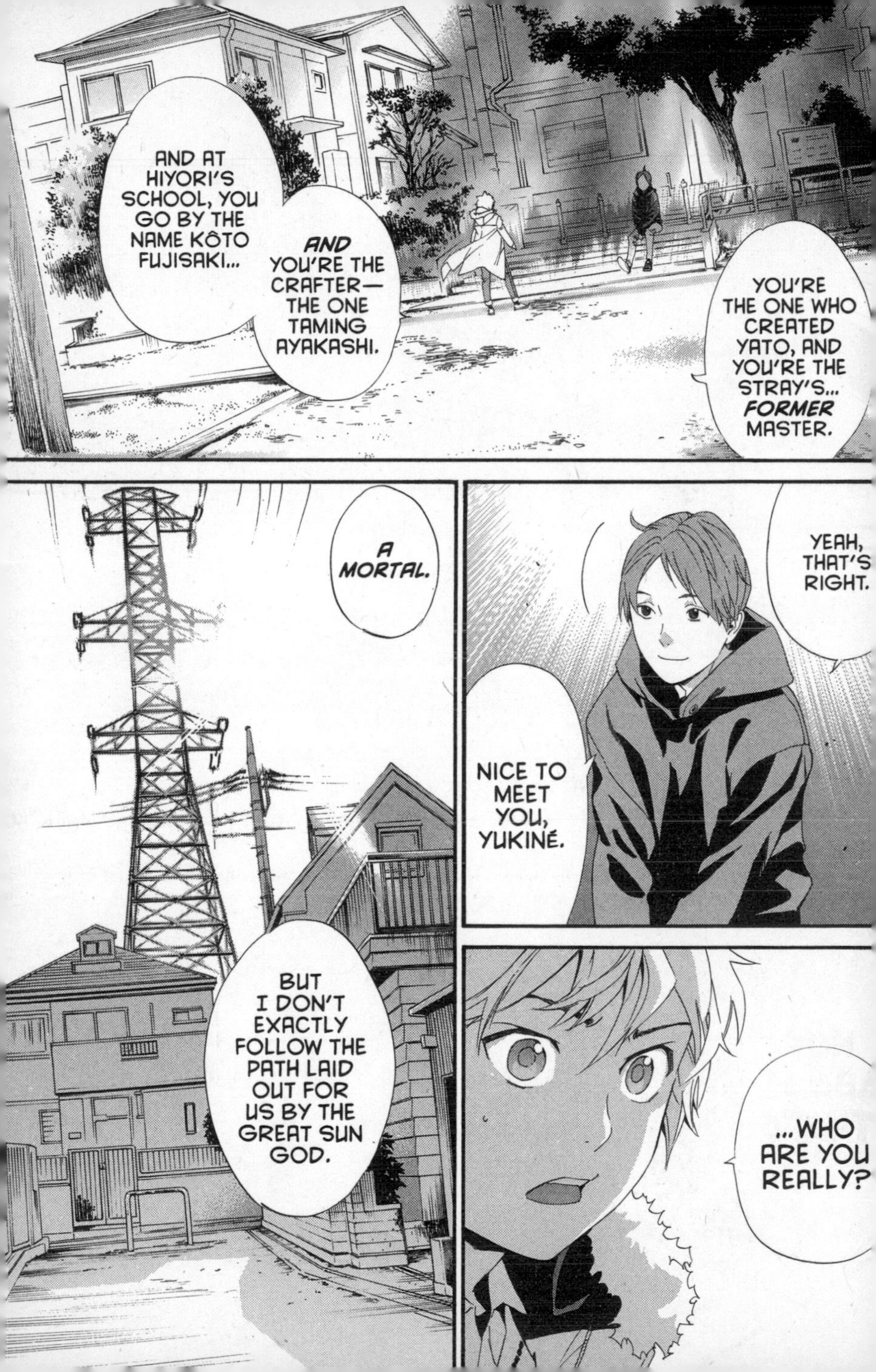
YOU'RE THE ONE WHO CREATED YATO, AND YOU'RE THE STRAY'S... *FORMER* MASTER.
AND YOU'RE THE CRAFTER—THE ONE TAMING AYAKASHI.
AND AT HIYORI'S SCHOOL, YOU GO BY THE NAME KÔTO FUJISAKI...
YEAH, THAT'S RIGHT.
NICE TO MEET YOU, YUKINÉ.
...WHO ARE YOU REALLY?
A MORTAL.
BUT I DON'T EXACTLY FOLLOW THE PATH LAID OUT FOR US BY THE GREAT SUN GOD.

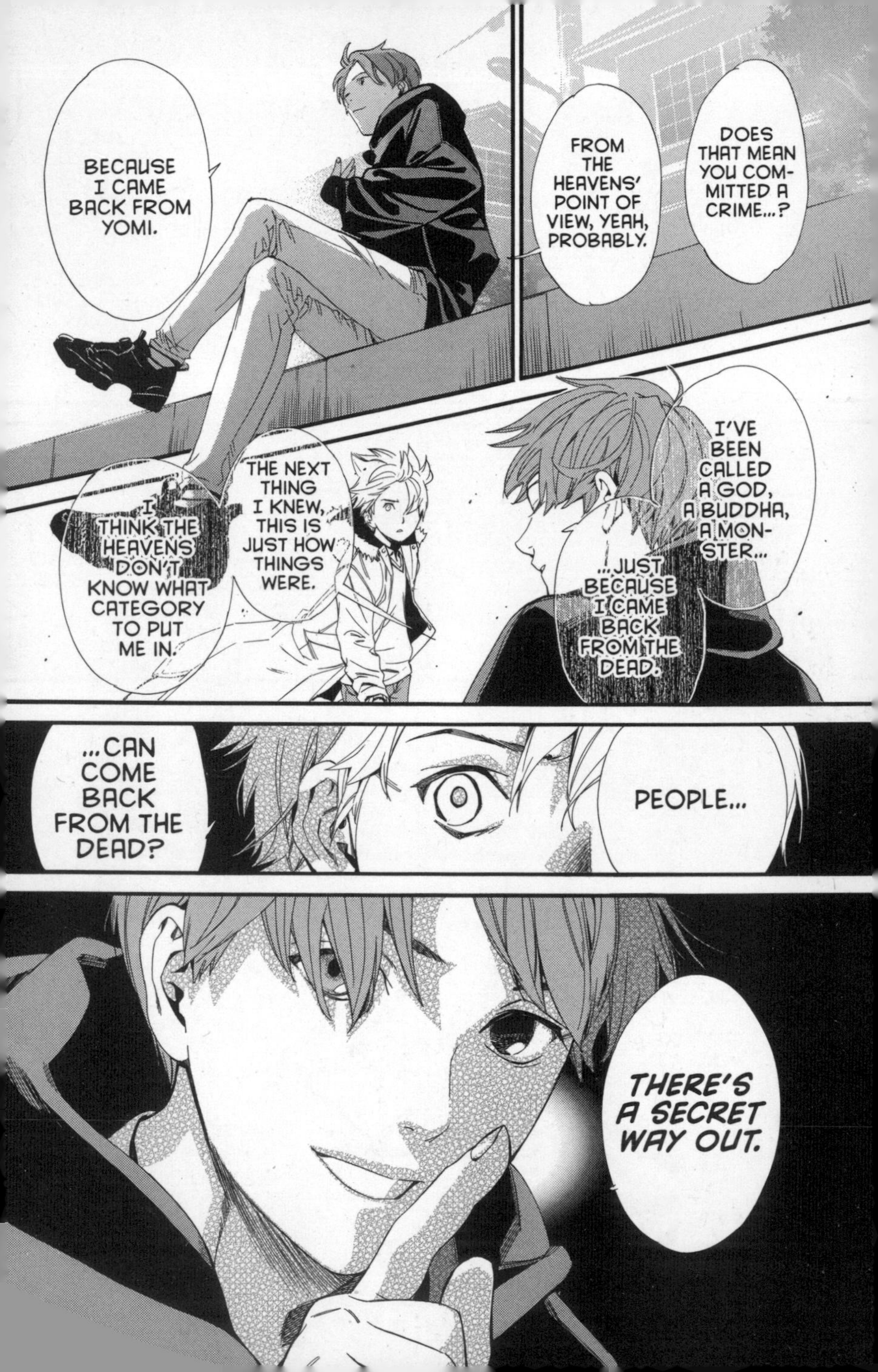
DOES THAT MEAN YOU COMMITTED A CRIME...?
FROM THE HEAVENS' POINT OF VIEW, YEAH, PROBABLY.
BECAUSE I CAME BACK FROM YOMI.
I'VE BEEN CALLED A GOD, A BUDDHA, A MONSTER...
...JUST BECAUSE I CAME BACK FROM THE DEAD.
THE NEXT THING I KNEW, THIS IS JUST HOW THINGS WERE.
I THINK THE HEAVENS DON'T KNOW WHAT CATEGORY TO PUT ME IN.
PEOPLE...
...CAN COME BACK FROM THE DEAD?
THERE'S A SECRET WAY OUT.

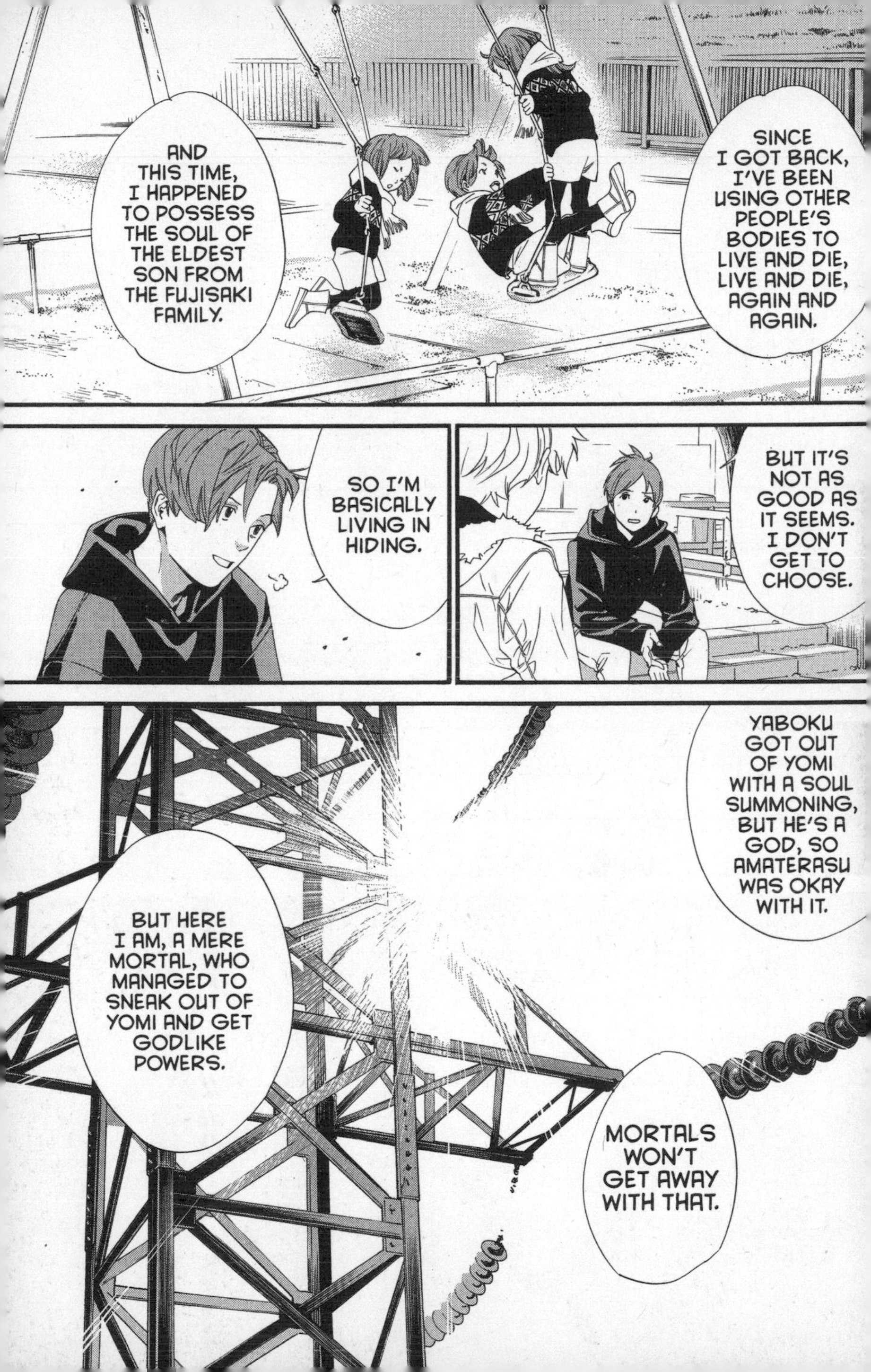
SINCE I GOT BACK, I'VE BEEN USING OTHER PEOPLE'S BODIES TO LIVE AND DIE, LIVE AND DIE, AGAIN AND AGAIN.
AND THIS TIME, I HAPPENED TO POSSESS THE SOUL OF THE ELDEST SON FROM THE FUJISAKI FAMILY.
BUT IT'S NOT AS GOOD AS IT SEEMS. I DON'T GET TO CHOOSE.
SO I'M BASICALLY LIVING IN HIDING.
YABOKU GOT OUT OF YOMI WITH A SOUL SUMMONING, BUT HE'S A GOD, SO AMATERASU WAS OKAY WITH IT.
BUT HERE I AM, A MERE MORTAL, WHO MANAGED TO SNEAK OUT OF YOMI AND GET GODLIKE POWERS.
MORTALS WON'T GET AWAY WITH THAT.

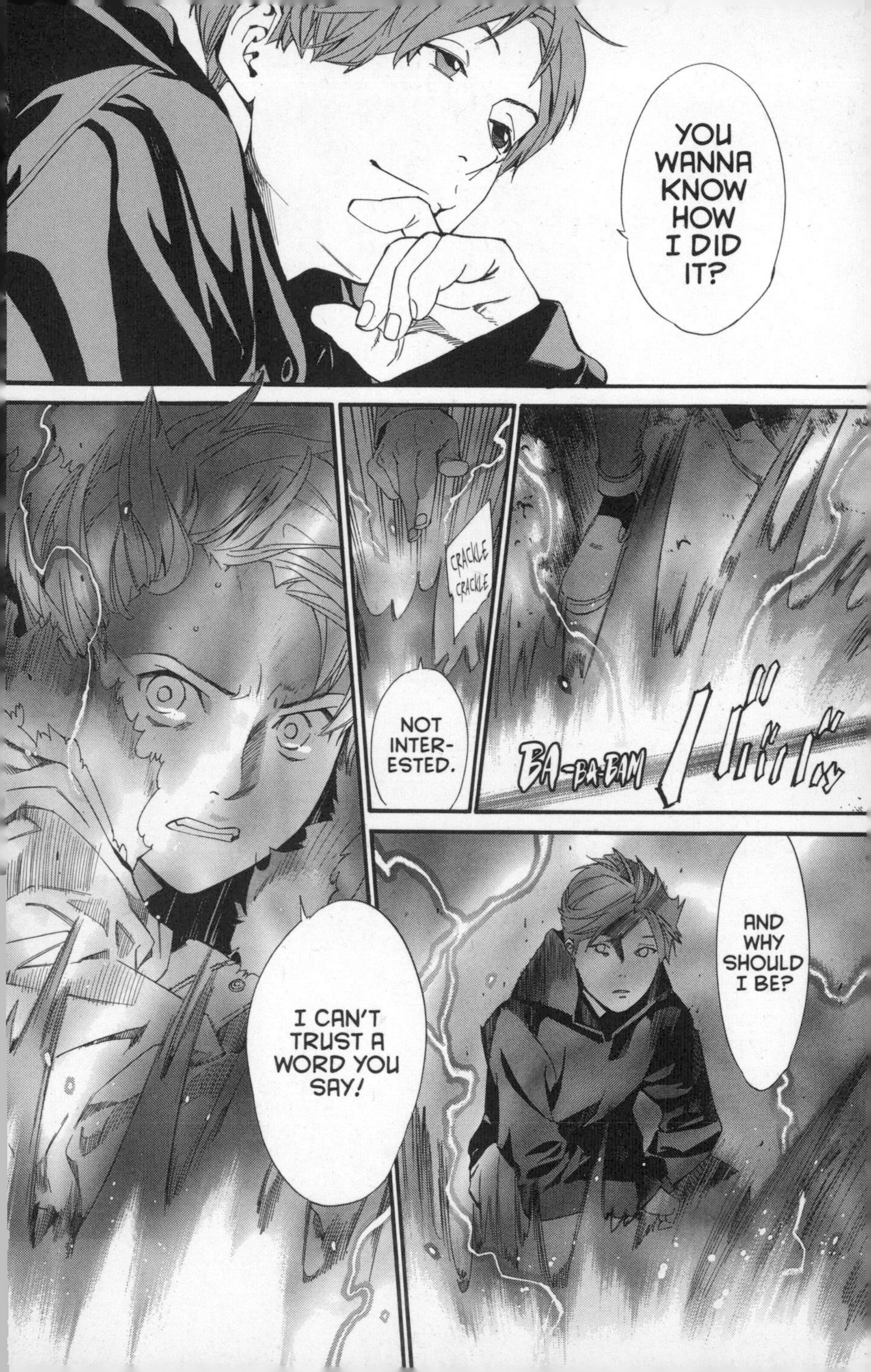
YOU WANNA KNOW HOW I DID IT?
BA-BA-BAM
CRACKLE CRACKLE
NOT INTER-ESTED.
AND WHY SHOULD I BE?
I CAN'T TRUST A WORD YOU SAY!

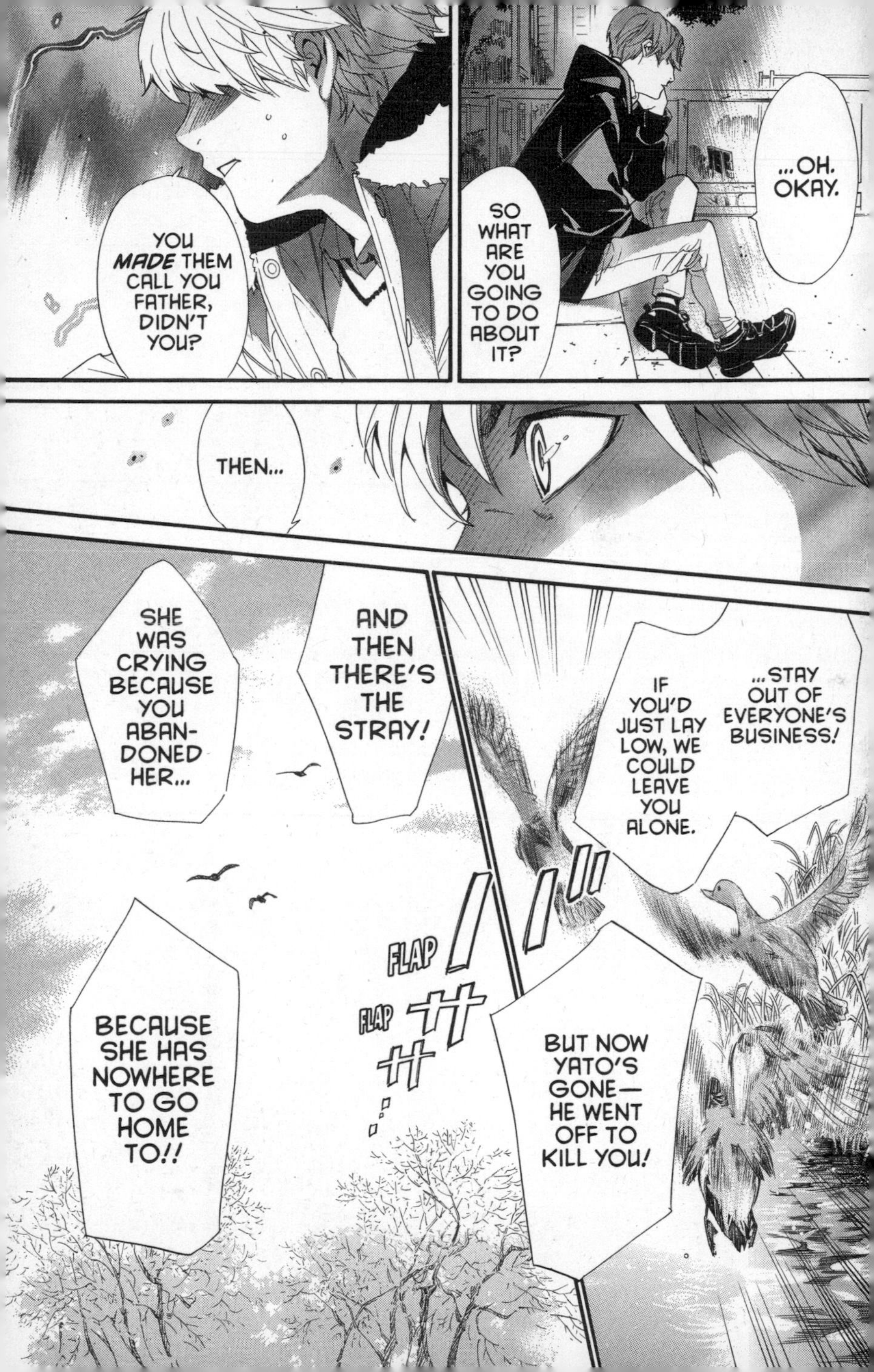
...OH. OKAY.
SO WHAT ARE YOU GOING TO DO ABOUT IT?
YOU *MADE* THEM CALL YOU FATHER, DIDN'T YOU?
THEN...
...STAY OUT OF EVERYONE'S BUSINESS!
IF YOU'D JUST LAY LOW, WE COULD LEAVE YOU ALONE.
BUT NOW YATO'S GONE— HE WENT OFF TO KILL YOU!
FLAP
FLAP
AND THEN THERE'S THE STRAY!
SHE WAS CRYING BECAUSE YOU ABAN-DONED HER...
BECAUSE SHE HAS NOWHERE TO GO HOME TO!!

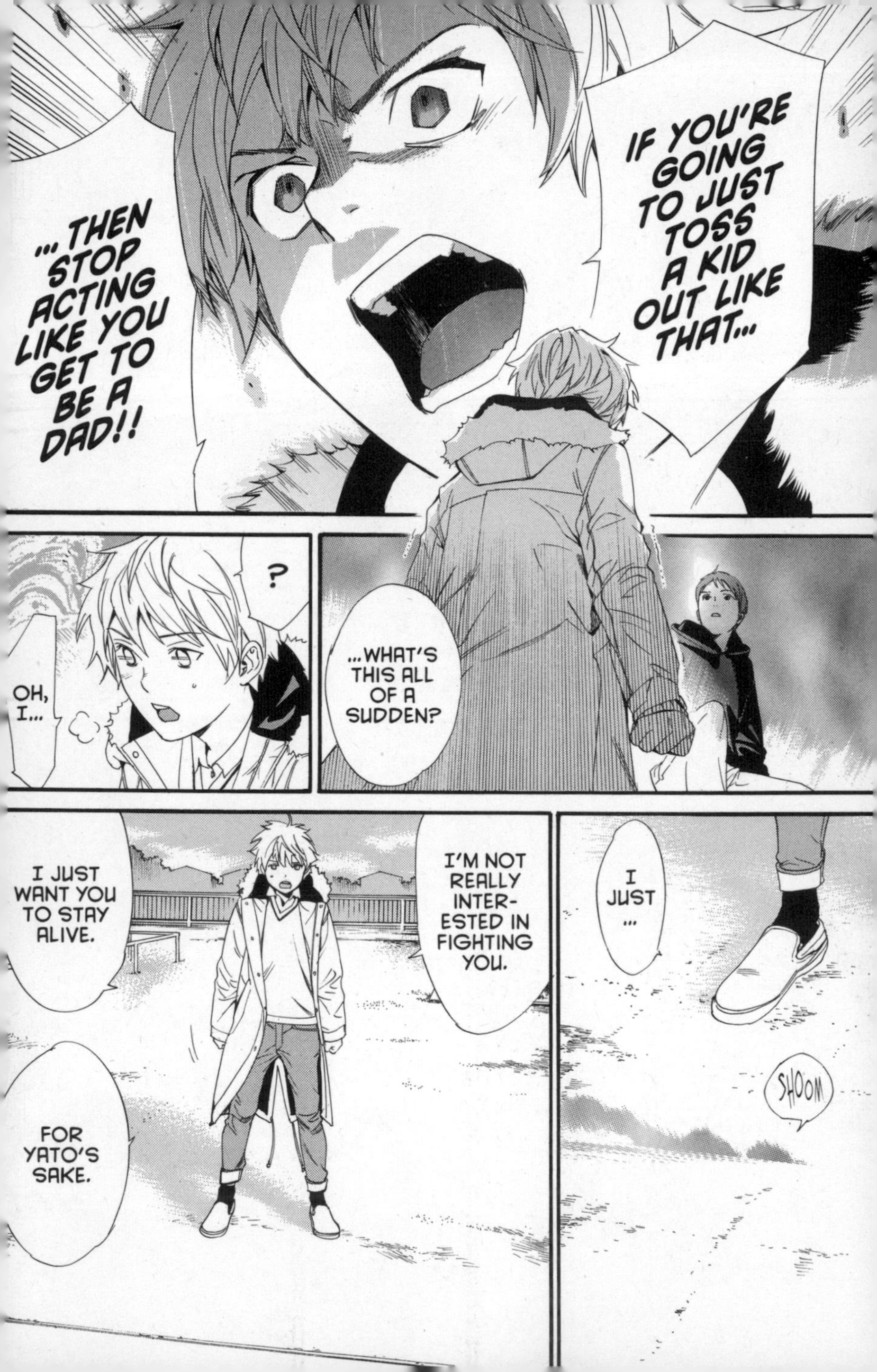
IF YOU'RE GOING TO JUST TOSS A KID OUT LIKE THAT...
...THEN STOP ACTING LIKE YOU GET TO BE A DAD!!
...WHAT'S THIS ALL OF A SUDDEN?
?
OH, I...
I JUST ...
SHOOM
I'M NOT REALLY INTER-ESTED IN FIGHTING YOU.
I JUST WANT YOU TO STAY ALIVE.
FOR YATO'S SAKE.

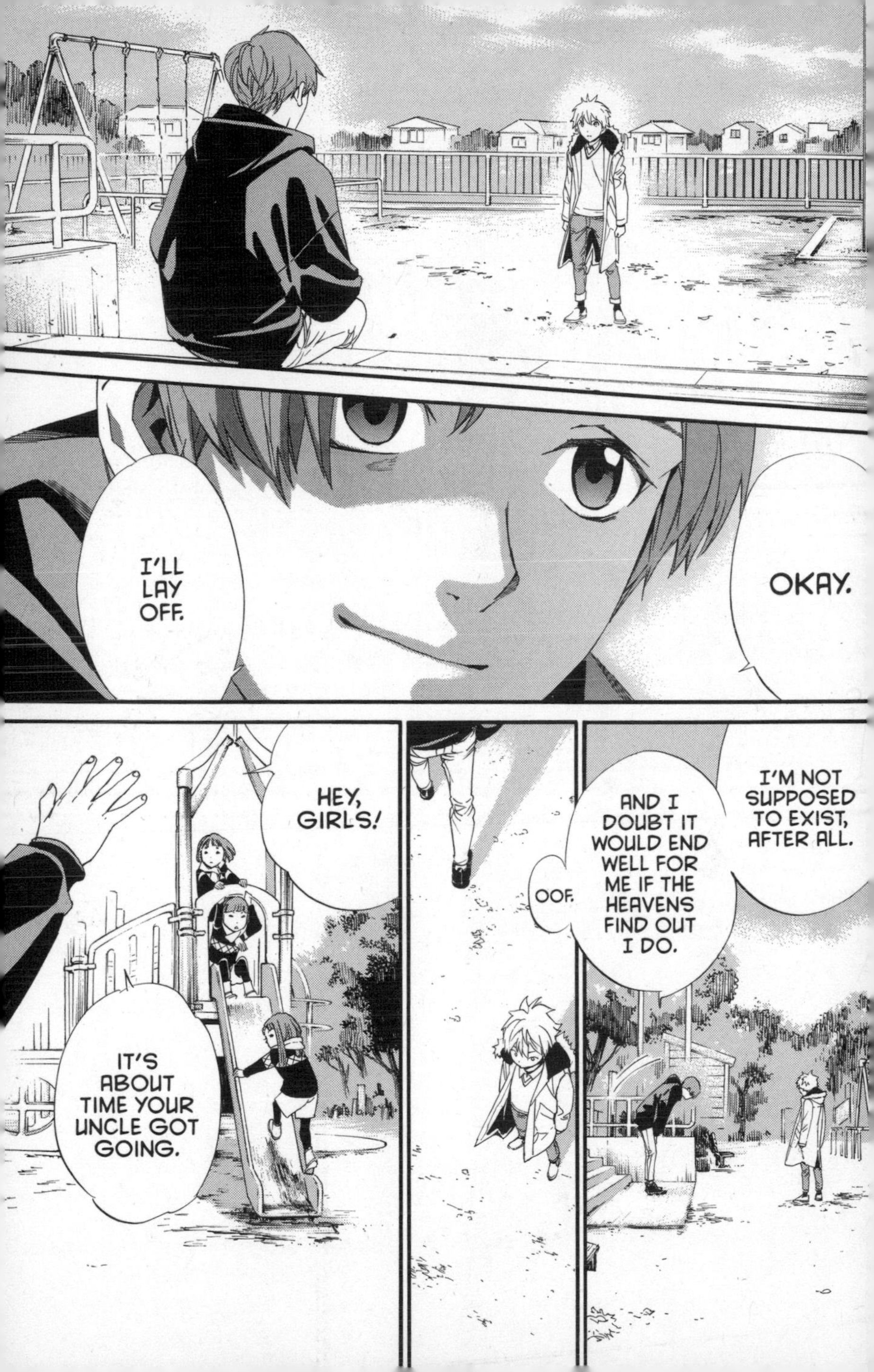
OKAY.
I'LL LAY OFF.
I'M NOT SUPPOSED TO EXIST, AFTER ALL.
AND I DOUBT IT WOULD END WELL FOR ME IF THE HEAVENS FIND OUT I DO.
OOF.
HEY, GIRLS!
IT'S ABOUT TIME YOUR UNCLE GOT GOING.

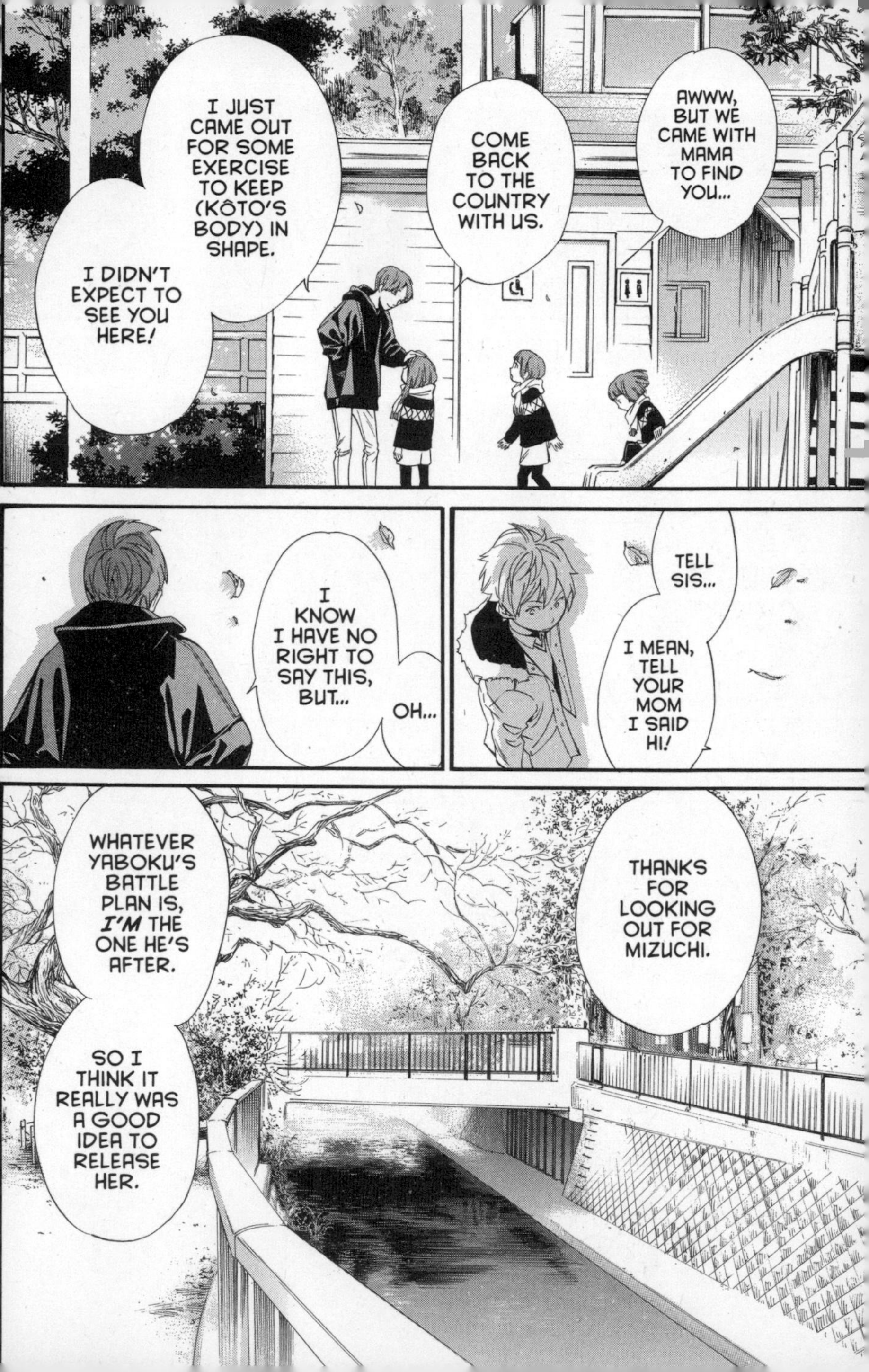
AWWW, BUT WE CAME WITH MAMA TO FIND YOU...
COME BACK TO THE COUNTRY WITH US.
I JUST CAME OUT FOR SOME EXERCISE TO KEEP (KÔTO'S BODY) IN SHAPE.
I DIDN'T EXPECT TO SEE YOU HERE!
TELL SIS...
I MEAN, TELL YOUR MOM I SAID HI!
I KNOW I HAVE NO RIGHT TO SAY THIS, BUT...
OH...
THANKS FOR LOOKING OUT FOR MIZUCHI.
WHATEVER YABOKU'S BATTLE PLAN IS, *I'M* THE ONE HE'S AFTER.
SO I THINK IT REALLY WAS A GOOD IDEA TO RELEASE HER.

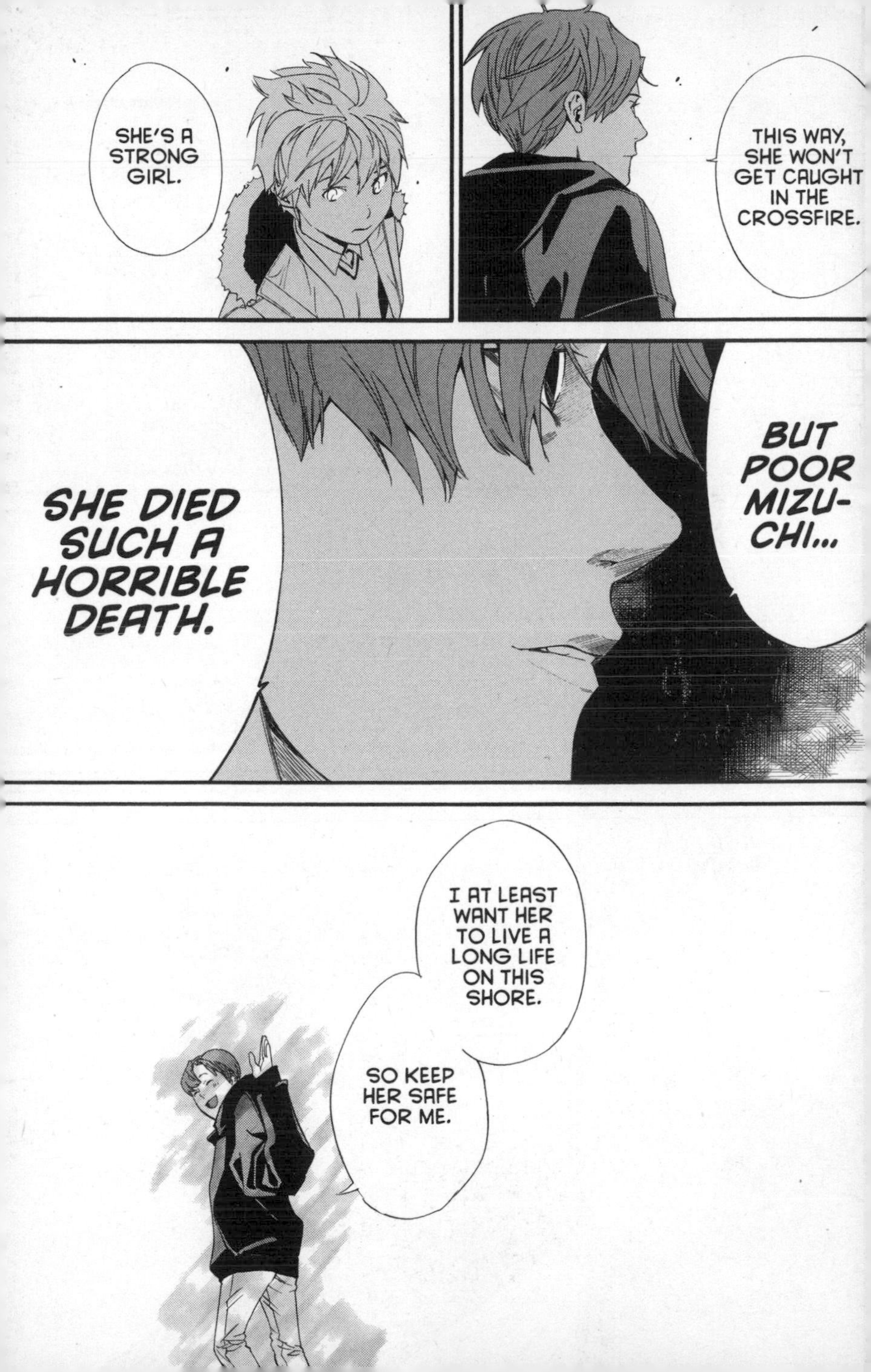
THIS WAY, SHE WON'T GET CAUGHT IN THE CROSSFIRE.
SHE'S A STRONG GIRL.
BUT POOR MIZU-CHI...
SHE DIED SUCH A HORRIBLE DEATH.
I AT LEAST WANT HER TO LIVE A LONG LIFE ON THIS SHORE.
SO KEEP HER SAFE FOR ME.

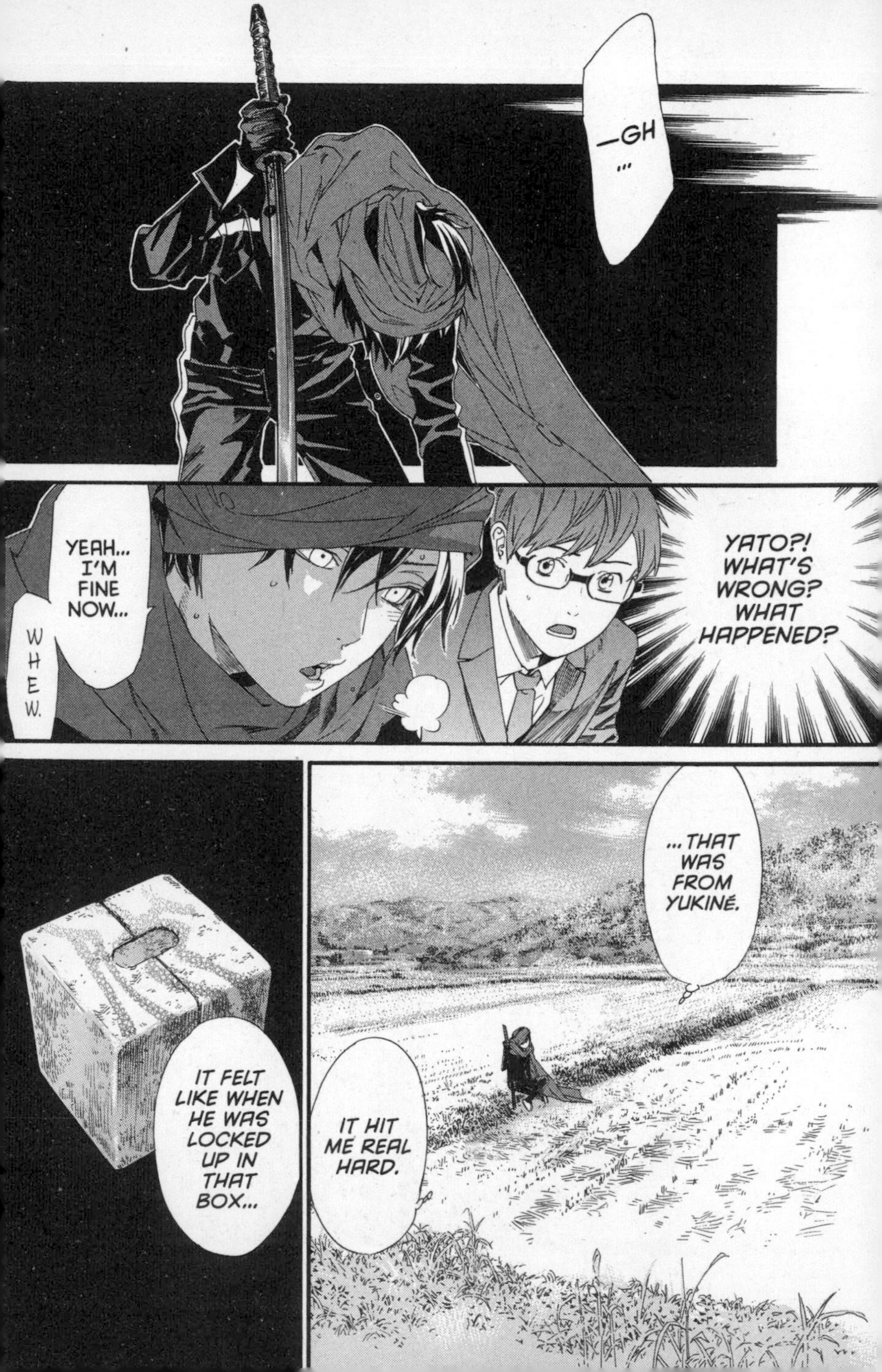
—GH ...
YATO?! WHAT'S WRONG? WHAT HAPPENED?
YEAH... I'M FINE NOW...
WHEW.
...THAT WAS FROM YUKINÉ.
IT HIT ME REAL HARD.
IT FELT LIKE WHEN HE WAS LOCKED UP IN THAT BOX...

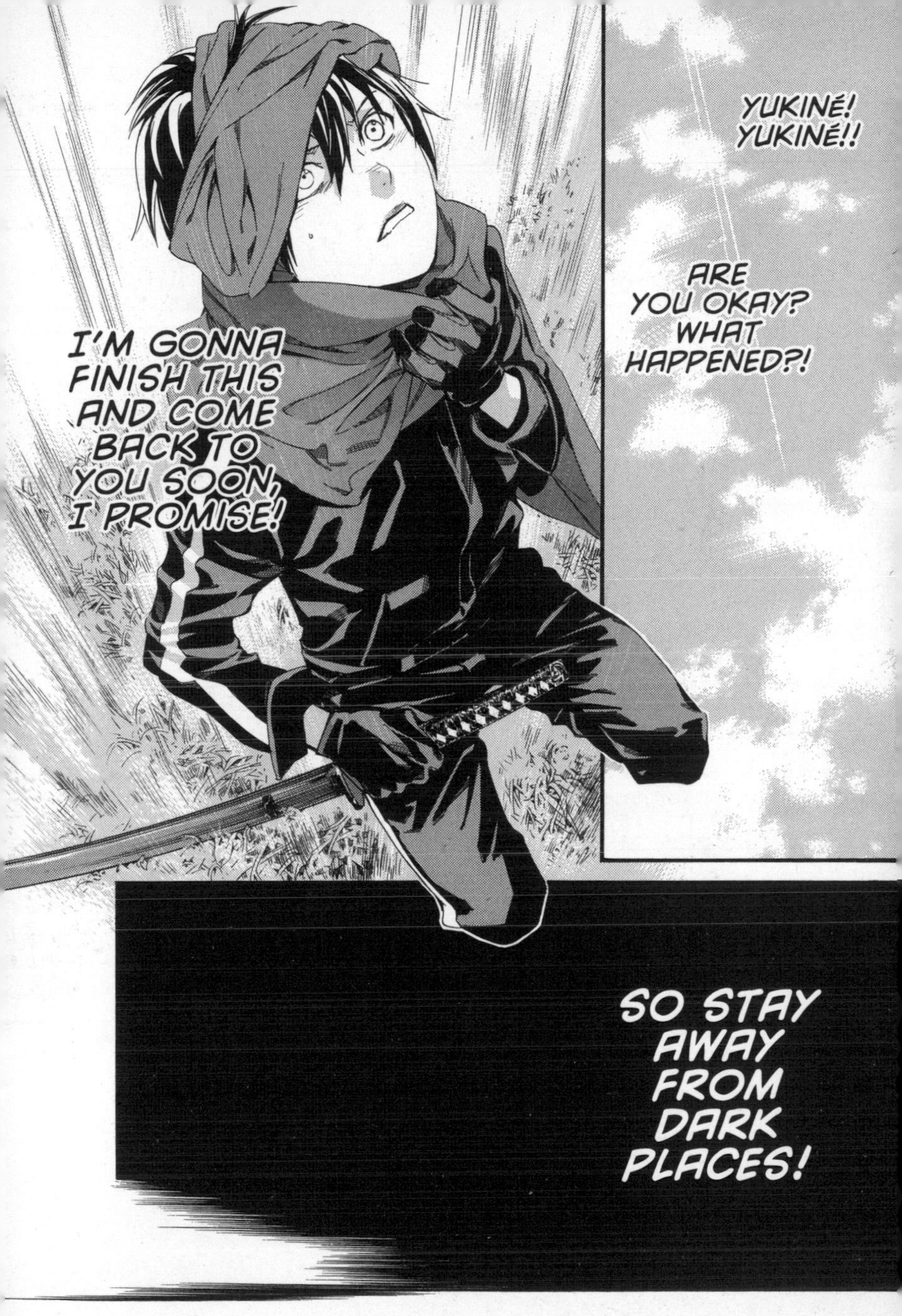
YUKINÉ! YUKINÉ!!
ARE YOU OKAY? WHAT HAPPENED?!
I'M GONNA FINISH THIS AND COME BACK TO YOU SOON, I PROMISE!
SO STAY AWAY FROM DARK PLACES!

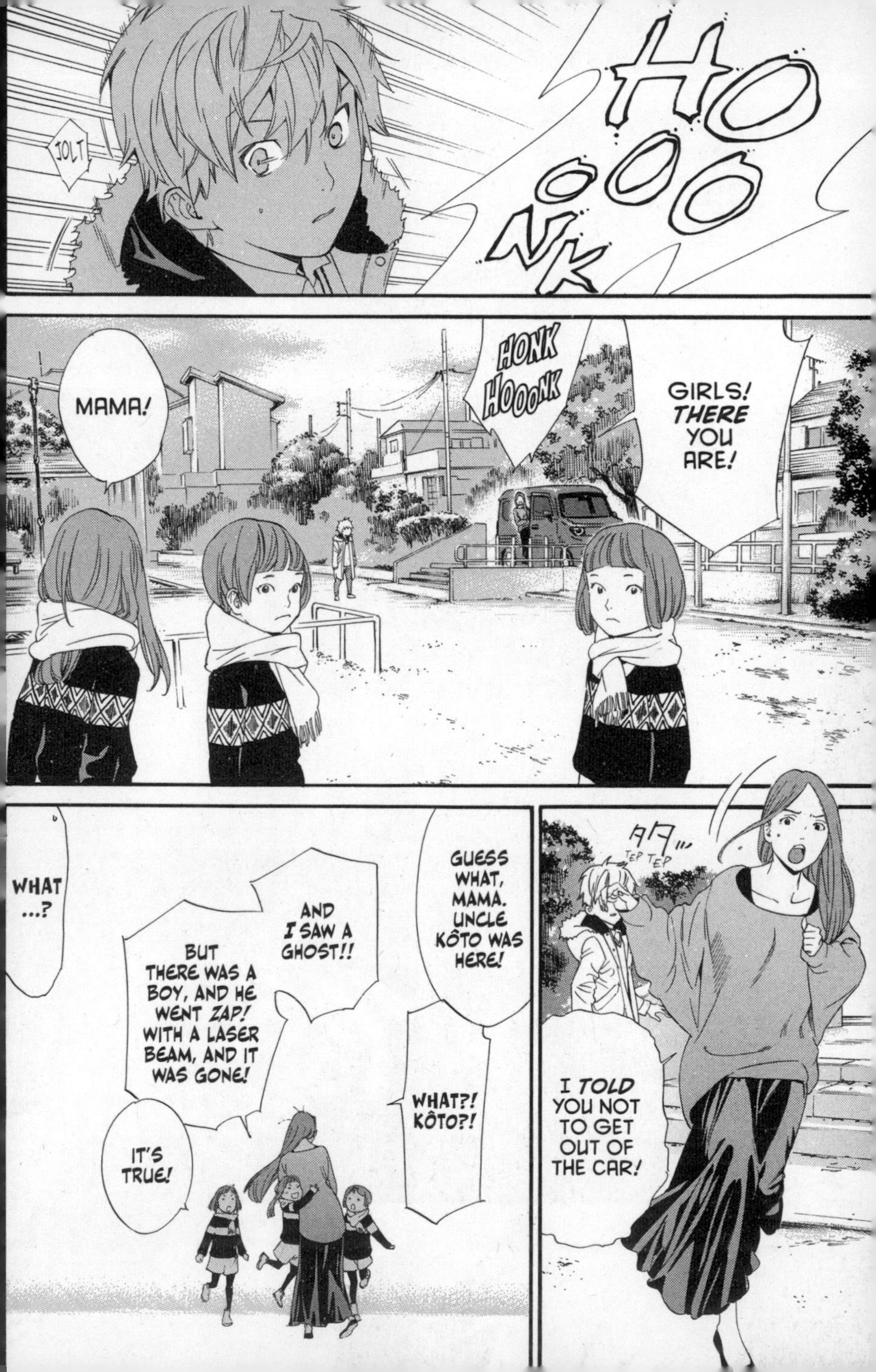
HOOOONK
JOLT
GIRLS! THERE YOU ARE!
HONK HOOONK
MAMA!
TEP TEP
I TOLD YOU NOT TO GET OUT OF THE CAR!
GUESS WHAT, MAMA. UNCLE KÔTO WAS HERE!
AND I SAW A GHOST!!
WHAT?! KÔTO?!
BUT THERE WAS A BOY, AND HE WENT ZAP! WITH A LASER BEAM, AND IT WAS GONE!
IT'S TRUE!
WHAT ...?

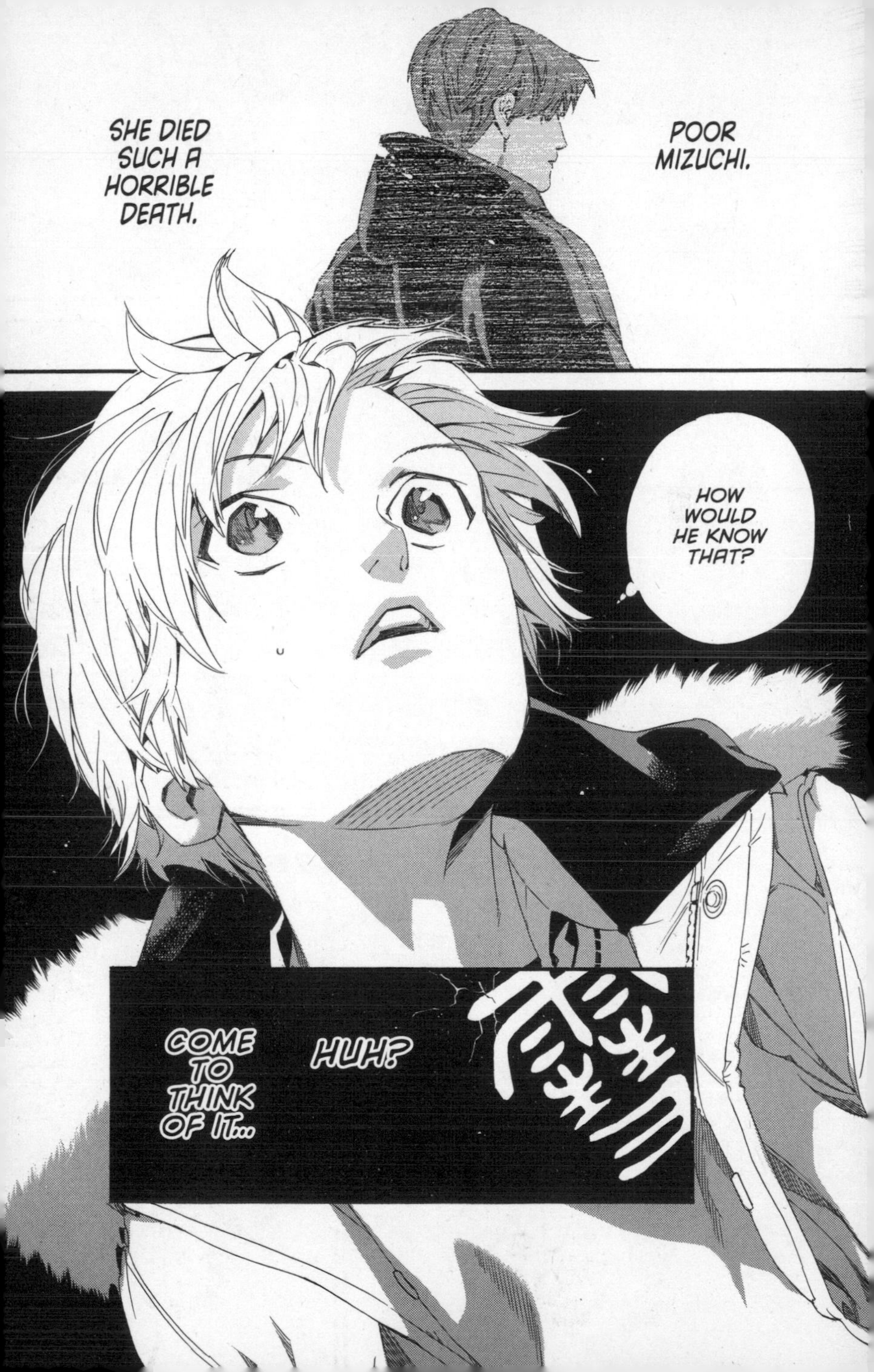
POOR MIZUCHI.
SHE DIED SUCH A HORRIBLE DEATH.
HOW WOULD HE KNOW THAT?
HUH?
COME TO THINK OF IT...

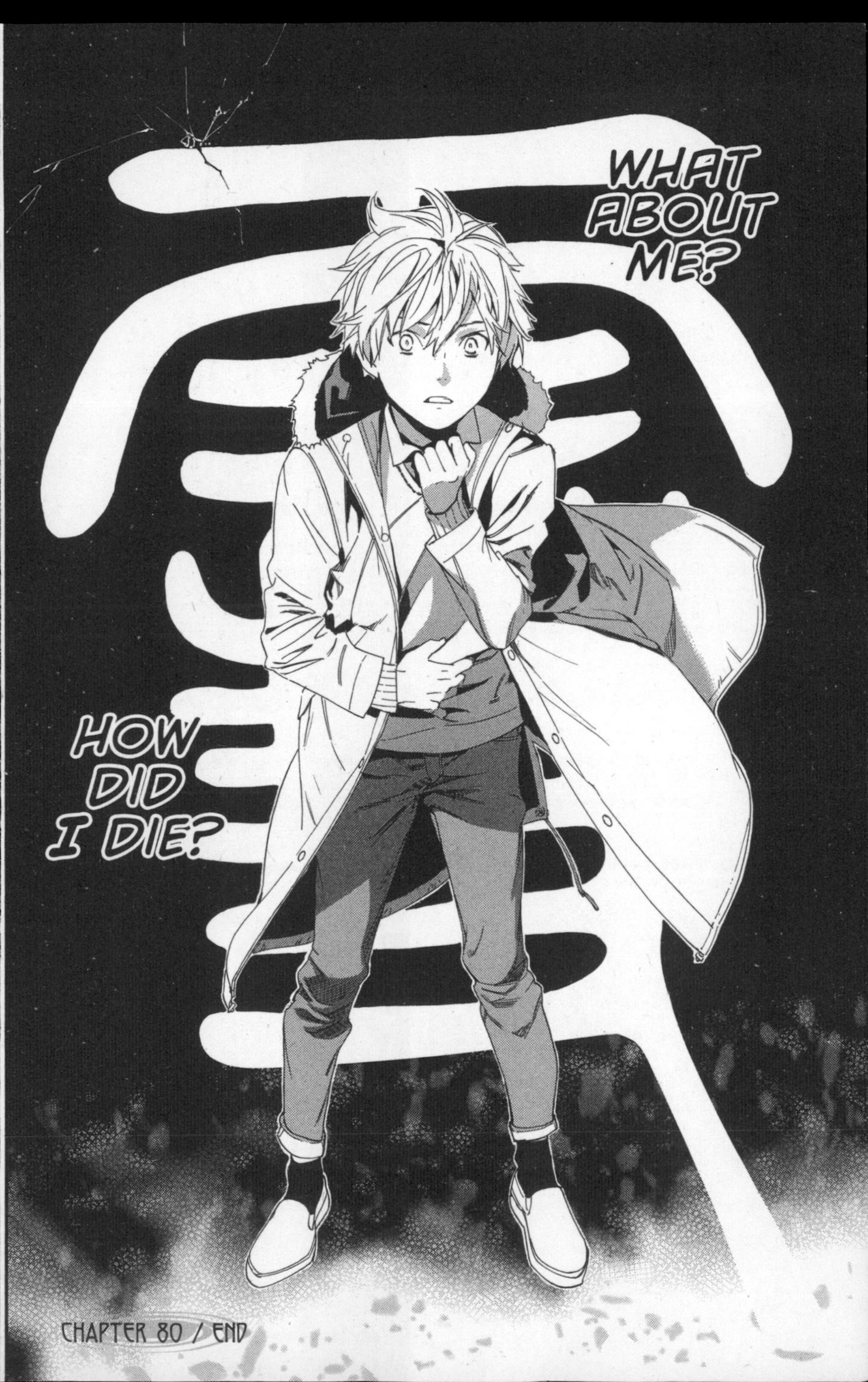
WHAT ABOUT ME?
HOW DID I DIE?

CHAPTER 80 / END

野

良

神

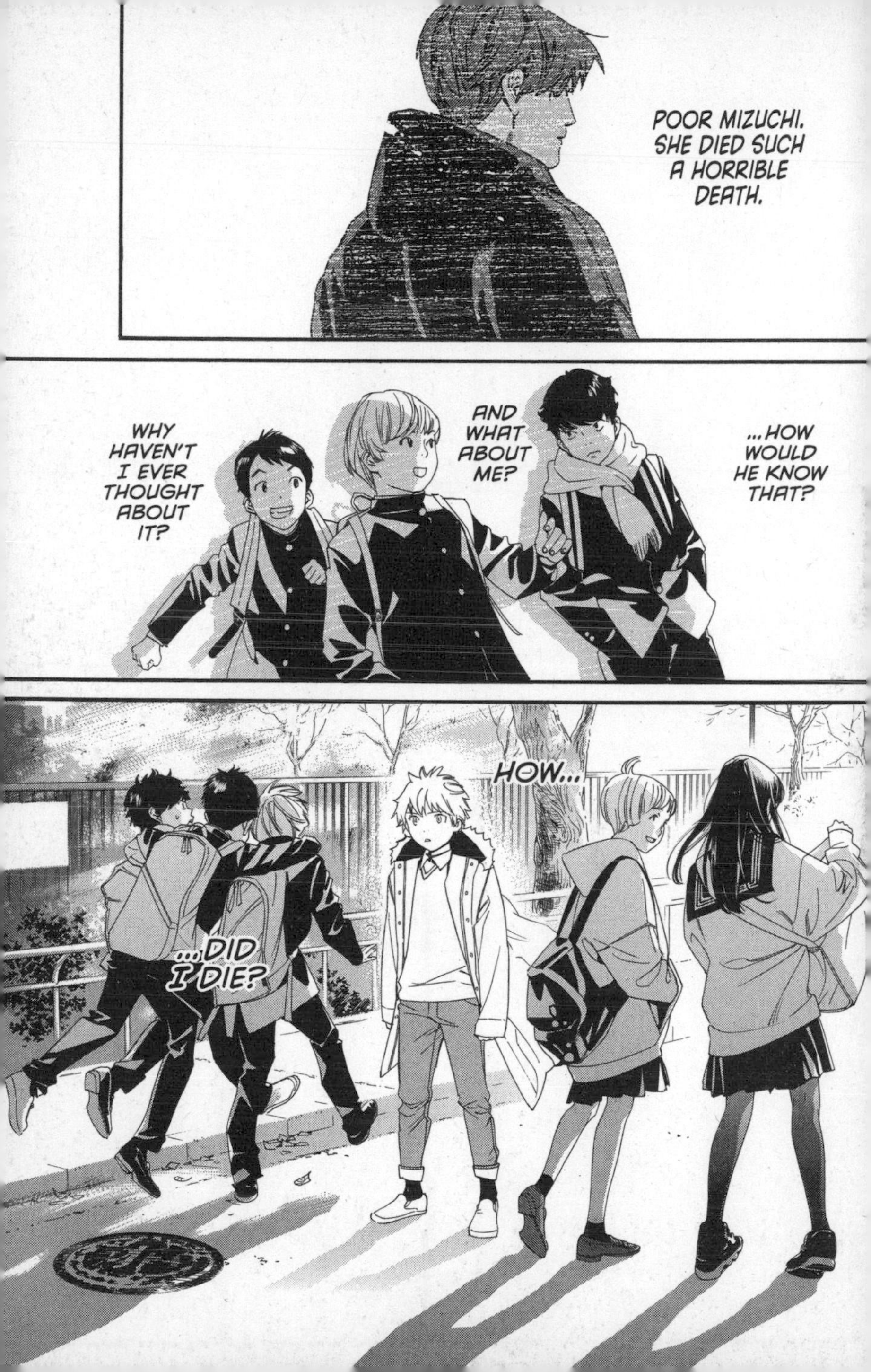
POOR MIZUCHI. SHE DIED SUCH A HORRIBLE DEATH.
...HOW WOULD HE KNOW THAT?
AND WHAT ABOUT ME?
WHY HAVEN'T I EVER THOUGHT ABOUT IT?
HOW...
...DID I DIE?

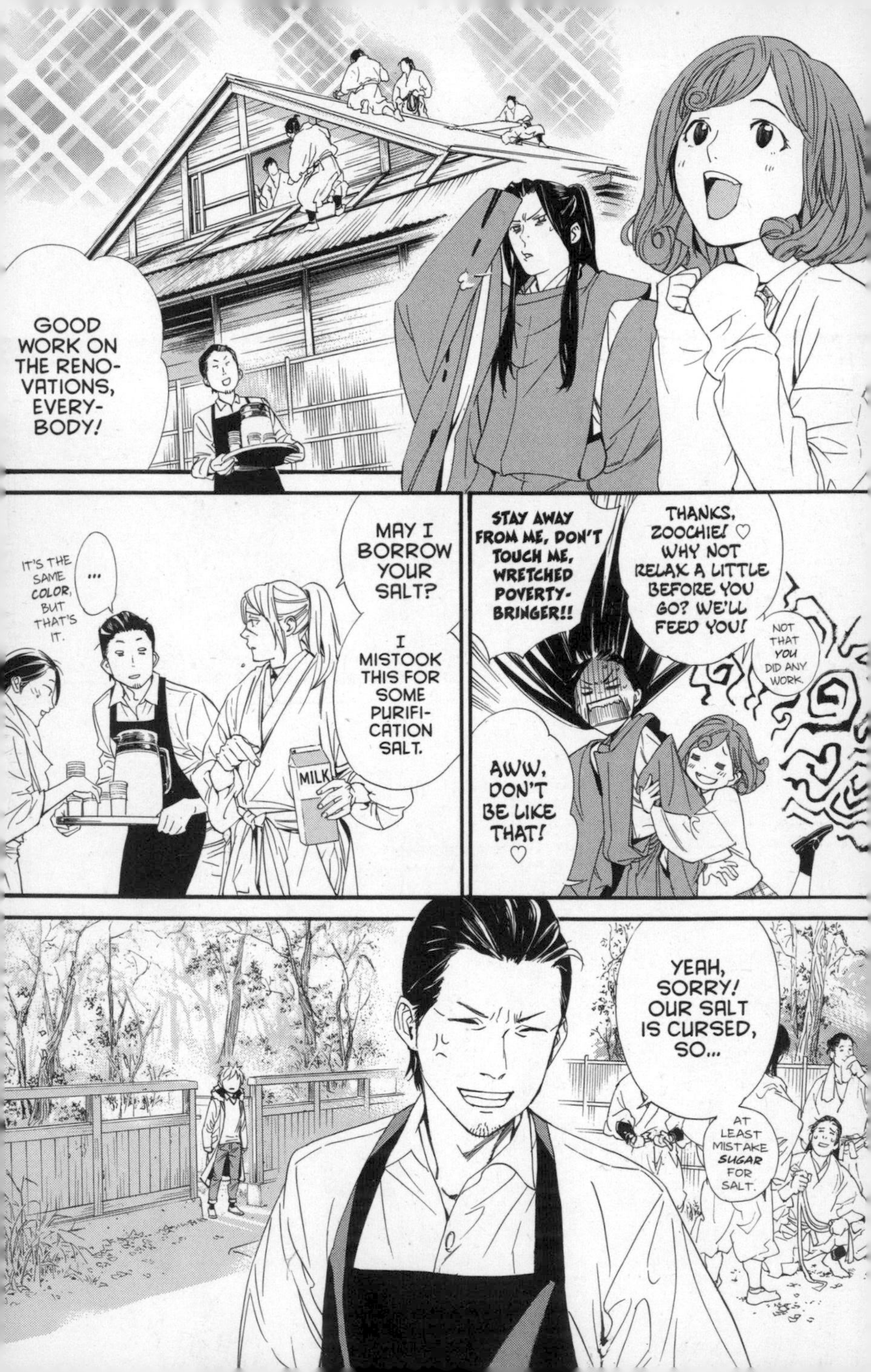

GOOD WORK ON THE RENOVATIONS, EVERYBODY!
THANKS, ZOOCHIE! ♡ WHY NOT RELAX A LITTLE BEFORE YOU GO? WE'LL FEED YOU!
NOT THAT YOU DID ANY WORK.
STAY AWAY FROM ME, DON'T TOUCH ME, WRETCHED POVERTY-BRINGER!!
AWW, DON'T BE LIKE THAT! ♡
MAY I BORROW YOUR SALT?
I MISTOOK THIS FOR SOME PURIFICATION SALT.
...
IT'S THE SAME COLOR, BUT THAT'S IT.
MILK
YEAH, SORRY! OUR SALT IS CURSED, SO...
AT LEAST MISTAKE SUGAR FOR SALT.

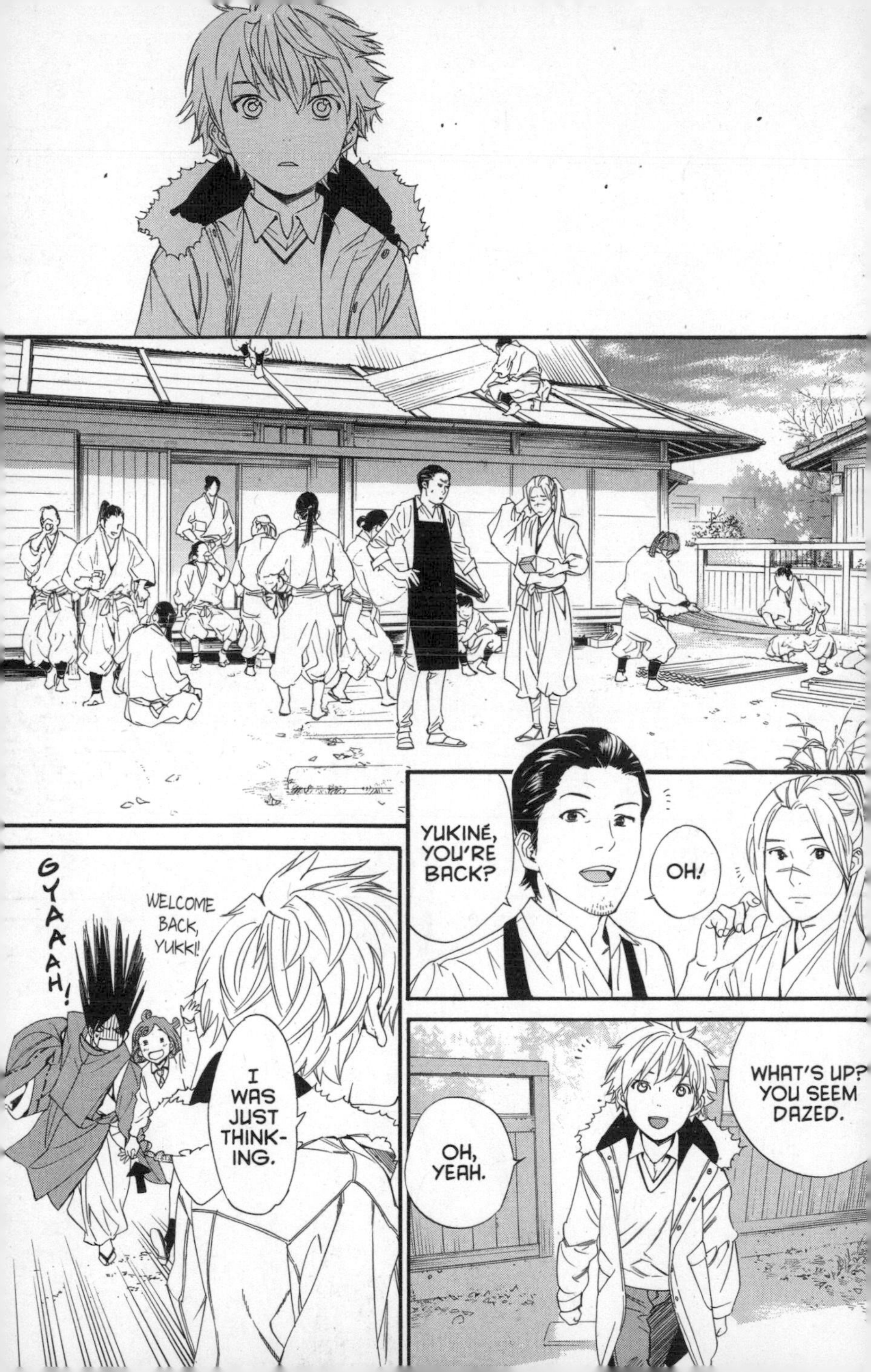
OH!
YUKINÉ, YOU'RE BACK?
WHAT'S UP? YOU SEEM DAZED.
OH, YEAH.
I WAS JUST THINKING.
WELCOME BACK, YUKKI!
GYAAAH!

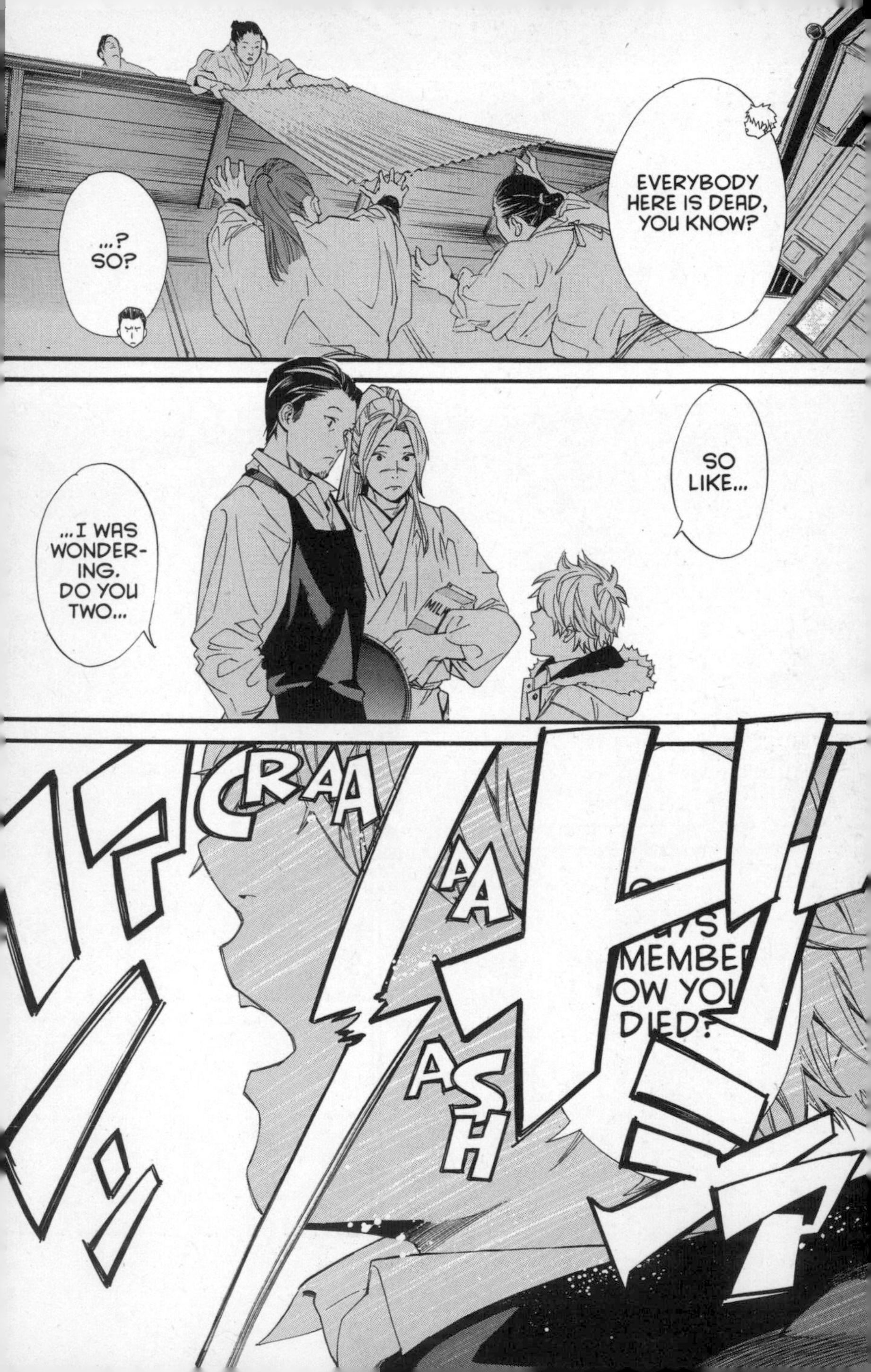
EVERYBODY HERE IS DEAD, YOU KNOW?
...? SO?
SO LIKE...
...I WAS WONDERING. DO YOU TWO...
CRAAAASH
MEMBE OW YOU DIED?

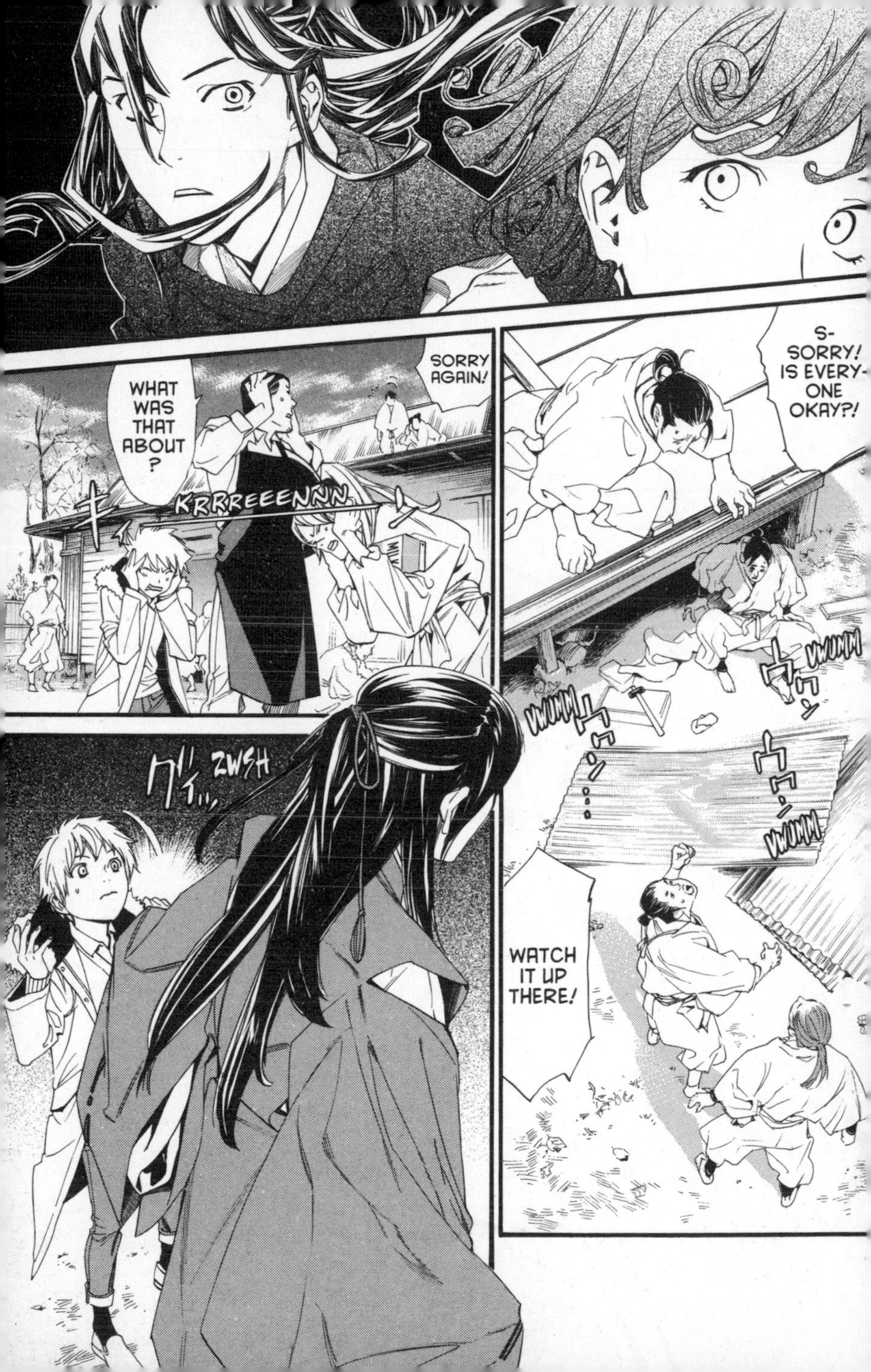
S-SORRY! IS EVERY-ONE OKAY?!
SORRY AGAIN!
WHAT WAS THAT ABOUT?
KRRREEENNN
VWUMM
VWUMM
VWUMM
WATCH IT UP THERE!
ZWSH

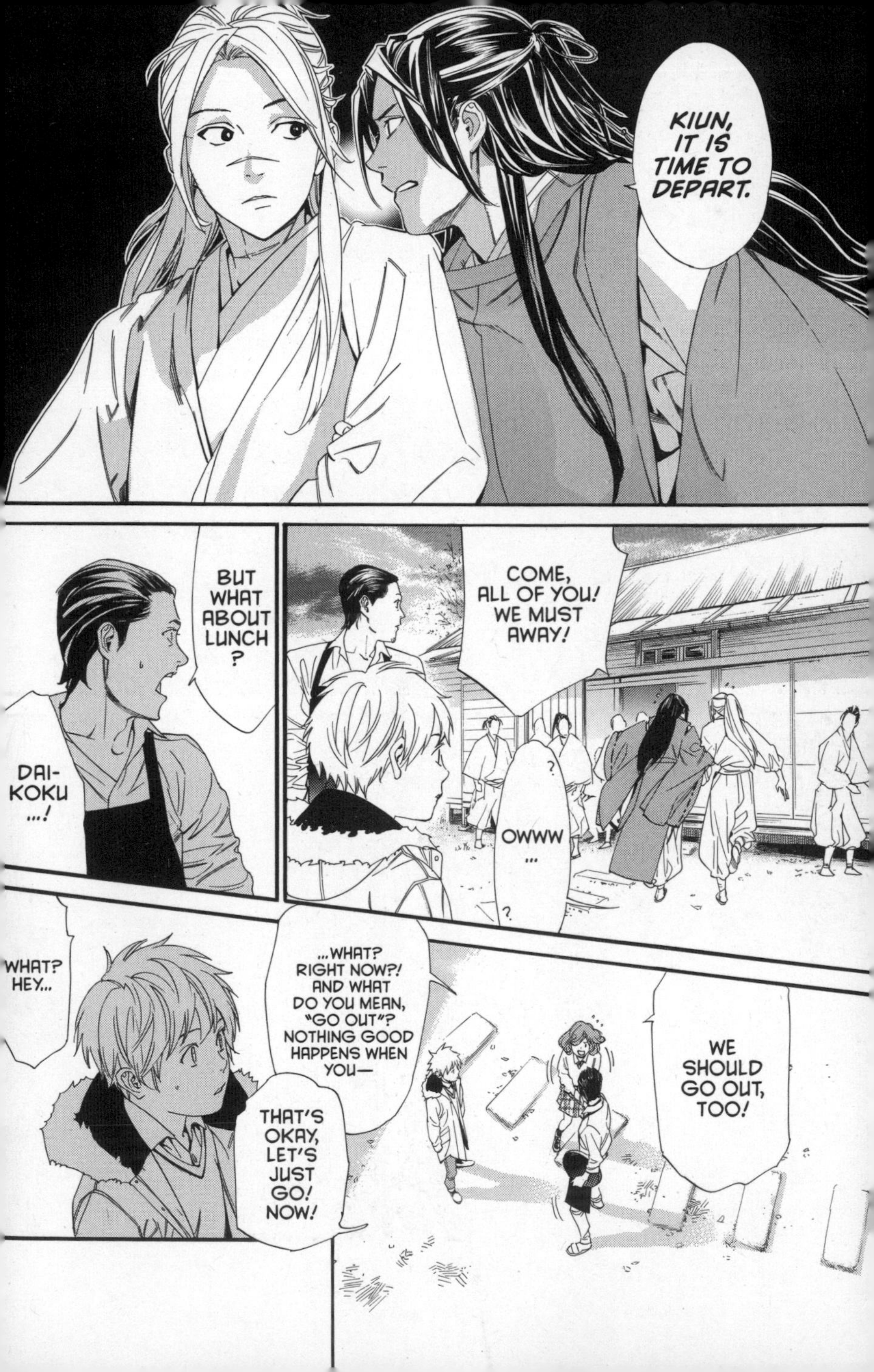
KIUN, IT IS TIME TO DEPART.
COME, ALL OF YOU! WE MUST AWAY!
? OWWW ... ?
BUT WHAT ABOUT LUNCH?
DAIKOKU ...!
WE SHOULD GO OUT, TOO!
WHAT? HEY...
...WHAT? RIGHT NOW?! AND WHAT DO YOU MEAN, "GO OUT"? NOTHING GOOD HAPPENS WHEN YOU—
THAT'S OKAY, LET'S JUST GO! NOW!

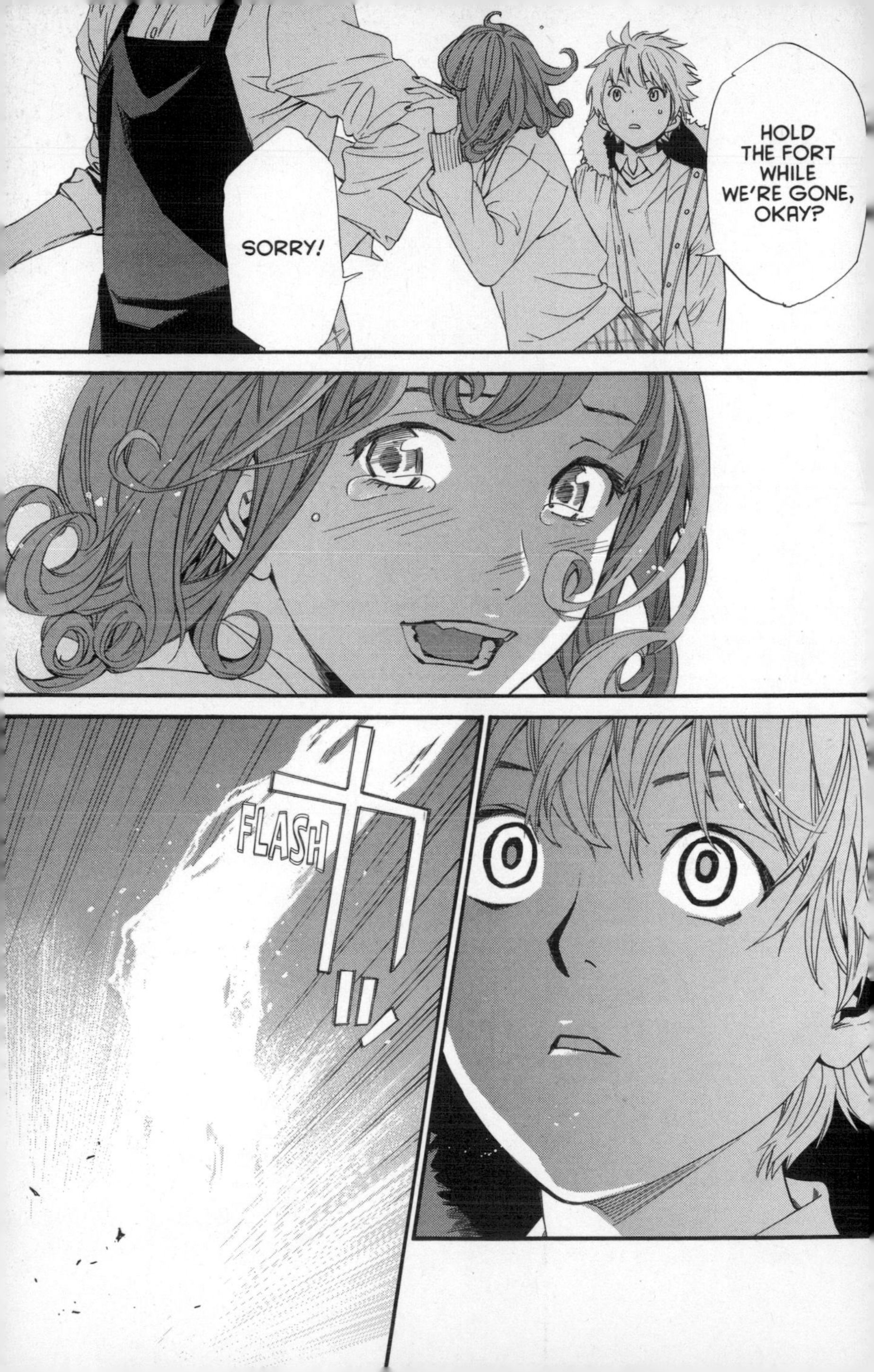
HOLD THE FORT WHILE WE'RE GONE, OKAY?
SORRY!
FLASH

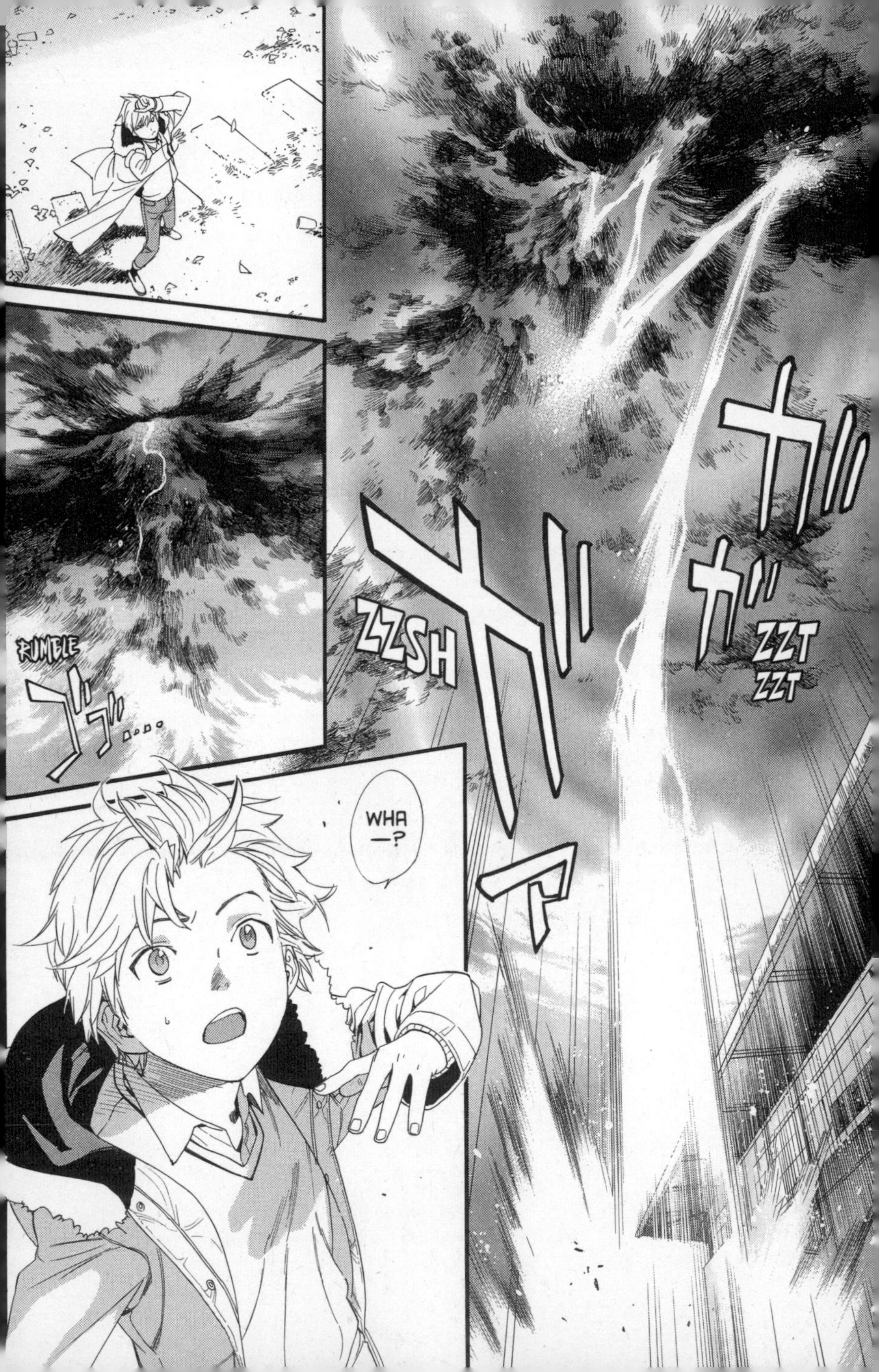
ZZT
ZZT
ZZSH
RUMBLE
WHA—?

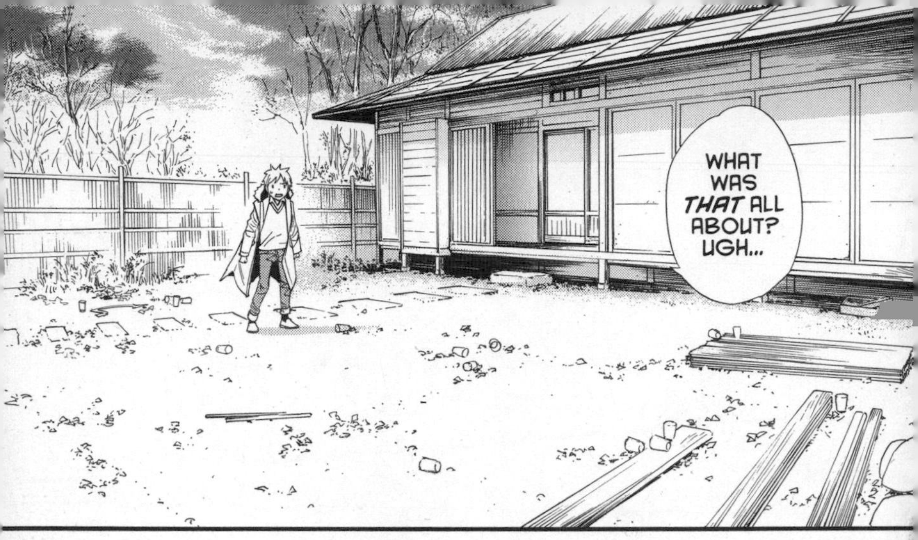
WHAT WAS *THAT* ALL ABOUT? UGH...

CHAPTER 81: ALONE

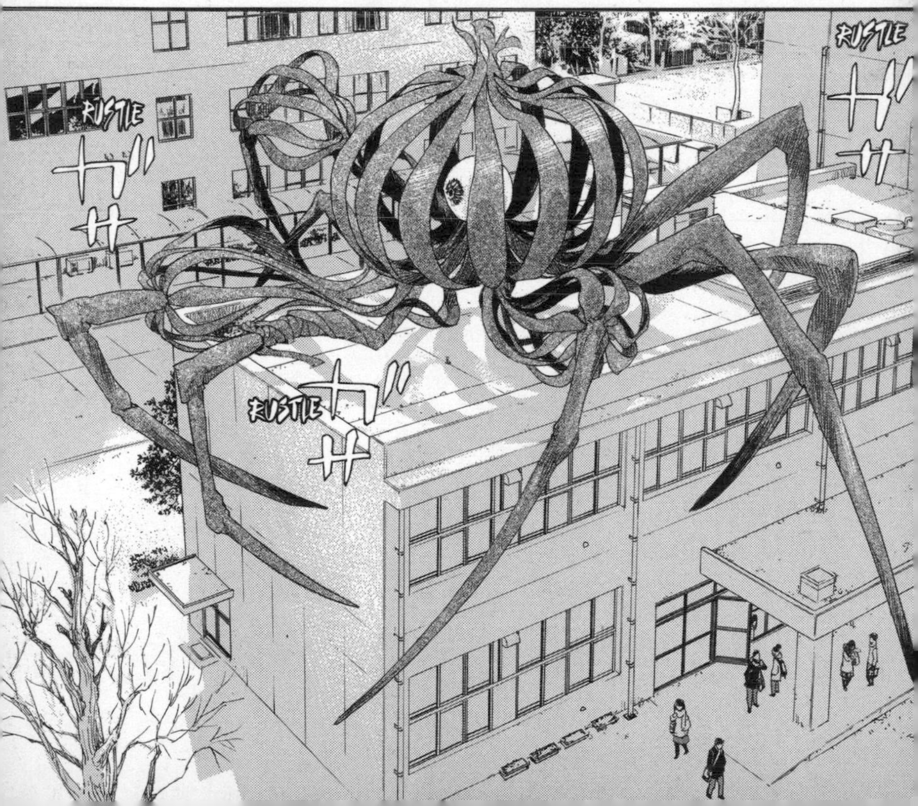
RUSTLE
RUSTLE
RUSTLE

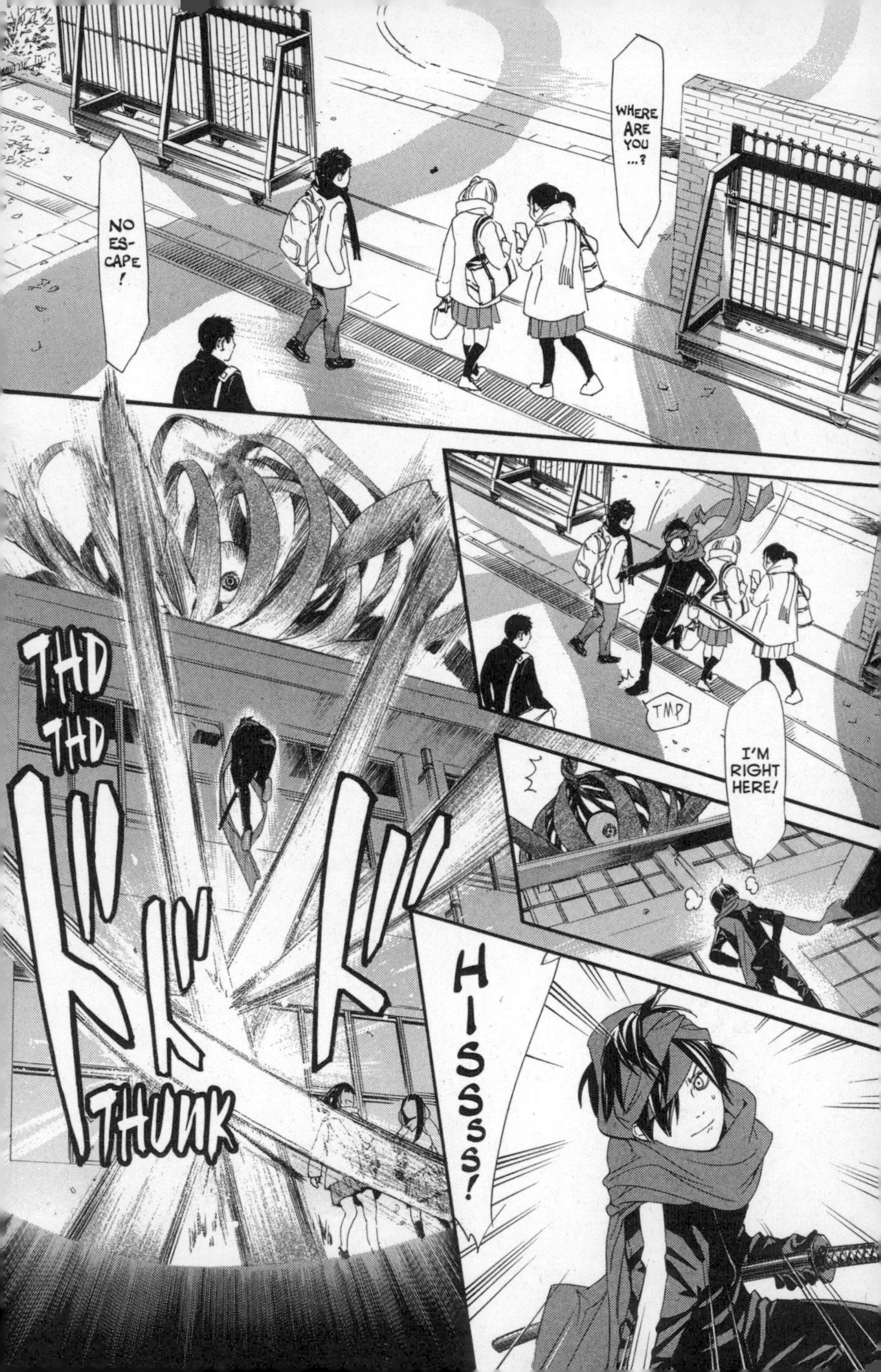
WHERE ARE YOU ...?
NO ES-CAPE!
TMP
I'M RIGHT HERE!
HISSSS!
THD THD
ドドド
THUNK

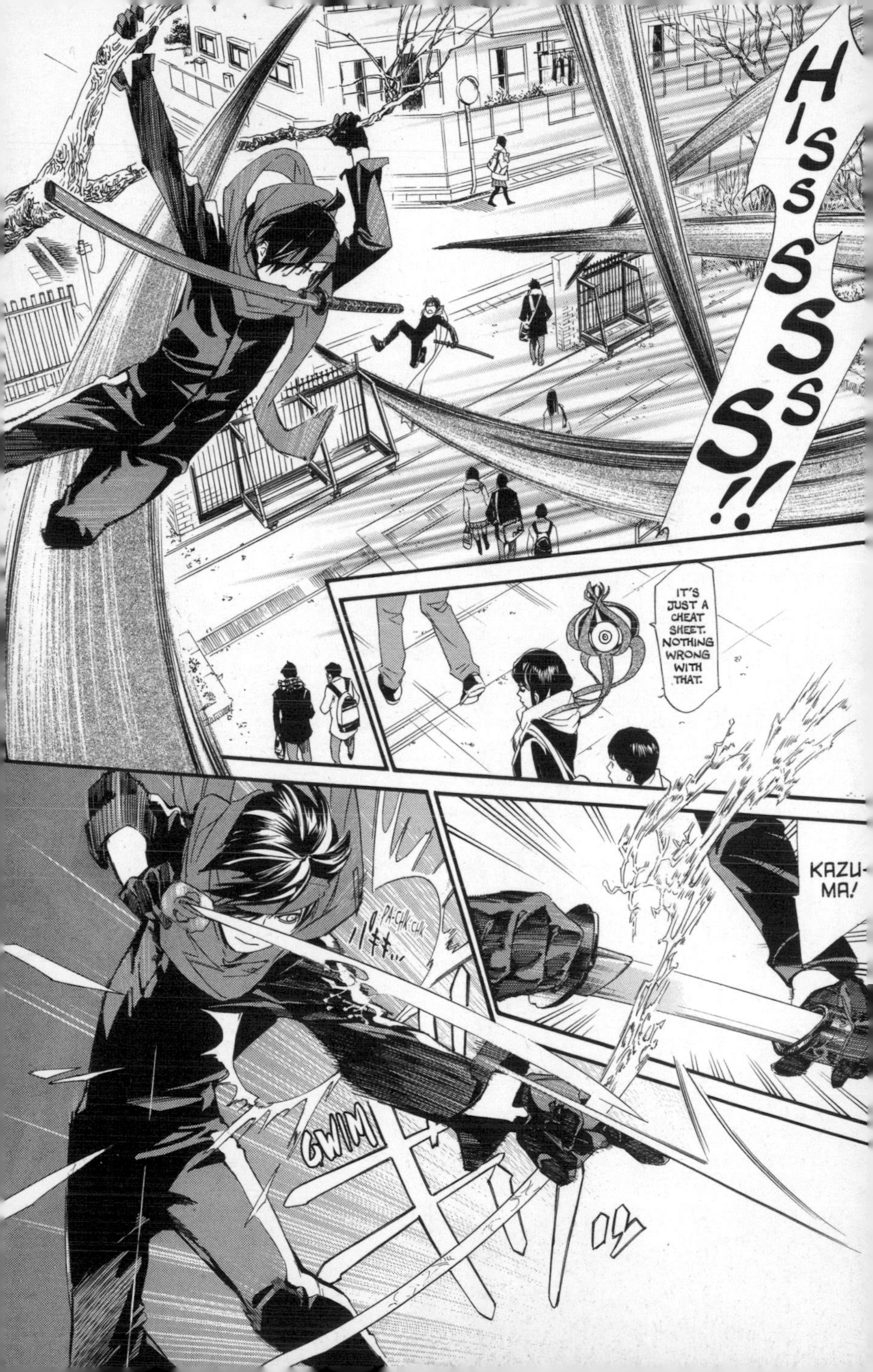
HISSSSSS!!
IT'S JUST A CHEAT SHEET. NOTHING WRONG WITH THAT.
KAZU-MA!
PA-CHA-CHA
GWIM

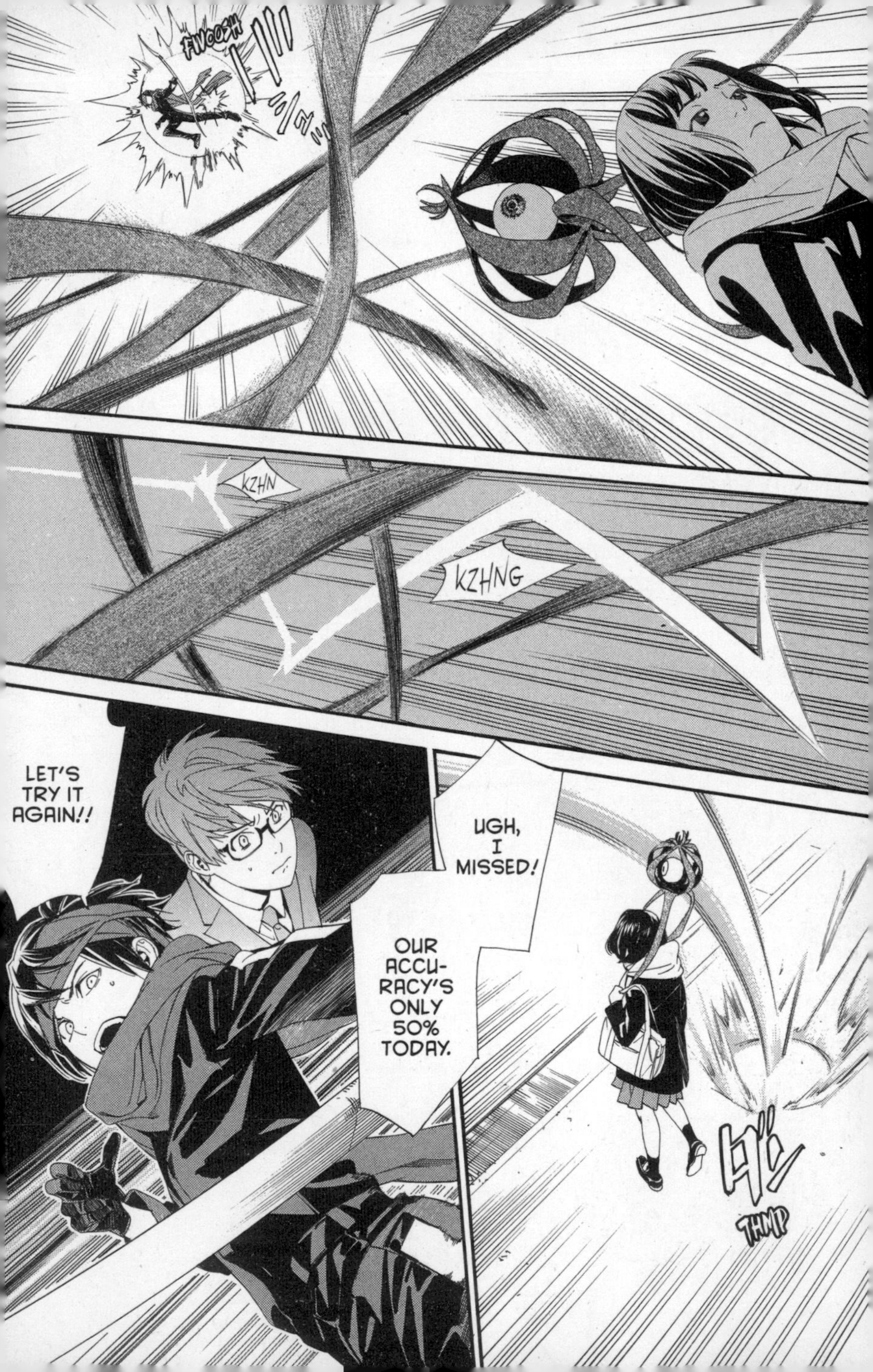
FWOOSH
KZHN
KZHNG
THMP
UGH, I MISSED!
OUR ACCURACY'S ONLY 50% TODAY.
LET'S TRY IT AGAIN!!

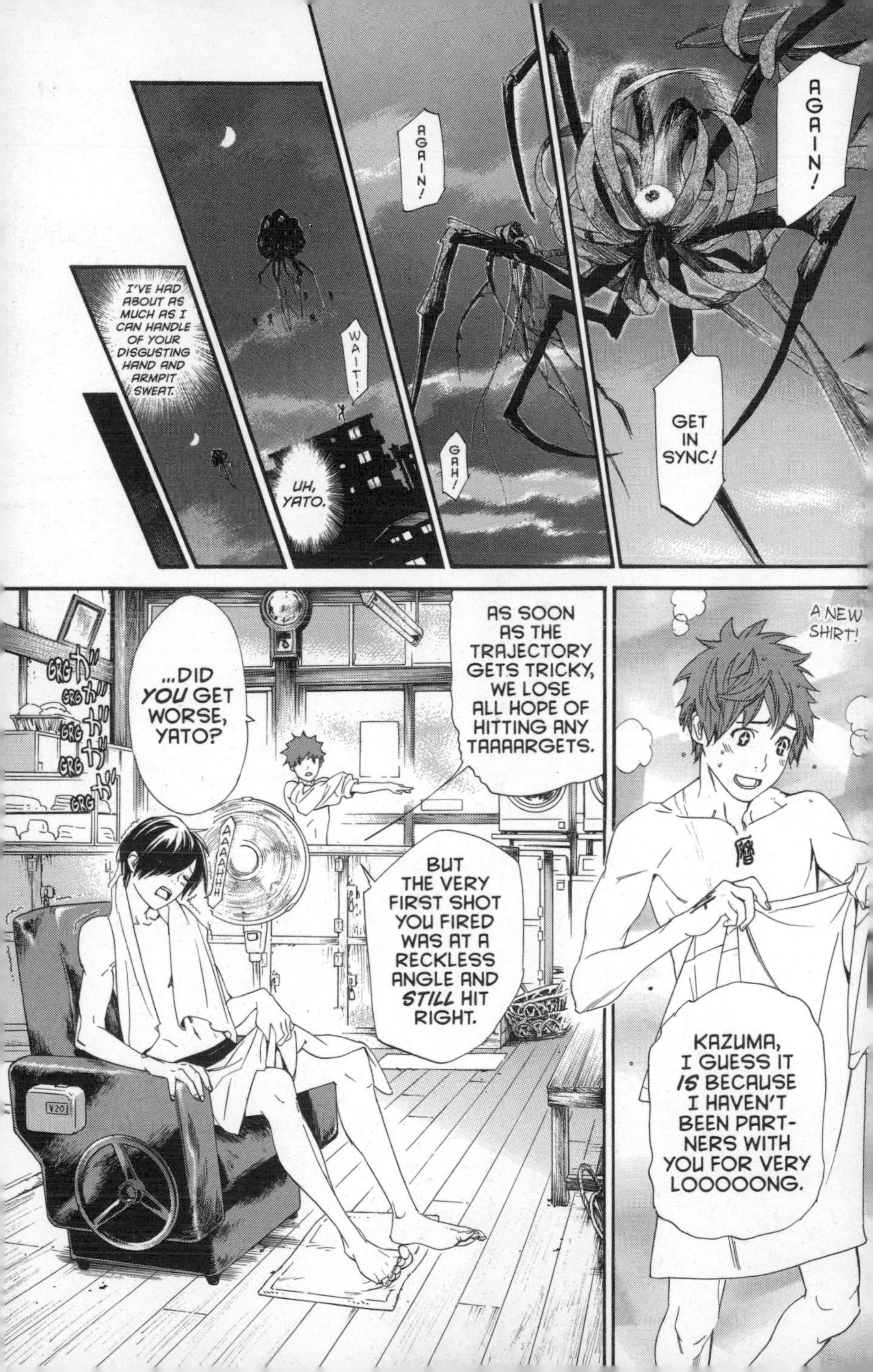

AGAIN!
GET IN SYNC!
AGAIN!
GAH!
WAIT!
UH, YATO.
I'VE HAD ABOUT AS MUCH AS I CAN HANDLE OF YOUR DISGUSTING HAND AND ARMPIT SWEAT.
A NEW SHIRT!
KAZUMA, I GUESS IT IS BECAUSE I HAVEN'T BEEN PART-NERS WITH YOU FOR VERY LOOOOONG.
AS SOON AS THE TRAJECTORY GETS TRICKY, WE LOSE ALL HOPE OF HITTING ANY TAAAARGETS.
...DID YOU GET WORSE, YATO?
GRG GRG GRG GRG GRG
AAAAHHH
BUT THE VERY FIRST SHOT YOU FIRED WAS AT A RECKLESS ANGLE AND STILL HIT RIGHT.
¥20

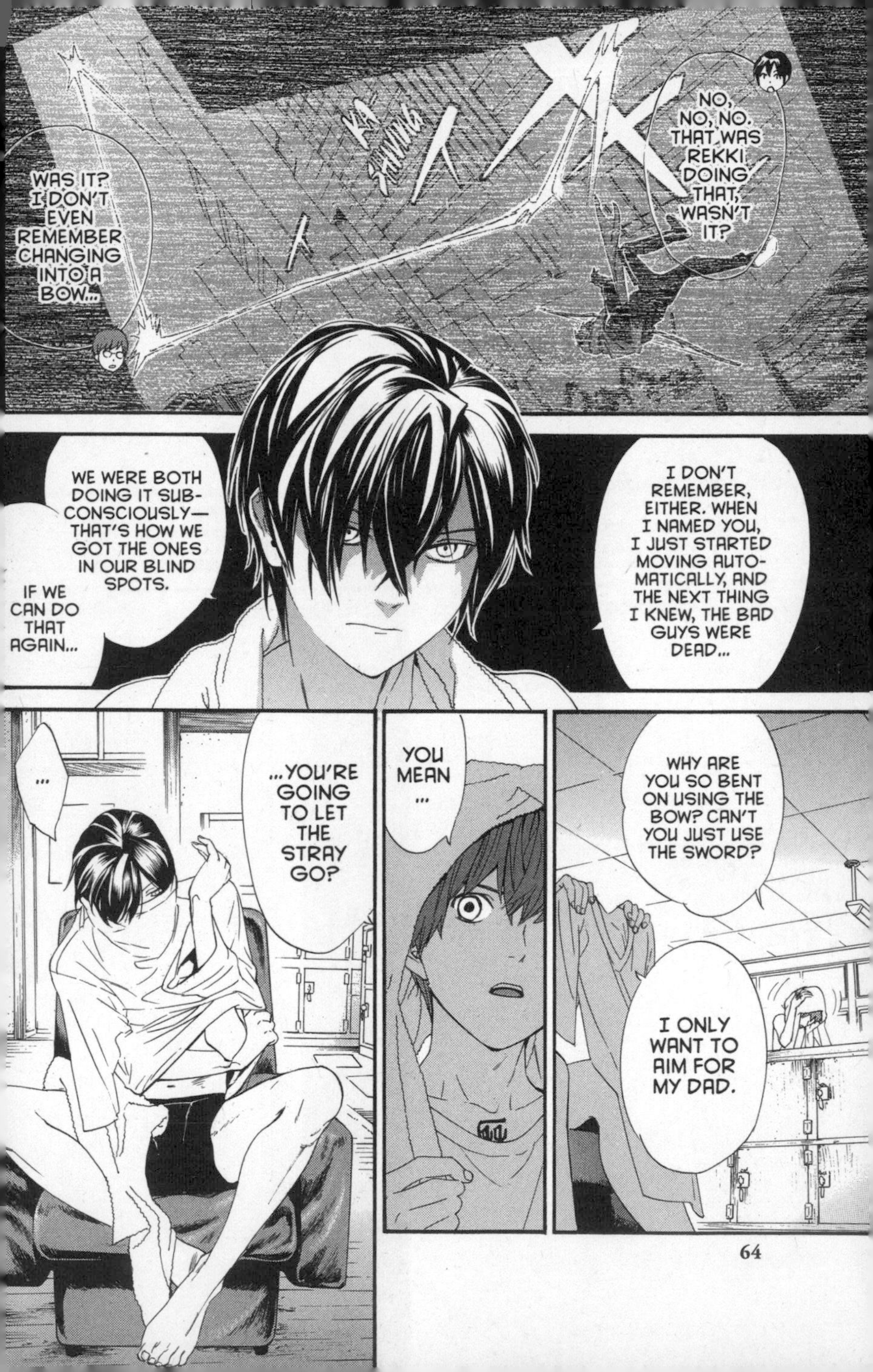
NO, NO, NO. THAT WAS REKKI DOING THAT, WASN'T IT?
WAS IT? I DON'T EVEN REMEMBER CHANGING INTO A BOW...
I DON'T REMEMBER, EITHER. WHEN I NAMED YOU, I JUST STARTED MOVING AUTOMATICALLY, AND THE NEXT THING I KNEW, THE BAD GUYS WERE DEAD...
WE WERE BOTH DOING IT SUBCONSCIOUSLY—THAT'S HOW WE GOT THE ONES IN OUR BLIND SPOTS.
IF WE CAN DO THAT AGAIN...
WHY ARE YOU SO BENT ON USING THE BOW? CAN'T YOU JUST USE THE SWORD?
I ONLY WANT TO AIM FOR MY DAD.
YOU MEAN ...
...YOU'RE GOING TO LET THE STRAY GO?
...

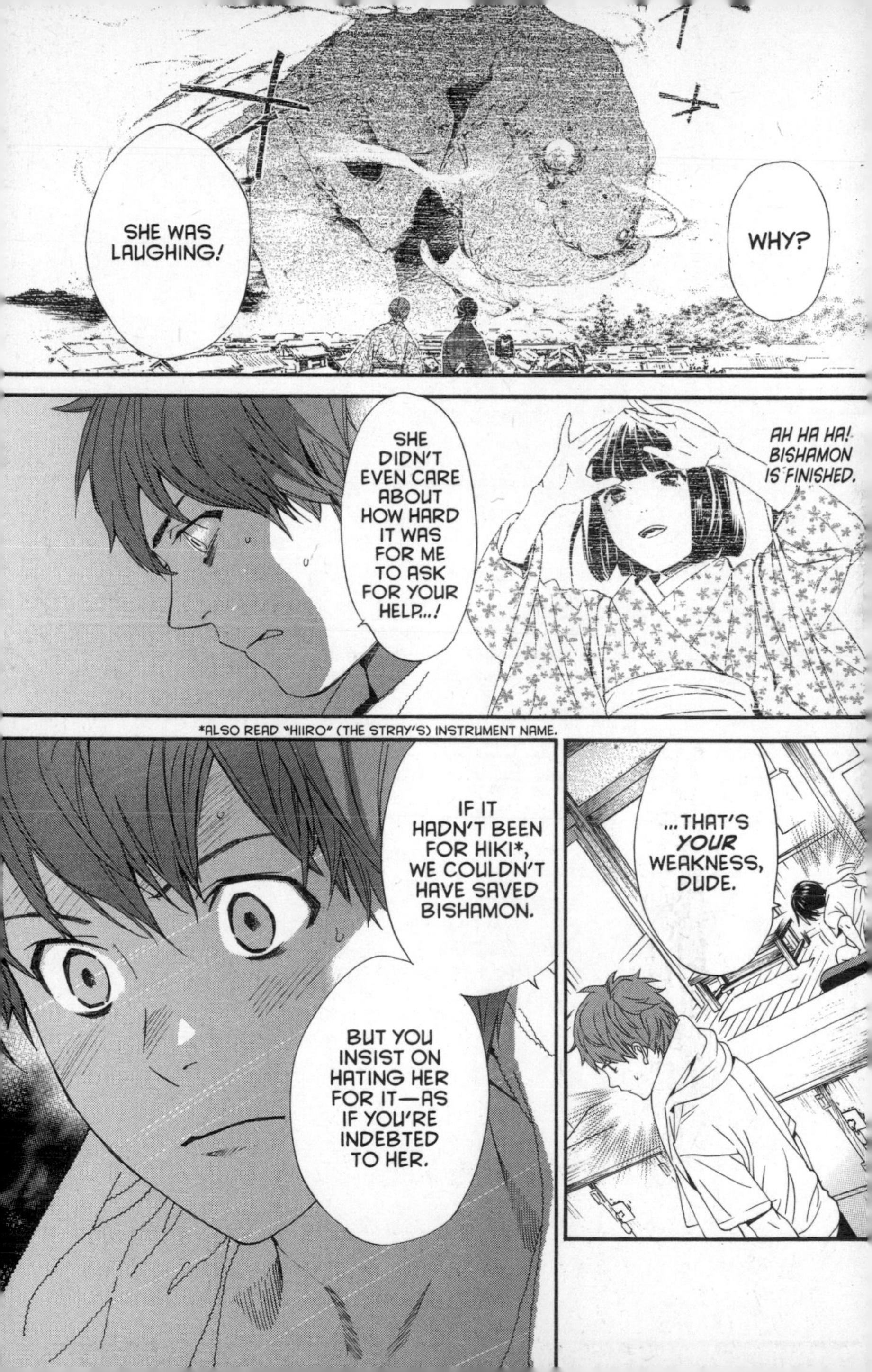
WHY?
SHE WAS LAUGHING!
AH HA HA! BISHAMON IS FINISHED.
SHE DIDN'T EVEN CARE ABOUT HOW HARD IT WAS FOR ME TO ASK FOR YOUR HELP...!
...THAT'S *YOUR* WEAKNESS, DUDE.
IF IT HADN'T BEEN FOR HIKI*, WE COULDN'T HAVE SAVED BISHAMON.
BUT YOU INSIST ON HATING HER FOR IT—AS IF YOU'RE INDEBTED TO HER.

*ALSO READ "HIIRO" (THE STRAY'S) INSTRUMENT NAME.

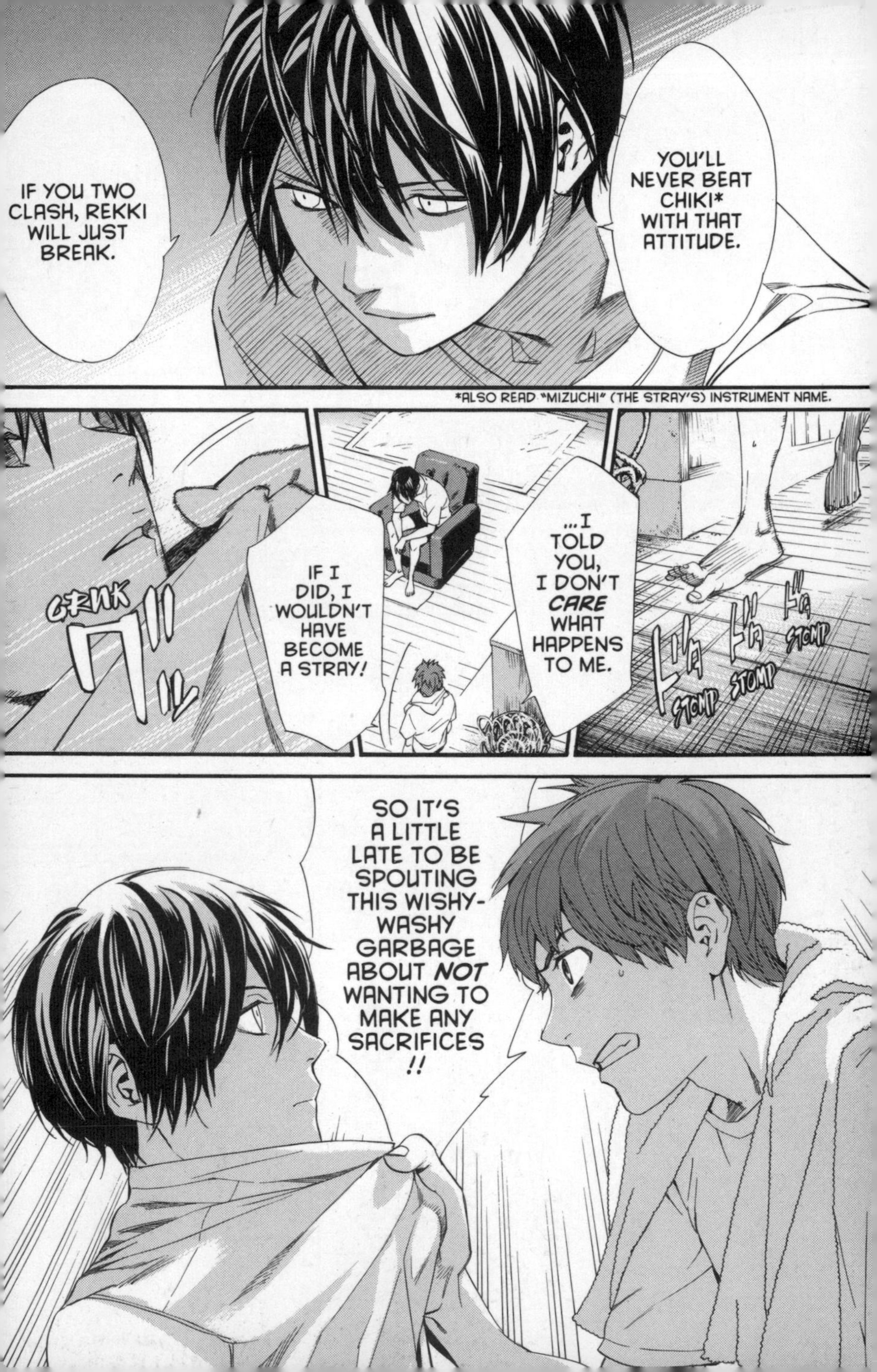
YOU'LL NEVER BEAT CHIKI* WITH THAT ATTITUDE.
IF YOU TWO CLASH, REKKI WILL JUST BREAK.
*ALSO READ "MIZUCHI" (THE STRAY'S) INSTRUMENT NAME.
STOMP STOMP STOMP
...I TOLD YOU, I DON'T *CARE* WHAT HAPPENS TO ME.
IF I DID, I WOULDN'T HAVE BECOME A STRAY!
GRNK
SO IT'S A LITTLE LATE TO BE SPOUTING THIS WISHY-WASHY GARBAGE ABOUT *NOT* WANTING TO MAKE ANY SACRIFICES!!

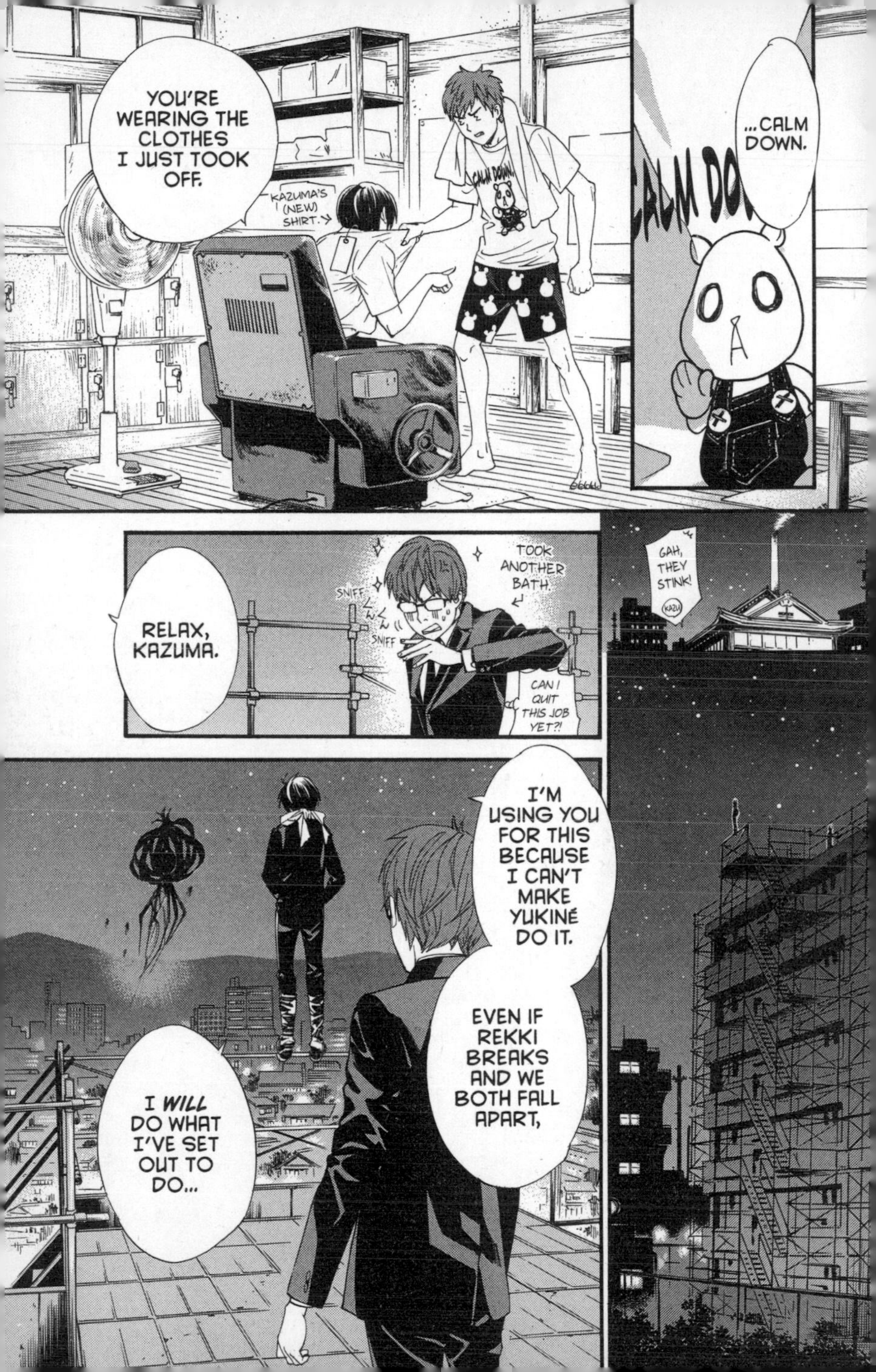

...CALM DOWN.
CALM DOW
YOU'RE WEARING THE CLOTHES I JUST TOOK OFF.
CALM DOWN.
KAZUMA'S (NEW) SHIRT.
GAH, THEY STINK!
KAZU
TOOK ANOTHER BATH.
SNIFF
SNIFF
CAN I QUIT THIS JOB YET?!
RELAX, KAZUMA.
I'M USING YOU FOR THIS BECAUSE I CAN'T MAKE YUKINÉ DO IT.
EVEN IF REKKI BREAKS AND WE BOTH FALL APART,
I *WILL* DO WHAT I'VE SET OUT TO DO...

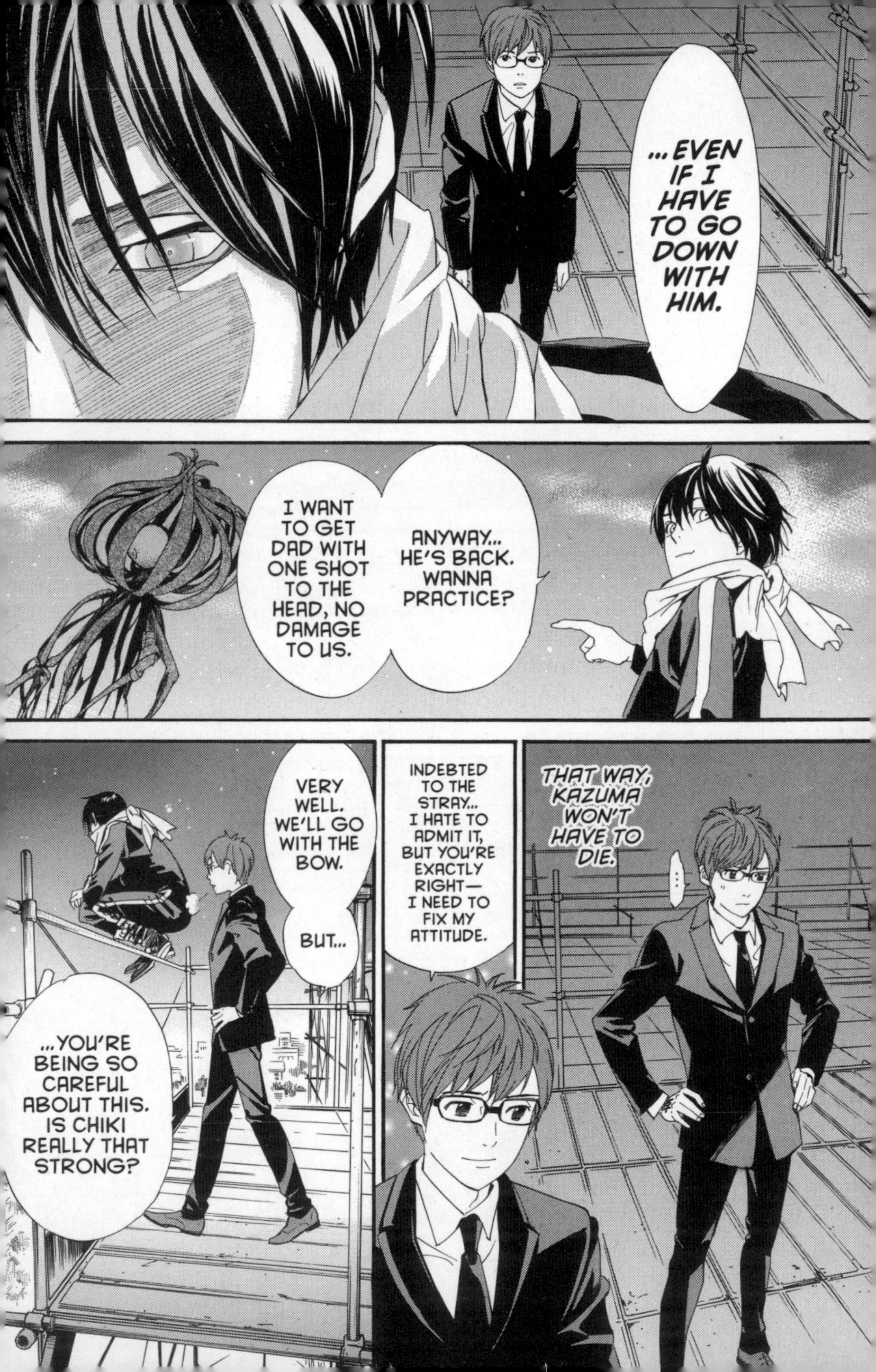
...EVEN IF I HAVE TO GO DOWN WITH HIM.
ANYWAY... HE'S BACK. WANNA PRACTICE?
I WANT TO GET DAD WITH ONE SHOT TO THE HEAD, NO DAMAGE TO US.
THAT WAY, KAZUMA WON'T HAVE TO DIE.
...
INDEBTED TO THE STRAY... I HATE TO ADMIT IT, BUT YOU'RE EXACTLY RIGHT— I NEED TO FIX MY ATTITUDE.
VERY WELL. WE'LL GO WITH THE BOW.
BUT...
...YOU'RE BEING SO CAREFUL ABOUT THIS. IS CHIKI REALLY THAT STRONG?

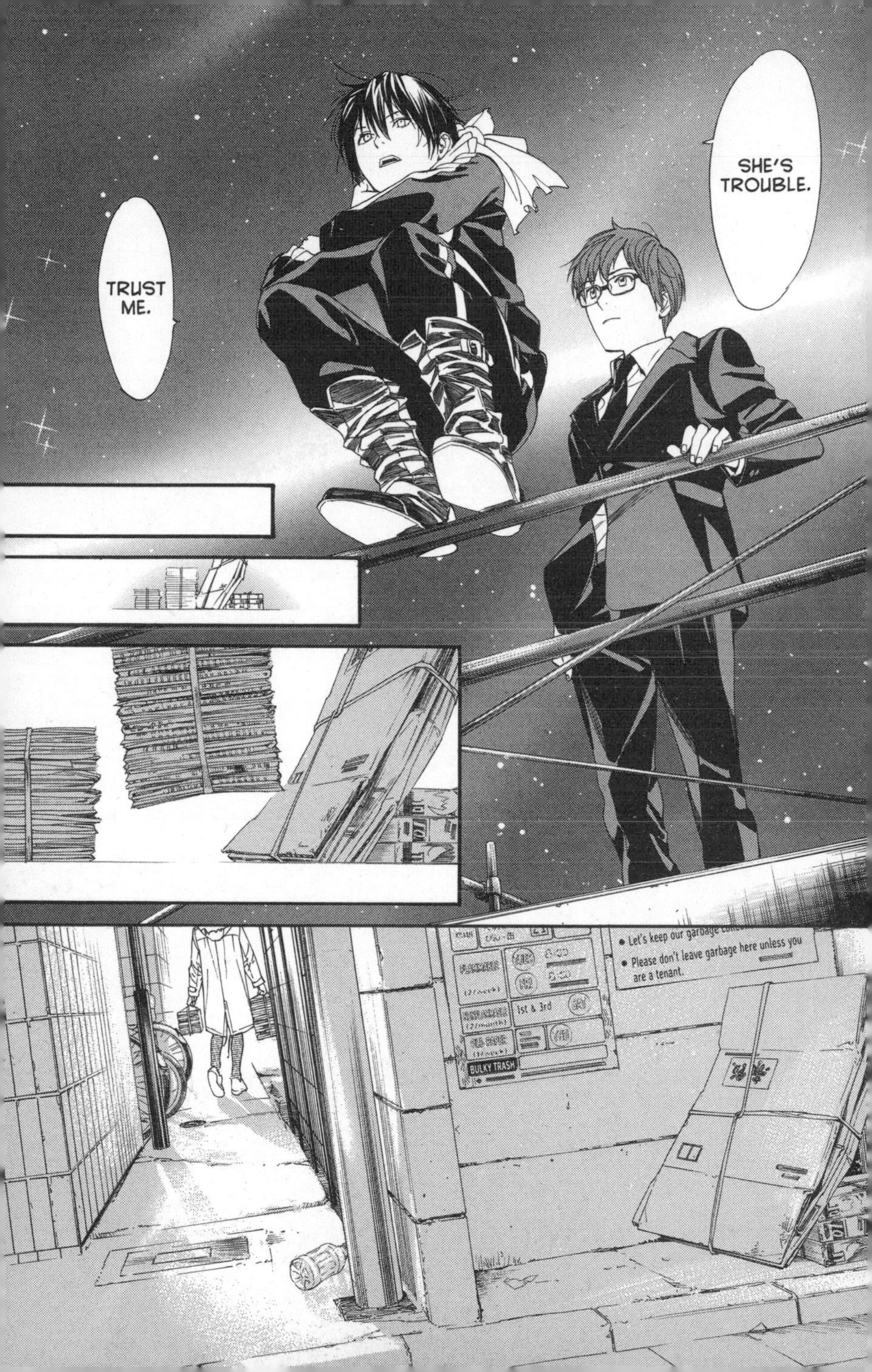
SHE'S TROUBLE.
TRUST ME.
• Let's keep our garbage
• Please don't leave garbage here unless you are a tenant.
1st & 3rd
(2/month)
BULKY TRASH

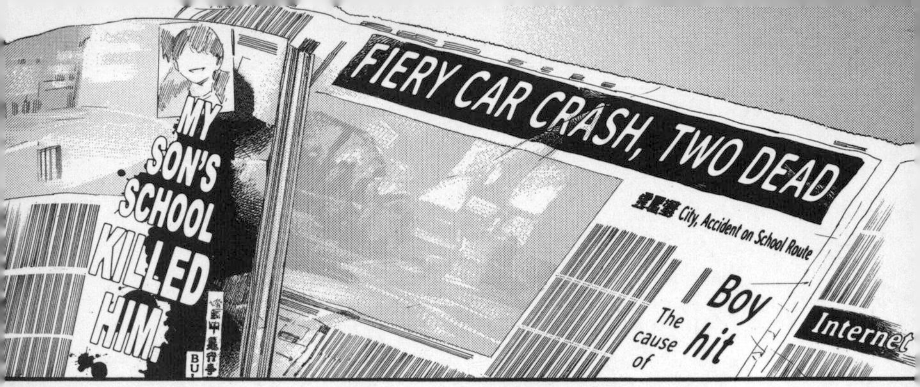
FIERY CAR CRASH, TWO DEAD
City, Accident on School Route
Boy hit
The cause of
Internet
MY SON'S SCHOOL KILLED HIM!

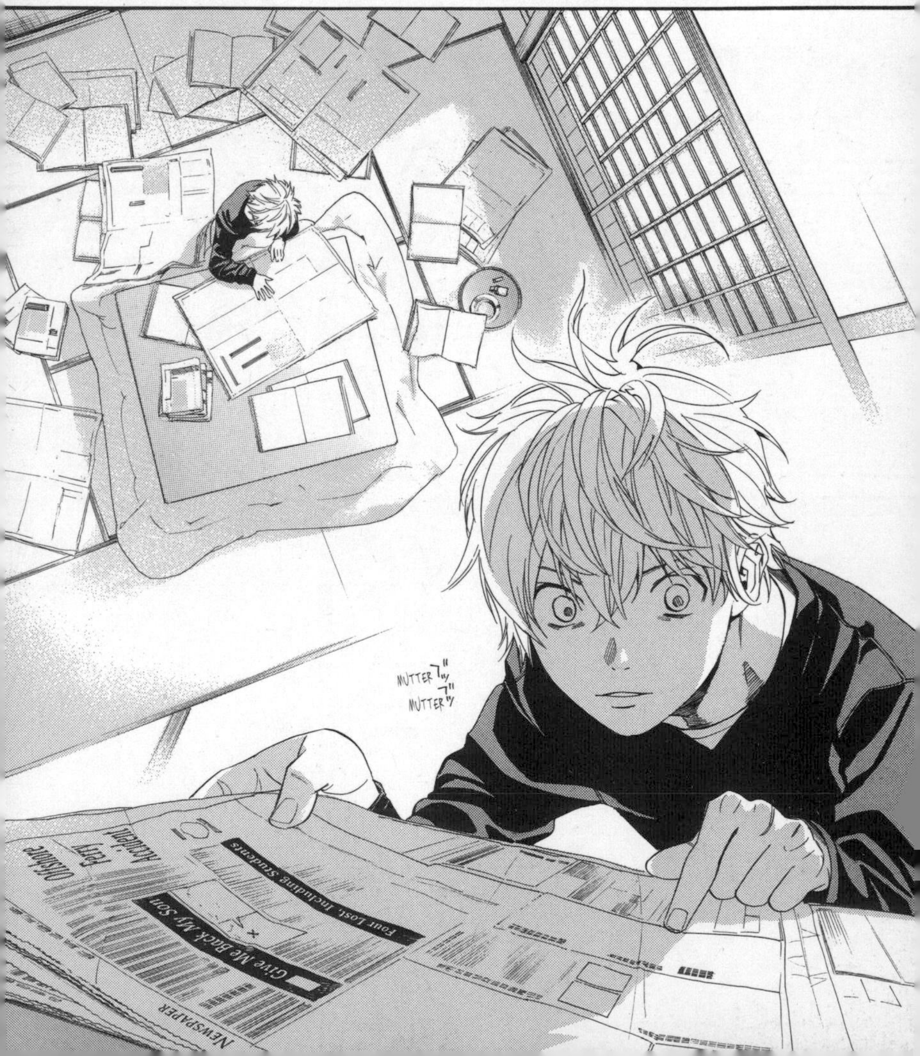
MUTTER MUTTER
Give Me Back My Son
Four Lost, Including Students
Offshore ferry accident
NEWSPAPER

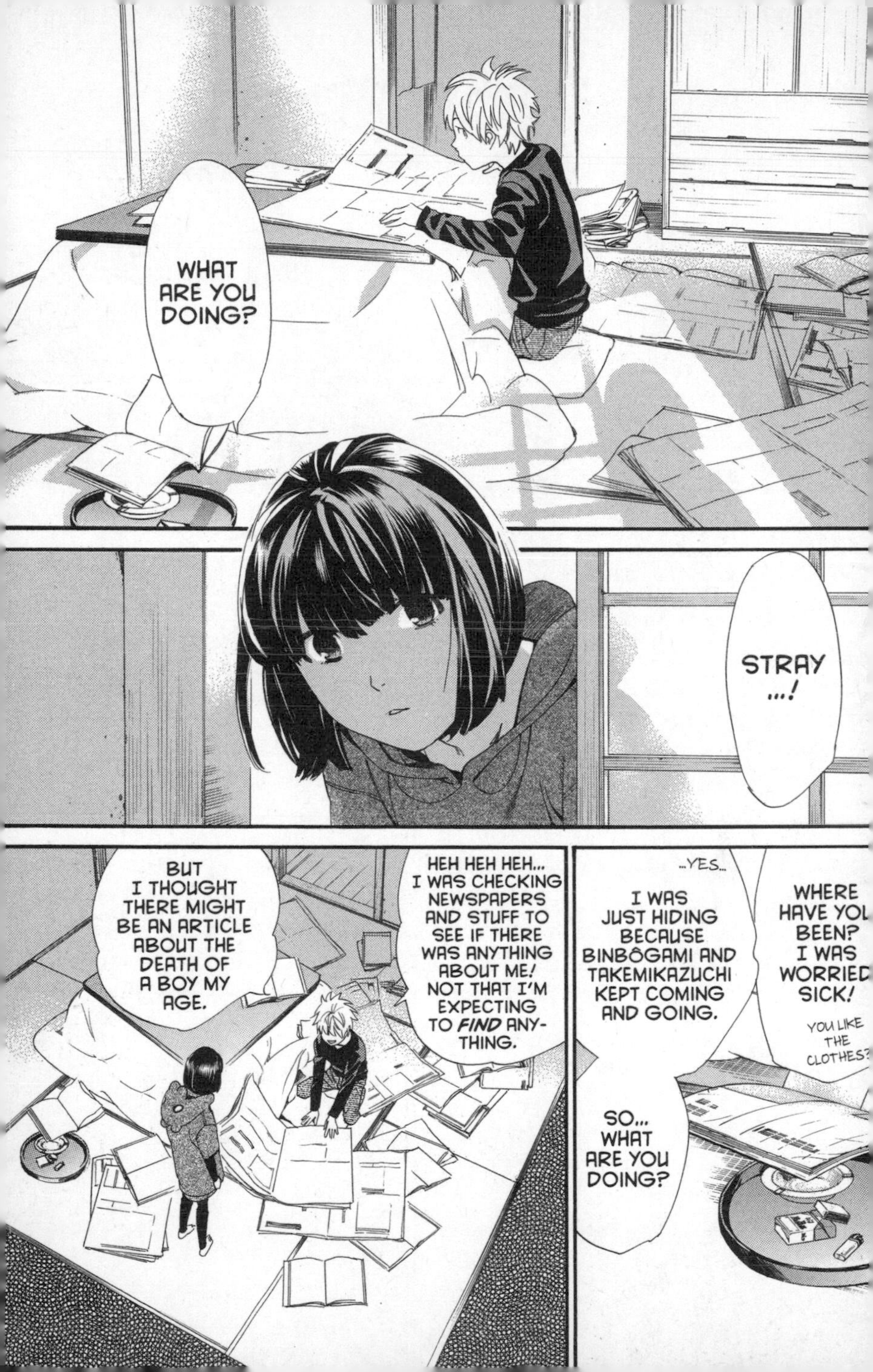
WHAT ARE YOU DOING?
STRAY ...!
WHERE HAVE YOU BEEN? I WAS WORRIED SICK!
YOU LIKE THE CLOTHES?
...YES...
I WAS JUST HIDING BECAUSE BINBÔGAMI AND TAKEMIKAZUCHI KEPT COMING AND GOING.
SO... WHAT ARE YOU DOING?
HEH HEH HEH... I WAS CHECKING NEWSPAPERS AND STUFF TO SEE IF THERE WAS ANYTHING ABOUT ME! NOT THAT I'M EXPECTING TO *FIND* ANYTHING.
BUT I THOUGHT THERE MIGHT BE AN ARTICLE ABOUT THE DEATH OF A BOY MY AGE.

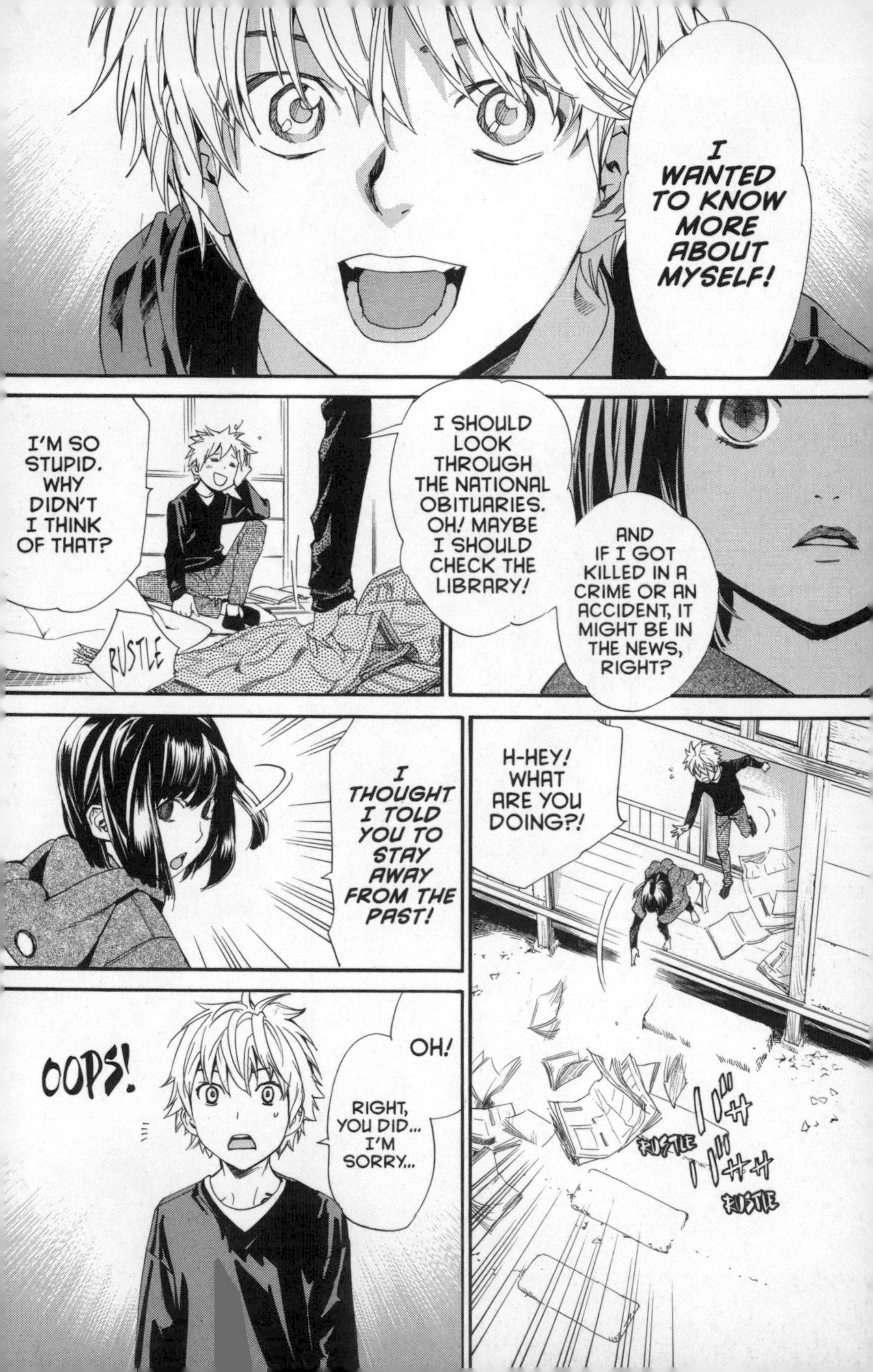
I WANTED TO KNOW MORE ABOUT MYSELF!
AND IF I GOT KILLED IN A CRIME OR AN ACCIDENT, IT MIGHT BE IN THE NEWS, RIGHT?
I SHOULD LOOK THROUGH THE NATIONAL OBITUARIES. OH! MAYBE I SHOULD CHECK THE LIBRARY!
I'M SO STUPID. WHY DIDN'T I THINK OF THAT?
RUSTLE
H-HEY! WHAT ARE YOU DOING?!
RUSTLE
RUSTLE
I THOUGHT I TOLD YOU TO STAY AWAY FROM THE PAST!
OH!
RIGHT, YOU DID... I'M SORRY...
OOPS!

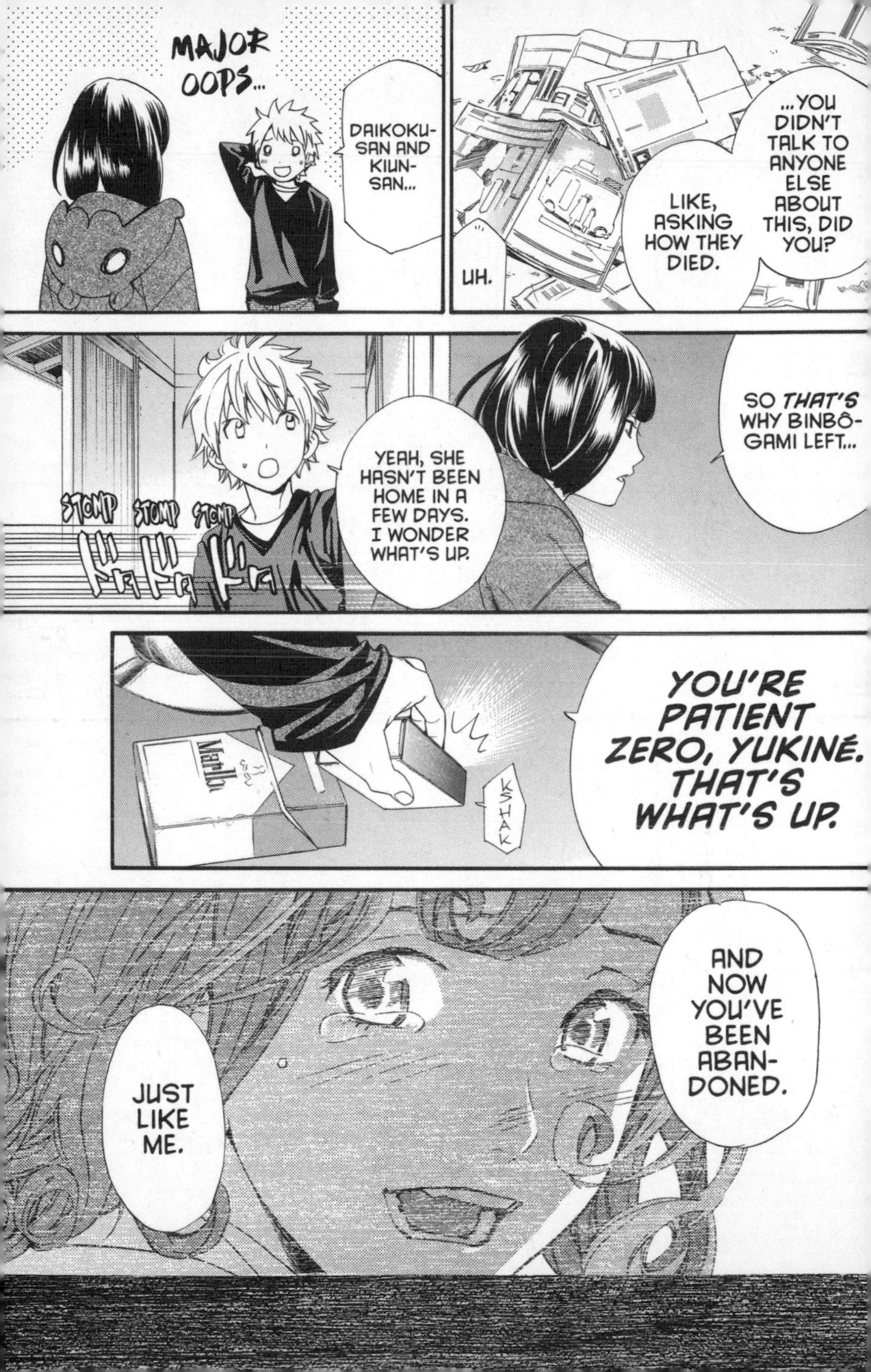
...YOU DIDN'T TALK TO ANYONE ELSE ABOUT THIS, DID YOU?
LIKE, ASKING HOW THEY DIED.
UH.
DAIKOKU-SAN AND KIUN-SAN...
MAJOR OOPS...
SO *THAT'S* WHY BINBÔGAMI LEFT...
YEAH, SHE HASN'T BEEN HOME IN A FEW DAYS. I WONDER WHAT'S UP.
STOMP STOMP STOMP
YOU'RE PATIENT ZERO, YUKINÉ. THAT'S WHAT'S UP.
KSHAK
AND NOW YOU'VE BEEN ABANDONED.
JUST LIKE ME.

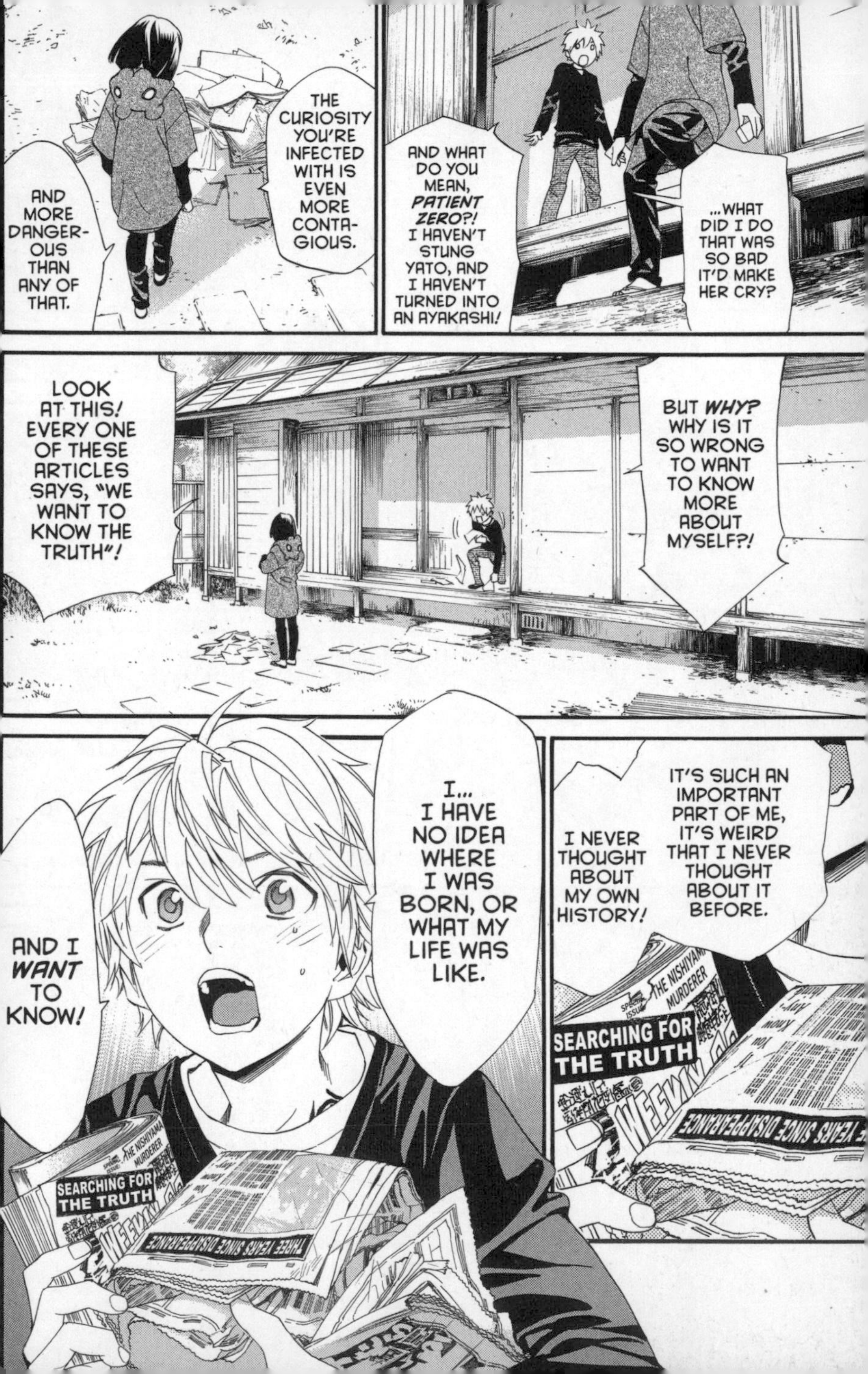
...WHAT DID I DO THAT WAS SO BAD IT'D MAKE HER CRY?
AND WHAT DO YOU MEAN, *PATIENT ZERO*?! I HAVEN'T STUNG YATO, AND I HAVEN'T TURNED INTO AN AYAKASHI!
THE CURIOSITY YOU'RE INFECTED WITH IS EVEN MORE CONTAGIOUS.
AND MORE DANGEROUS THAN ANY OF THAT.
BUT *WHY?* WHY IS IT SO WRONG TO WANT TO KNOW MORE ABOUT MYSELF?!
LOOK AT THIS! EVERY ONE OF THESE ARTICLES SAYS, "WE WANT TO KNOW THE TRUTH"!
IT'S SUCH AN IMPORTANT PART OF ME, IT'S WEIRD THAT I NEVER THOUGHT ABOUT IT BEFORE.
I NEVER THOUGHT ABOUT MY OWN HISTORY!
THE NISHIYAMA MURDERER
SEARCHING FOR THE TRUTH
I... I HAVE NO IDEA WHERE I WAS BORN, OR WHAT MY LIFE WAS LIKE.
AND I *WANT* TO KNOW!
THE NISHIYAMA MURDERER
SEARCHING FOR THE TRUTH
THREE YEARS SINCE DISAPPEARANCE

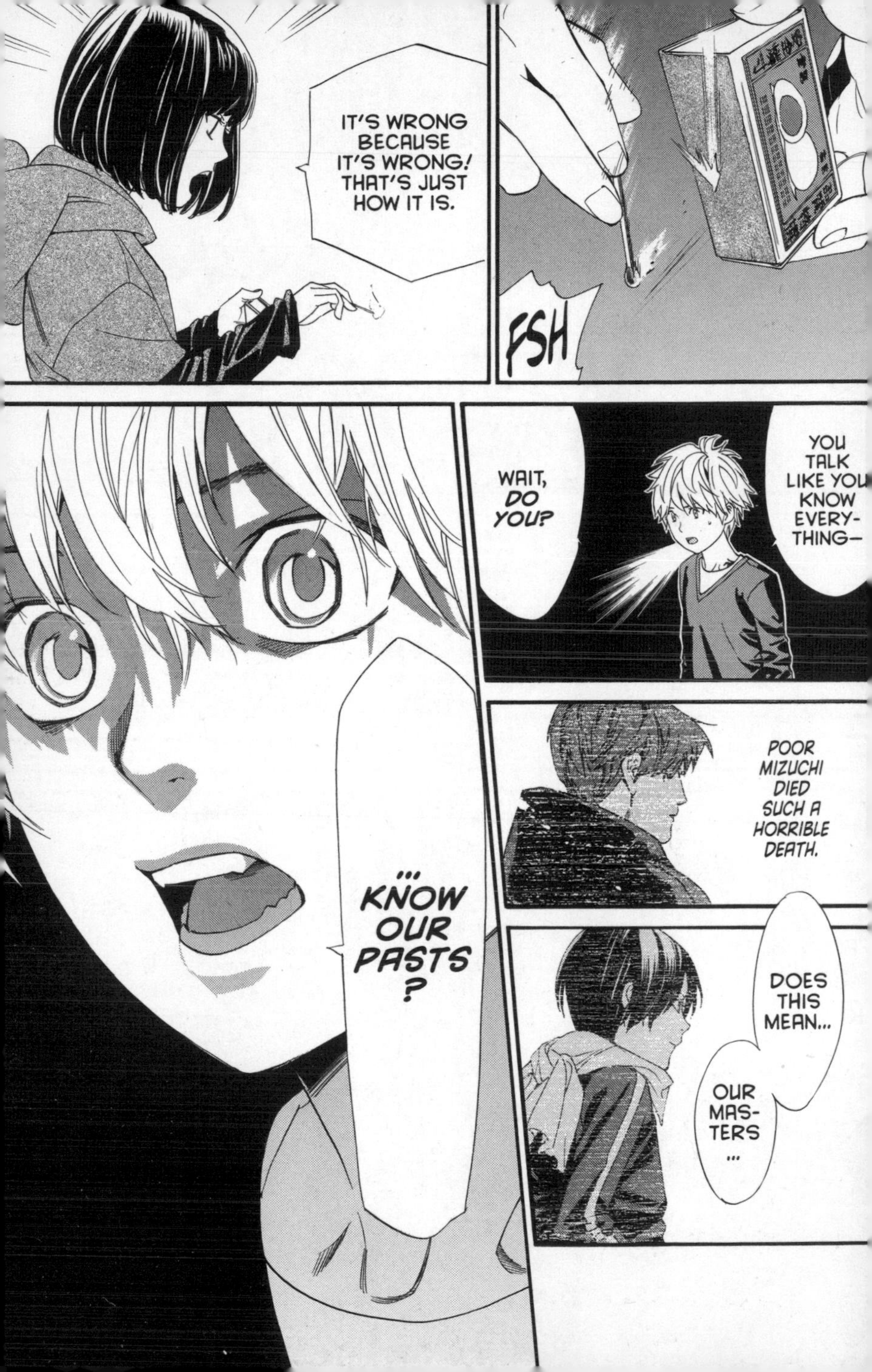
FSH
IT'S WRONG BECAUSE IT'S WRONG! THAT'S JUST HOW IT IS.
YOU TALK LIKE YOU KNOW EVERY-THING—
WAIT, DO YOU?
POOR MIZUCHI DIED SUCH A HORRIBLE DEATH.
DOES THIS MEAN...
OUR MAS-TERS...
...KNOW OUR PASTS?

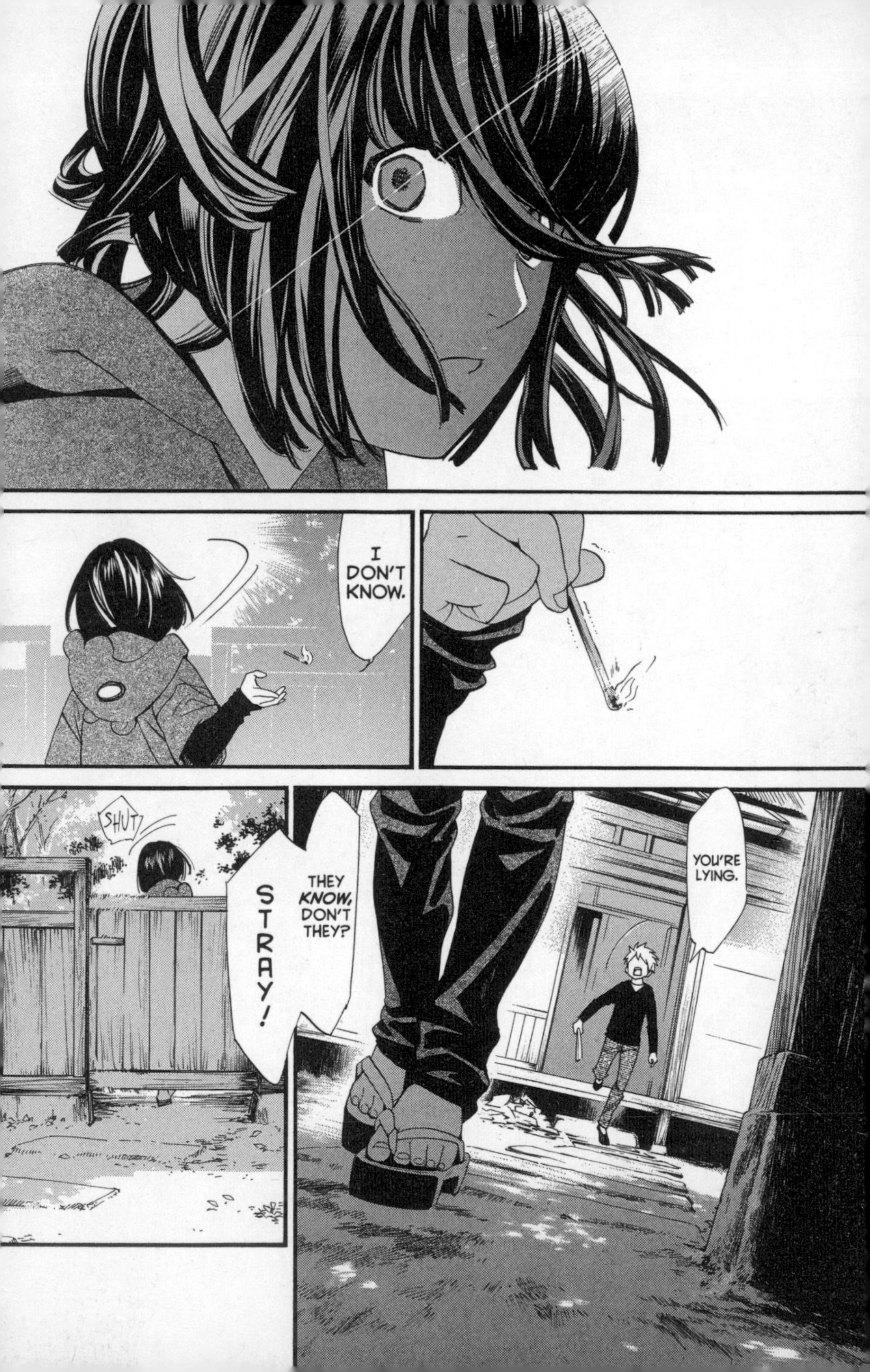
I DON'T KNOW.
YOU'RE LYING.
THEY *KNOW,* DON'T THEY?
STRAY!
SHUT

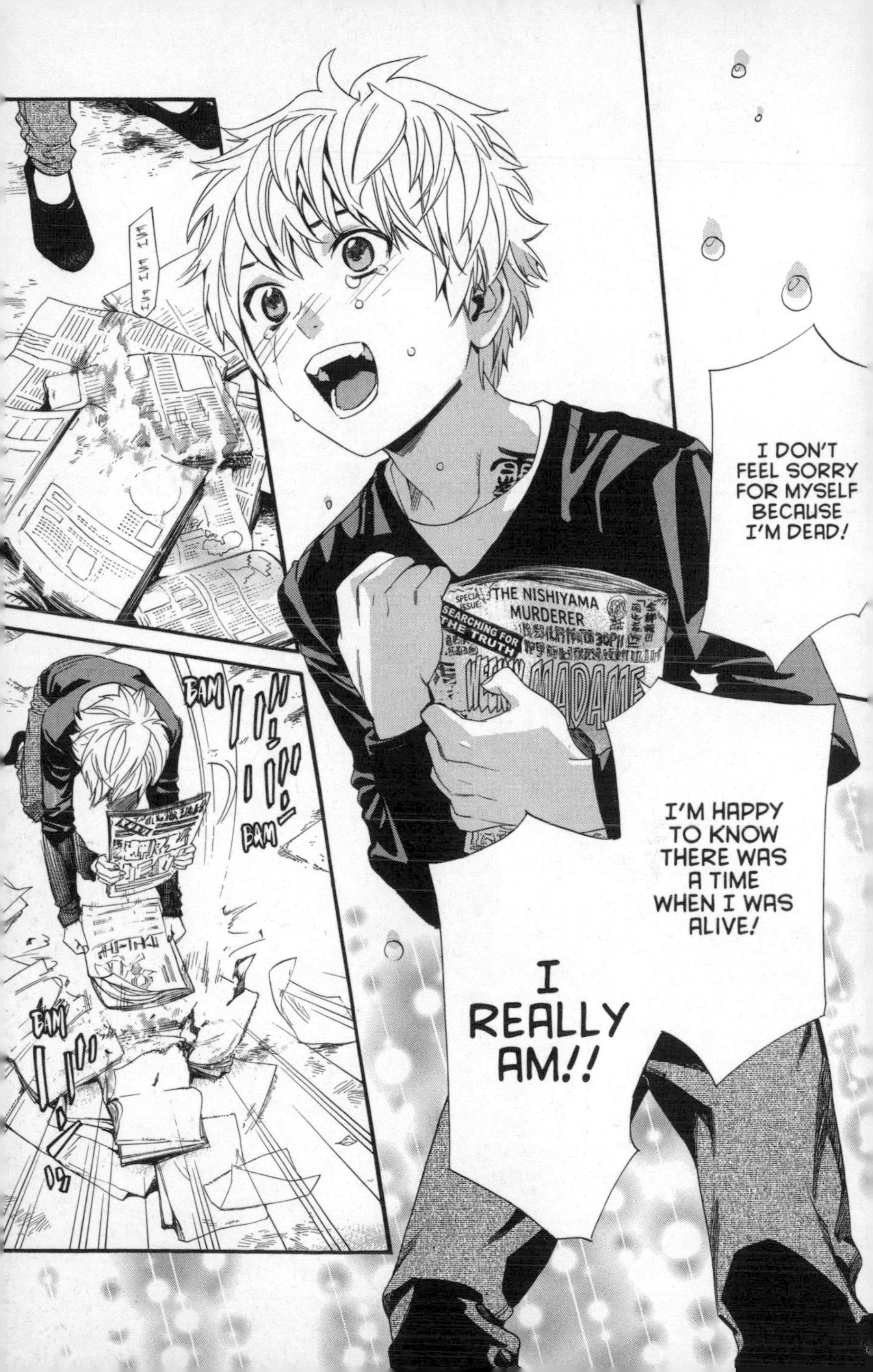
SPECIAL ISSUE
THE NISHIYAMA MURDERER
SEARCHING FOR THE TRUTH
MADAME
I DON'T FEEL SORRY FOR MYSELF BECAUSE I'M DEAD!
I'M HAPPY TO KNOW THERE WAS A TIME WHEN I WAS ALIVE!
I REALLY AM!!
FSH FSH FSH
BAM
BAM
BAM

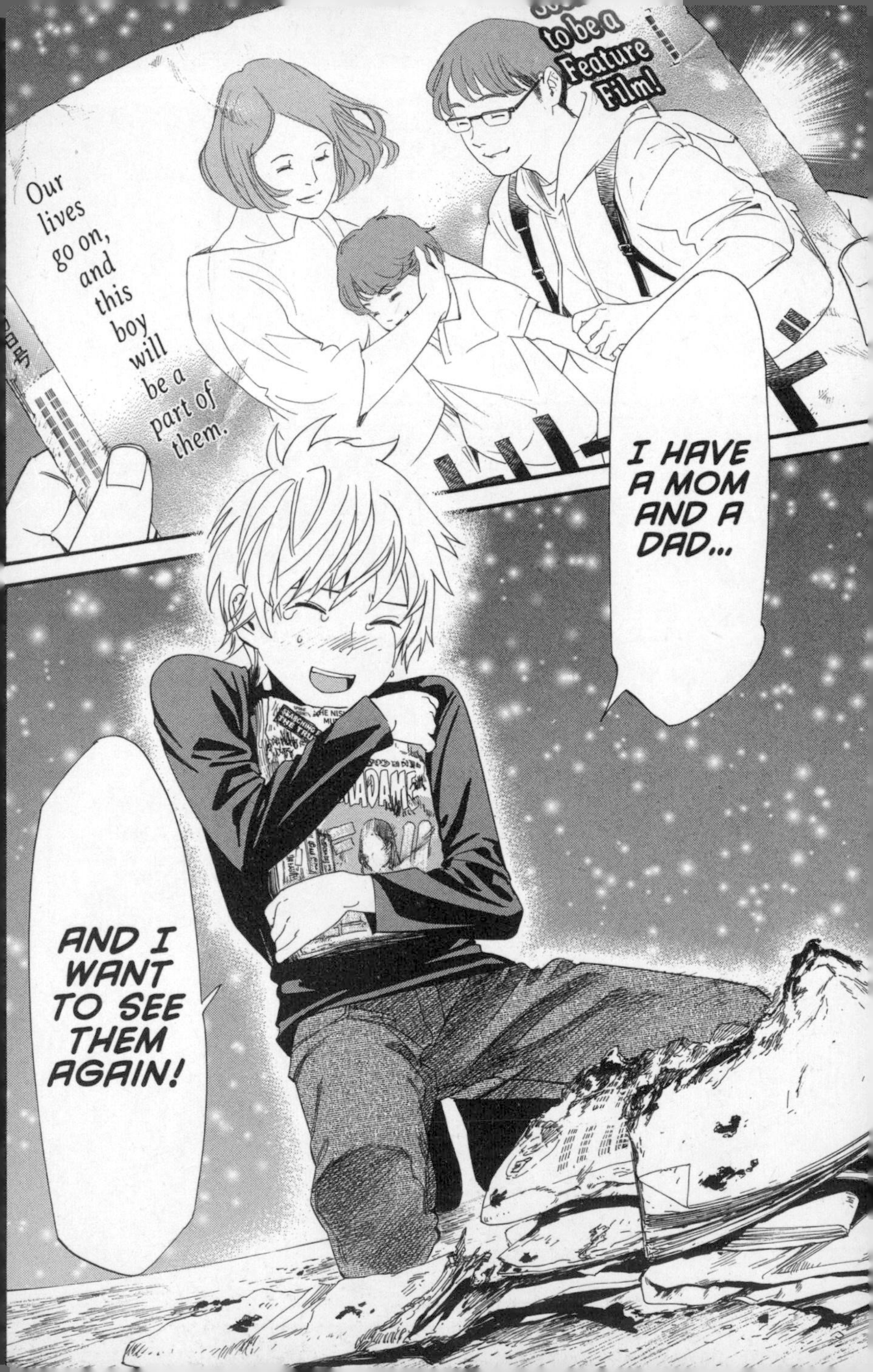
to be a Feature Film!
Our lives go on, and this boy will be a part of them.
I HAVE A MOM AND A DAD...
AND I WANT TO SEE THEM AGAIN!

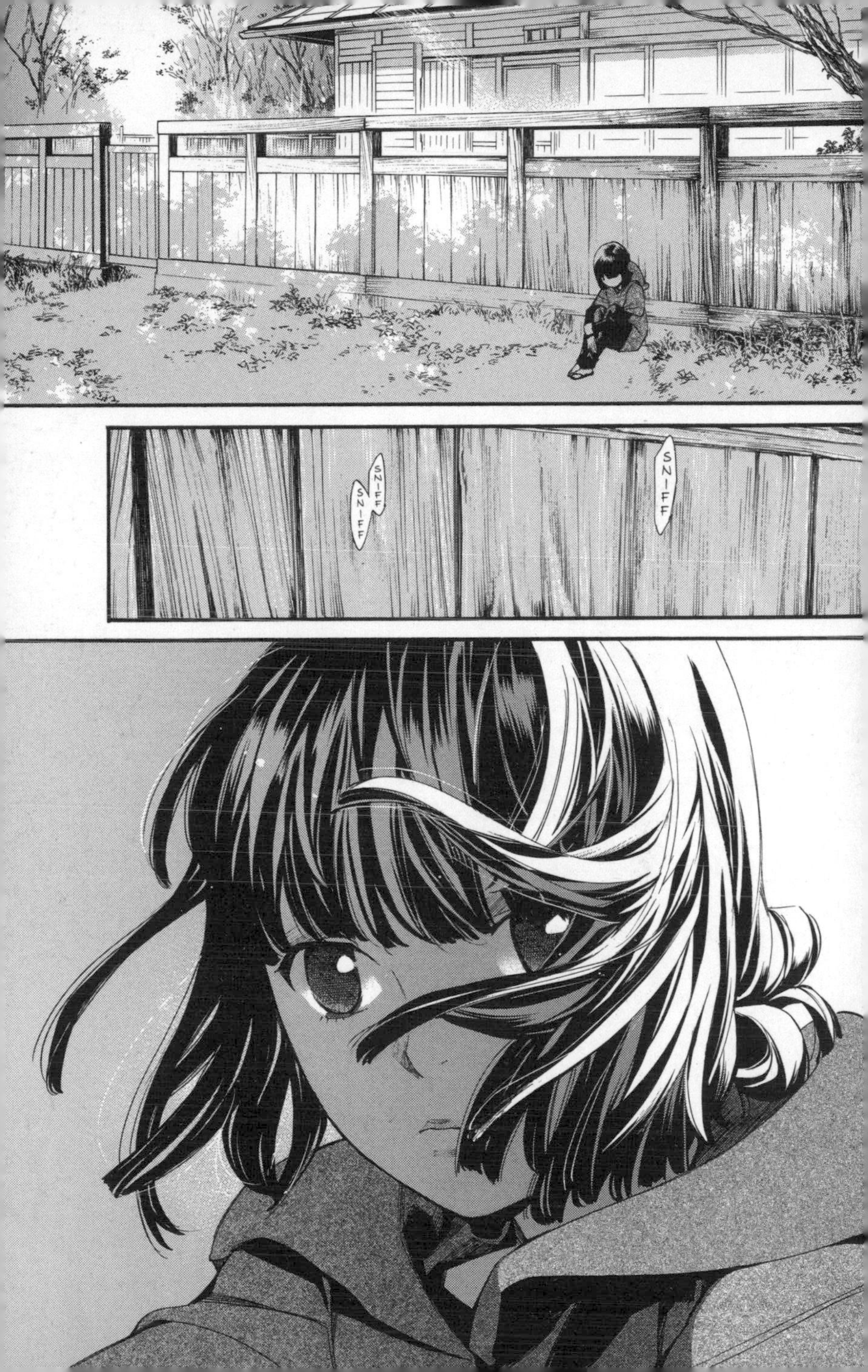
SNIFF
SNIFF
SNIFF

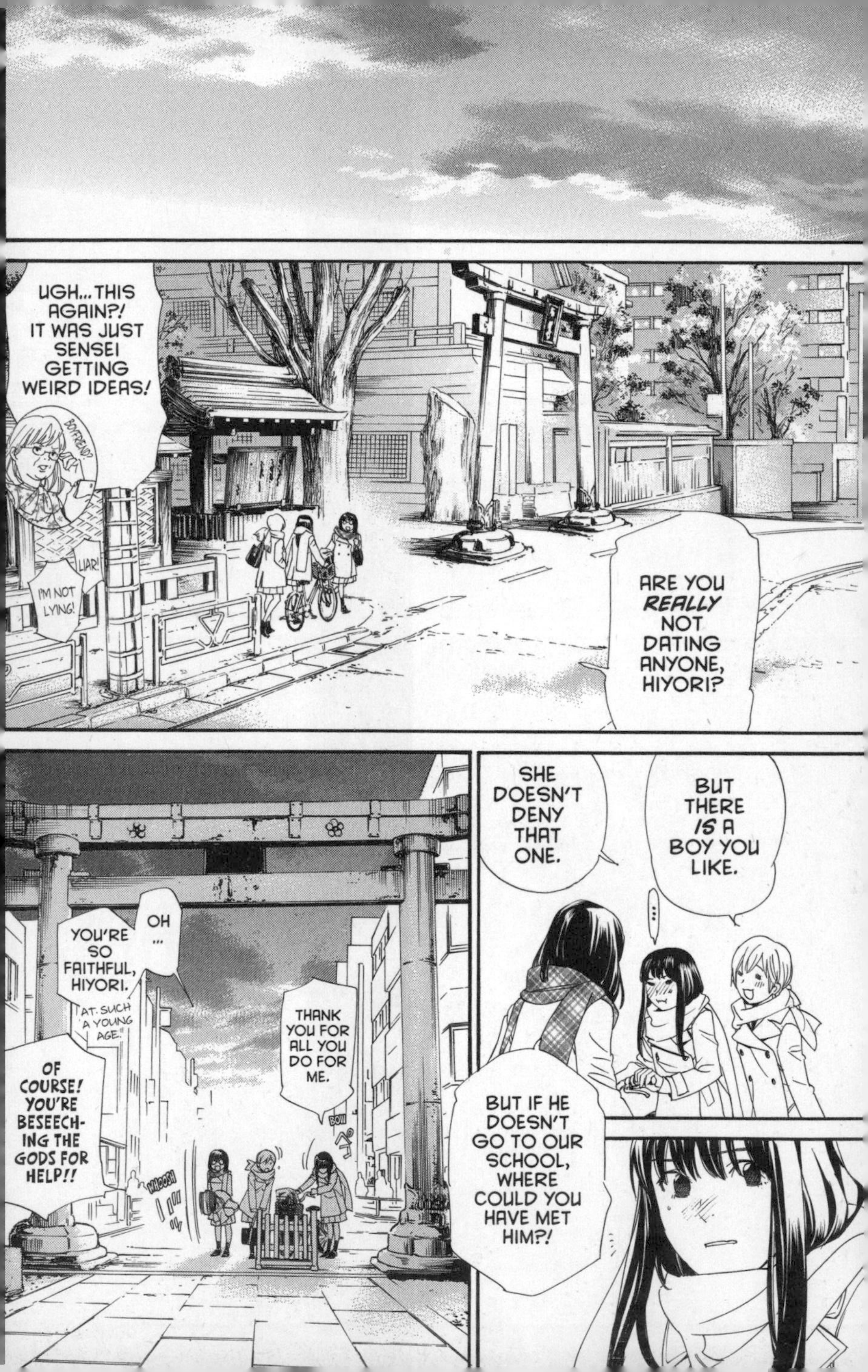
ARE YOU *REALLY* NOT DATING ANYONE, HIYORI?
UGH... THIS AGAIN?! IT WAS JUST SENSEI GETTING WEIRD IDEAS!
BOYFRIEND?
LIAR!
I'M NOT LYING!
BUT THERE *IS* A BOY YOU LIKE.
...
SHE DOESN'T DENY THAT ONE.
BUT IF HE DOESN'T GO TO OUR SCHOOL, WHERE COULD YOU HAVE MET HIM?!
THANK YOU FOR ALL YOU DO FOR ME.
BOW
OH ...
YOU'RE SO FAITHFUL, HIYORI.
AT SUCH A YOUNG AGE.
OF COURSE! YOU'RE BESEECHING THE GODS FOR HELP!!
WHOOSH

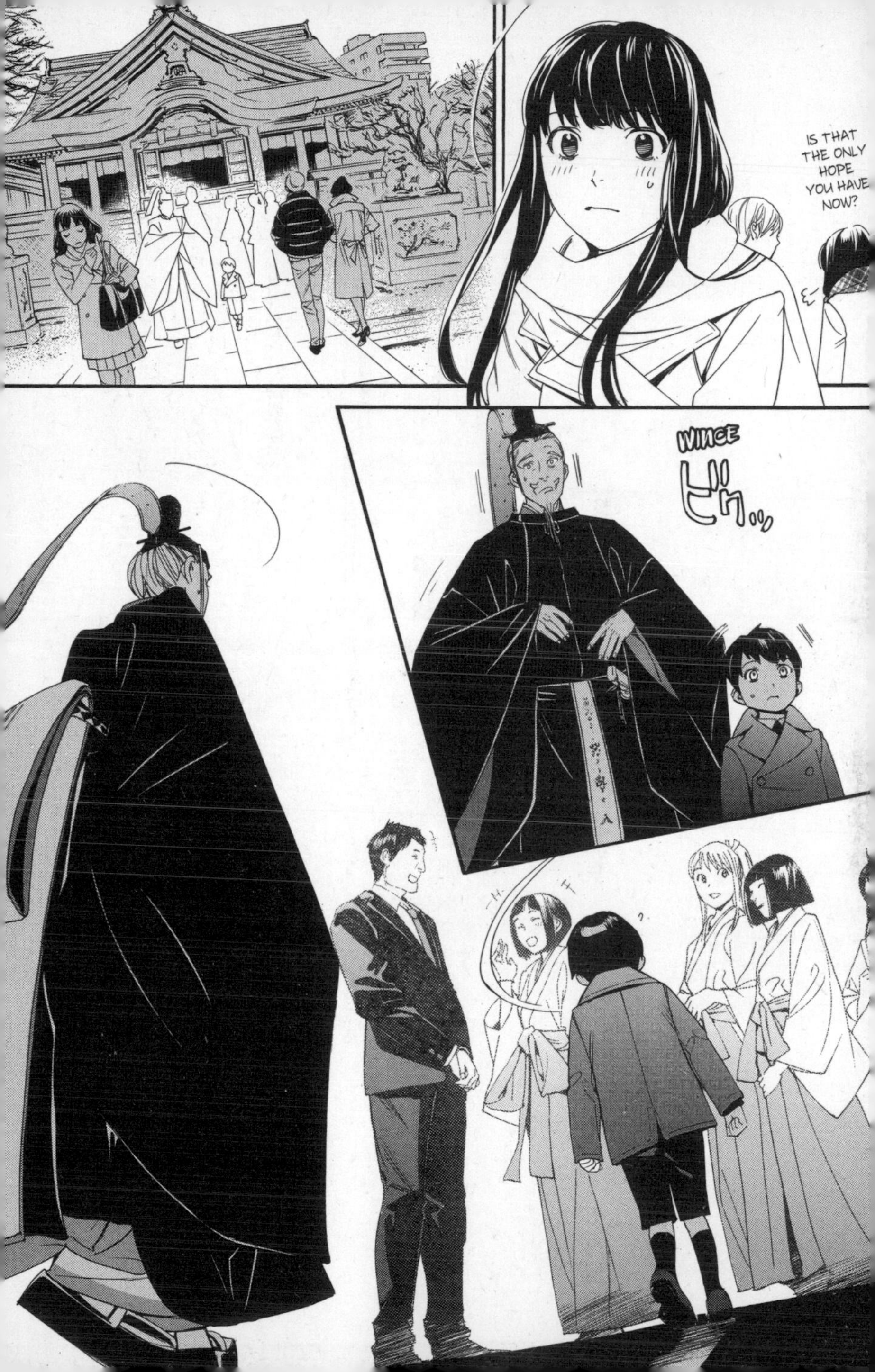
IS THAT THE ONLY HOPE YOU HAVE NOW?
WINCE

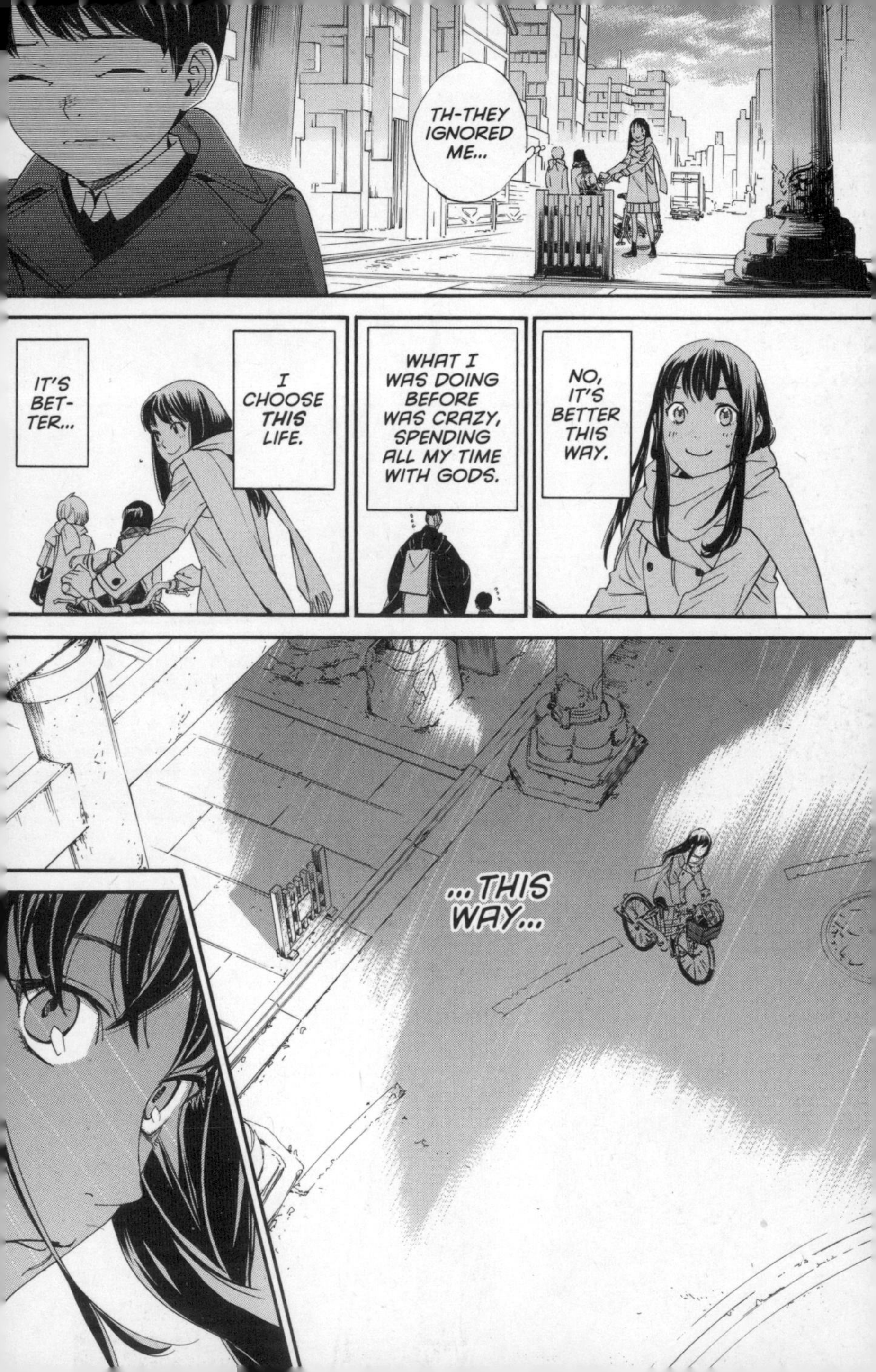
TH-THEY IGNORED ME...
NO, IT'S BETTER THIS WAY.
WHAT I WAS DOING BEFORE WAS CRAZY, SPENDING ALL MY TIME WITH GODS.
I CHOOSE THIS LIFE.
IT'S BET-TER...
...THIS WAY...

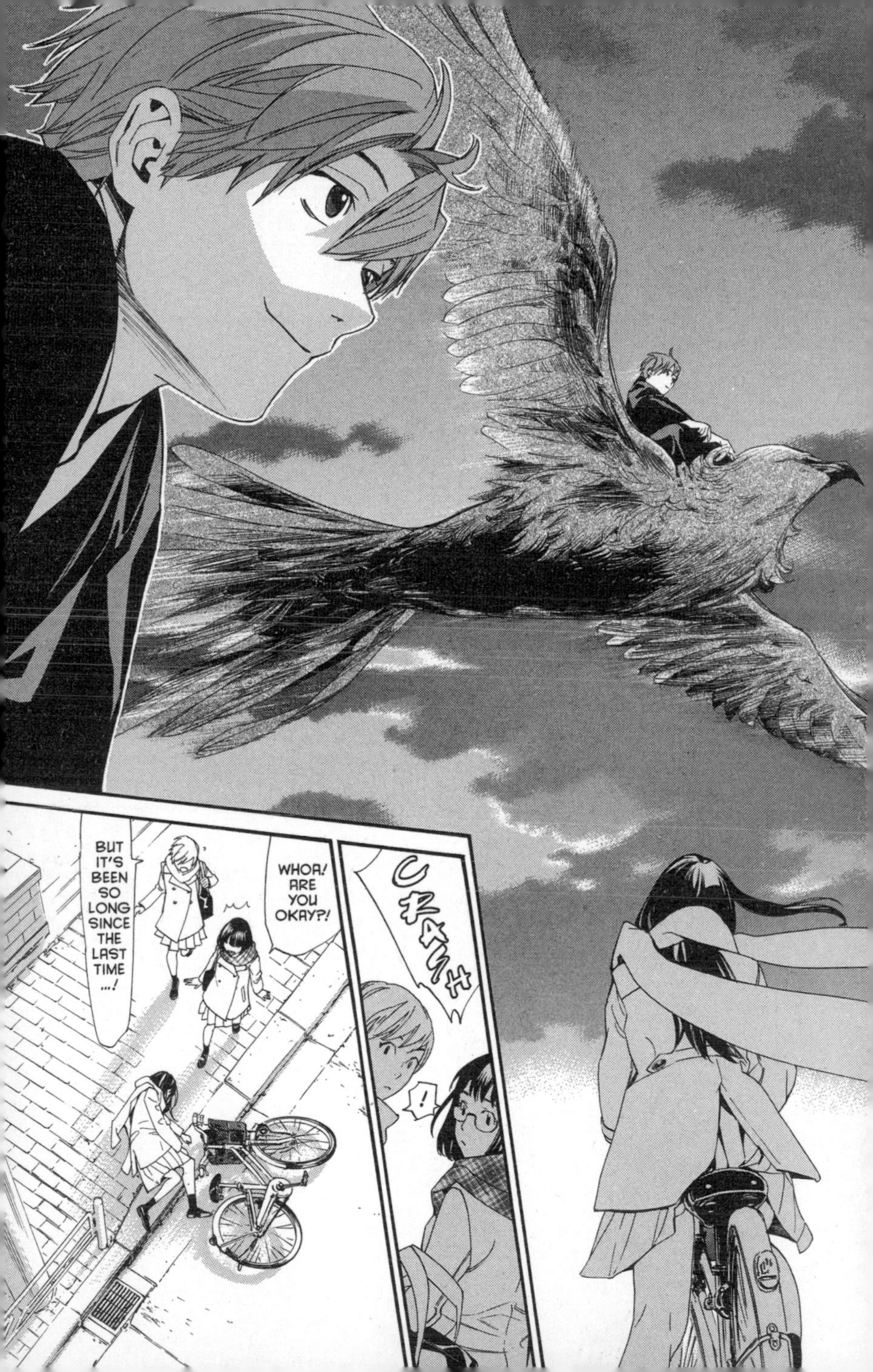
CRASH
!
WHOA! ARE YOU OKAY?!
BUT IT'S BEEN SO LONG SINCE THE LAST TIME ...!

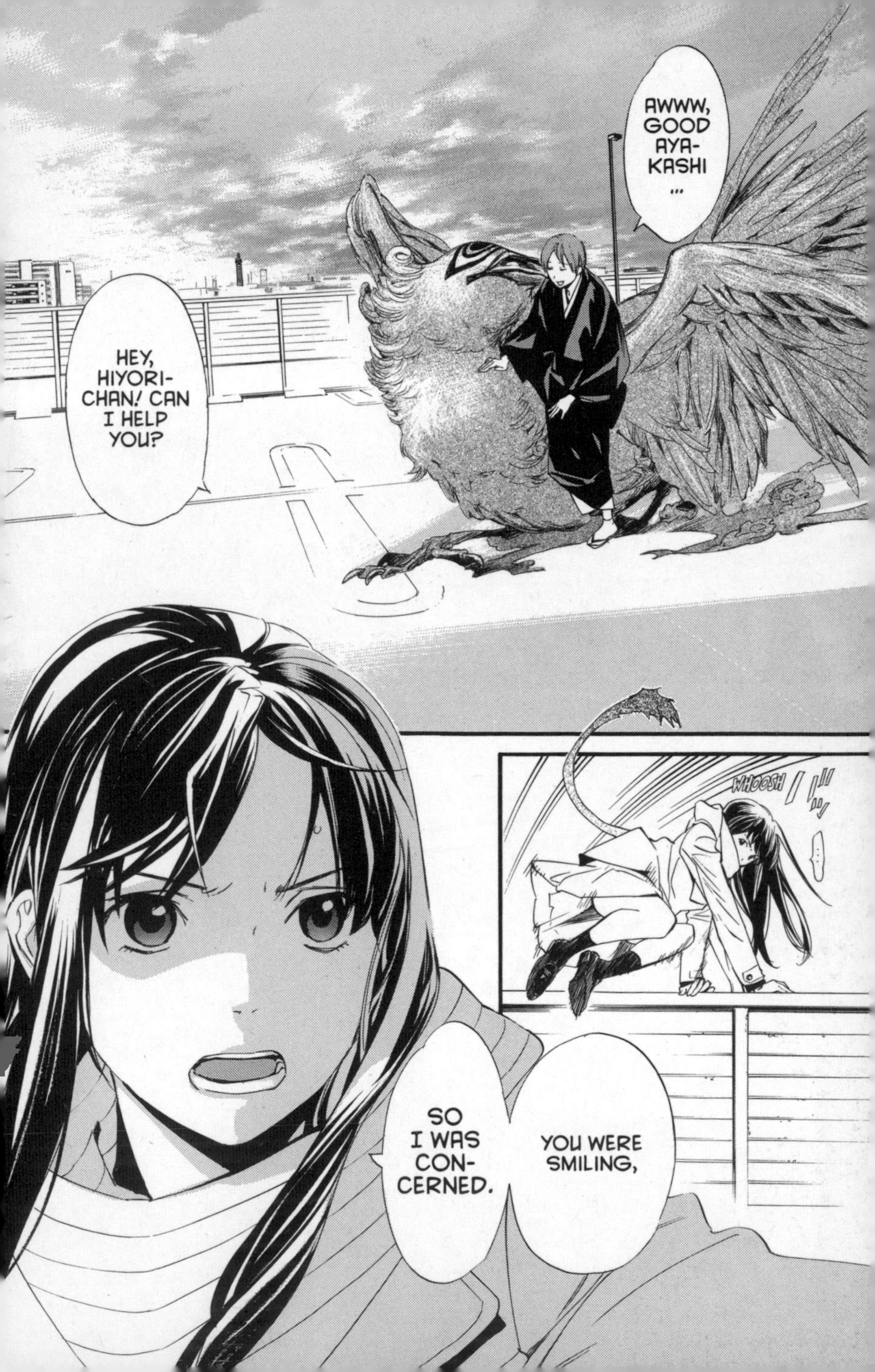
AWWW, GOOD AYA-KASHI ...
HEY, HIYORI-CHAN! CAN I HELP YOU?
WHOOSH
...
YOU WERE SMILING,
SO I WAS CON-CERNED.

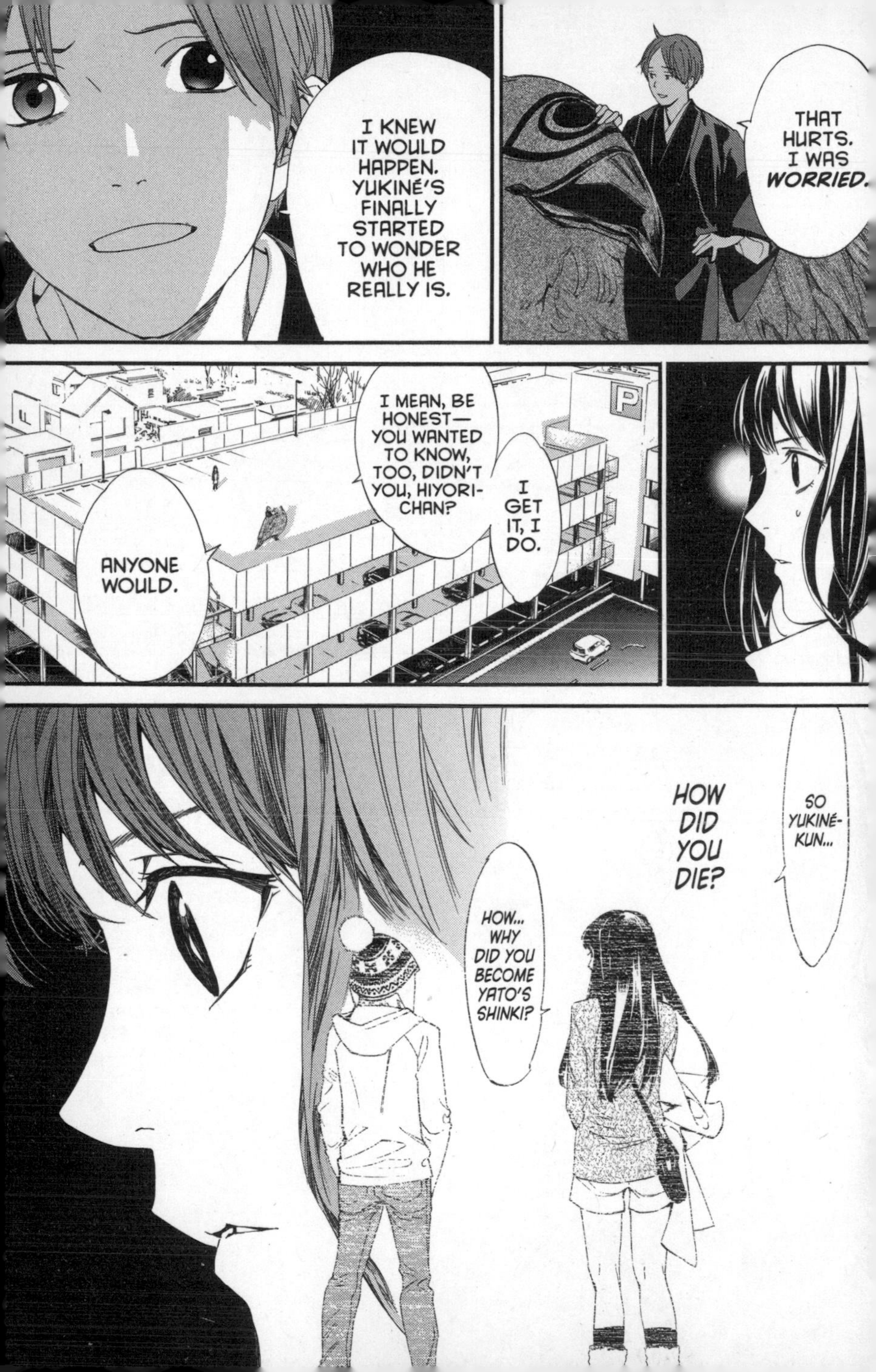
THAT HURTS. I WAS *WORRIED.*
I KNEW IT WOULD HAPPEN. YUKINÉ'S FINALLY STARTED TO WONDER WHO HE REALLY IS.
I MEAN, BE HONEST—YOU WANTED TO KNOW, TOO, DIDN'T YOU, HIYORI-CHAN?
I GET IT, I DO.
ANYONE WOULD.
SO YUKINÉ-KUN...
HOW DID YOU DIE?
HOW... WHY DID YOU BECOME YATO'S SHINKI?

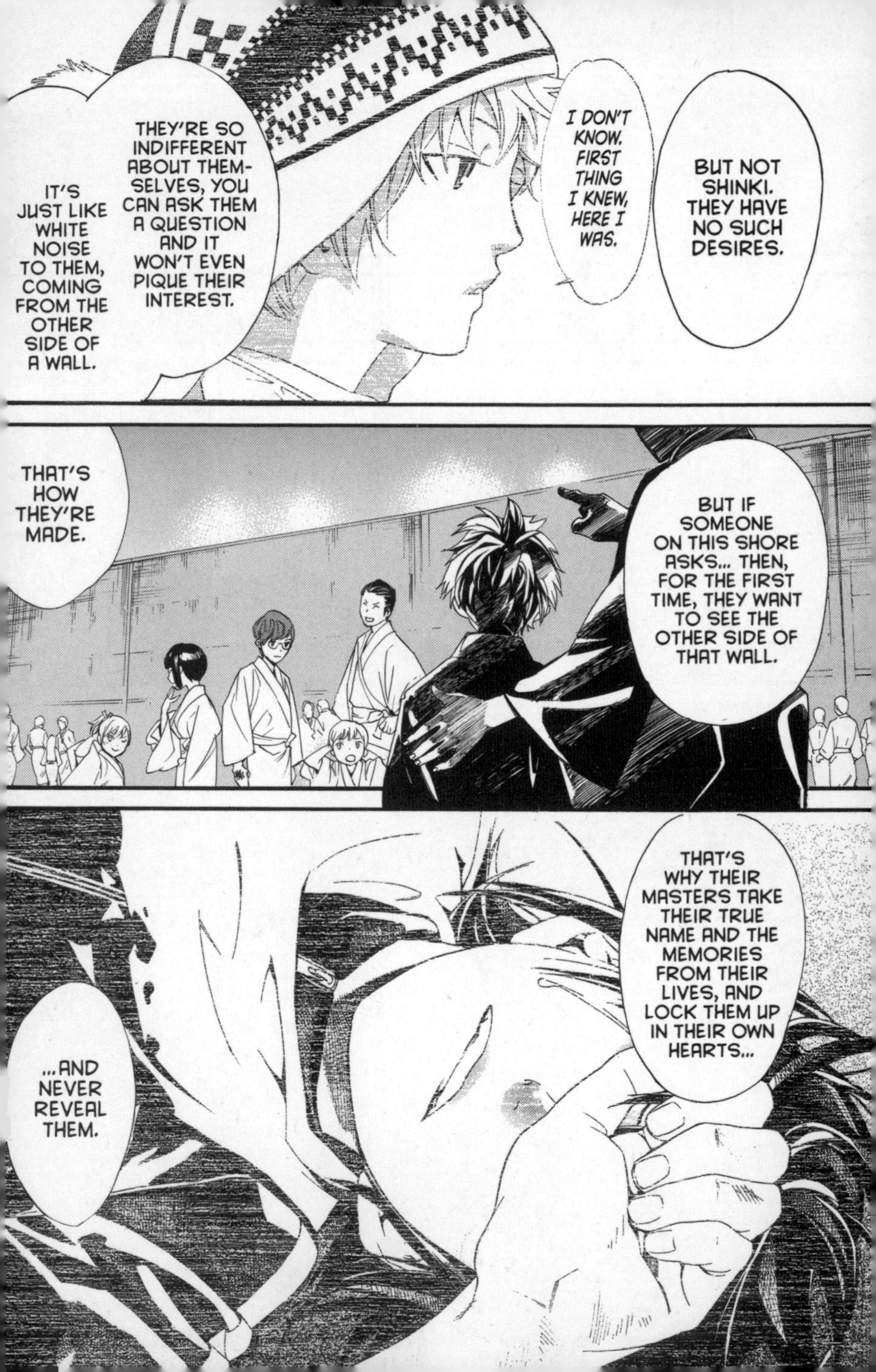
BUT NOT SHINKI. THEY HAVE NO SUCH DESIRES.
I DON'T KNOW. FIRST THING I KNEW, HERE I WAS.
THEY'RE SO INDIFFERENT ABOUT THEM-SELVES, YOU CAN ASK THEM A QUESTION AND IT WON'T EVEN PIQUE THEIR INTEREST.
IT'S JUST LIKE WHITE NOISE TO THEM, COMING FROM THE OTHER SIDE OF A WALL.
BUT IF SOMEONE ON THIS SHORE ASKS... THEN, FOR THE FIRST TIME, THEY WANT TO SEE THE OTHER SIDE OF THAT WALL.
THAT'S HOW THEY'RE MADE.
THAT'S WHY THEIR MASTERS TAKE THEIR TRUE NAME AND THE MEMORIES FROM THEIR LIVES, AND LOCK THEM UP IN THEIR OWN HEARTS...
...AND NEVER REVEAL THEM.

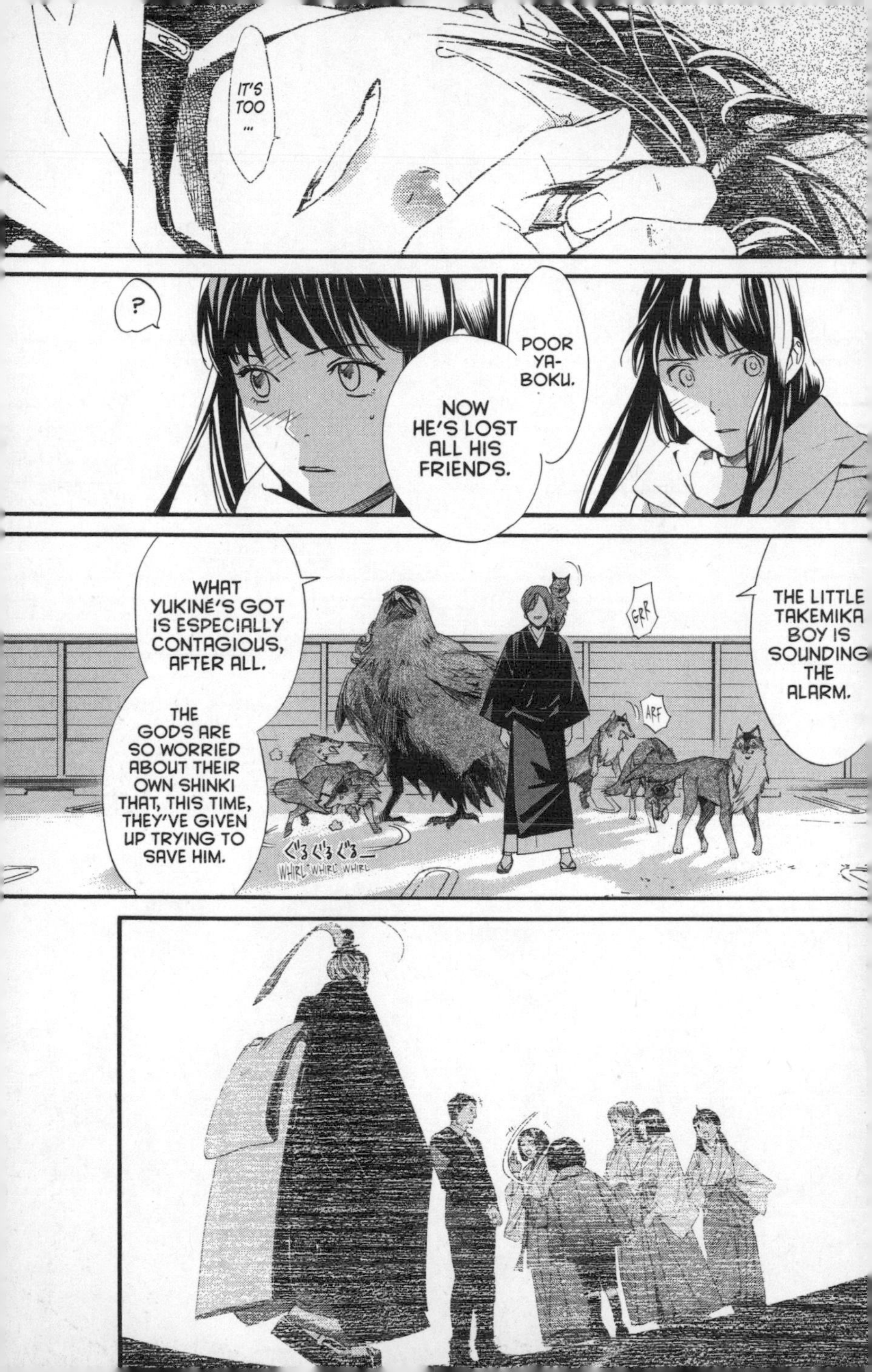
IT'S TOO ...
POOR YA-BOKU.
NOW HE'S LOST ALL HIS FRIENDS.
?
THE LITTLE TAKEMIKA BOY IS SOUNDING THE ALARM.
GRR
ARF
WHAT YUKINÉ'S GOT IS ESPECIALLY CONTAGIOUS, AFTER ALL.
THE GODS ARE SO WORRIED ABOUT THEIR OWN SHINKI THAT, THIS TIME, THEY'VE GIVEN UP TRYING TO SAVE HIM.
ぐるぐるぐる—
WHIRL WHIRL WHIRL

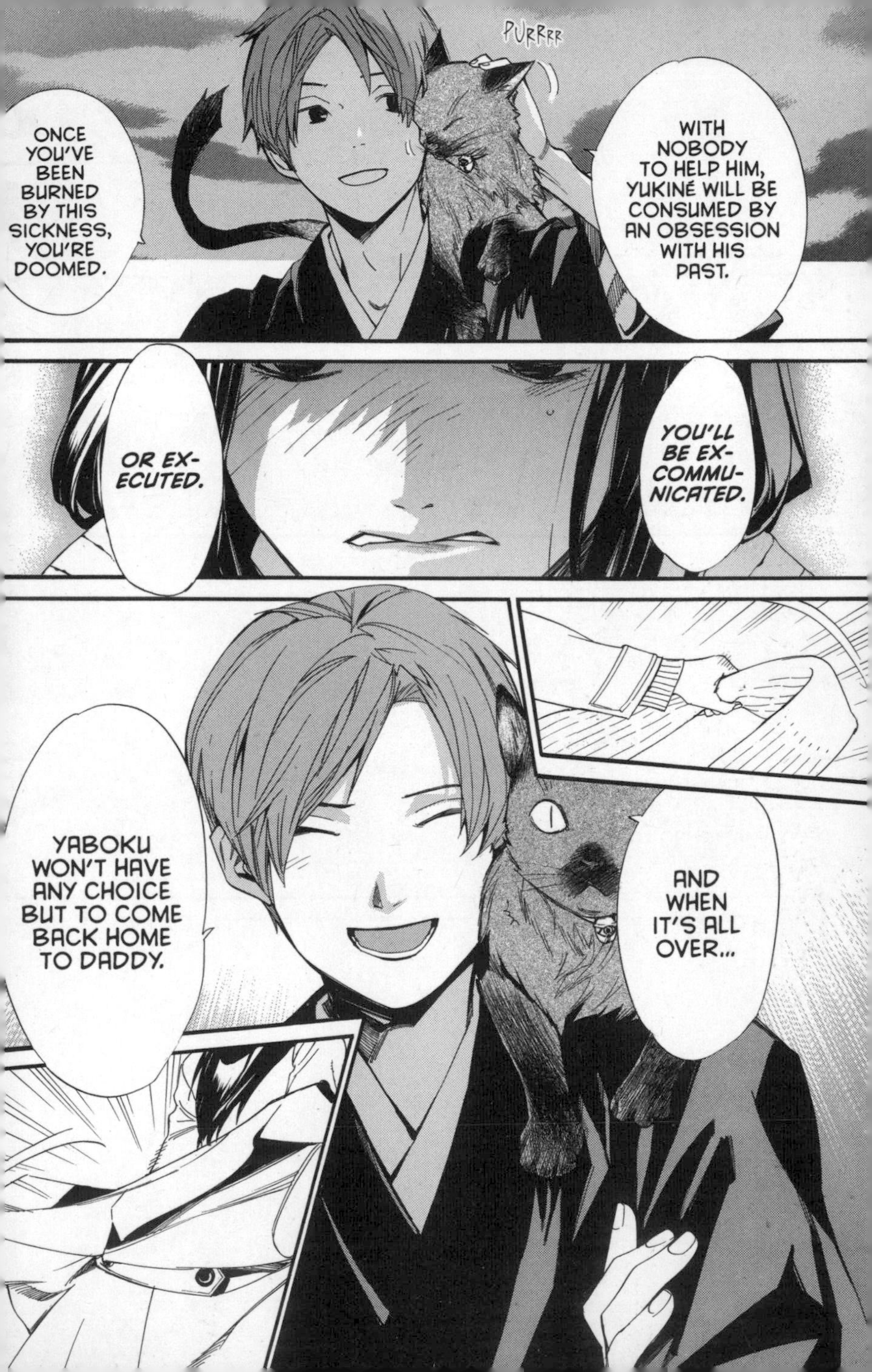
PURRRR
WITH NOBODY TO HELP HIM, YUKINÉ WILL BE CONSUMED BY AN OBSESSION WITH HIS PAST.
ONCE YOU'VE BEEN BURNED BY THIS SICKNESS, YOU'RE DOOMED.
YOU'LL BE EX-COMMUNICATED.
OR EX-ECUTED.
AND WHEN IT'S ALL OVER...
YABOKU WON'T HAVE ANY CHOICE BUT TO COME BACK HOME TO DADDY.

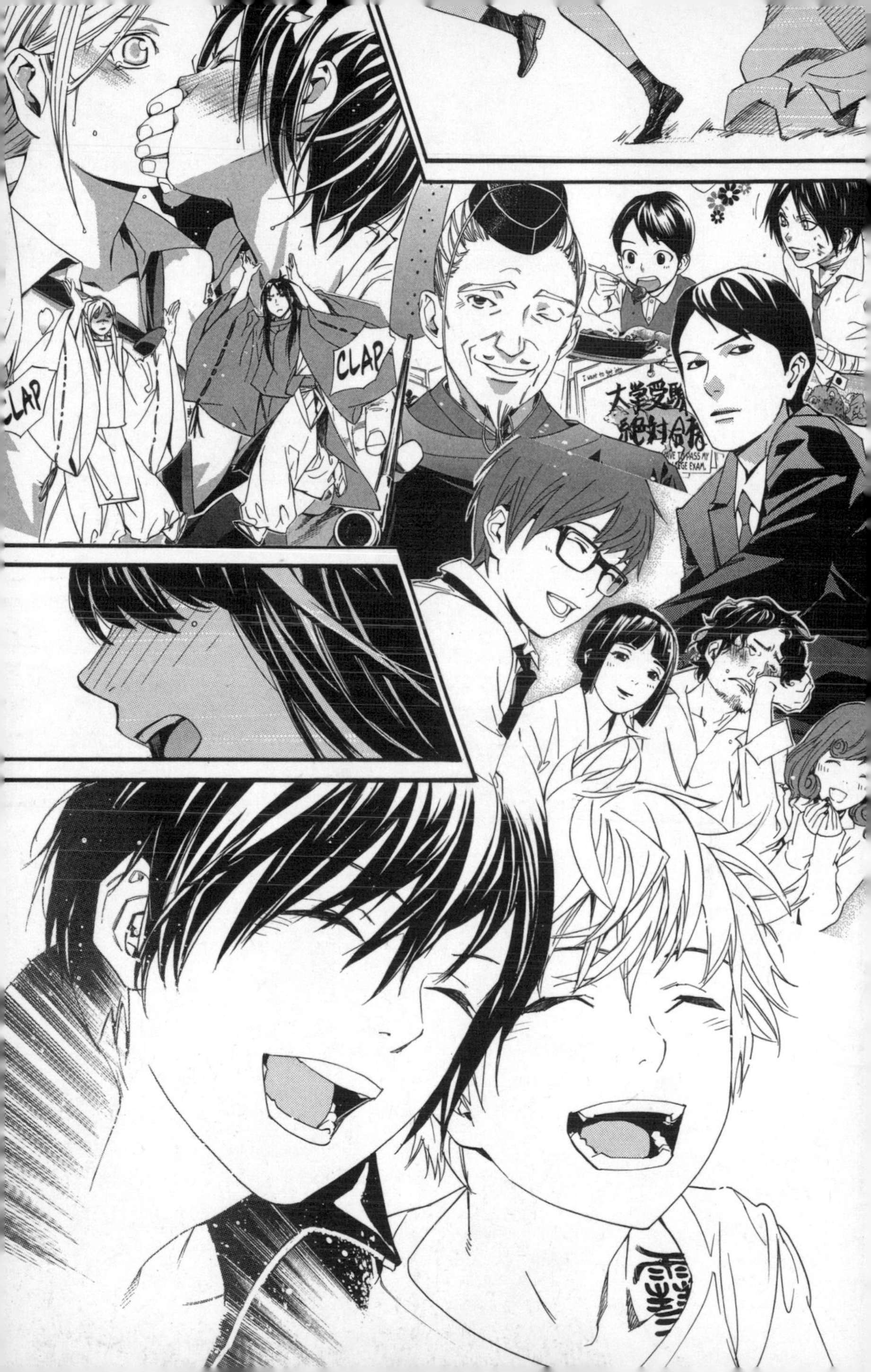
I want to get into
大学受験
絶対合格
PASS MY
EXAM.
CLAP
CLAP

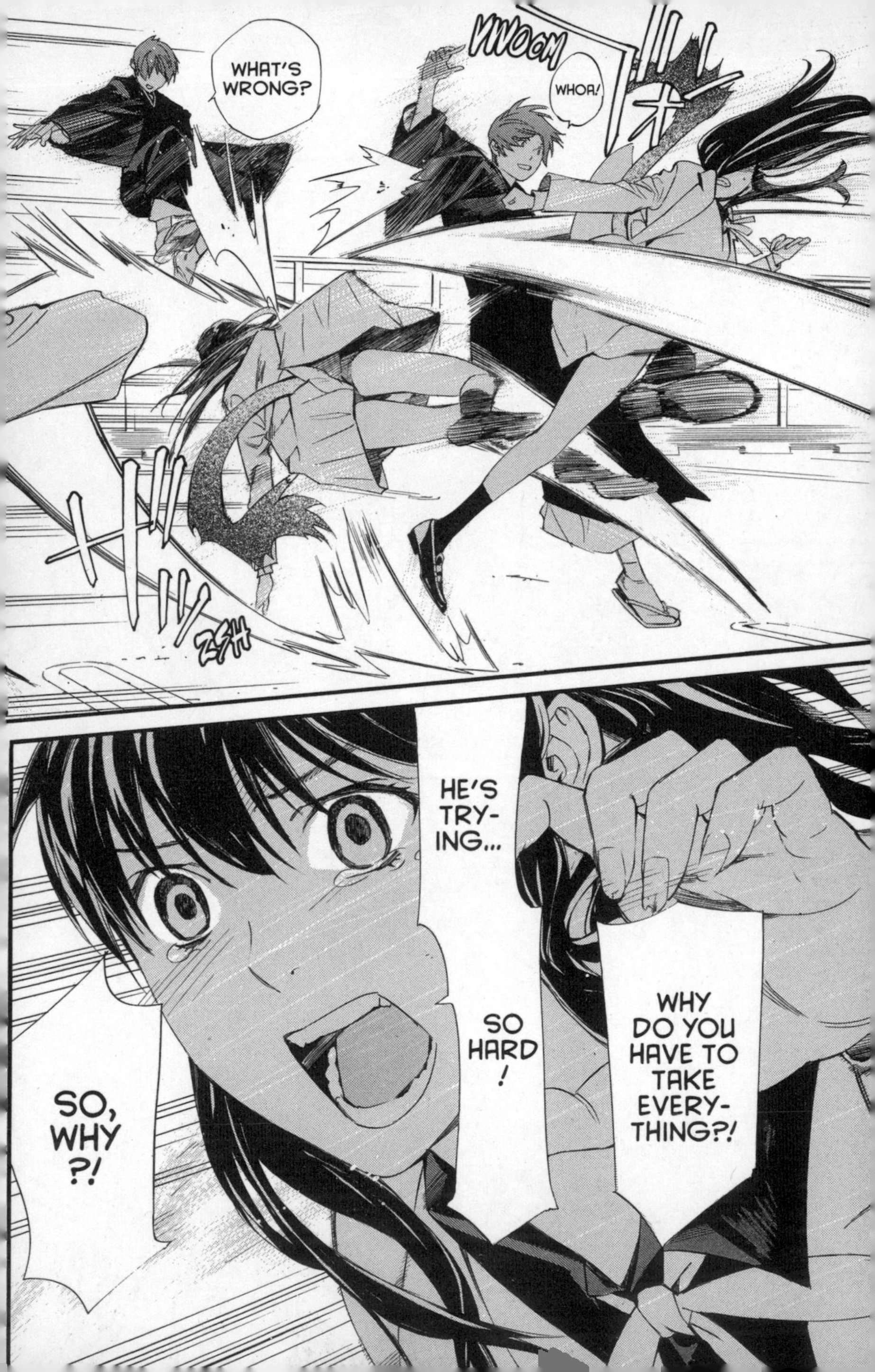
VVNOOM
WHOA!
WHAT'S WRONG?
ZSH
HE'S TRYING...
SO HARD!
WHY DO YOU HAVE TO TAKE EVERYTHING?!
SO, WHY?!

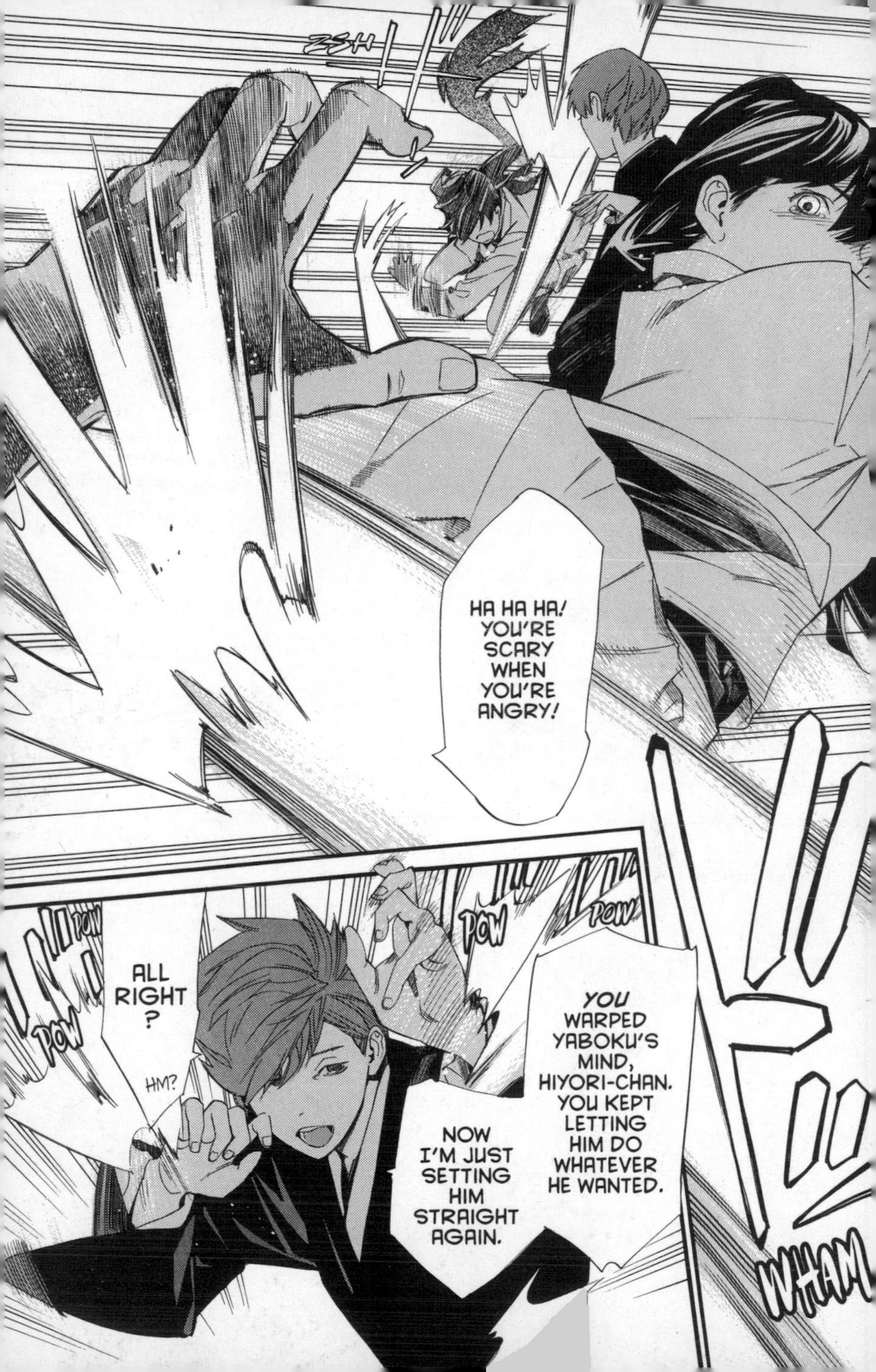
ZSH
HA HA HA! YOU'RE SCARY WHEN YOU'RE ANGRY!
WHAM
POW
POW
POW
POW
YOU WARPED YABOKU'S MIND, HIYORI-CHAN. YOU KEPT LETTING HIM DO WHATEVER HE WANTED.
NOW I'M JUST SETTING HIM STRAIGHT AGAIN.
ALL RIGHT?
HM?

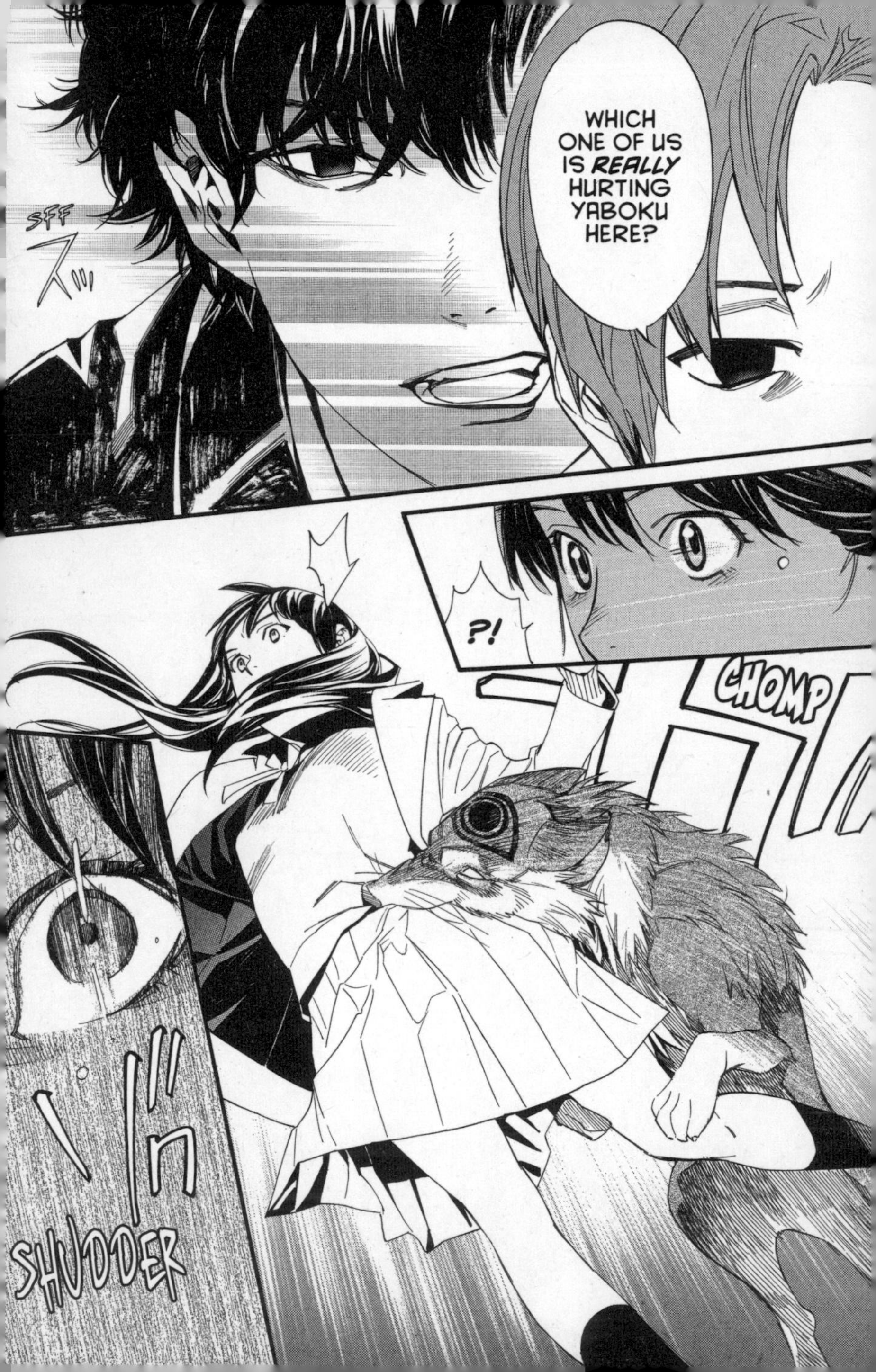
WHICH ONE OF US IS *REALLY* HURTING YABOKU HERE?
SFF
?!
CHOMP
SHUDDER

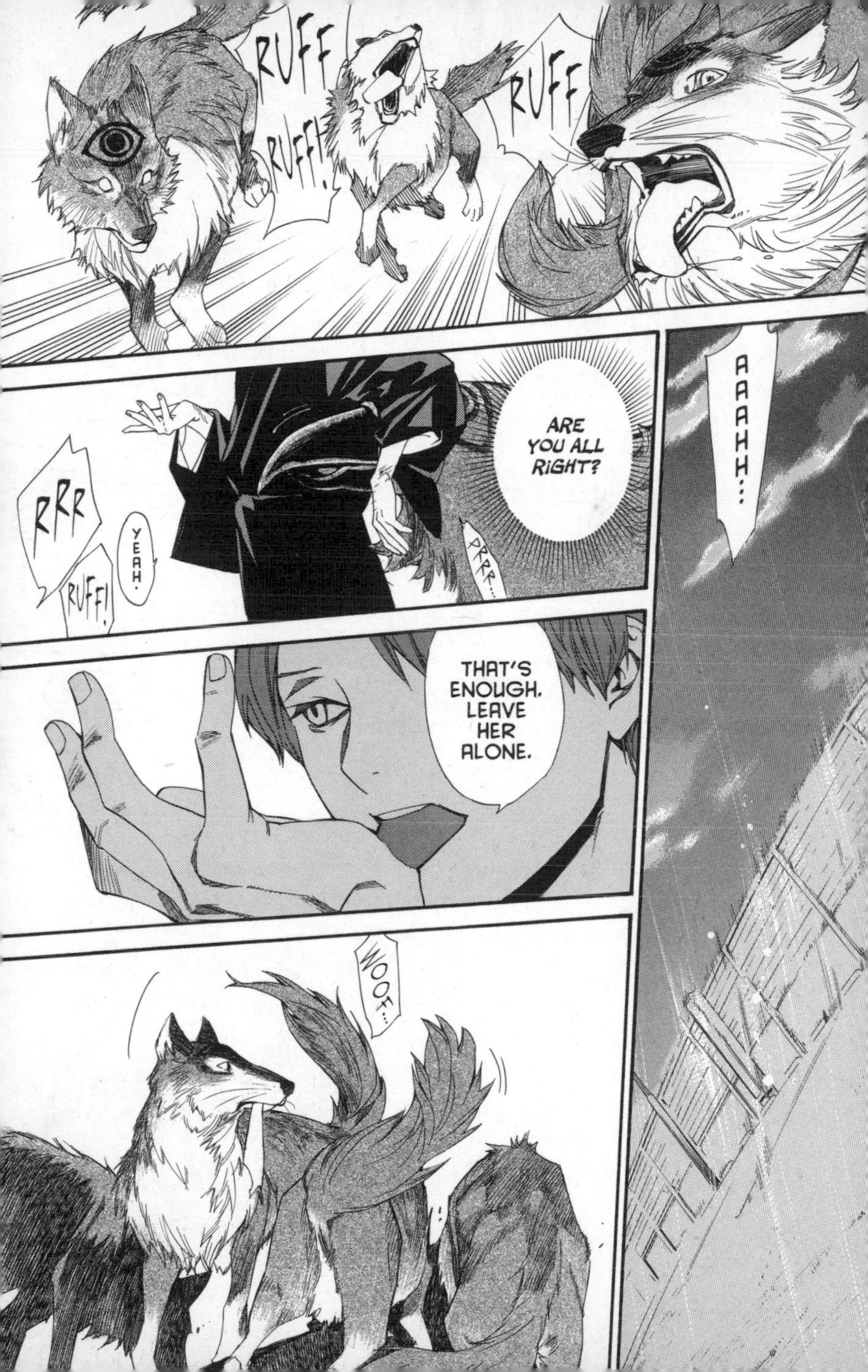
RUFF
RUFF
RUFF!
AAAAHH...
ARE YOU ALL RIGHT?
PRRR...
YEAH.
RRR
RUFF!
THAT'S ENOUGH. LEAVE HER ALONE.
WOOF...

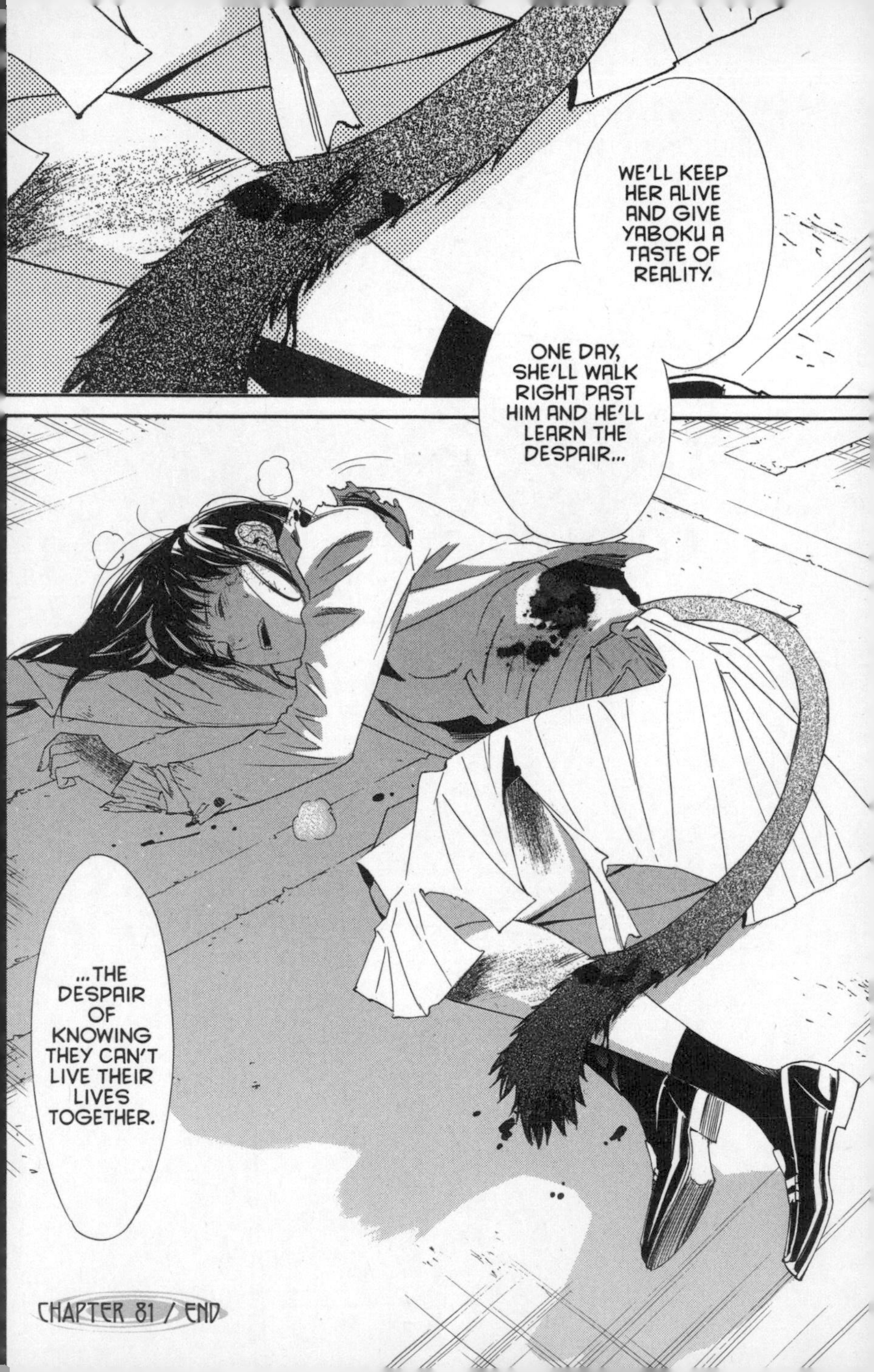

WE'LL KEEP HER ALIVE AND GIVE YABOKU A TASTE OF REALITY.
ONE DAY, SHE'LL WALK RIGHT PAST HIM AND HE'LL LEARN THE DESPAIR...
...THE DESPAIR OF KNOWING THEY CAN'T LIVE THEIR LIVES TOGETHER.
CHAPTER 81 / END

野

皀

神

[illegible]

[illegible]

神

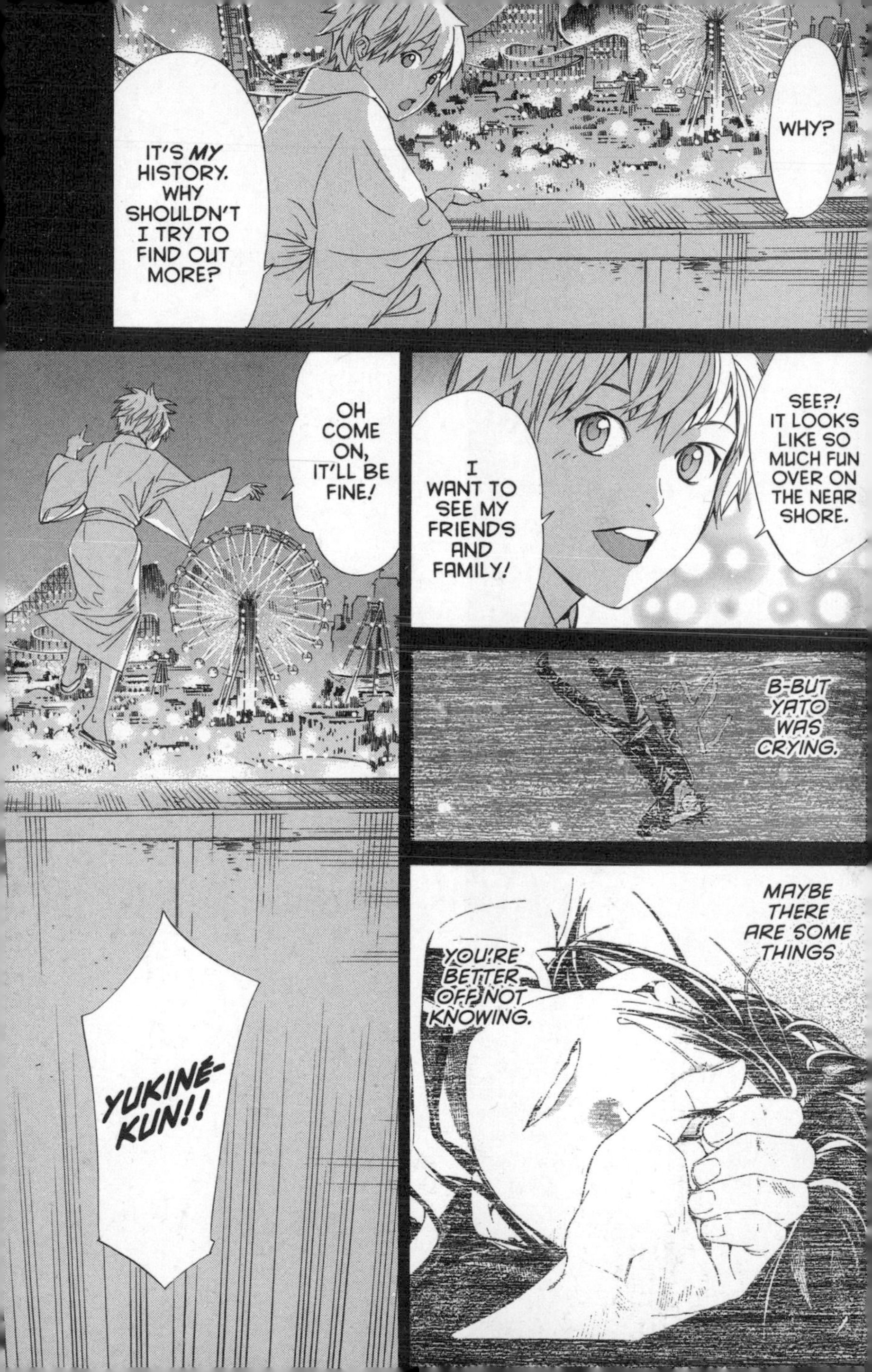
WHY?
IT'S *MY* HISTORY. WHY SHOULDN'T I TRY TO FIND OUT MORE?
SEE?! IT LOOKS LIKE SO MUCH FUN OVER ON THE NEAR SHORE.
I WANT TO SEE MY FRIENDS AND FAMILY!
B-BUT YATO WAS CRYING.
MAYBE THERE ARE SOME THINGS
YOU'RE BETTER OFF NOT KNOWING.
OH COME ON, IT'LL BE FINE!
YUKINE-KUN!!

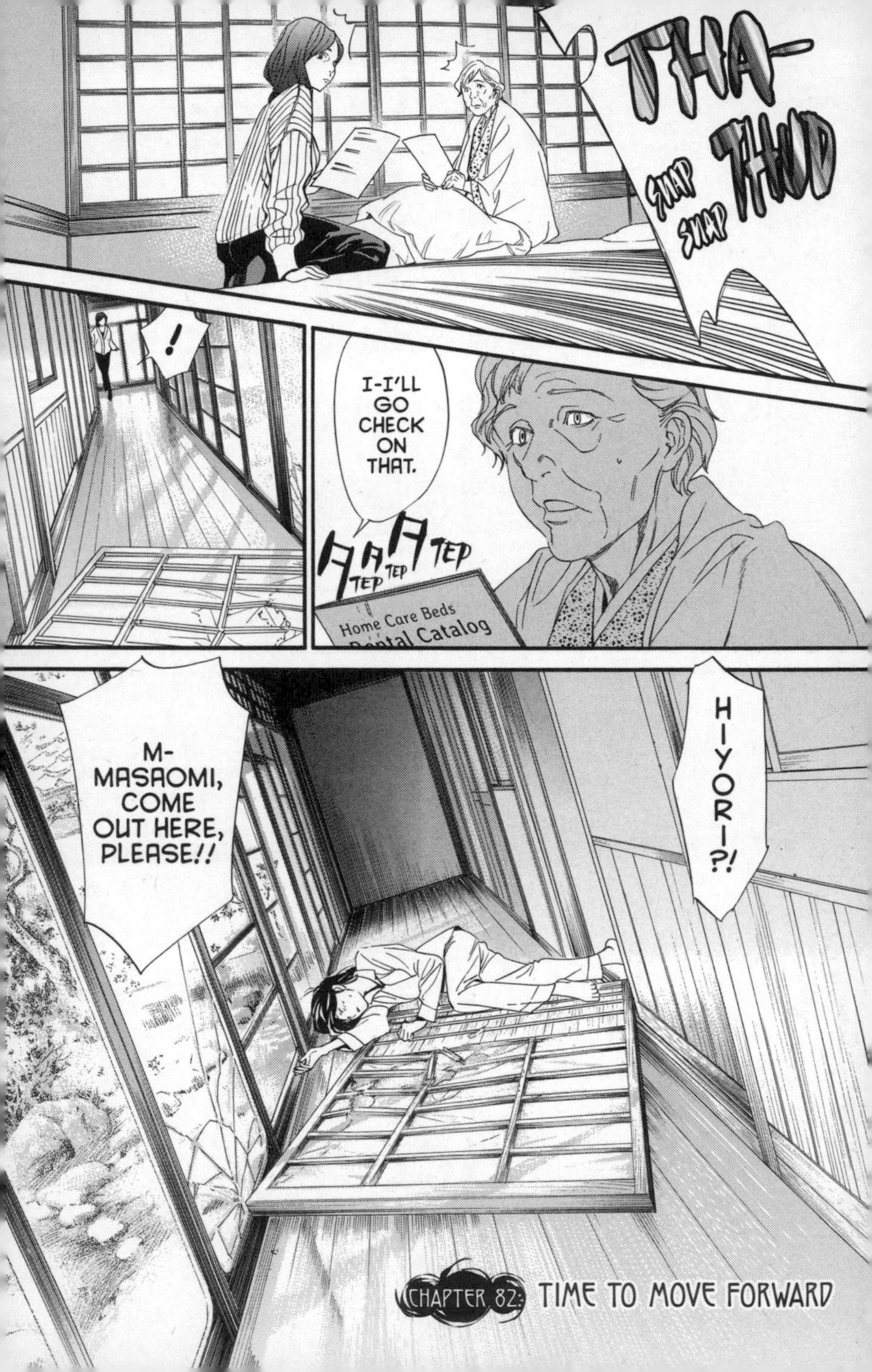
THA-THUD
SNAP SNAP
I-I'LL GO CHECK ON THAT.
TEP TEP TEP TEP
Home Care Beds Rental Catalog
!
HIYORI?!
M-MASAOMI, COME OUT HERE, PLEASE!!
CHAPTER 82: TIME TO MOVE FORWARD

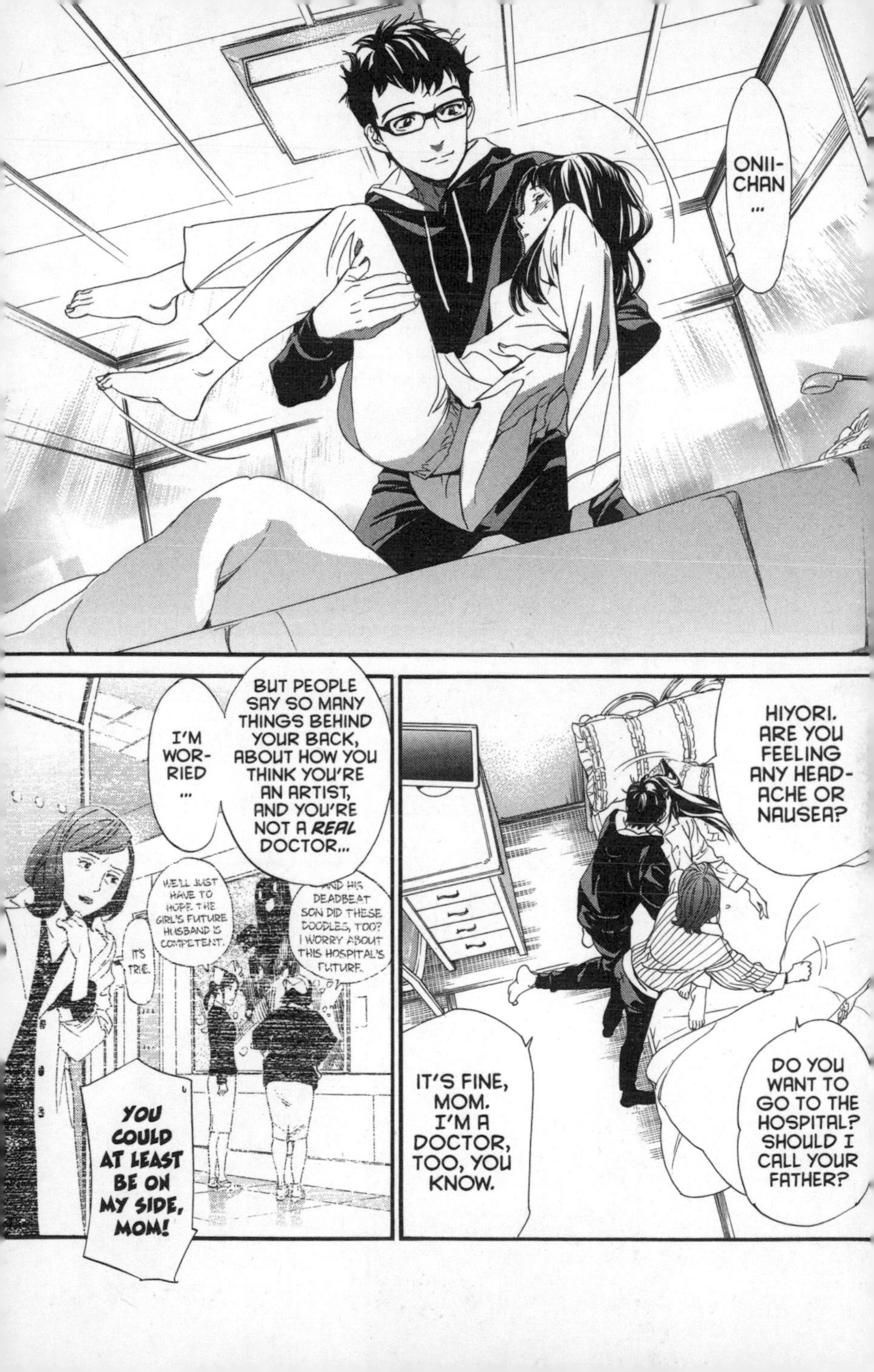
ONII-CHAN ...
HIYORI. ARE YOU FEELING ANY HEADACHE OR NAUSEA?
DO YOU WANT TO GO TO THE HOSPITAL? SHOULD I CALL YOUR FATHER?
IT'S FINE, MOM. I'M A DOCTOR, TOO, YOU KNOW.
BUT PEOPLE SAY SO MANY THINGS BEHIND YOUR BACK, ABOUT HOW YOU THINK YOU'RE AN ARTIST, AND YOU'RE NOT A *REAL* DOCTOR...
I'M WORRIED ...
...AND HIS DEADBEAT SON DID THESE DOODLES, TOO? I WORRY ABOUT THIS HOSPITAL'S FUTURE.
WE'LL JUST HAVE TO HOPE THE GIRL'S FUTURE HUSBAND IS COMPETENT.
IT'S TRUE.
YOU COULD AT LEAST BE ON MY SIDE, MOM!

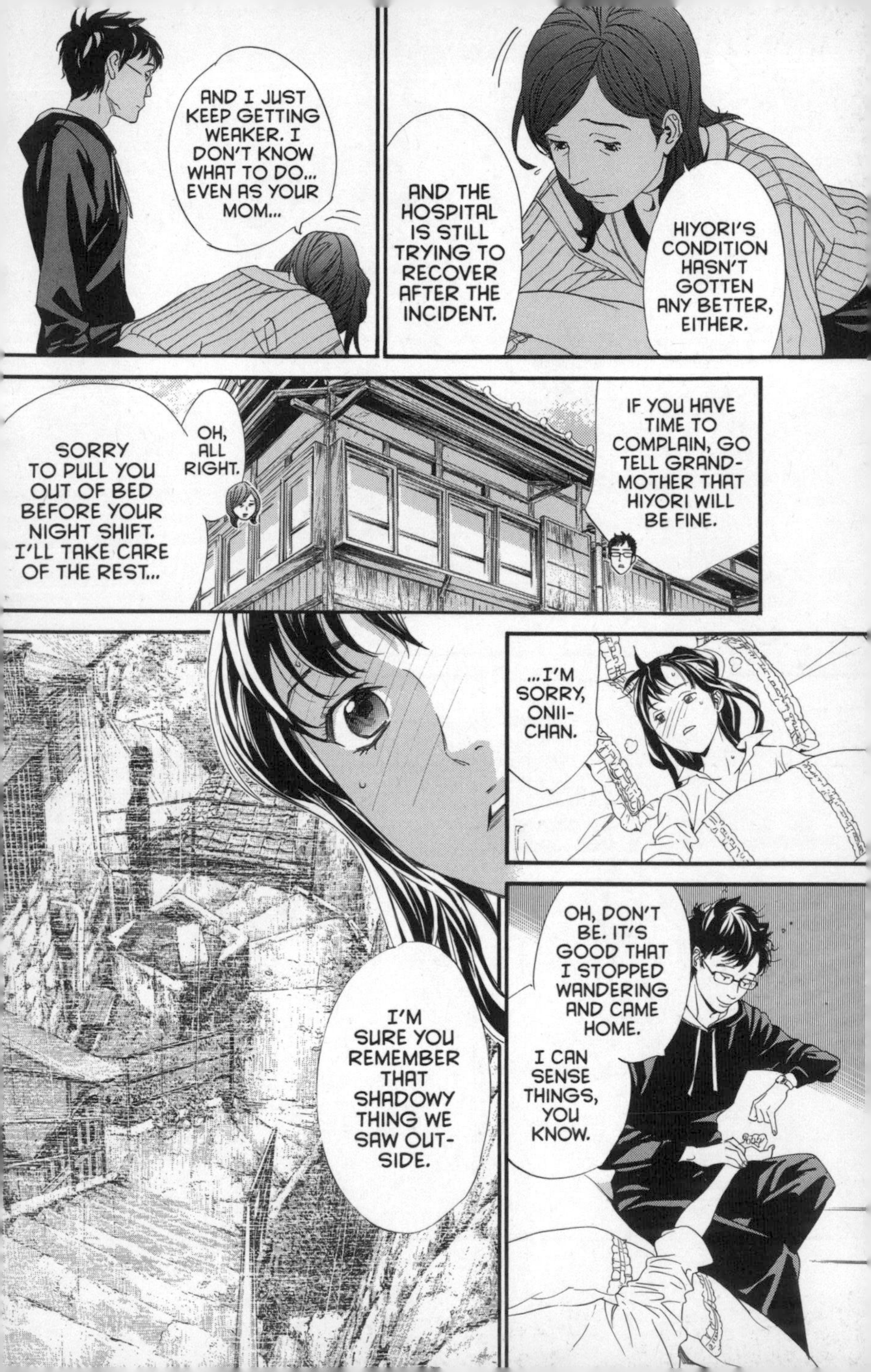
HIYORI'S CONDITION HASN'T GOTTEN ANY BETTER, EITHER.
AND THE HOSPITAL IS STILL TRYING TO RECOVER AFTER THE INCIDENT.
AND I JUST KEEP GETTING WEAKER. I DON'T KNOW WHAT TO DO... EVEN AS YOUR MOM...
IF YOU HAVE TIME TO COMPLAIN, GO TELL GRAND-MOTHER THAT HIYORI WILL BE FINE.
OH, ALL RIGHT.
SORRY TO PULL YOU OUT OF BED BEFORE YOUR NIGHT SHIFT. I'LL TAKE CARE OF THE REST...
...I'M SORRY, ONII-CHAN.
OH, DON'T BE. IT'S GOOD THAT I STOPPED WANDERING AND CAME HOME.
I CAN SENSE THINGS, YOU KNOW.
I'M SURE YOU REMEMBER THAT SHADOWY THING WE SAW OUT-SIDE.

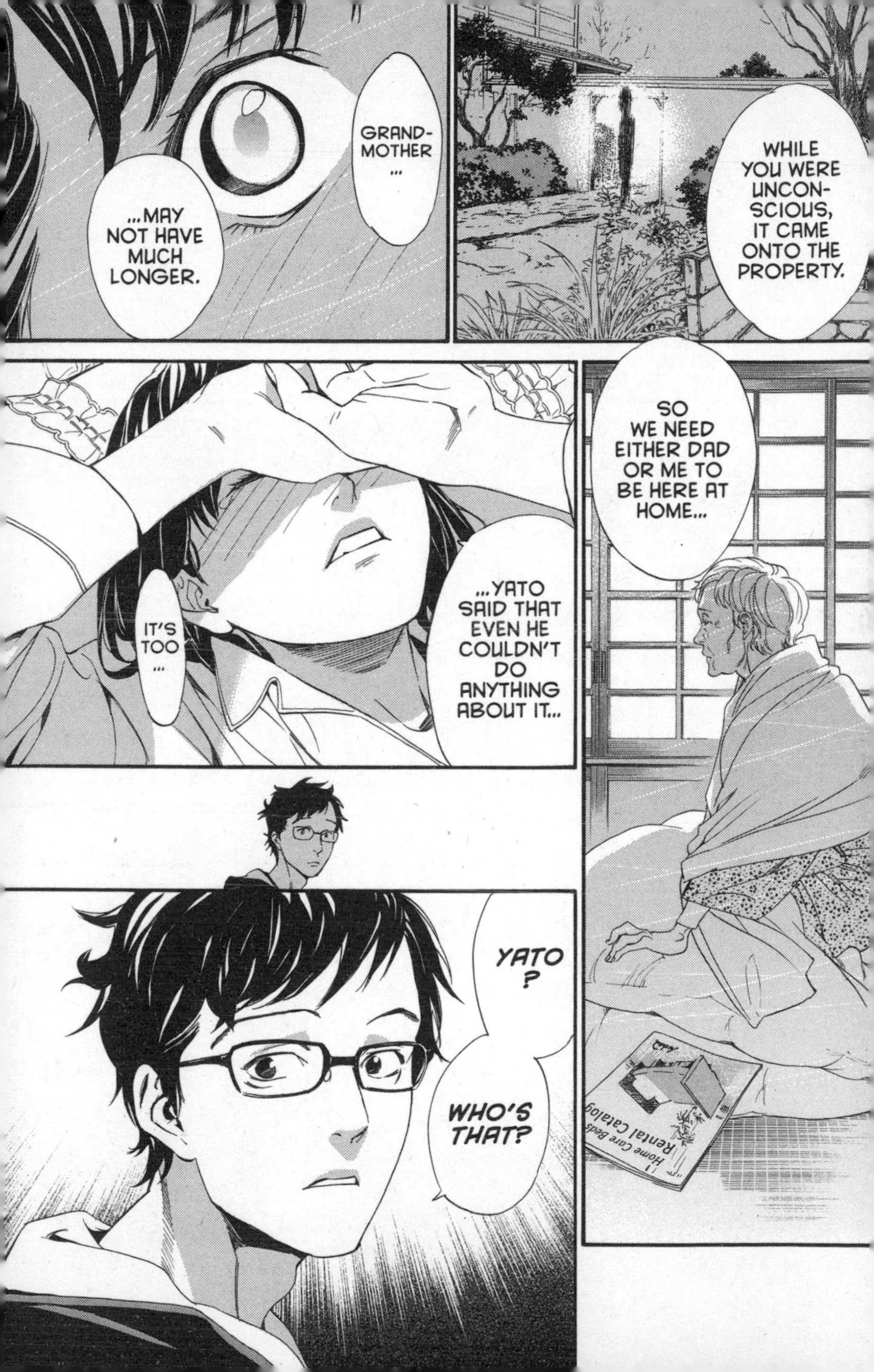
WHILE YOU WERE UNCONSCIOUS, IT CAME ONTO THE PROPERTY.
GRAND-MOTHER ...
...MAY NOT HAVE MUCH LONGER.
SO WE NEED EITHER DAD OR ME TO BE HERE AT HOME...
Home Care Beds Rental Catalog
...YATO SAID THAT EVEN HE COULDN'T DO ANYTHING ABOUT IT...
IT'S TOO ...
YATO ?
WHO'S THAT?

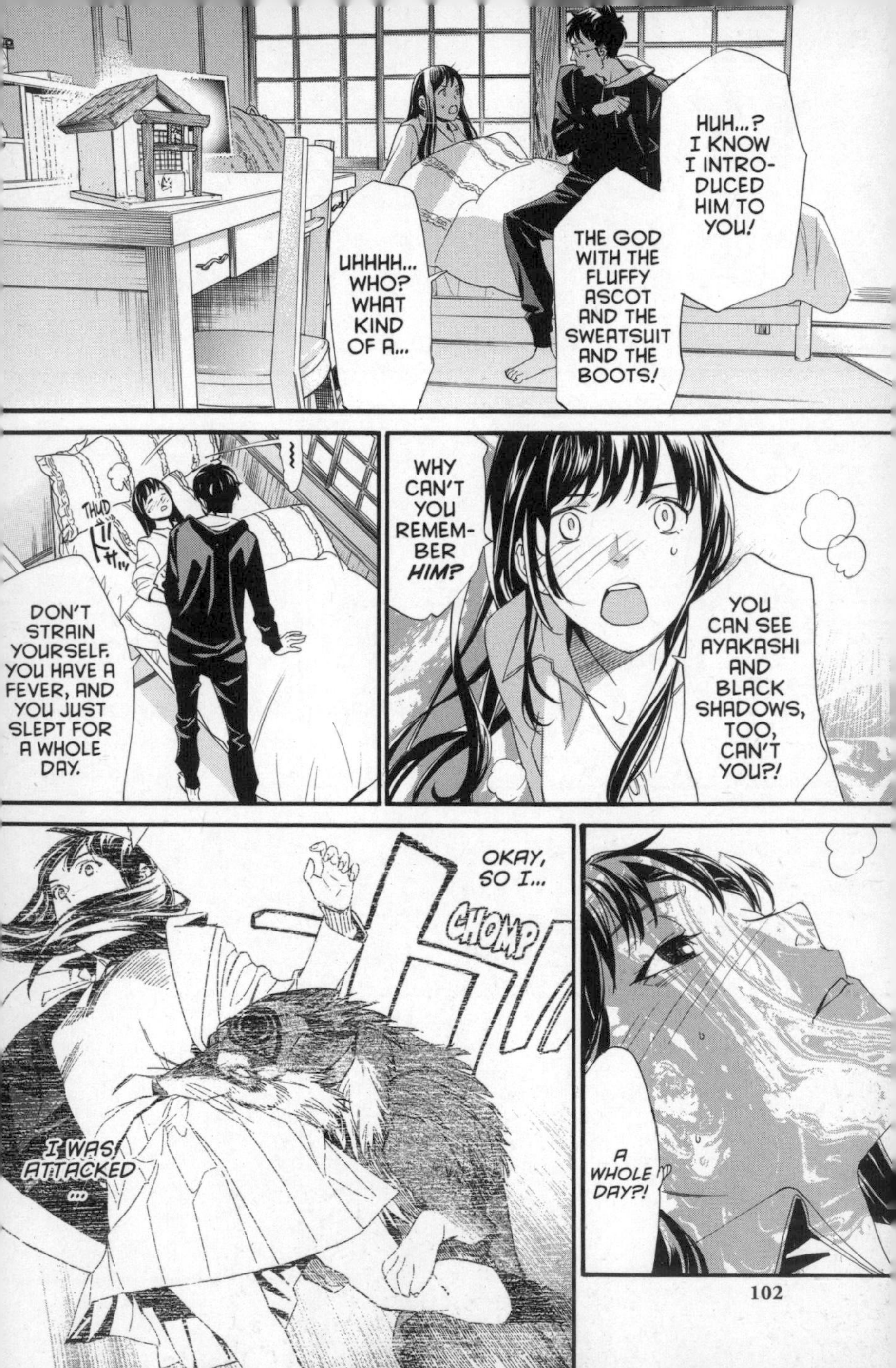
HUH...? I KNOW I INTRO-DUCED HIM TO YOU!
THE GOD WITH THE FLUFFY ASCOT AND THE SWEATSUIT AND THE BOOTS!
UHHHH... WHO? WHAT KIND OF A...
YOU CAN SEE AYAKASHI AND BLACK SHADOWS, TOO, CAN'T YOU?!
WHY CAN'T YOU REMEM-BER *HIM?*
THUD
DON'T STRAIN YOURSELF. YOU HAVE A FEVER, AND YOU JUST SLEPT FOR A WHOLE DAY.
A WHOLE DAY?!
OKAY, SO I...
CHOMP
I WAS ATTACKED ...

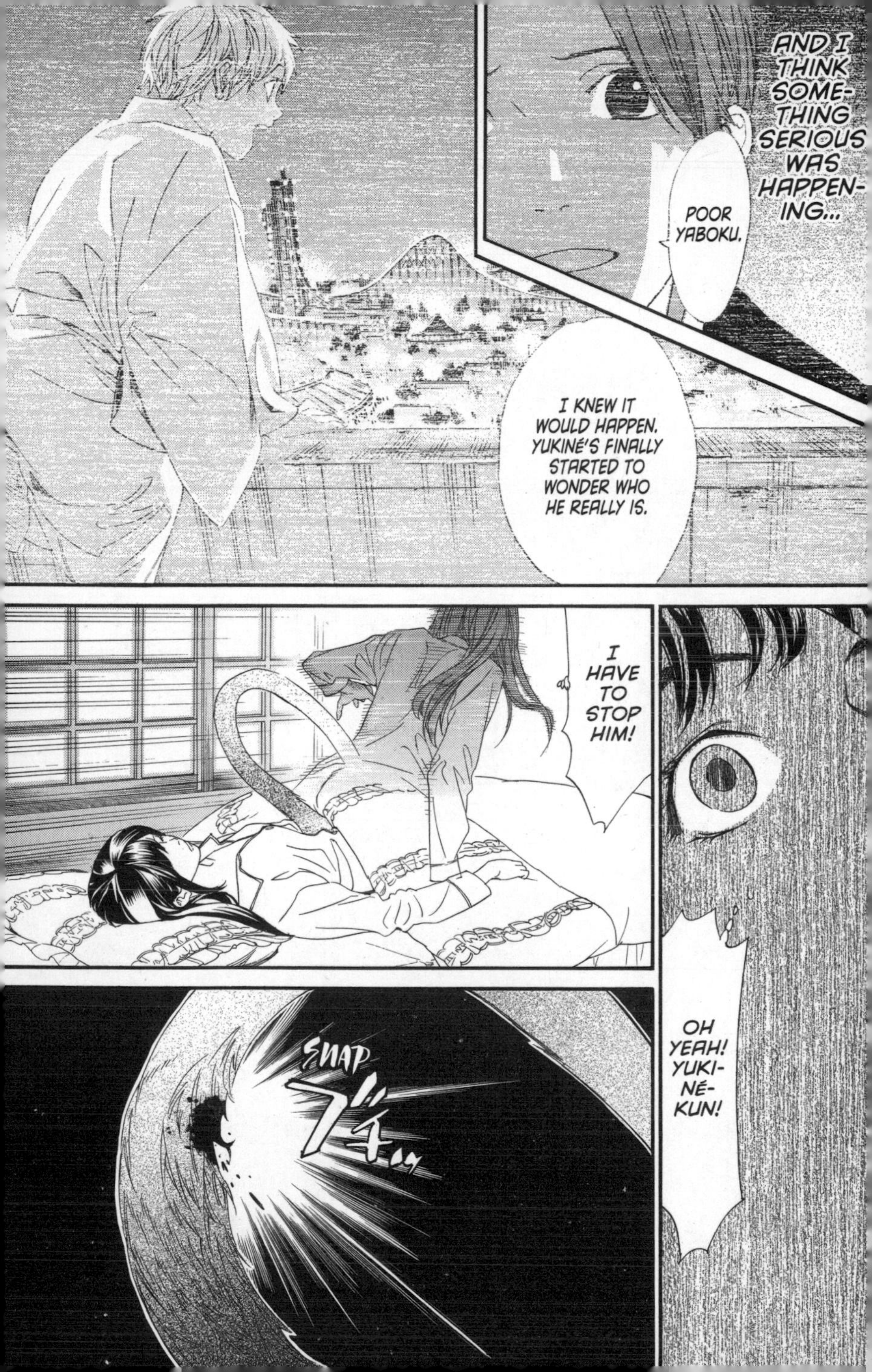
AND I THINK SOMETHING SERIOUS WAS HAPPENING...
POOR YABOKU.
I KNEW IT WOULD HAPPEN. YUKINÉ'S FINALLY STARTED TO WONDER WHO HE REALLY IS.
OH YEAH! YUKINÉ-KUN!
I HAVE TO STOP HIM!
SNAP

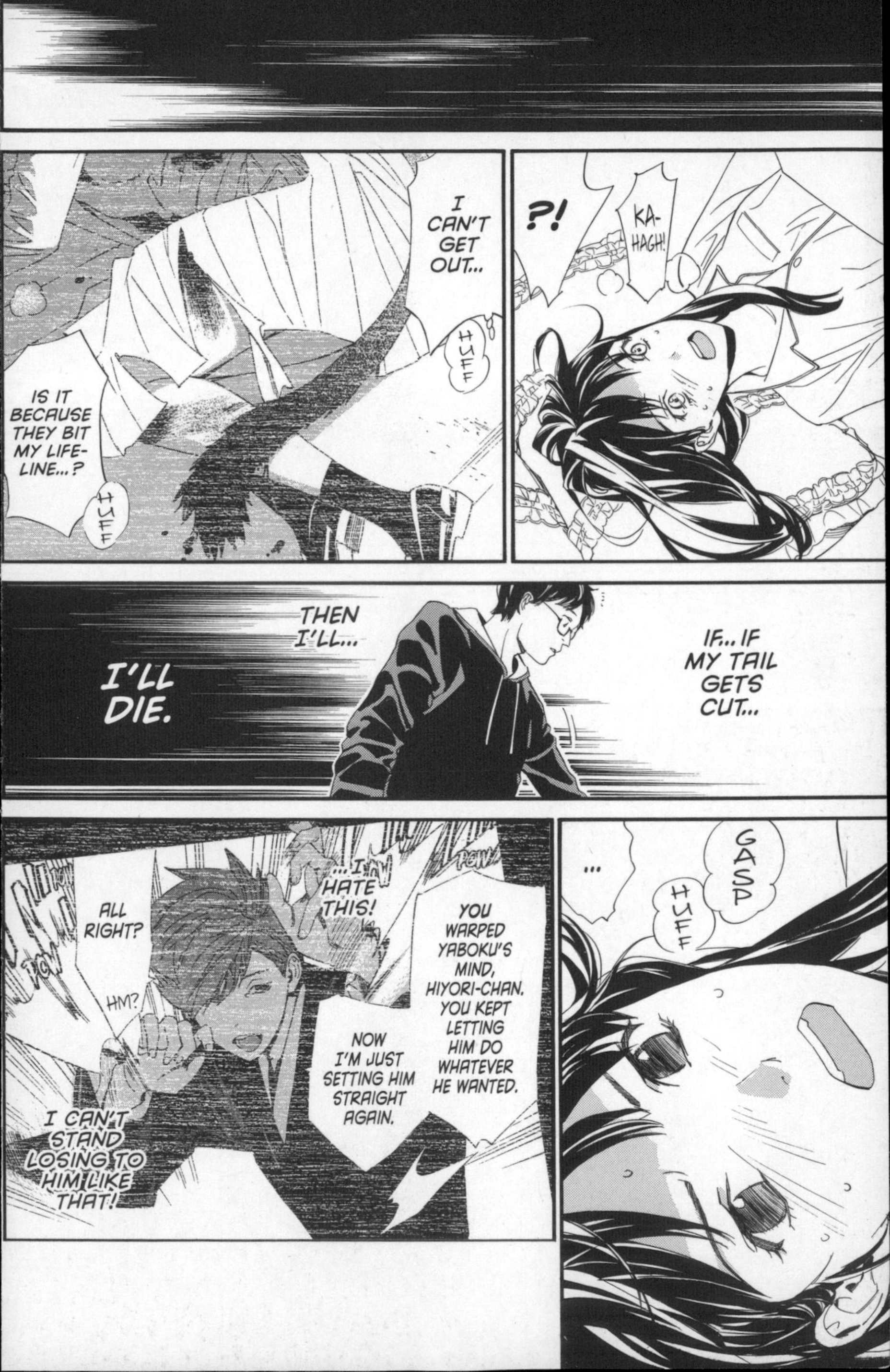
?!
KA-HAGH!
I CAN'T GET OUT...
HUFF
IS IT BECAUSE THEY BIT MY LIFE-LINE...?
HUFF
IF... IF MY TAIL GETS CUT...
THEN I'LL...
I'LL DIE.
GASP
HUFF
...
...I HATE THIS!
YOU WARPED YABOKU'S MIND, HIYORI-CHAN. YOU KEPT LETTING HIM DO WHATEVER HE WANTED.
ALL RIGHT?
HM?
NOW I'M JUST SETTING HIM STRAIGHT AGAIN.
I CAN'T STAND LOSING TO HIM LIKE THAT!

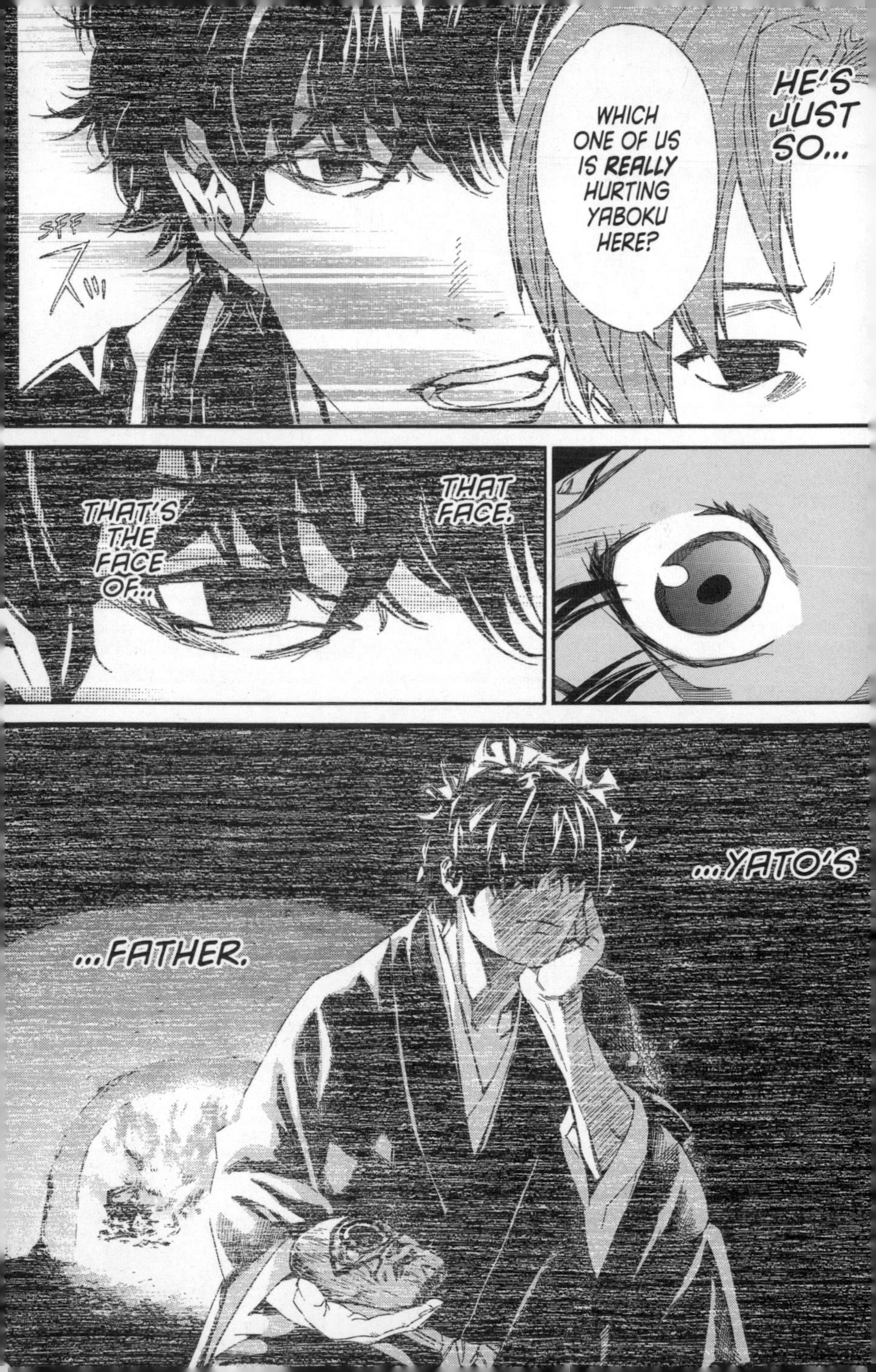
HE'S JUST SO...
WHICH ONE OF US IS **REALLY** HURTING YABOKU HERE?
SFF
THAT FACE.
THAT'S THE FACE OF...
...YATO'S
...FATHER.

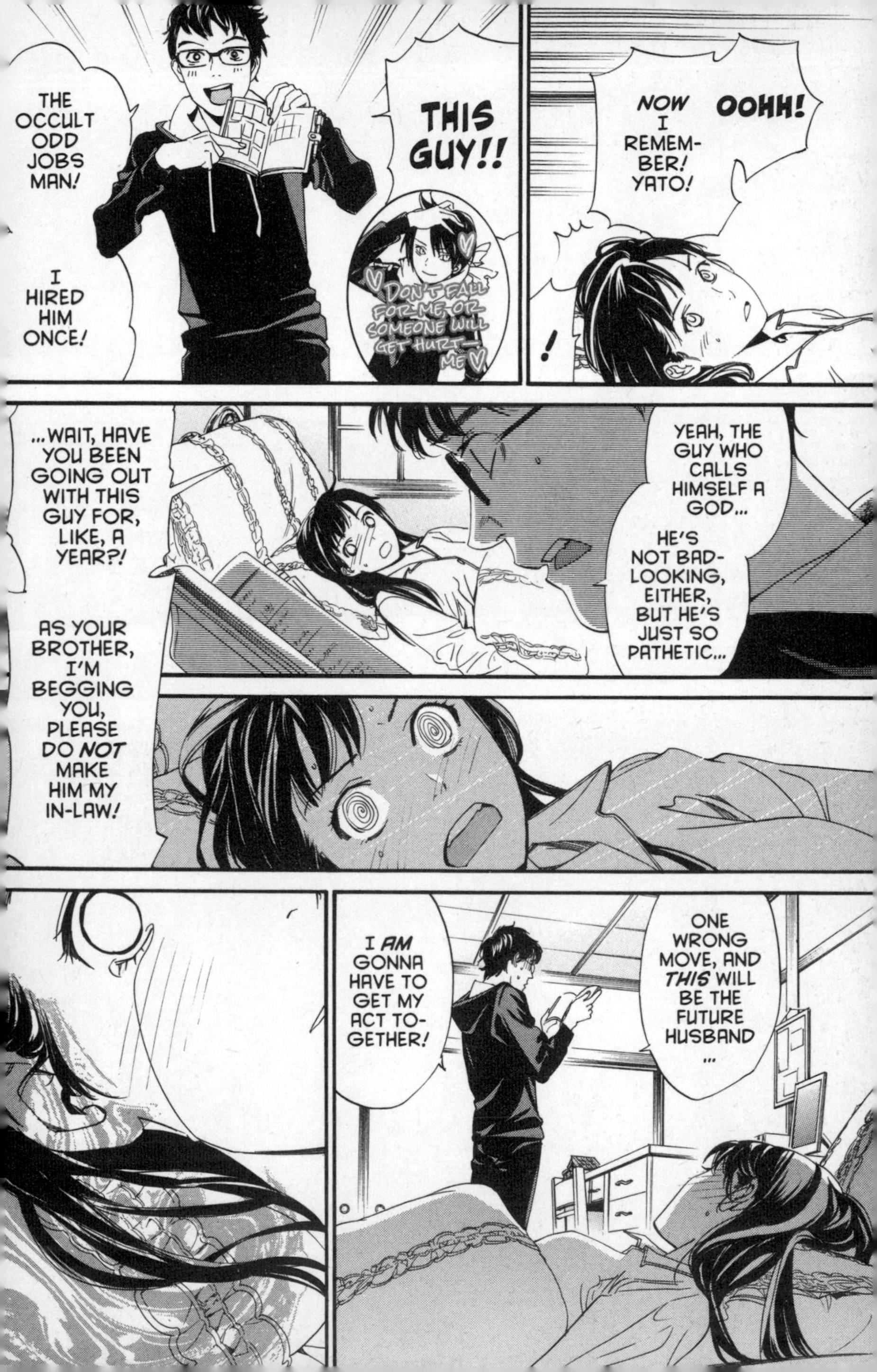

NOW I REMEMBER! YATO!
OOHH!
!
THIS GUY!!
DON'T FALL FOR ME OR SOMEONE WILL GET HURT—ME♥
THE OCCULT ODD JOBS MAN!
I HIRED HIM ONCE!
YEAH, THE GUY WHO CALLS HIMSELF A GOD...
HE'S NOT BAD-LOOKING, EITHER, BUT HE'S JUST SO PATHETIC...
...WAIT, HAVE YOU BEEN GOING OUT WITH THIS GUY FOR, LIKE, A YEAR?!
AS YOUR BROTHER, I'M BEGGING YOU, PLEASE DO NOT MAKE HIM MY IN-LAW!
ONE WRONG MOVE, AND THIS WILL BE THE FUTURE HUSBAND ...
I AM GONNA HAVE TO GET MY ACT TOGETHER!

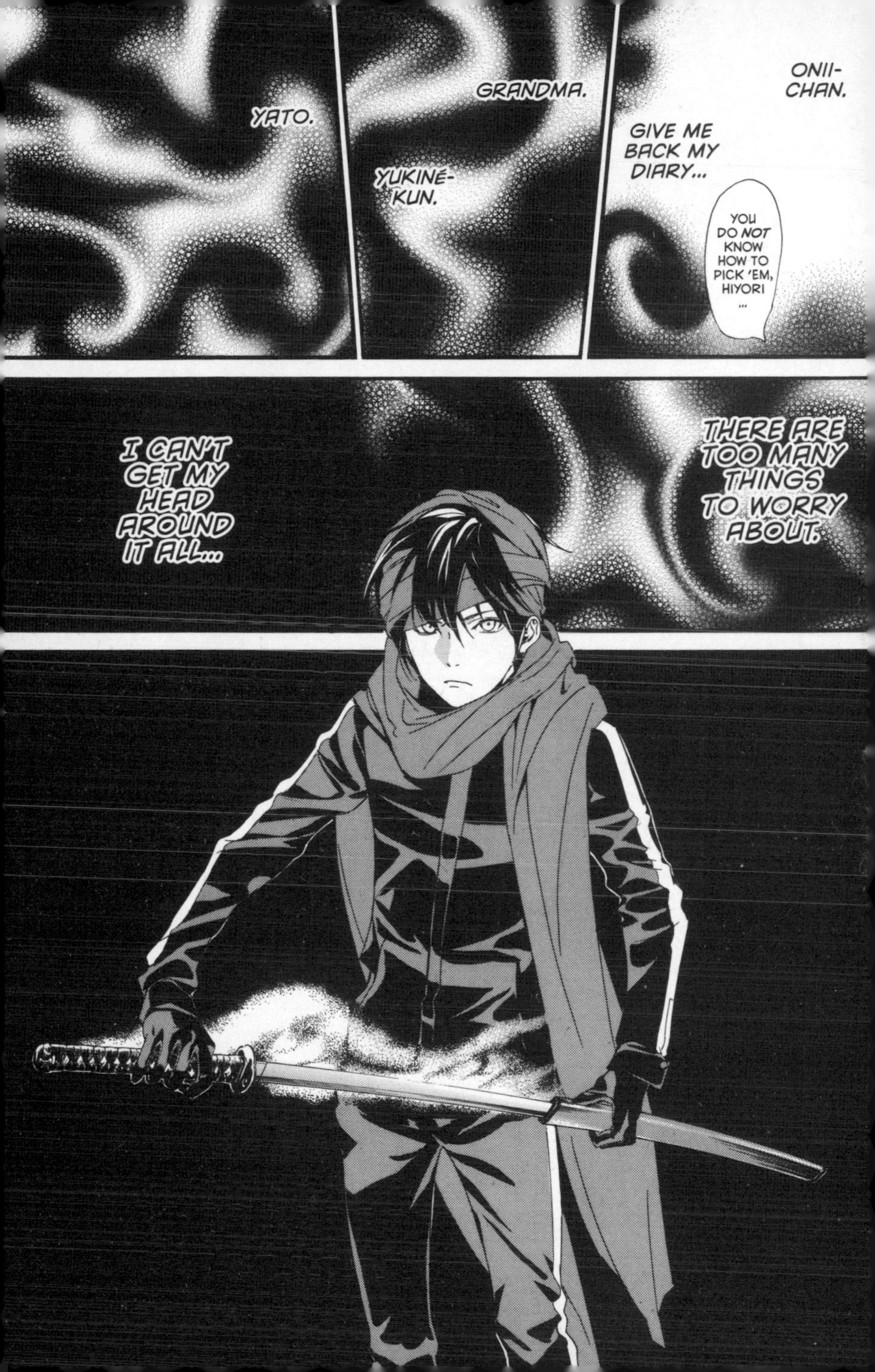
ONII-CHAN.
GIVE ME BACK MY DIARY...
YOU DO *NOT* KNOW HOW TO PICK 'EM, HIYORI ...
GRANDMA.
YUKINÉ-KUN.
YATO.
THERE ARE TOO MANY THINGS TO WORRY ABOUT.
I CAN'T GET MY HEAD AROUND IT ALL...

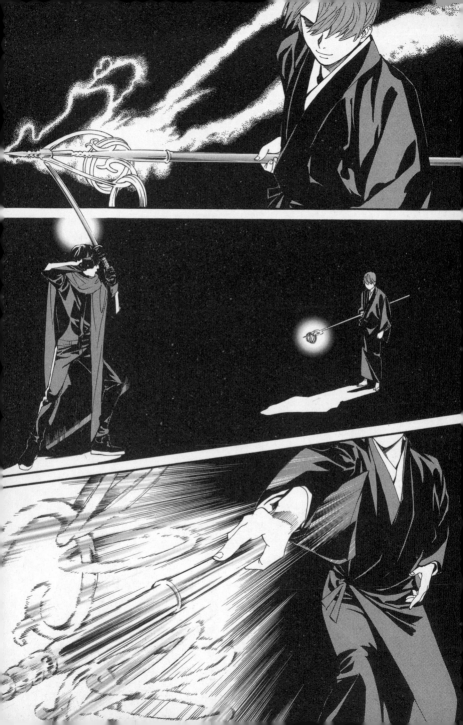

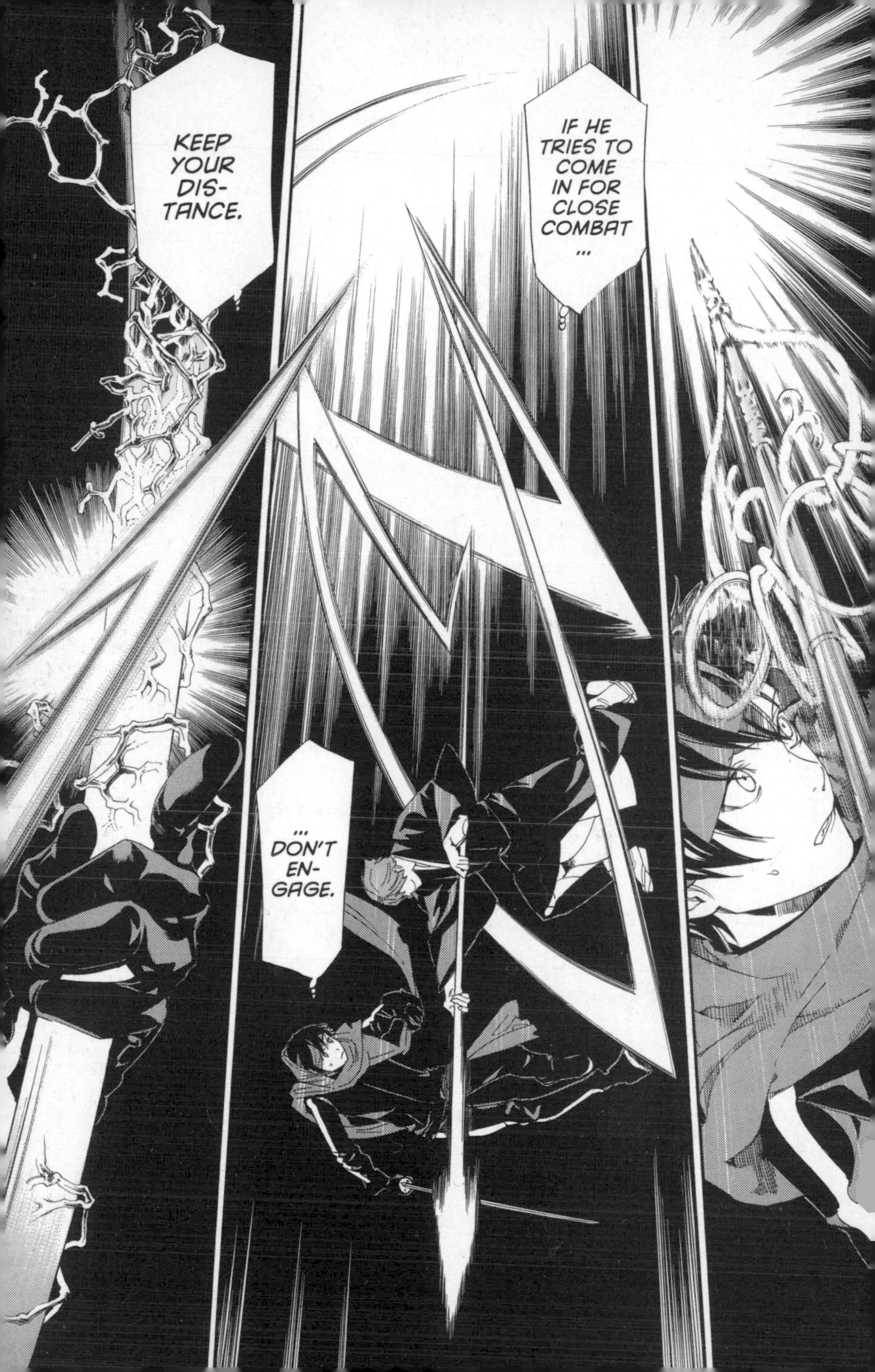
IF HE TRIES TO COME IN FOR CLOSE COMBAT ...
... DON'T EN-GAGE.
KEEP YOUR DIS-TANCE.

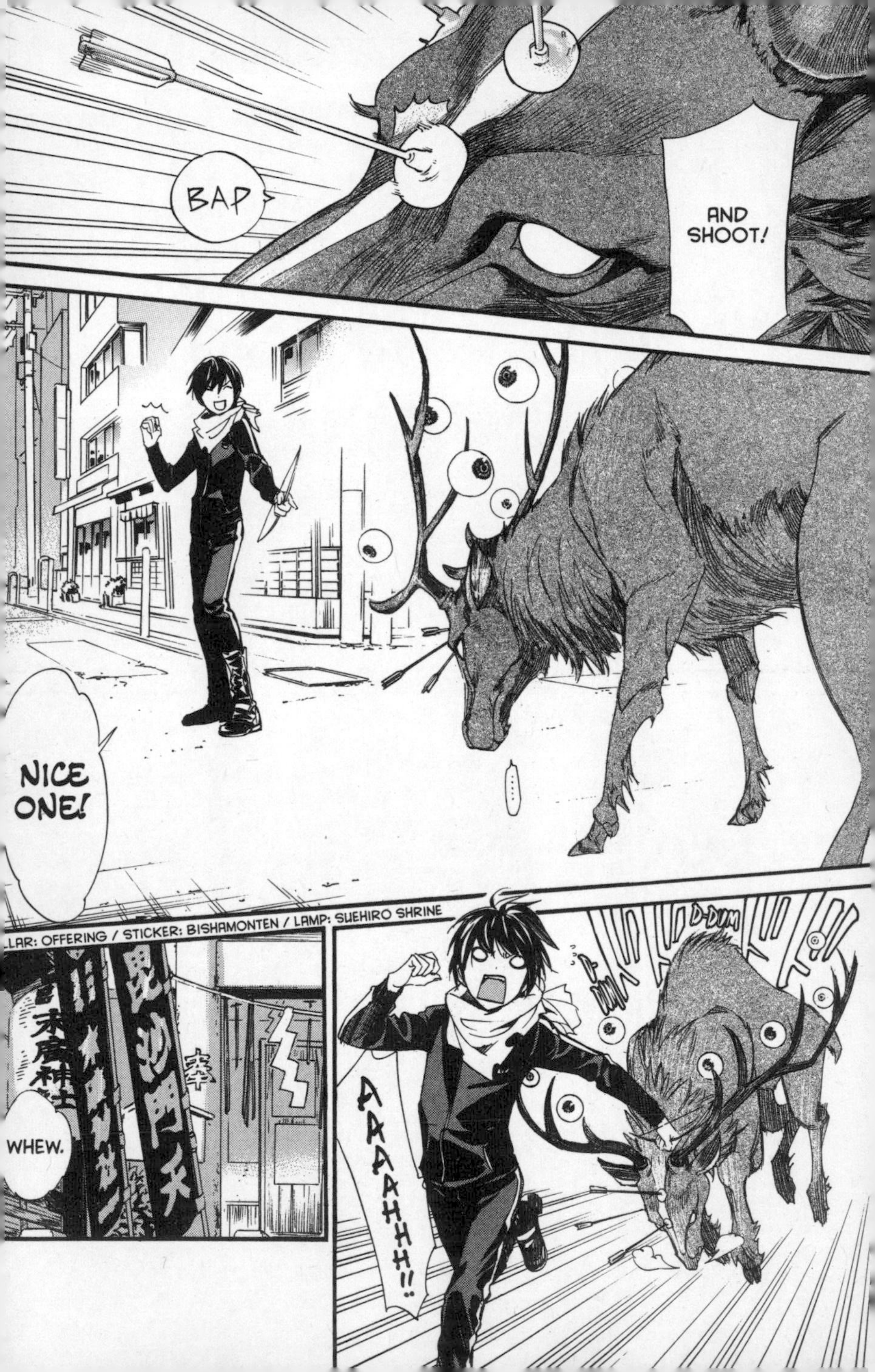
AND SHOOT!
BAP
NICE ONE!
......
D-DUM
AAAAAHHH!!
LLAR: OFFERING / STICKER: BISHAMONTEN / LAMP: SUEHIRO SHRINE
WHEW.

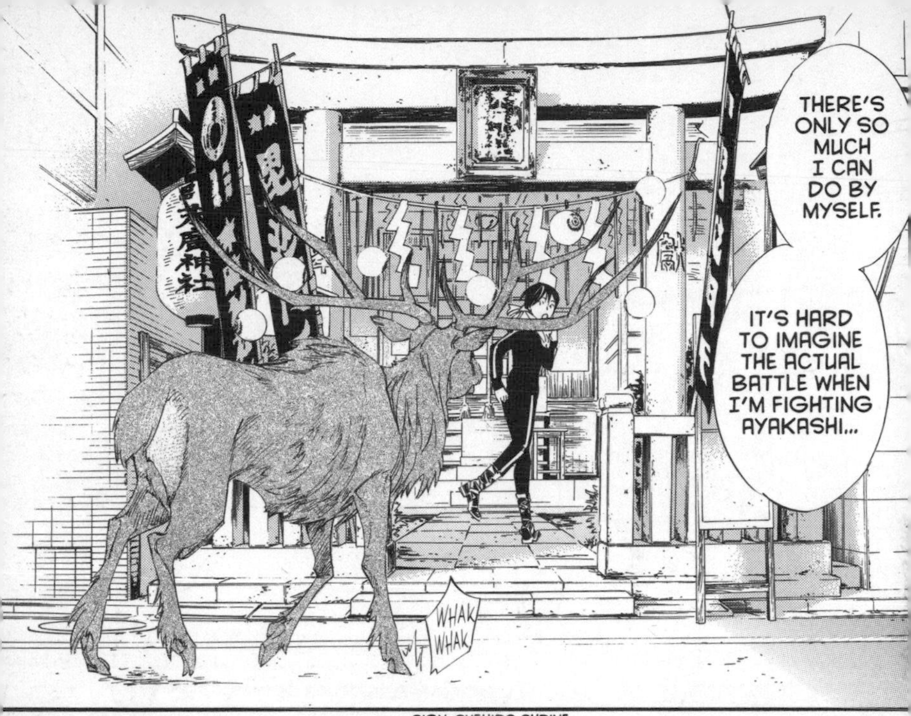
THERE'S ONLY SO MUCH I CAN DO BY MYSELF.
IT'S HARD TO IMAGINE THE ACTUAL BATTLE WHEN I'M FIGHTING AYAKASHI...
WHAK WHAK

SIGN: SUEHIRO SHRINE

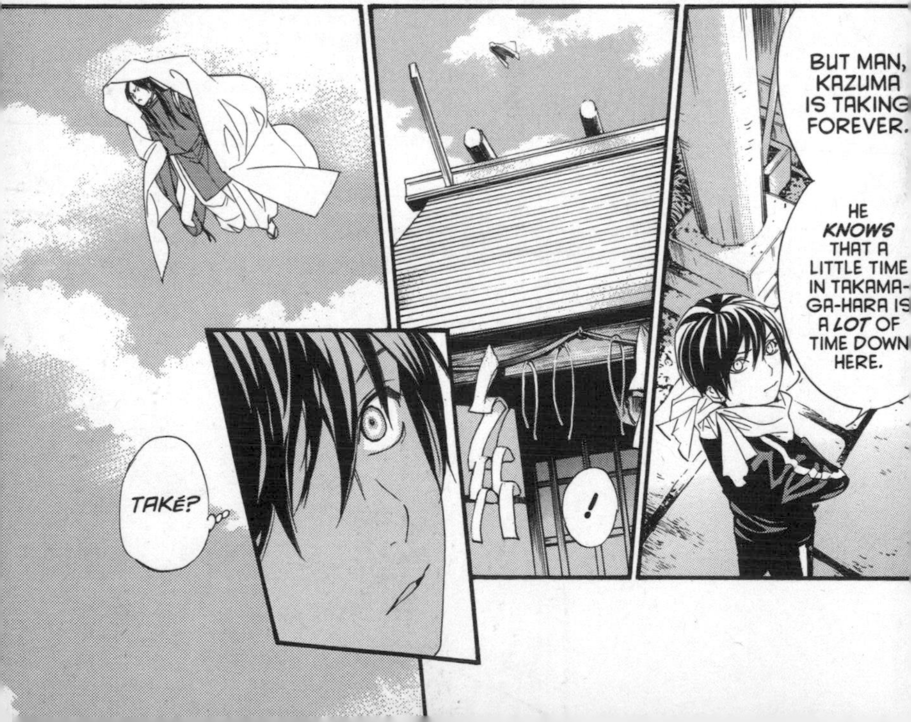
BUT MAN, KAZUMA IS TAKING FOREVER.
HE *KNOWS* THAT A LITTLE TIME IN TAKAMA-GA-HARA IS A *LOT* OF TIME DOWN HERE.
!
TAKÉ?

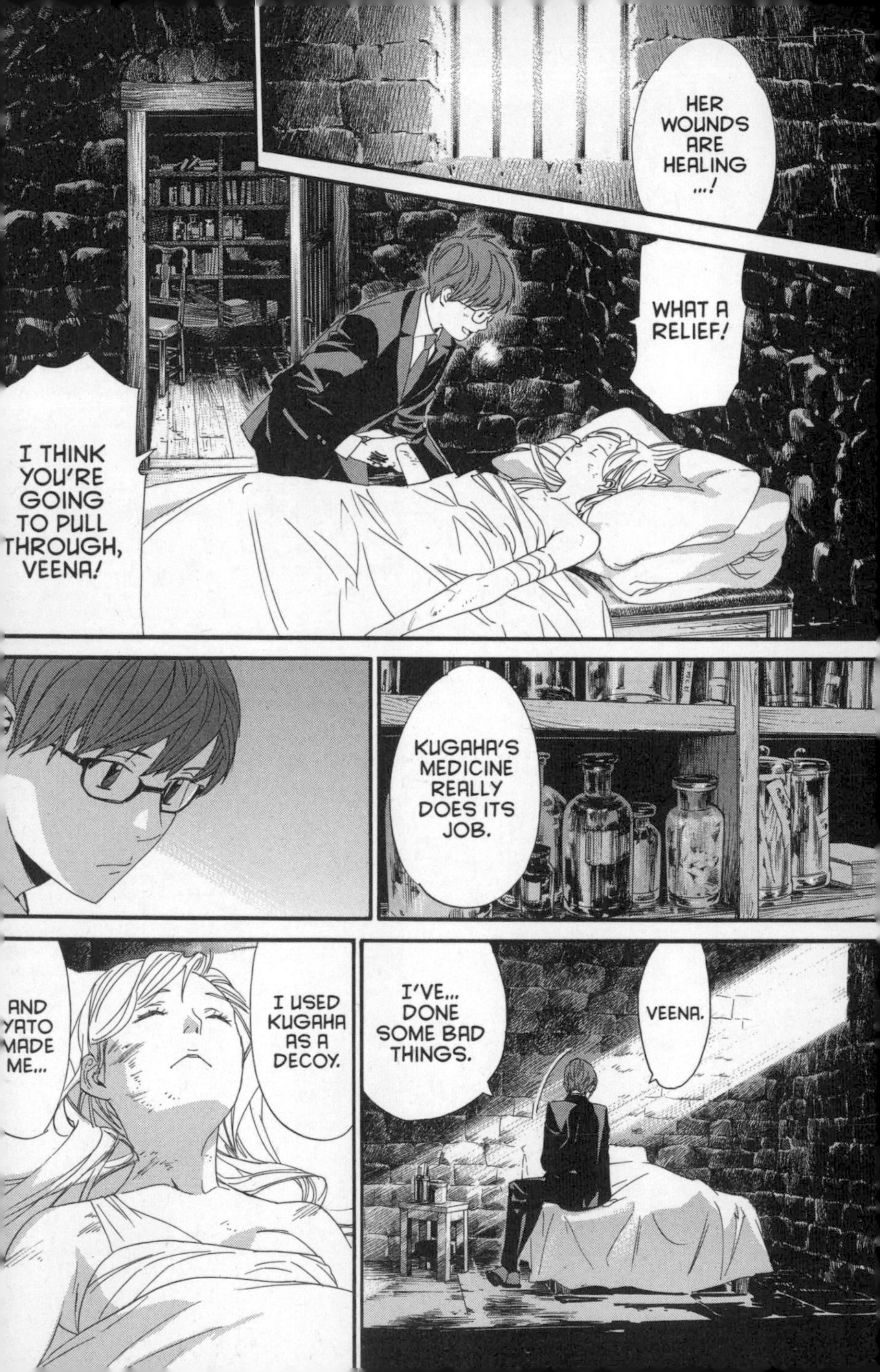
HER WOUNDS ARE HEALING ...!
WHAT A RELIEF!
I THINK YOU'RE GOING TO PULL THROUGH, VEENA!
KUGAHA'S MEDICINE REALLY DOES ITS JOB.
VEENA.
I'VE... DONE SOME BAD THINGS.
I USED KUGAHA AS A DECOY.
AND YATO MADE ME...

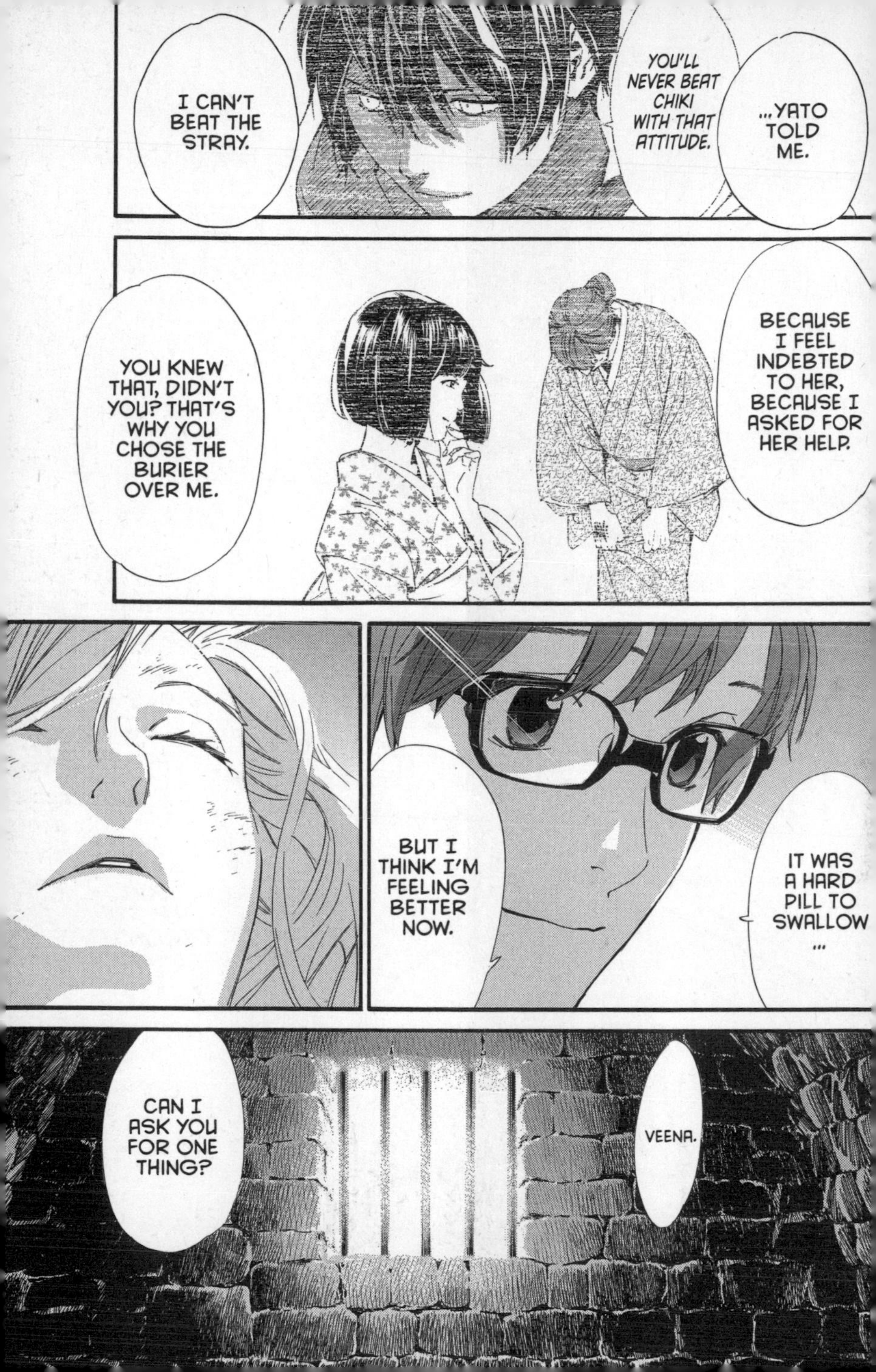
...YATO TOLD ME.
YOU'LL NEVER BEAT CHIKI WITH THAT ATTITUDE.
I CAN'T BEAT THE STRAY.
BECAUSE I FEEL INDEBTED TO HER, BECAUSE I ASKED FOR HER HELP.
YOU KNEW THAT, DIDN'T YOU? THAT'S WHY YOU CHOSE THE BURIER OVER ME.
IT WAS A HARD PILL TO SWALLOW ...
BUT I THINK I'M FEELING BETTER NOW.
VEENA.
CAN I ASK YOU FOR ONE THING?

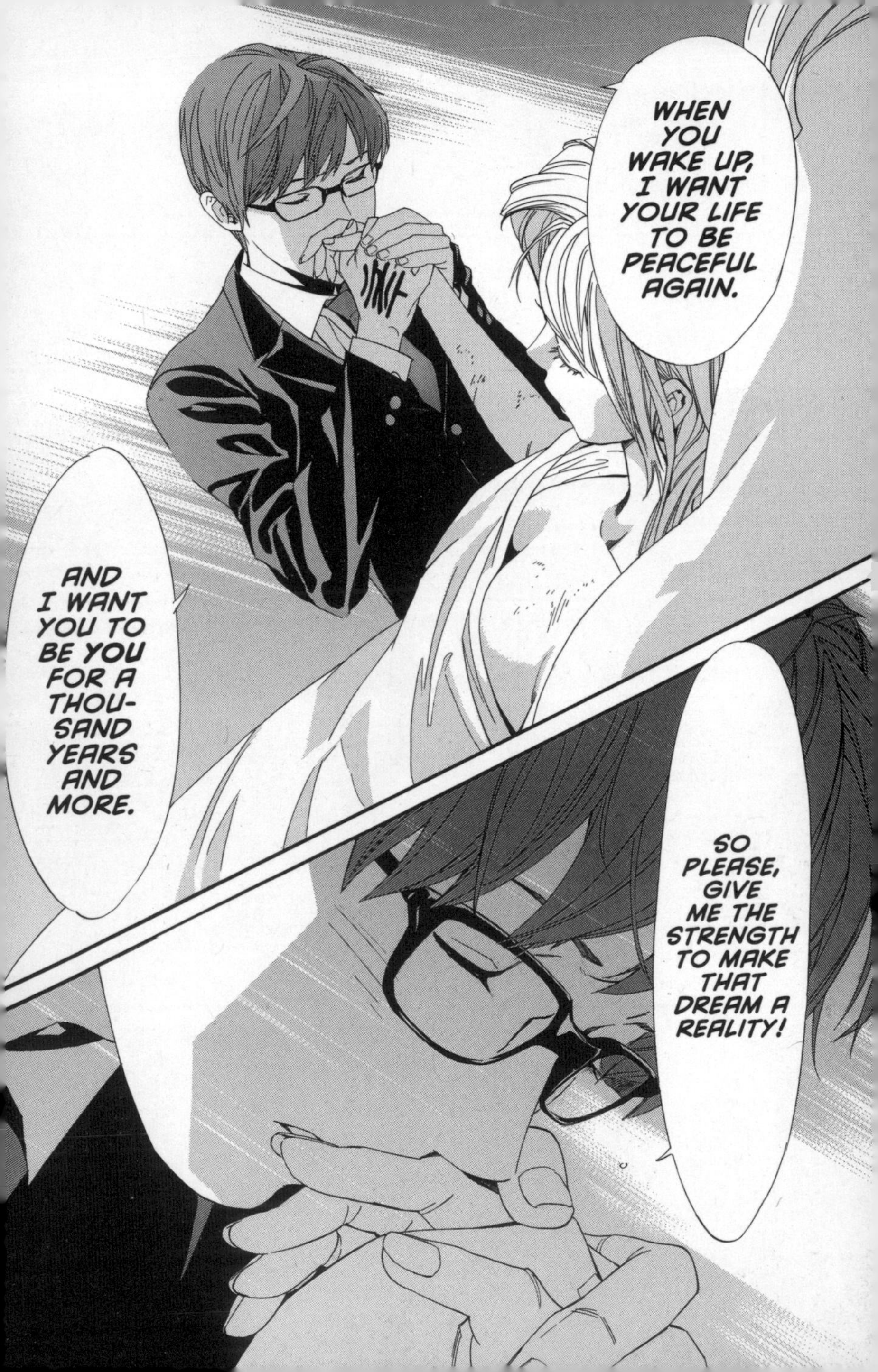
WHEN YOU WAKE UP, I WANT YOUR LIFE TO BE PEACEFUL AGAIN.
AND I WANT YOU TO BE YOU FOR A THOU-SAND YEARS AND MORE.
SO PLEASE, GIVE ME THE STRENGTH TO MAKE THAT DREAM A REALITY!

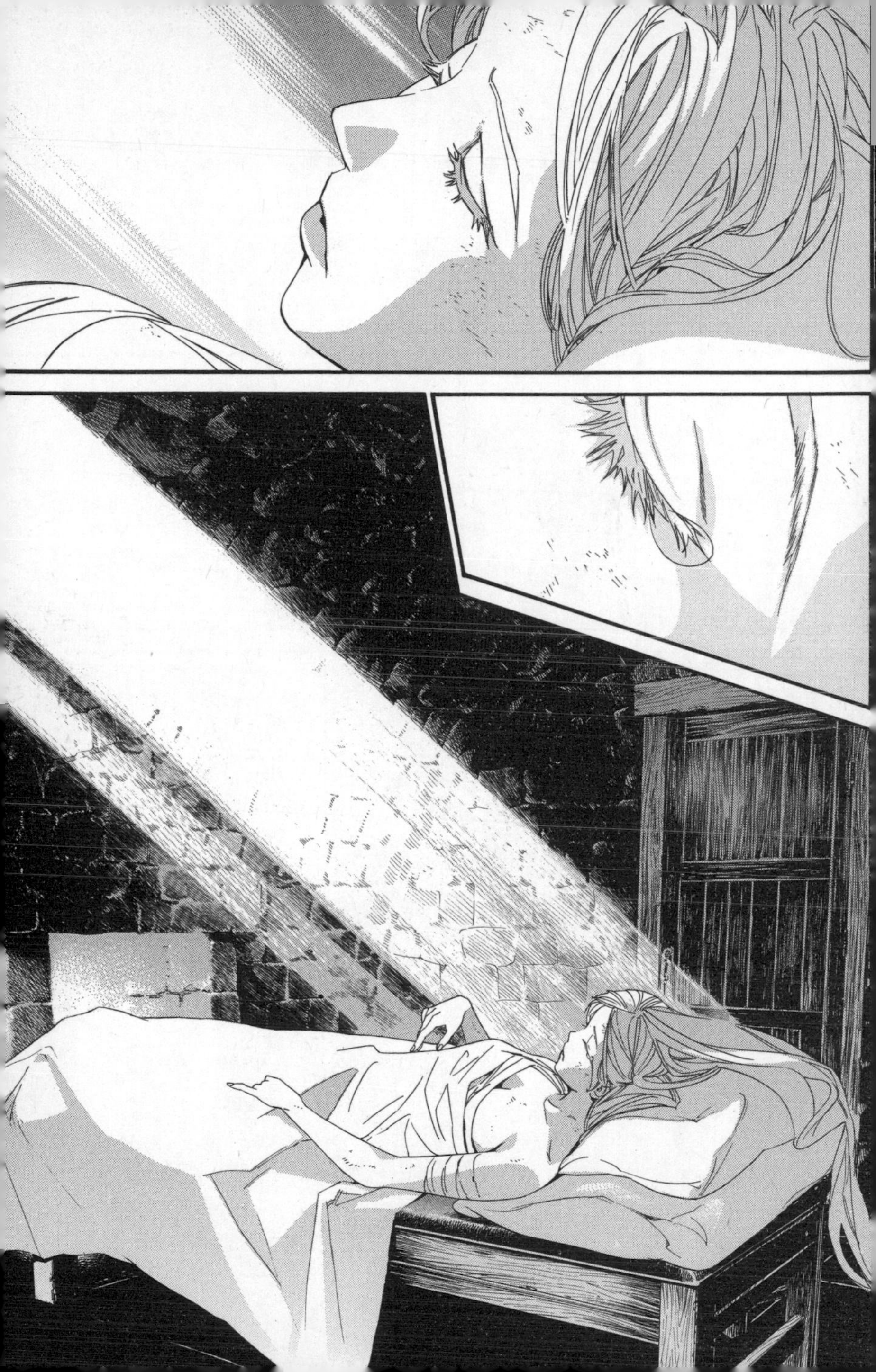

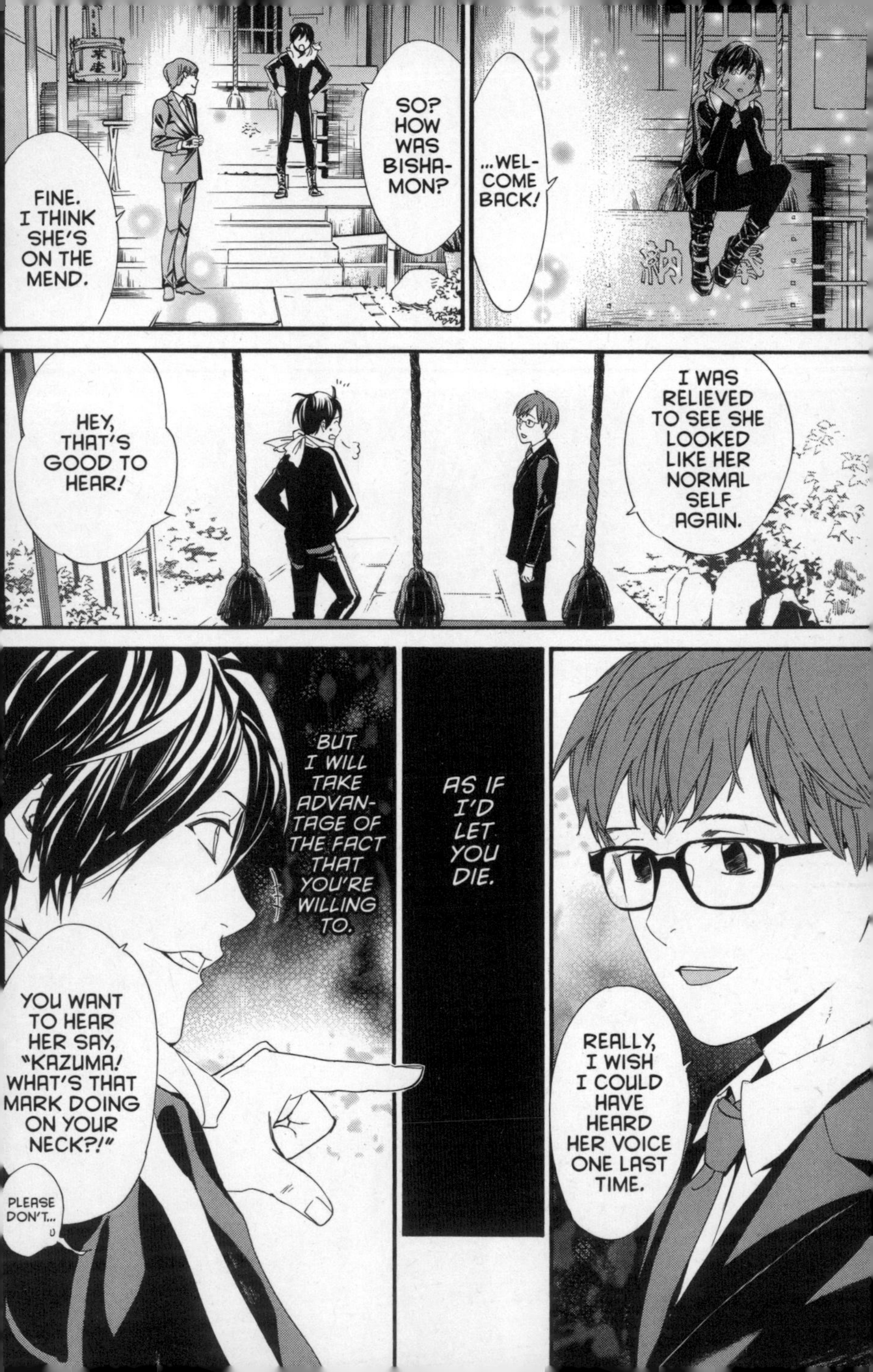
...WELCOME BACK!
SO? HOW WAS BISHAMON?
FINE. I THINK SHE'S ON THE MEND.
I WAS RELIEVED TO SEE SHE LOOKED LIKE HER NORMAL SELF AGAIN.
HEY, THAT'S GOOD TO HEAR!
REALLY, I WISH I COULD HAVE HEARD HER VOICE ONE LAST TIME.
AS IF I'D LET YOU DIE.
BUT I WILL TAKE ADVANTAGE OF THE FACT THAT YOU'RE WILLING TO.
YOU WANT TO HEAR HER SAY, "KAZUMA! WHAT'S THAT MARK DOING ON YOUR NECK?!"
PLEASE DON'T...

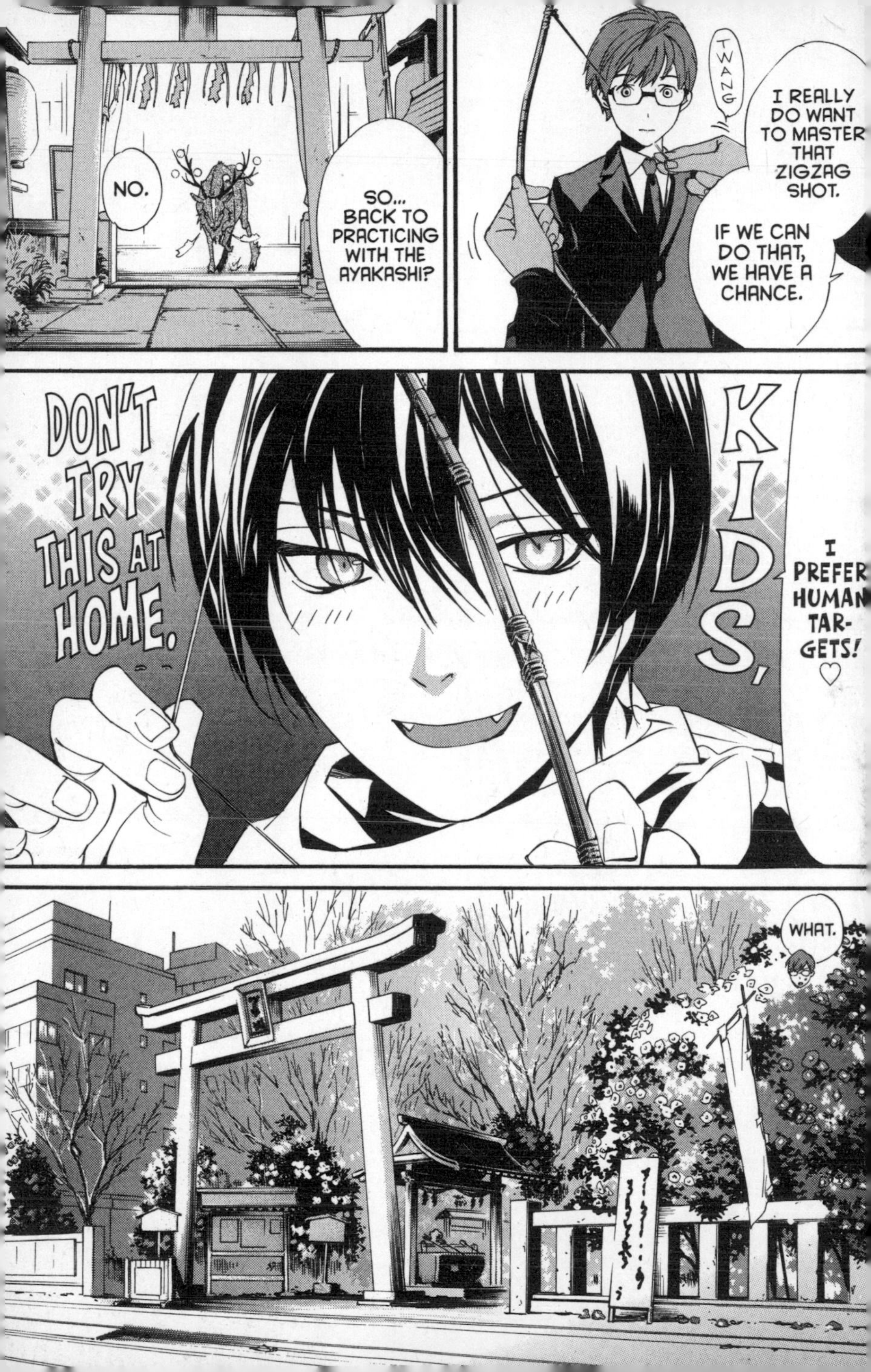
TWANG
I REALLY DO WANT TO MASTER THAT ZIGZAG SHOT.
IF WE CAN DO THAT, WE HAVE A CHANCE.
SO... BACK TO PRACTICING WITH THE AYAKASHI?
NO.
KIDS,
DON'T TRY THIS AT HOME.
I PREFER HUMAN TARGETS! ♡
WHAT.

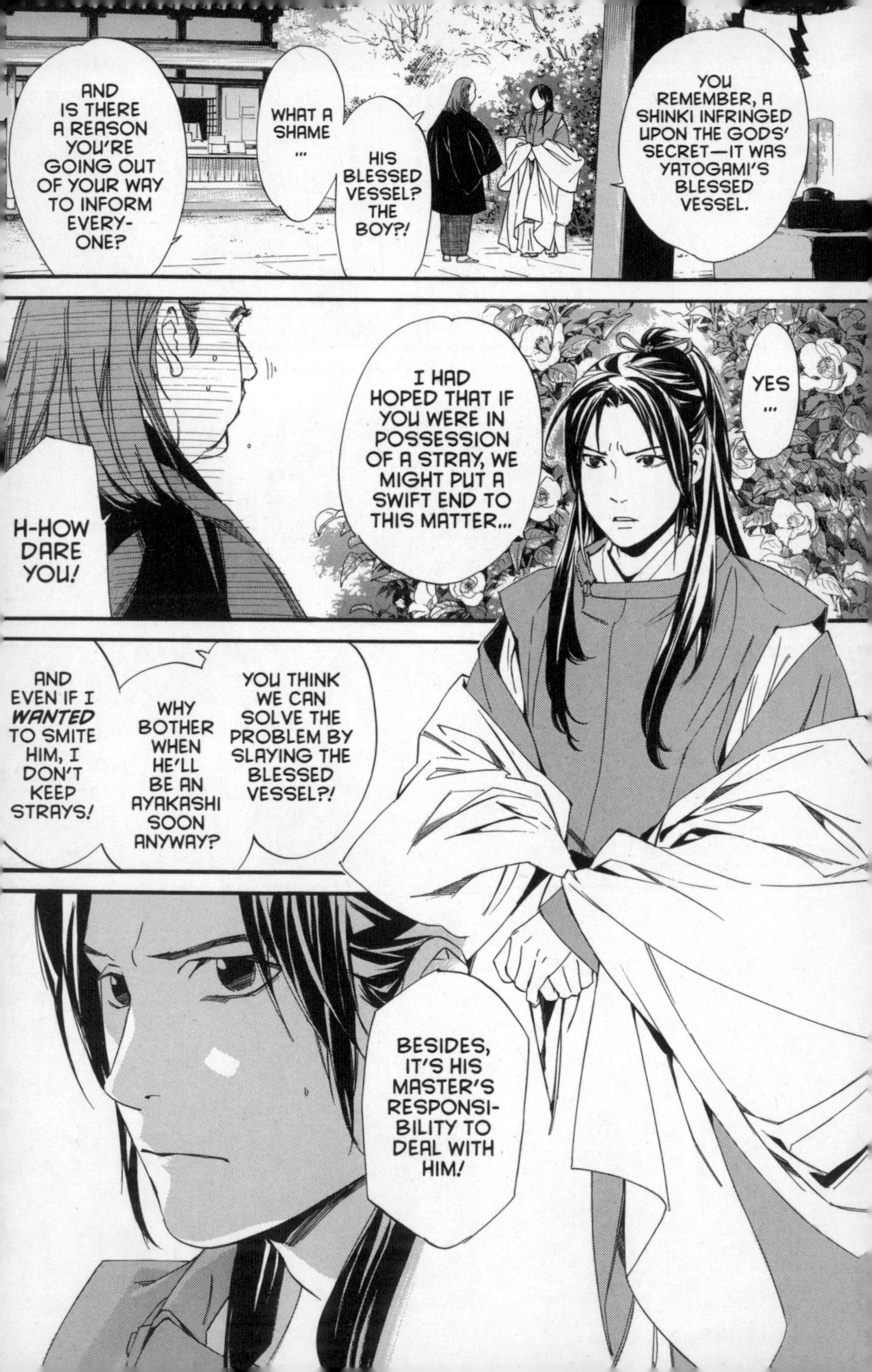
YOU REMEMBER, A SHINKI INFRINGED UPON THE GODS' SECRET—IT WAS YATOGAMI'S BLESSED VESSEL.
HIS BLESSED VESSEL? THE BOY?!
WHAT A SHAME ...
AND IS THERE A REASON YOU'RE GOING OUT OF YOUR WAY TO INFORM EVERY-ONE?
YES ...
I HAD HOPED THAT IF YOU WERE IN POSSESSION OF A STRAY, WE MIGHT PUT A SWIFT END TO THIS MATTER...
H-HOW DARE YOU!
YOU THINK WE CAN SOLVE THE PROBLEM BY SLAYING THE BLESSED VESSEL?!
WHY BOTHER WHEN HE'LL BE AN AYAKASHI SOON ANYWAY?
AND EVEN IF I *WANTED* TO SMITE HIM, I DON'T KEEP STRAYS!
BESIDES, IT'S HIS MASTER'S RESPONSI-BILITY TO DEAL WITH HIM!

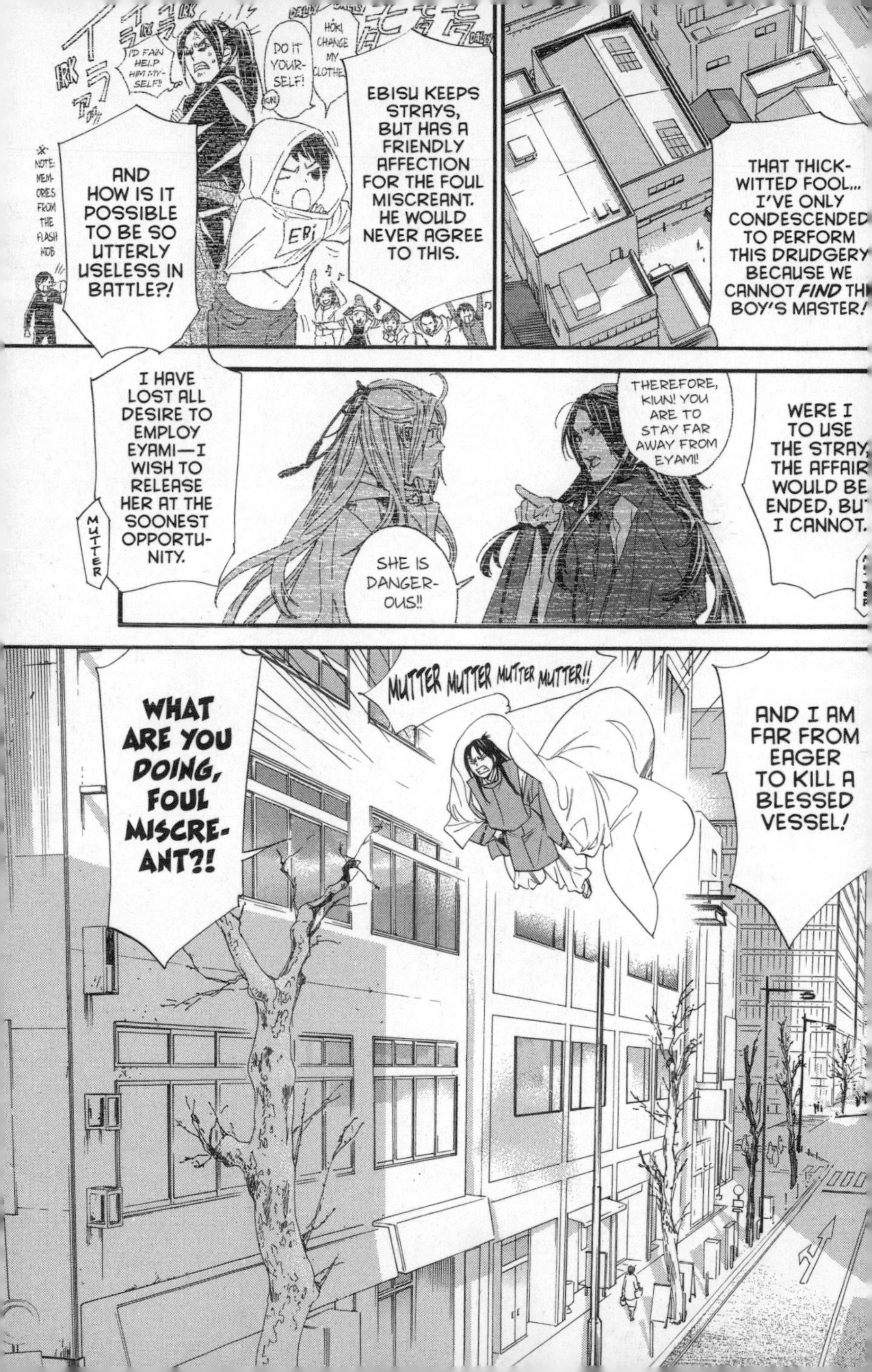
THAT THICK-WITTED FOOL... I'VE ONLY CONDESCENDED TO PERFORM THIS DRUDGERY BECAUSE WE CANNOT *FIND* TH BOY'S MASTER!
EBISU KEEPS STRAYS, BUT HAS A FRIENDLY AFFECTION FOR THE FOUL MISCREANT. HE WOULD NEVER AGREE TO THIS.
DALLY
HŌKI, CHANGE MY CLOTHE
DO IT YOURSELF!
I'D FAIN HELP HIM MYSELF!!
IRK
AND HOW IS IT POSSIBLE TO BE SO UTTERLY USELESS IN BATTLE?!
※NOTE: MEMORIES FROM THE FLASH MOB
EBi
WERE I TO USE THE STRAY, THE AFFAIR WOULD BE ENDED, BUT I CANNOT.
THEREFORE, KIUN! YOU ARE TO STAY FAR AWAY FROM EYAMI!
SHE IS DANGEROUS!!
I HAVE LOST ALL DESIRE TO EMPLOY EYAMI—I WISH TO RELEASE HER AT THE SOONEST OPPORTUNITY.
MUTTER
AND I AM FAR FROM EAGER TO KILL A BLESSED VESSEL!
MUTTER MUTTER MUTTER MUTTER!!
WHAT ARE YOU DOING, FOUL MISCREANT?!

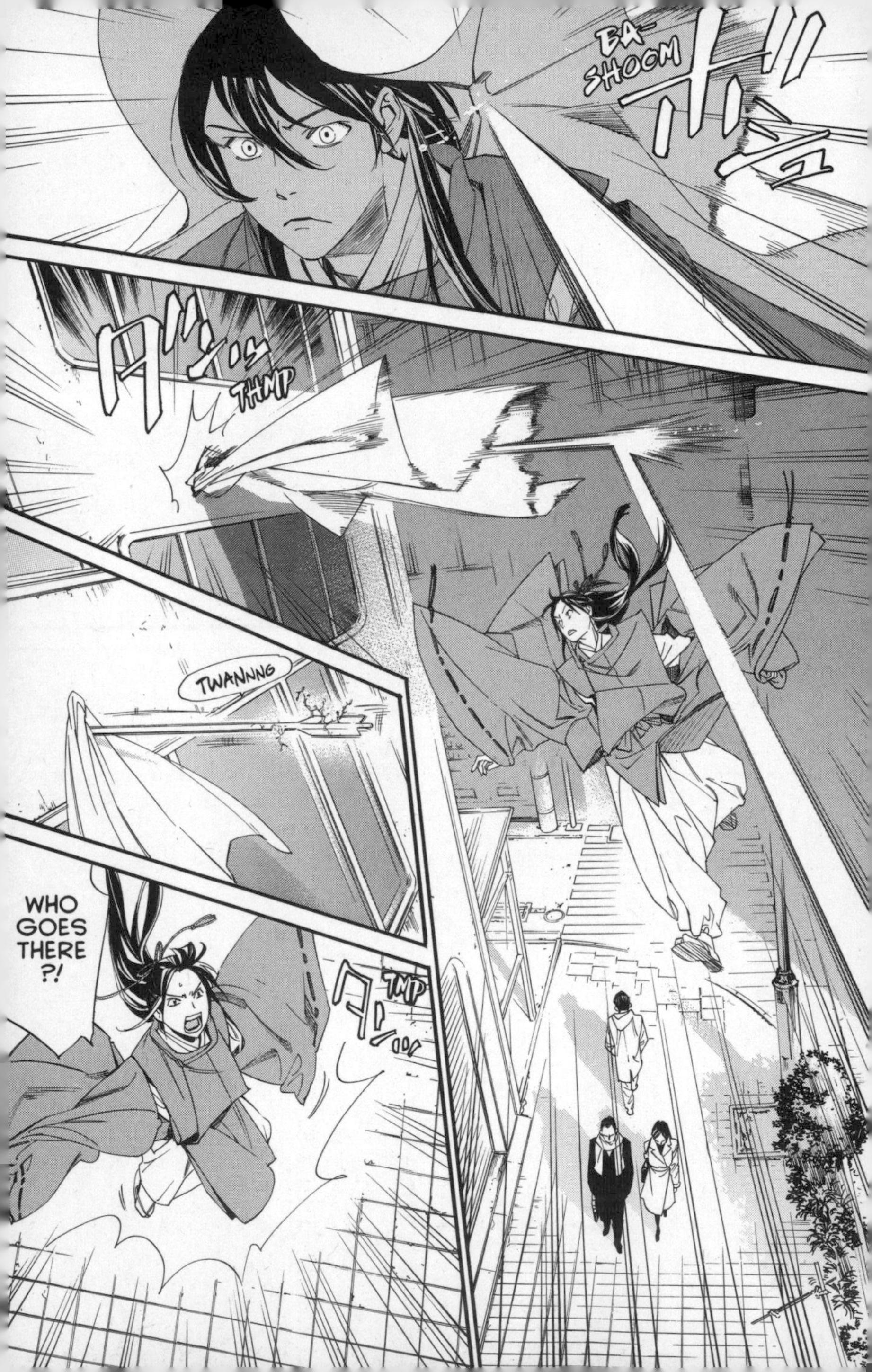
BA-SHOOM
THMP
TWANNNG
TMP
WHO GOES THERE ?!

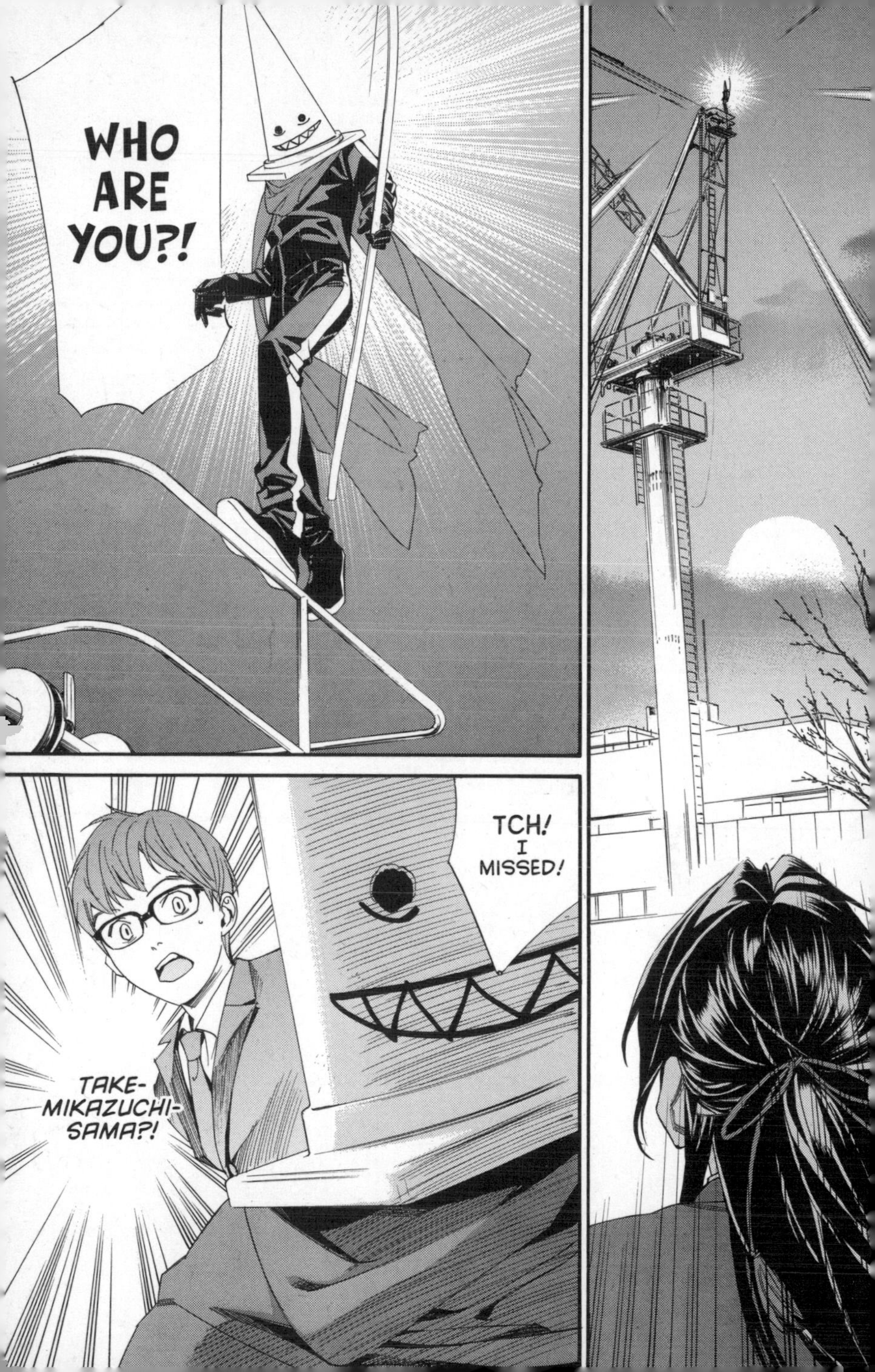
WHO ARE YOU?!
TCH! I MISSED!
TAKE-MIKAZUCHI-SAMA?!

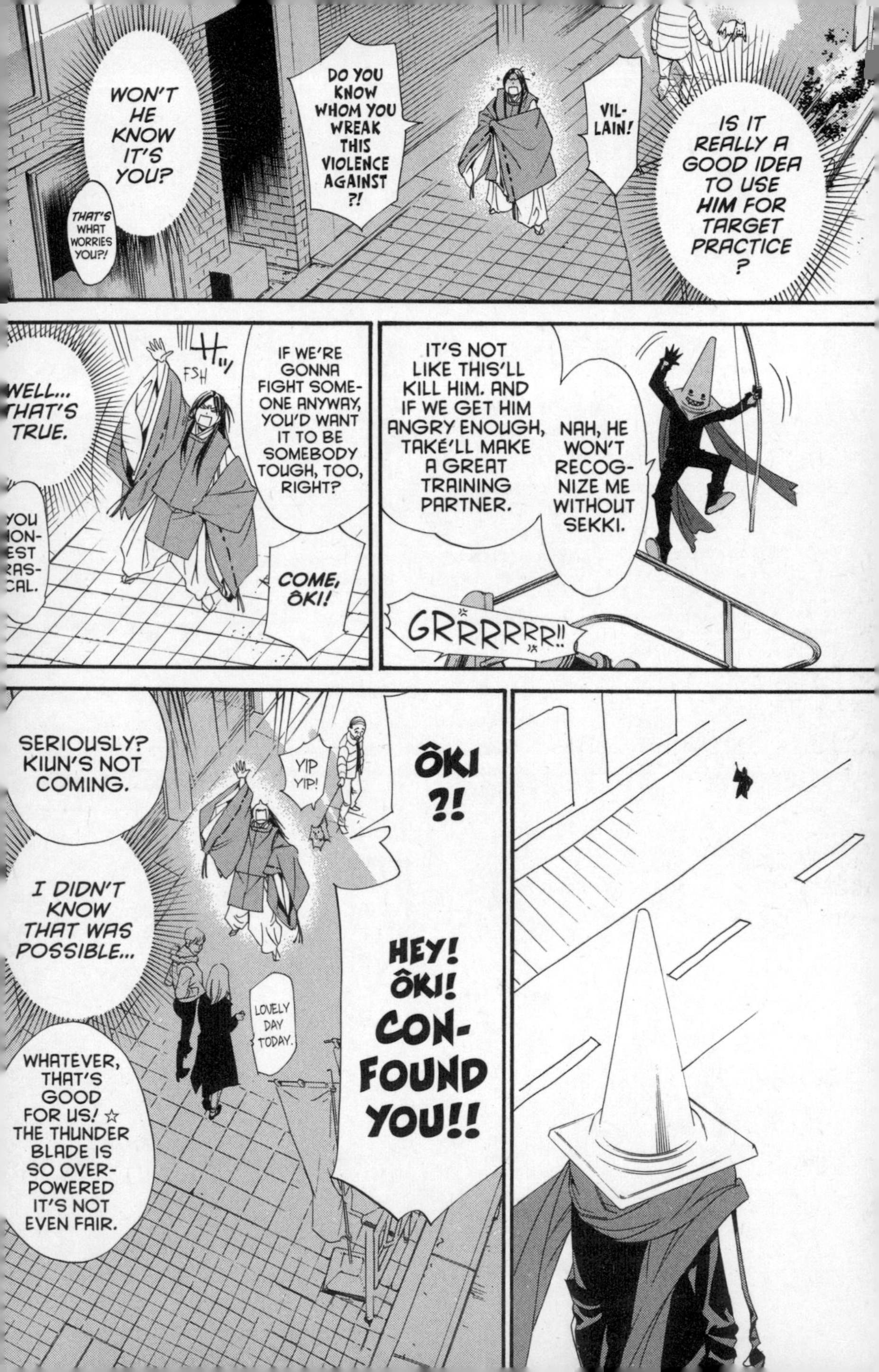
IS IT REALLY A GOOD IDEA TO USE HIM FOR TARGET PRACTICE?
VIL-LAIN!
DO YOU KNOW WHOM YOU WREAK THIS VIOLENCE AGAINST?!
WON'T HE KNOW IT'S YOU?
THAT'S WHAT WORRIES YOU?!
NAH, HE WON'T RECOG-NIZE ME WITHOUT SEKKI.
IT'S NOT LIKE THIS'LL KILL HIM. AND IF WE GET HIM ANGRY ENOUGH, TAKÉ'LL MAKE A GREAT TRAINING PARTNER.
GRRRRRR!!
IF WE'RE GONNA FIGHT SOME-ONE ANYWAY, YOU'D WANT IT TO BE SOMEBODY TOUGH, TOO, RIGHT?
FSH
WELL... THAT'S TRUE.
COME, ÔKI!
YOU ON-EST AS-CAL.
ÔKI?!
YIP YIP!
HEY! ÔKI! CON-FOUND YOU!!
SERIOUSLY? KIUN'S NOT COMING.
I DIDN'T KNOW THAT WAS POSSIBLE...
LOVELY DAY TODAY.
WHATEVER, THAT'S GOOD FOR US! ☆ THE THUNDER BLADE IS SO OVER-POWERED IT'S NOT EVEN FAIR.

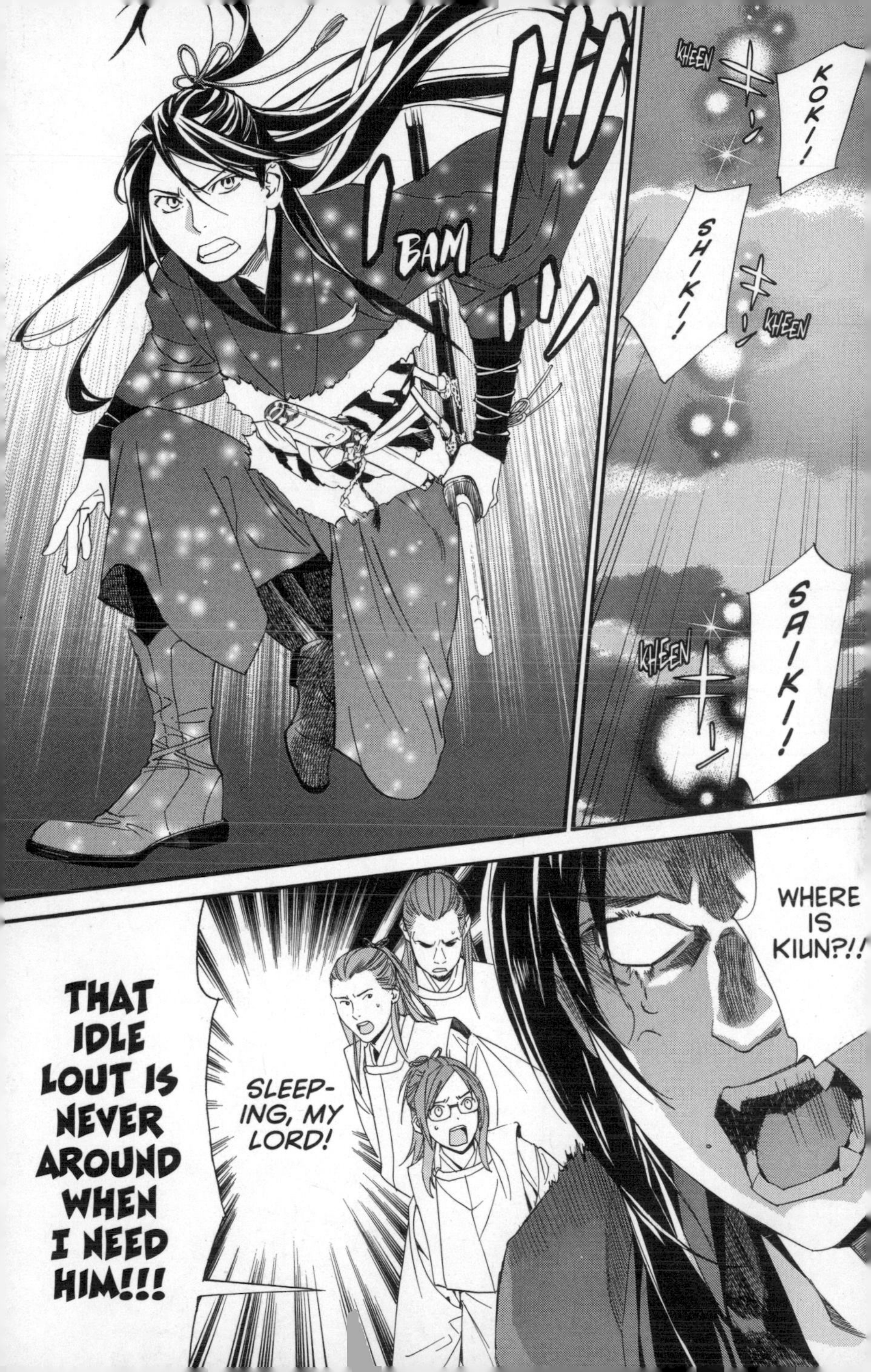
KHEEN
KOKI!!
SHIKI!!
KHEEN
SAIKI!!
KHEEN
BAM
WHERE IS KIUN?!!
SLEEP-ING, MY LORD!
THAT IDLE LOUT IS NEVER AROUND WHEN I NEED HIM!!!

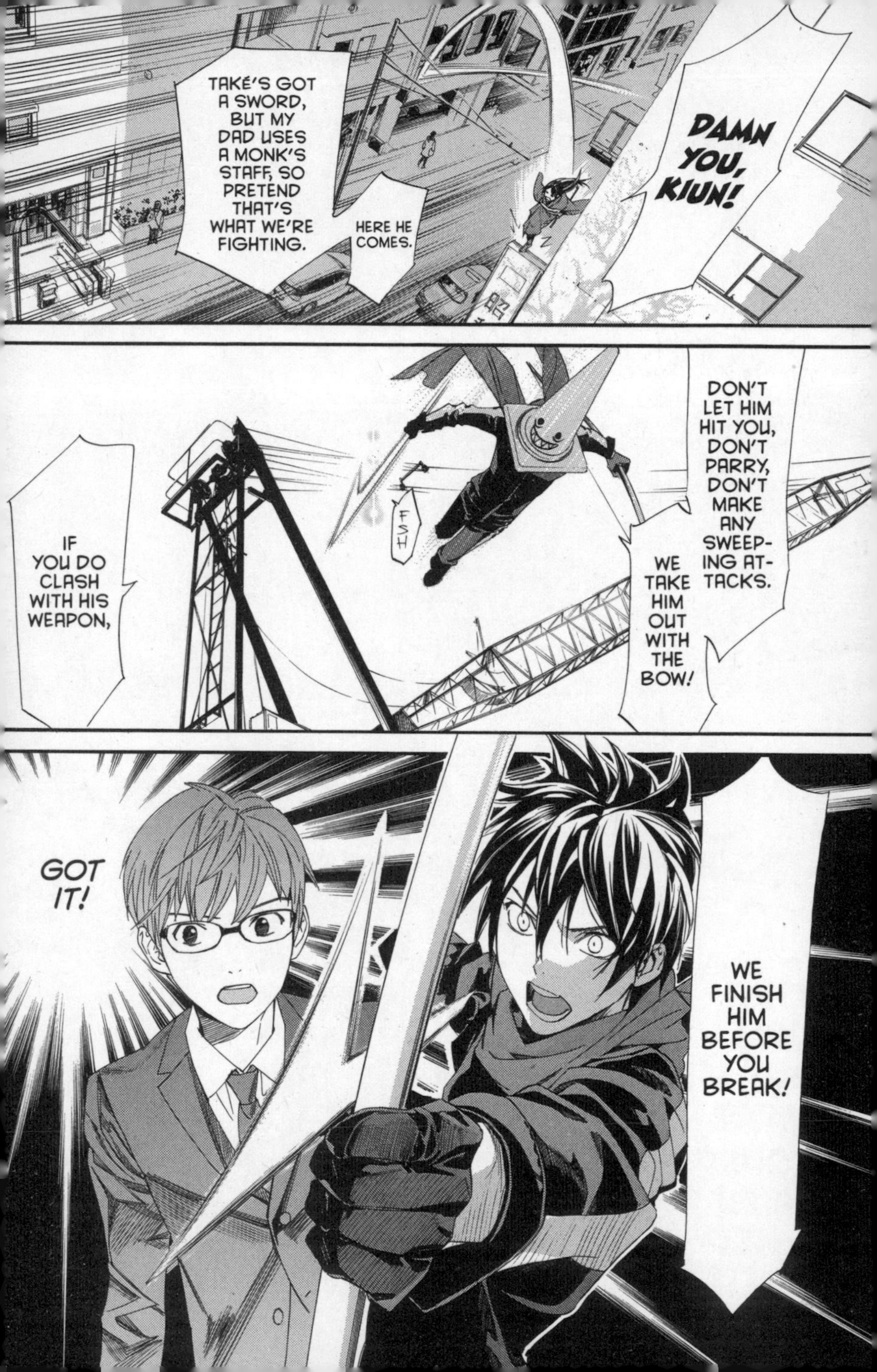
DAMN YOU, KIUN!
TAKÉ'S GOT A SWORD, BUT MY DAD USES A MONK'S STAFF, SO PRETEND THAT'S WHAT WE'RE FIGHTING.
HERE HE COMES.
DON'T LET HIM HIT YOU, DON'T PARRY, DON'T MAKE ANY SWEEP-ING AT-TACKS.
WE TAKE HIM OUT WITH THE BOW!
FSH
IF YOU DO CLASH WITH HIS WEAPON,
WE FINISH HIM BEFORE YOU BREAK!
GOT IT!

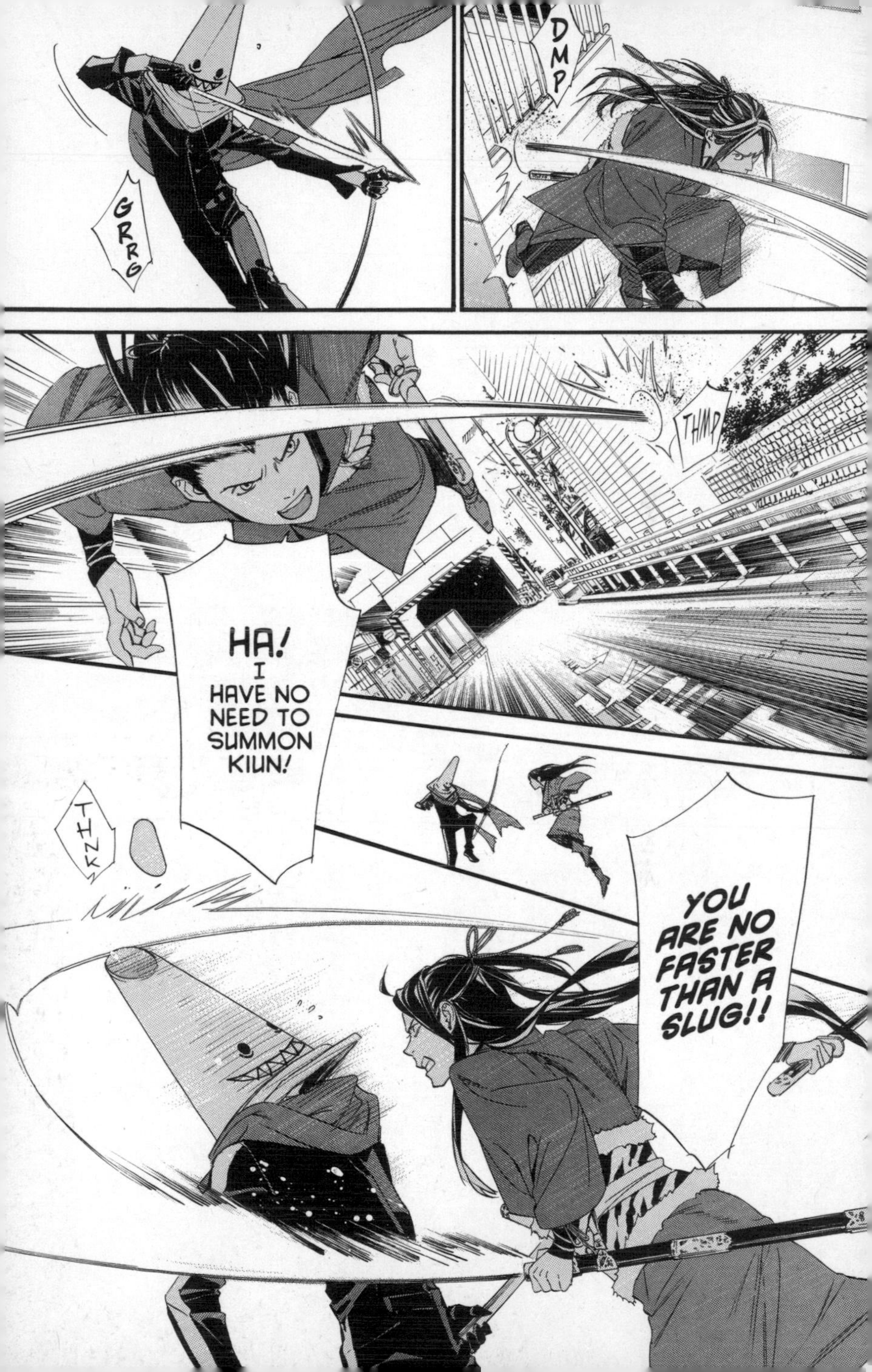
DMP
GRRG
THMP
HA! I HAVE NO NEED TO SUMMON KIUN!
YOU ARE NO FASTER THAN A SLUG!!
THNK

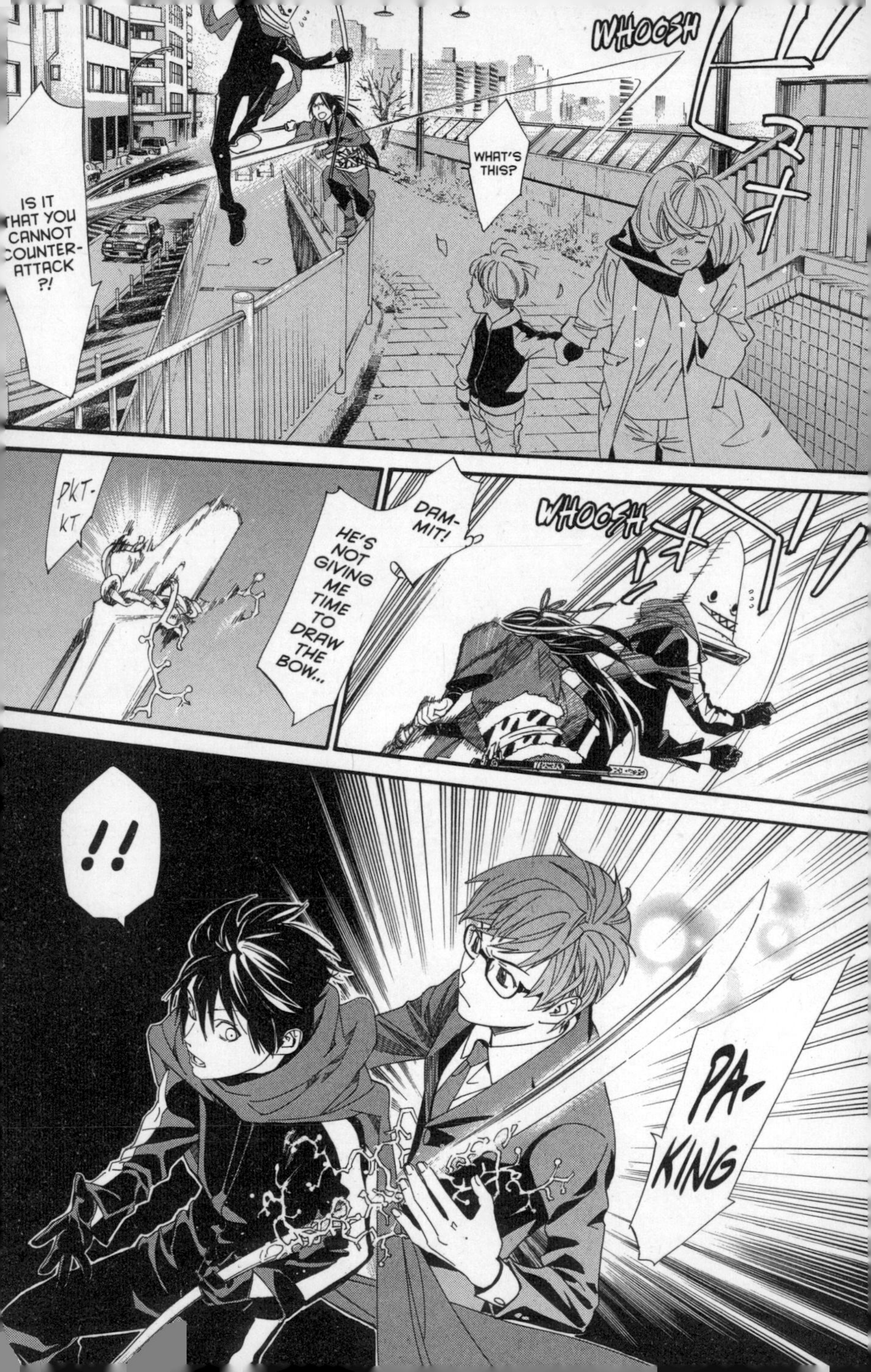
WHOOSH
WHAT'S THIS?
IS IT THAT YOU CANNOT COUNTER-ATTACK?!
WHOOSH
DAM-MIT!
HE'S NOT GIVING ME TIME TO DRAW THE BOW...
PKT-KT
PA-KING
!!

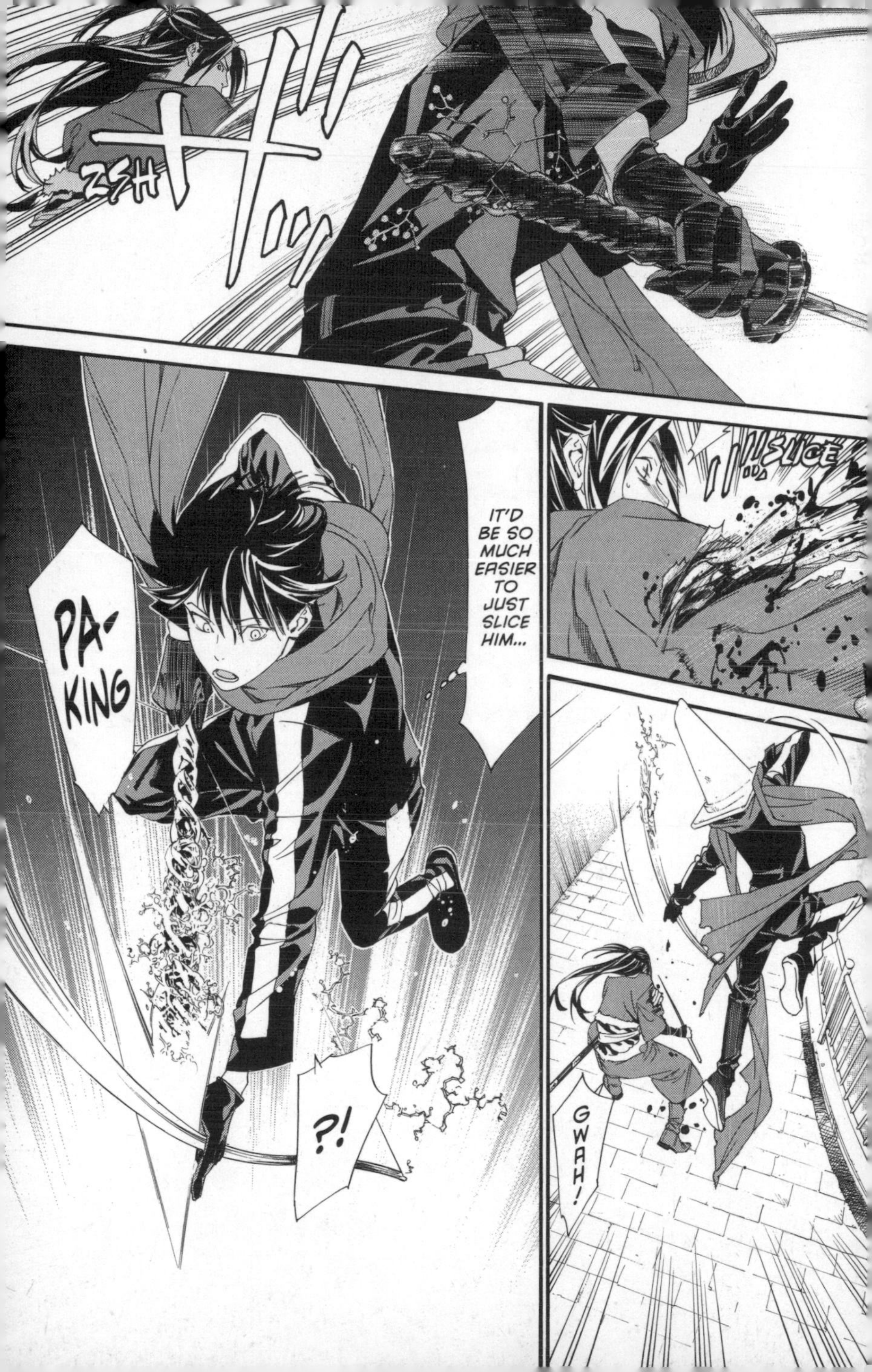
ZSH
SLICE
GWAH!
IT'D BE SO MUCH EASIER TO JUST SLICE HIM...
PA-KING
?!

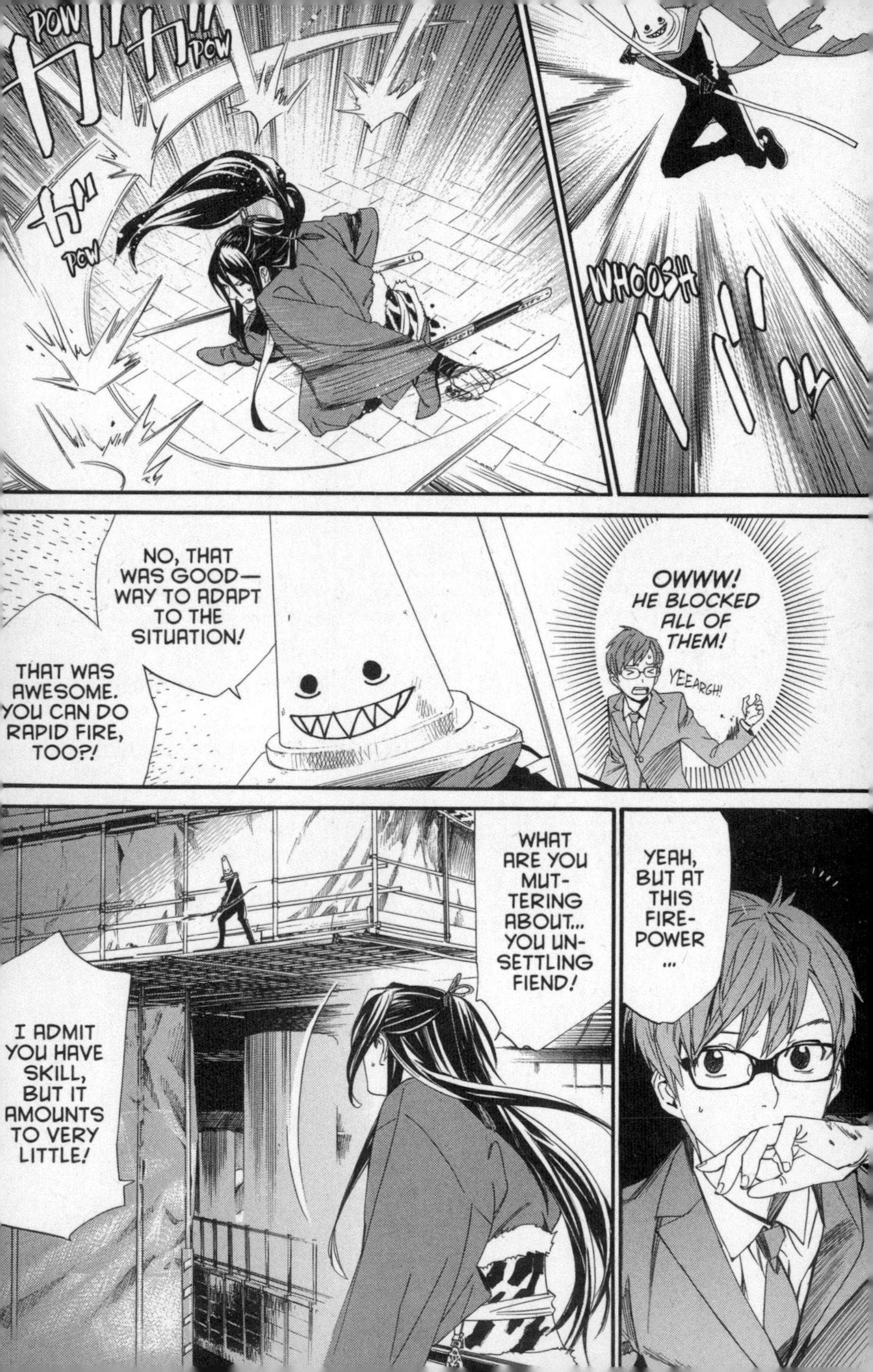
WHOOSH
POW
POW
POW
OWWW! HE BLOCKED ALL OF THEM!
YEEARGH!
NO, THAT WAS GOOD— WAY TO ADAPT TO THE SITUATION!
THAT WAS AWESOME. YOU CAN DO RAPID FIRE, TOO?!
YEAH, BUT AT THIS FIRE-POWER...
WHAT ARE YOU MUT-TERING ABOUT... YOU UN-SETTLING FIEND!
I ADMIT YOU HAVE SKILL, BUT IT AMOUNTS TO VERY LITTLE!

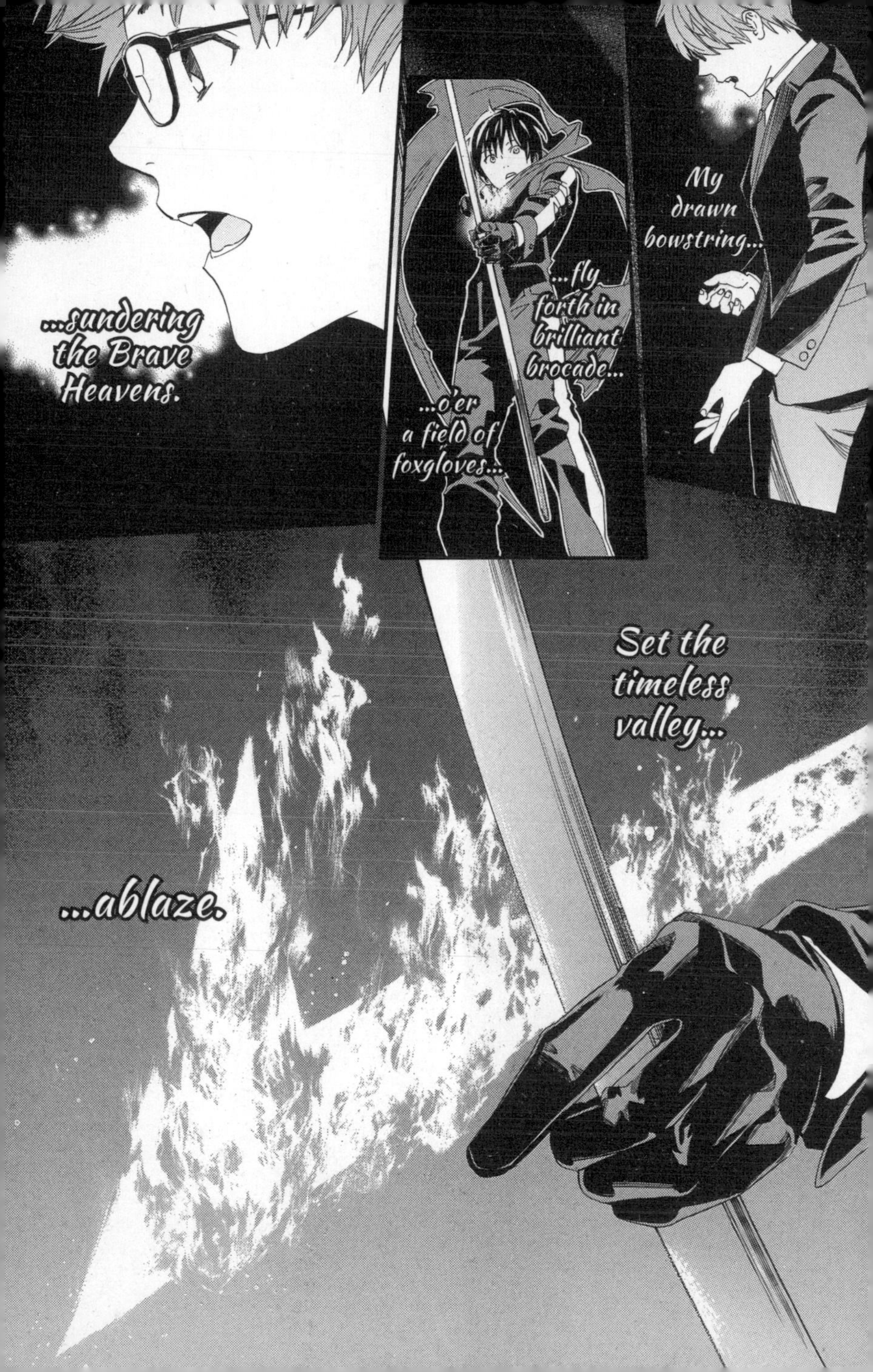
My drawn bowstring...
...fly forth in brilliant brocade...
...o'er a field of foxgloves...
...sundering the Brave Heavens.
Set the timeless valley...
...ablaze.

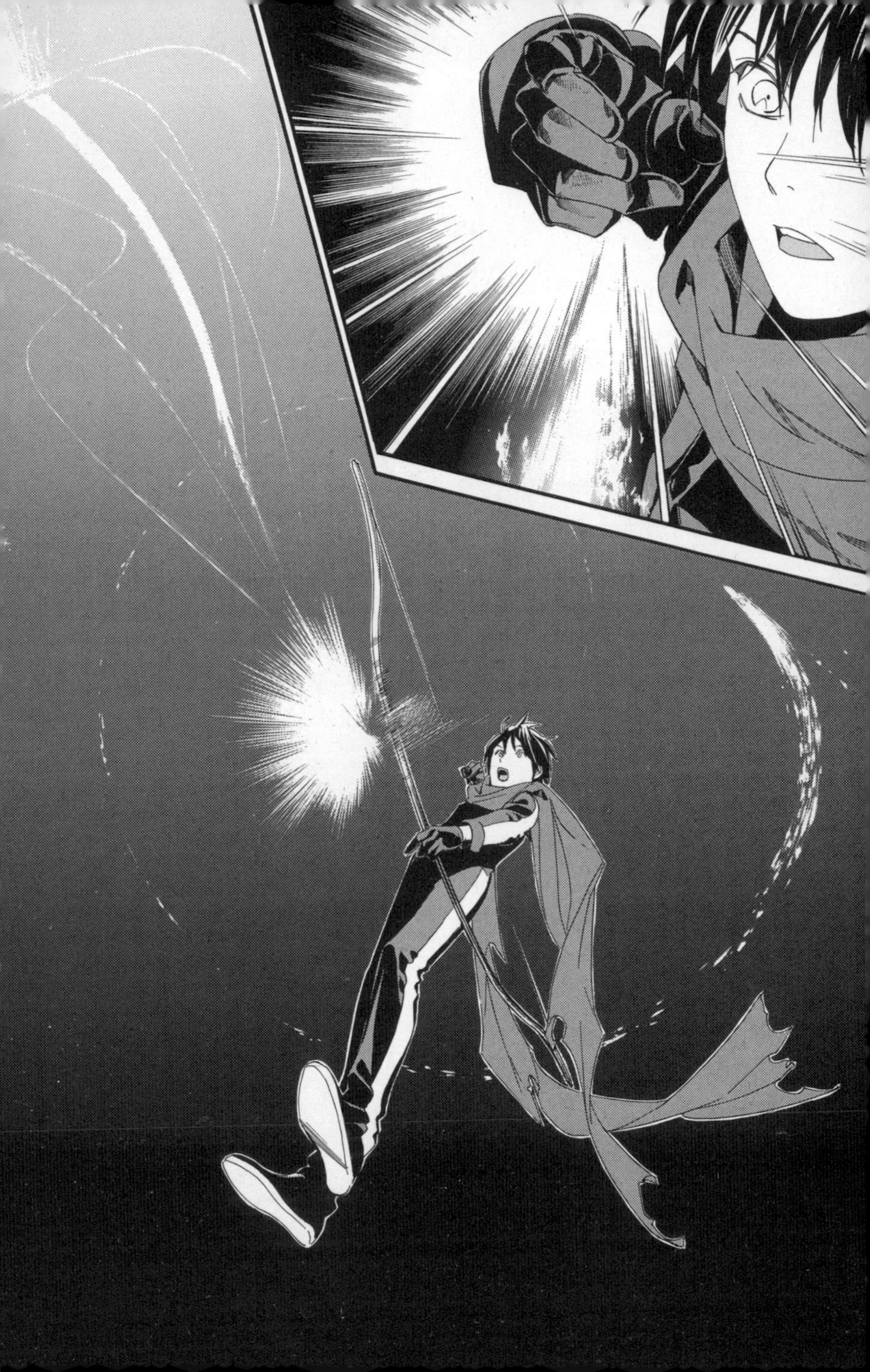

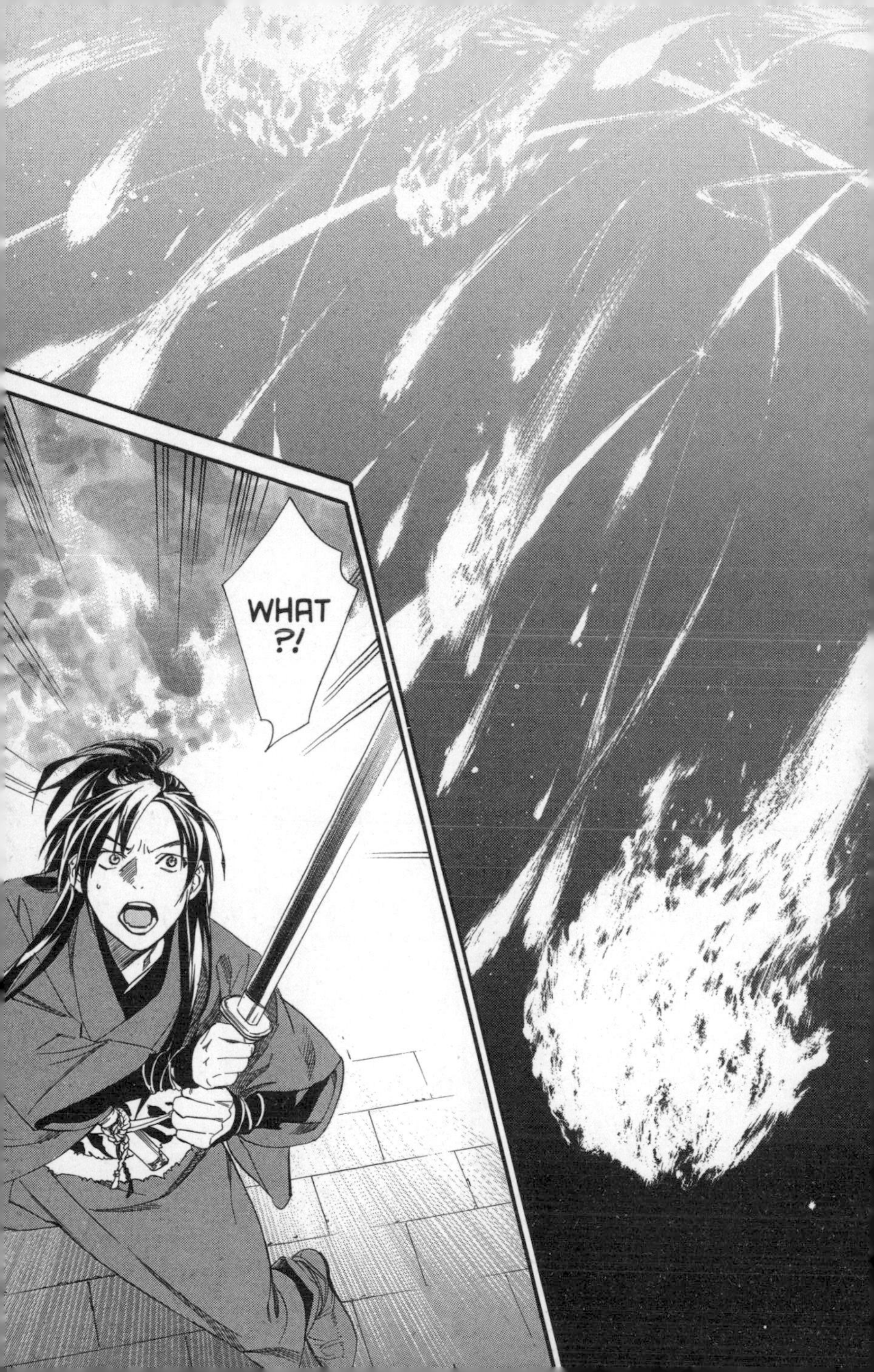
WHAT ?!

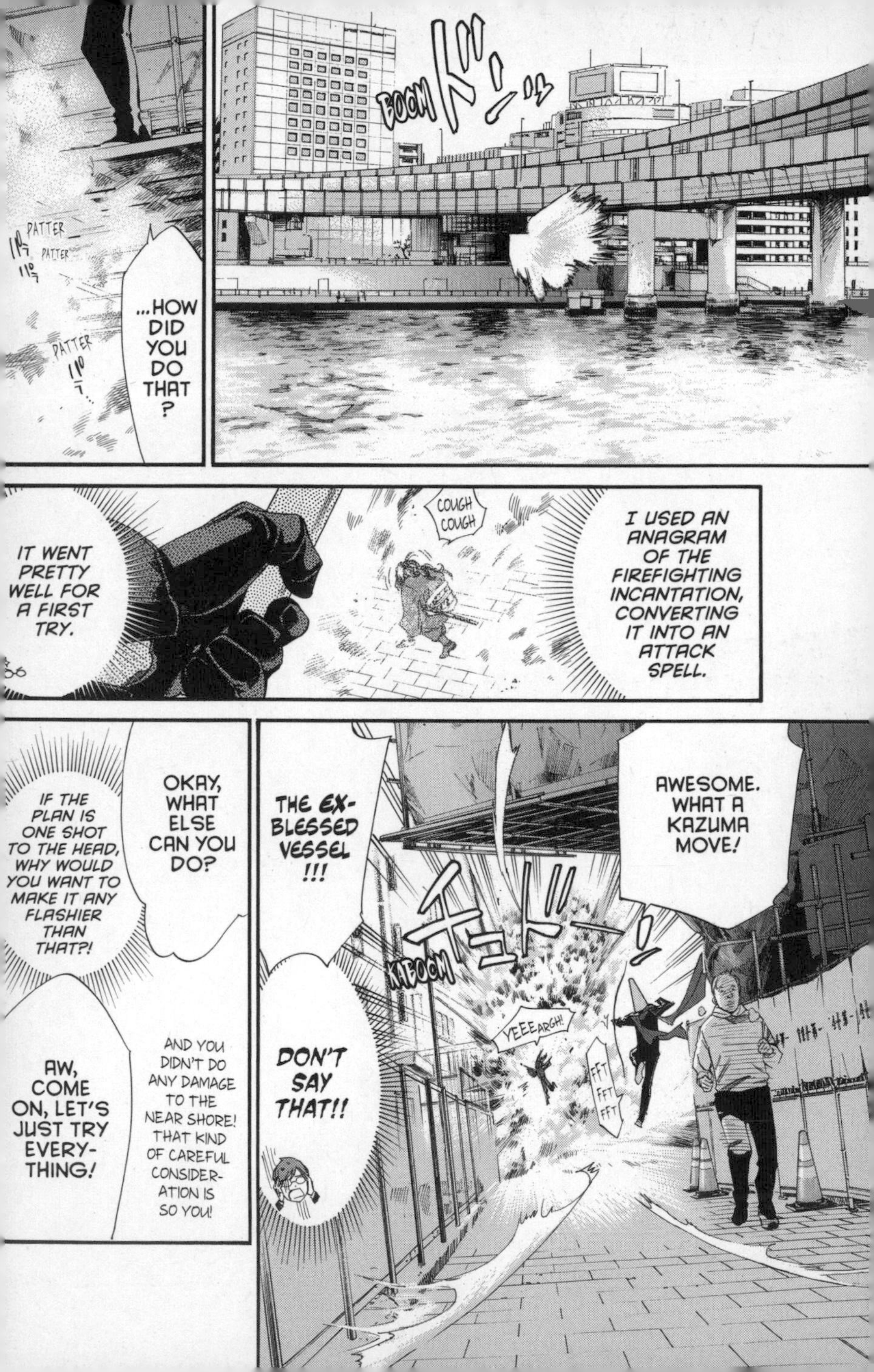
BOOM
PATTER
PATTER
PATTER
...HOW DID YOU DO THAT?
I USED AN ANAGRAM OF THE FIREFIGHTING INCANTATION, CONVERTING IT INTO AN ATTACK SPELL.
COUGH COUGH
IT WENT PRETTY WELL FOR A FIRST TRY.
AWESOME. WHAT A KAZUMA MOVE!
THE EX-BLESSED VESSEL!!!
KABOOM
YEEEARGH!
FFT FFT FFT
DON'T SAY THAT!!
OKAY, WHAT ELSE CAN YOU DO?
IF THE PLAN IS ONE SHOT TO THE HEAD, WHY WOULD YOU WANT TO MAKE IT ANY FLASHIER THAN THAT?!
AND YOU DIDN'T DO ANY DAMAGE TO THE NEAR SHORE! THAT KIND OF CAREFUL CONSIDERATION IS SO YOU!
AW, COME ON, LET'S JUST TRY EVERYTHING!

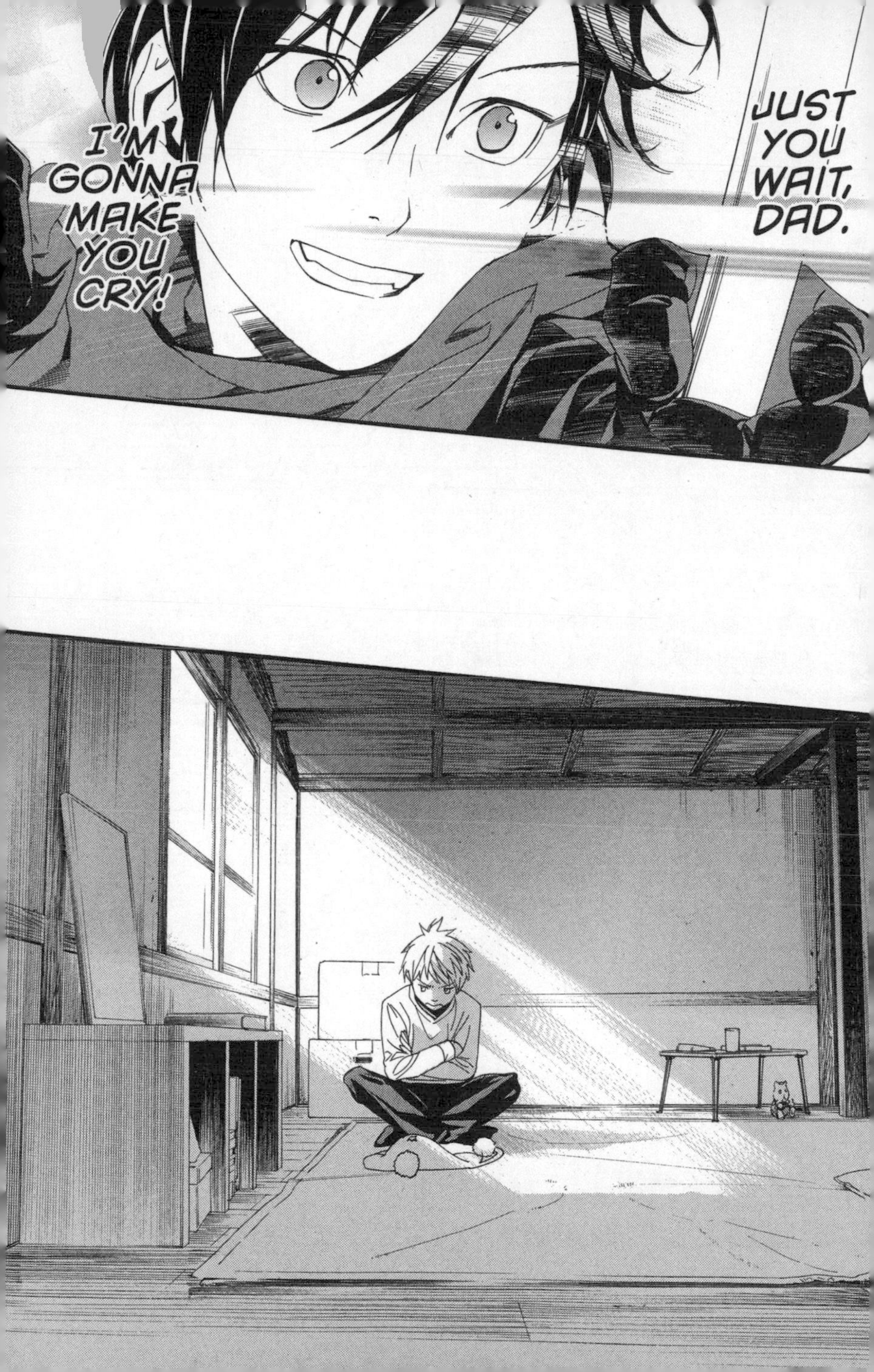
JUST YOU WAIT, DAD.
I'M GONNA MAKE YOU CRY!

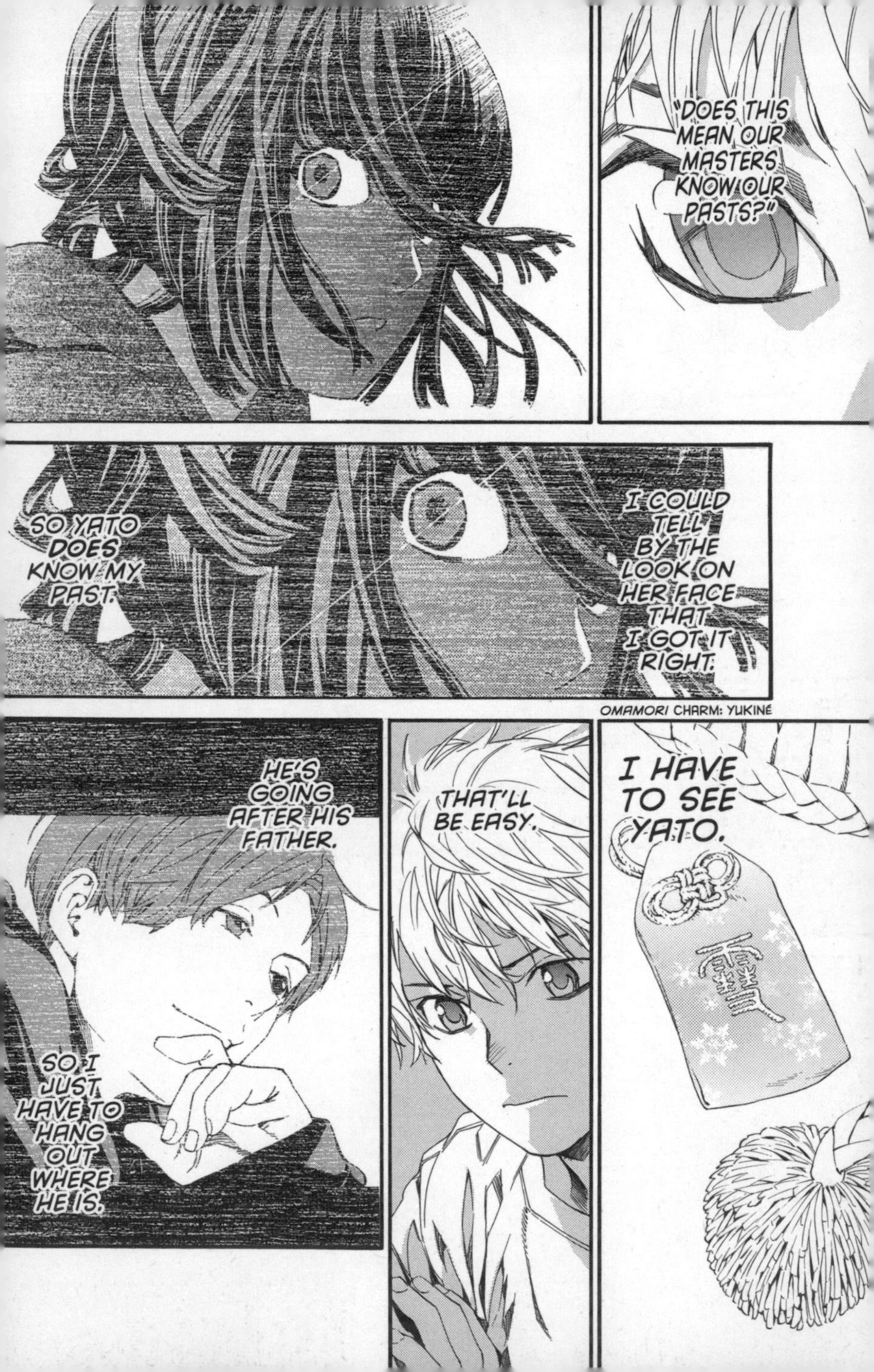
"DOES THIS MEAN OUR MASTERS KNOW OUR PASTS?"
I COULD TELL BY THE LOOK ON HER FACE THAT I GOT IT RIGHT.
SO YATO DOES KNOW MY PAST.
OMAMORI CHARM: YUKINÉ
I HAVE TO SEE YATO.
THAT'LL BE EASY.
HE'S GOING AFTER HIS FATHER.
SO I JUST HAVE TO HANG OUT WHERE HE IS.

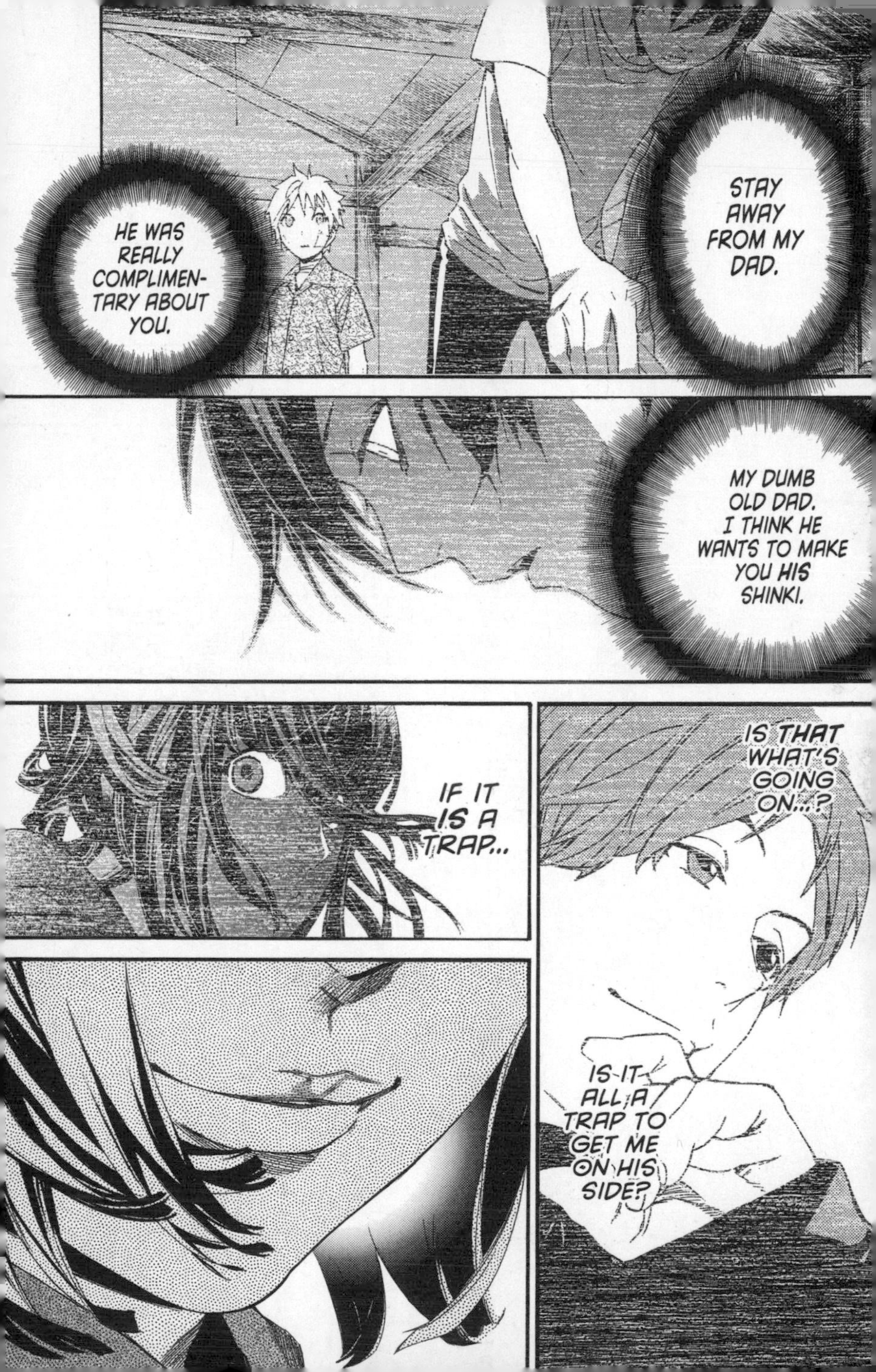
STAY AWAY FROM MY DAD.
HE WAS REALLY COMPLIMENTARY ABOUT YOU.
MY DUMB OLD DAD. I THINK HE WANTS TO MAKE YOU HIS SHINKI.
IS THAT WHAT'S GOING ON...?
IS IT ALL A TRAP TO GET ME ON HIS SIDE?
IF IT IS A TRAP...

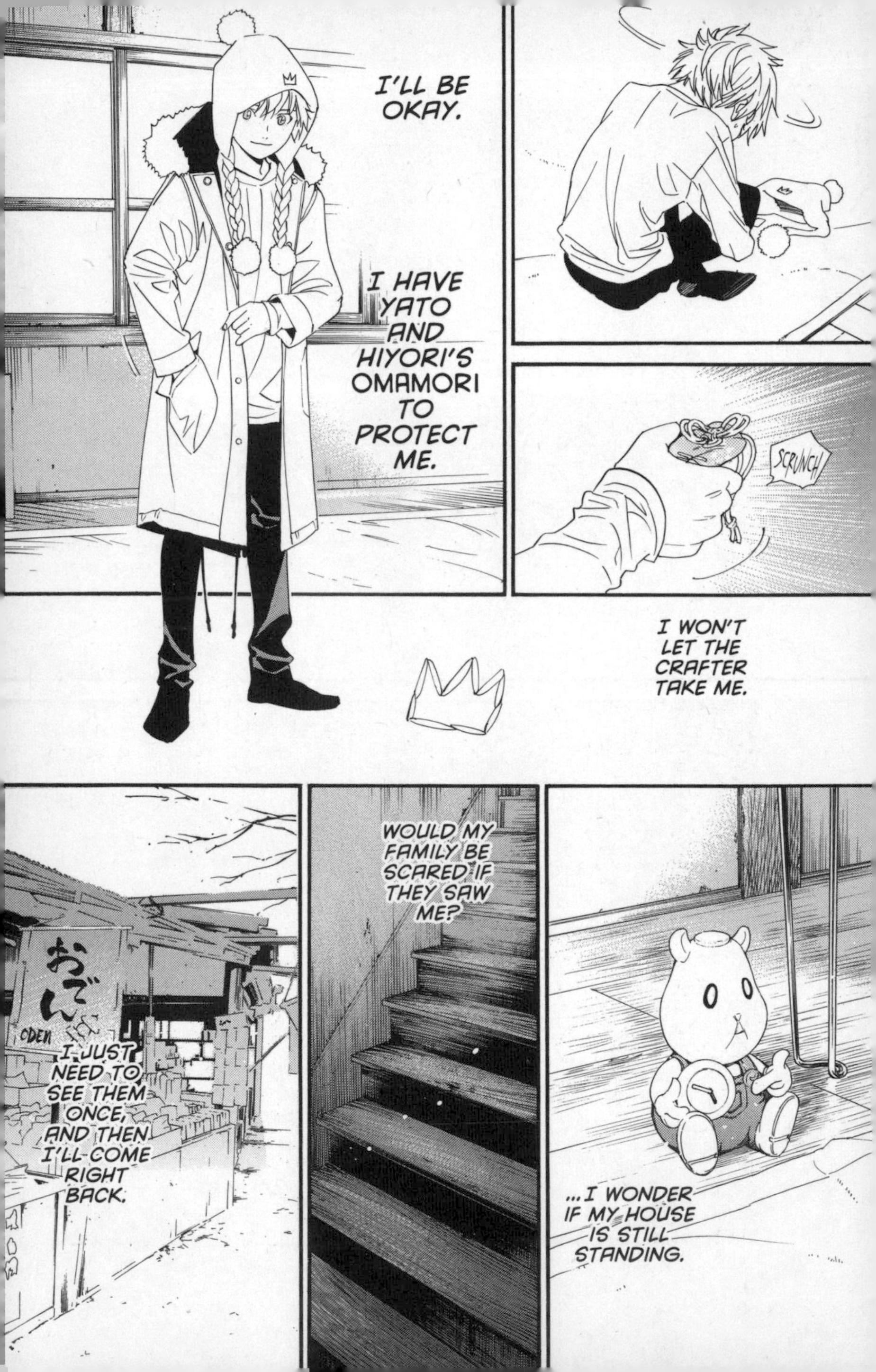

SCRUNCH
I'LL BE OKAY.
I HAVE YATO AND HIYORI'S OMAMORI TO PROTECT ME.
I WON'T LET THE CRAFTER TAKE ME.
...I WONDER IF MY HOUSE IS STILL STANDING.
WOULD MY FAMILY BE SCARED IF THEY SAW ME?
おでん
ODEN
I JUST NEED TO SEE THEM ONCE, AND THEN I'LL COME RIGHT BACK.

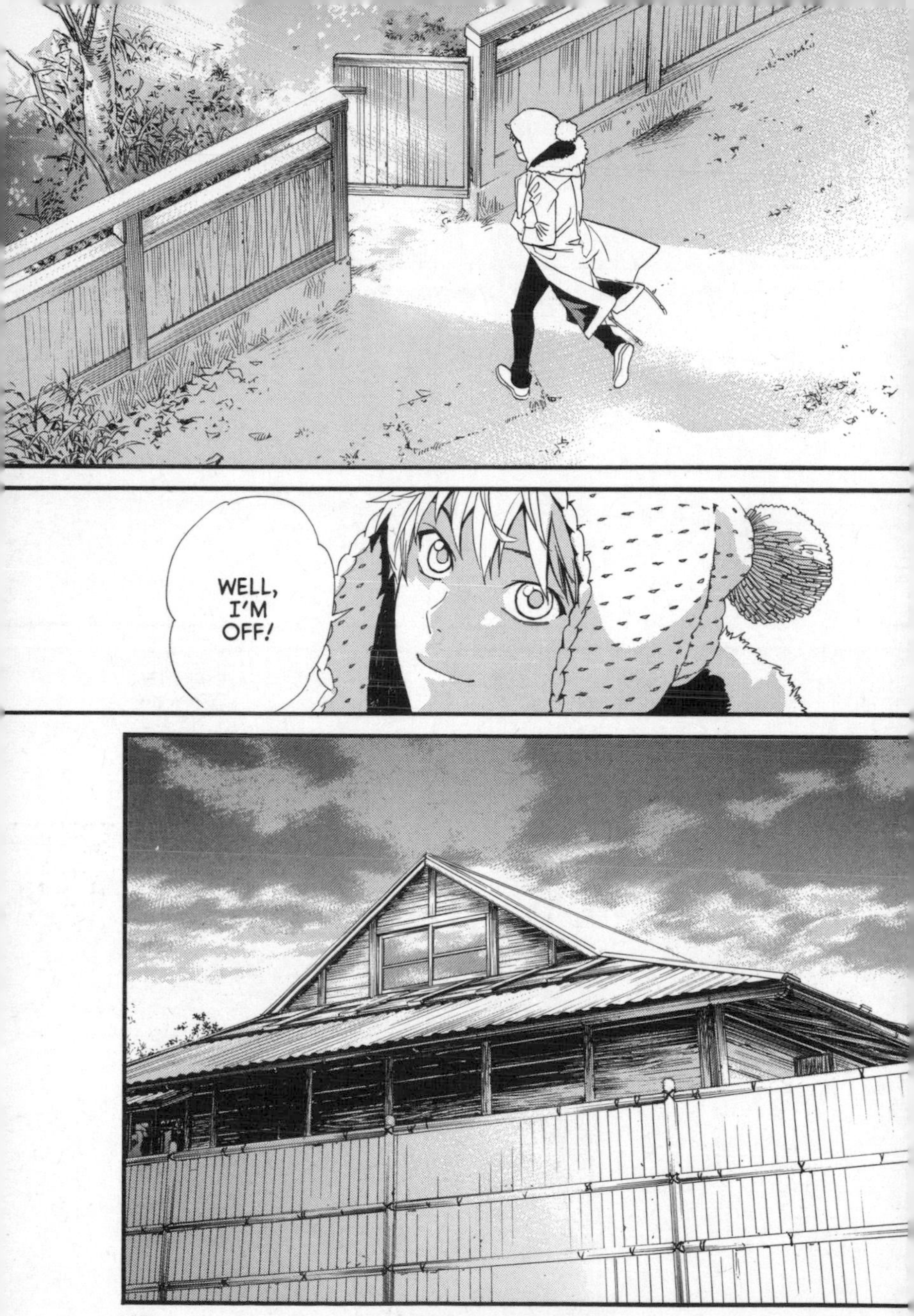
WELL, I'M OFF!

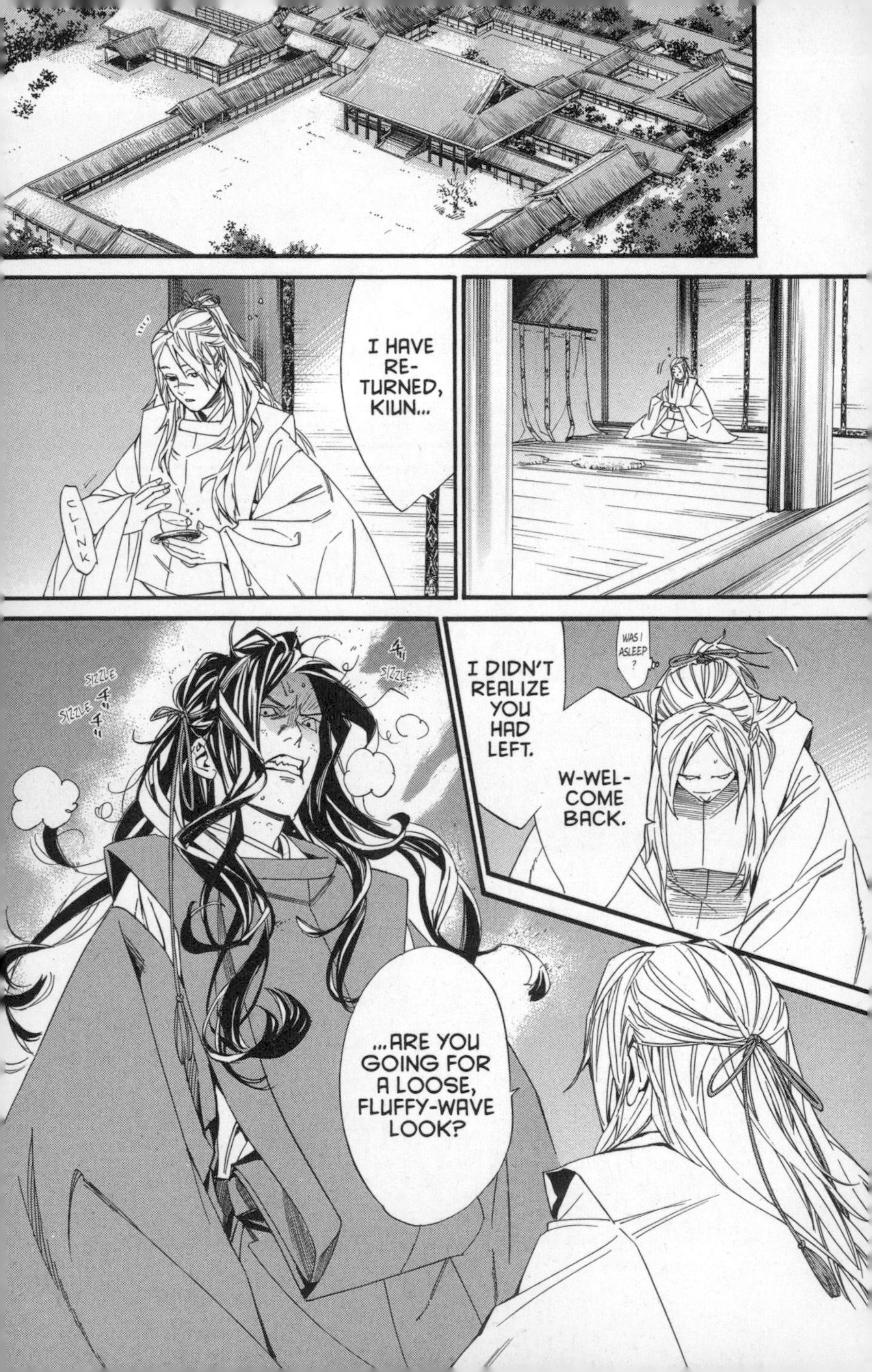
I HAVE RE-TURNED, KIUN...
CLINK
WAS I ASLEEP?
I DIDN'T REALIZE YOU HAD LEFT.
W-WEL-COME BACK.
SIZZLE
SIZZLE
SIZZLE
...ARE YOU GOING FOR A LOOSE, FLUFFY-WAVE LOOK?

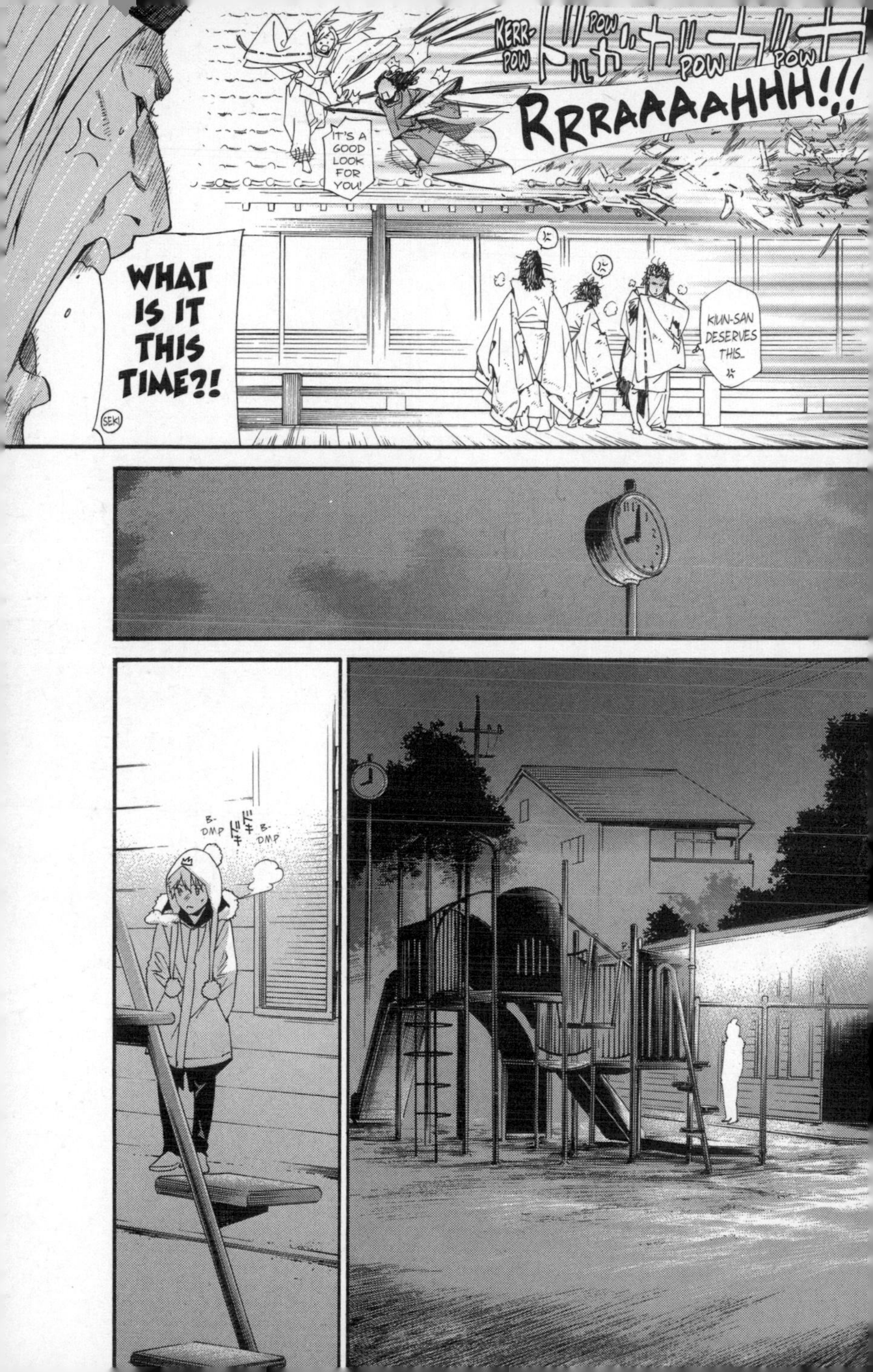

KERR-POW
POW
POW
POW
RRRAAAAHHH!!!
IT'S A GOOD LOOK FOR YOU!
KIUN-SAN DESERVES THIS...
WHAT IS IT THIS TIME?!
SEKI
B-DMP
B-DMP

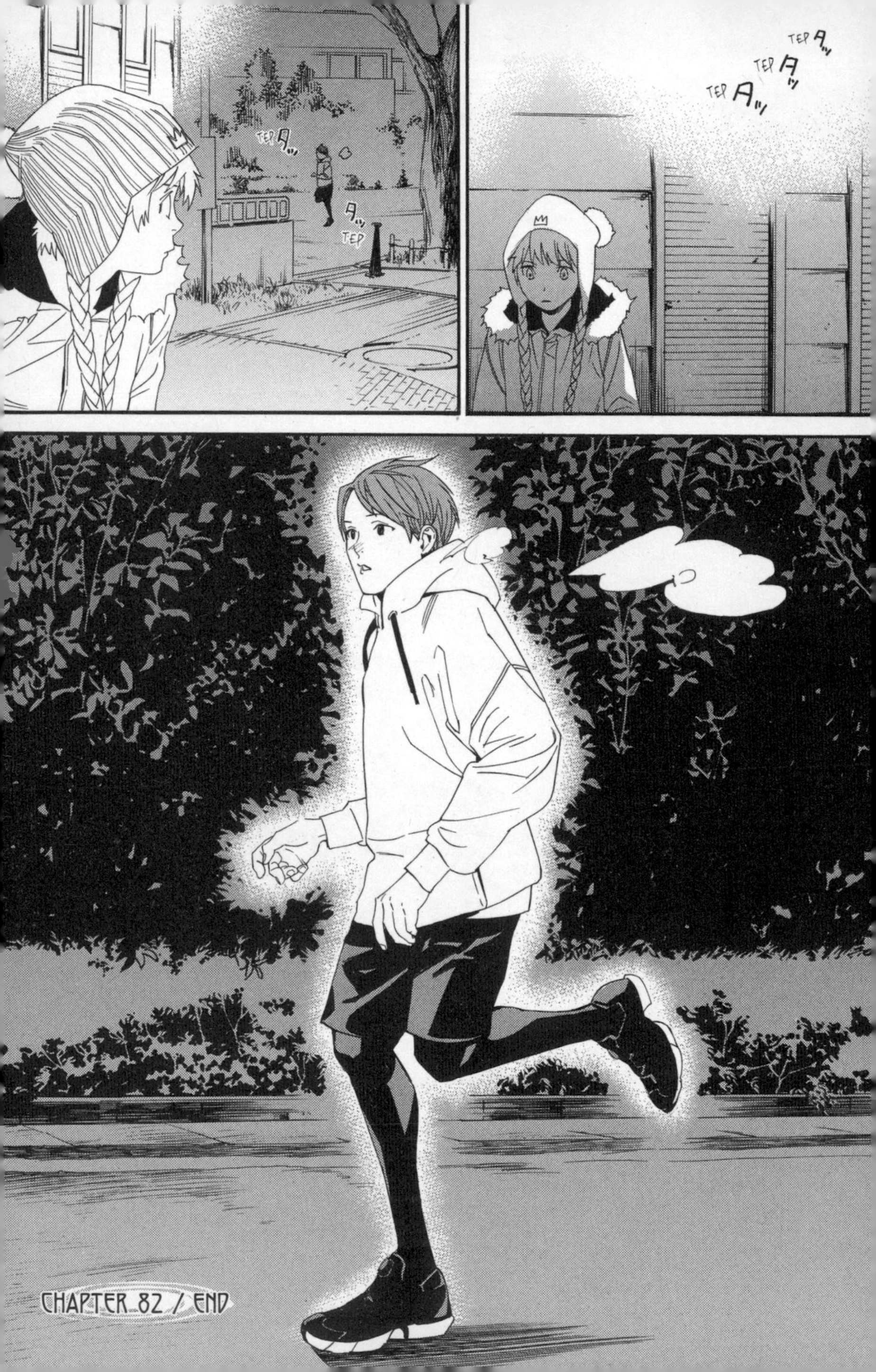
TEP タッ
TEP タッ
TEP タッ
TEP タッ
タッ TEP
CHAPTER 82 / END

野

皂

神

[illegible]

首

神

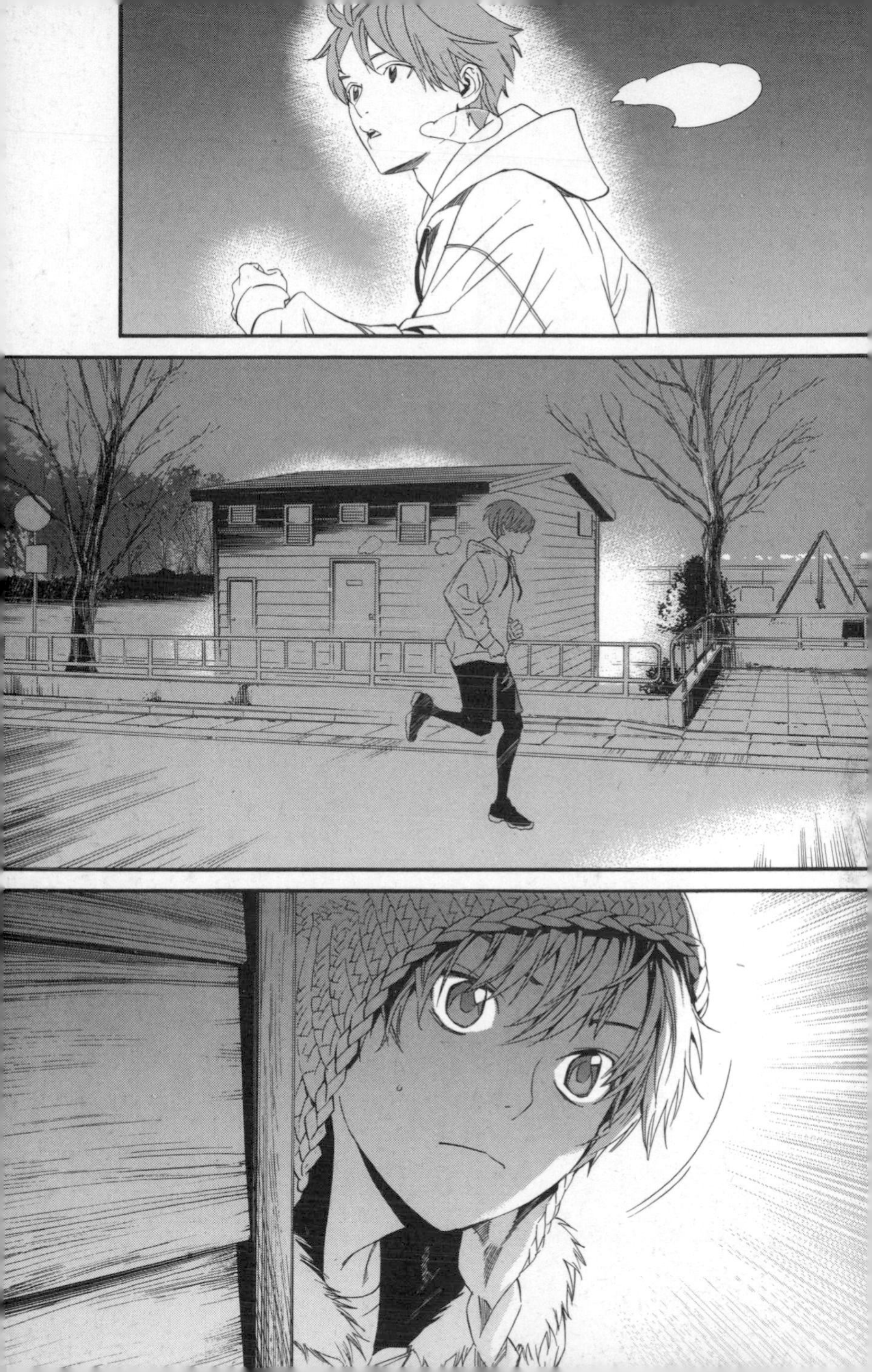

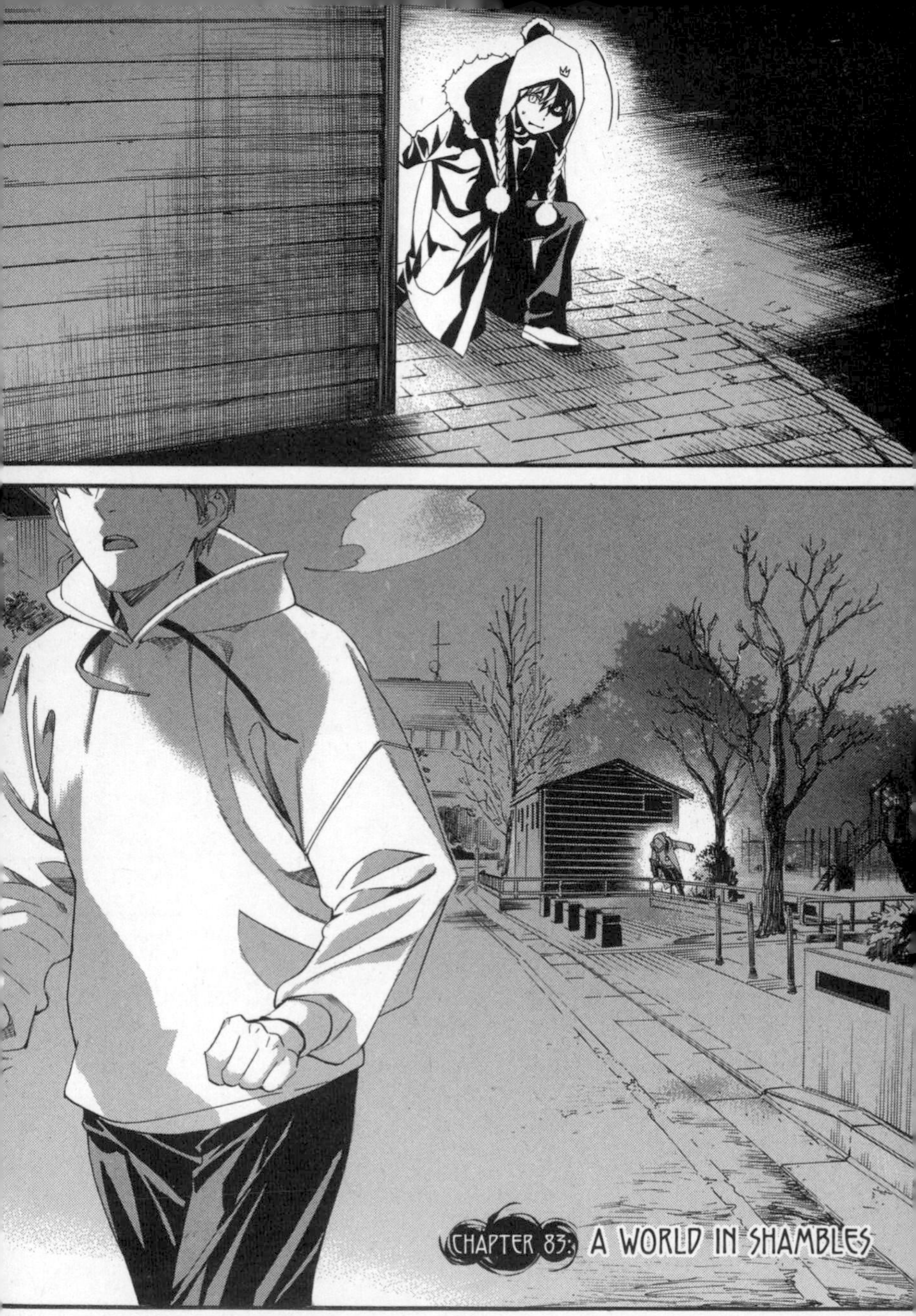
CHAPTER 83: A WORLD IN SHAMBLES

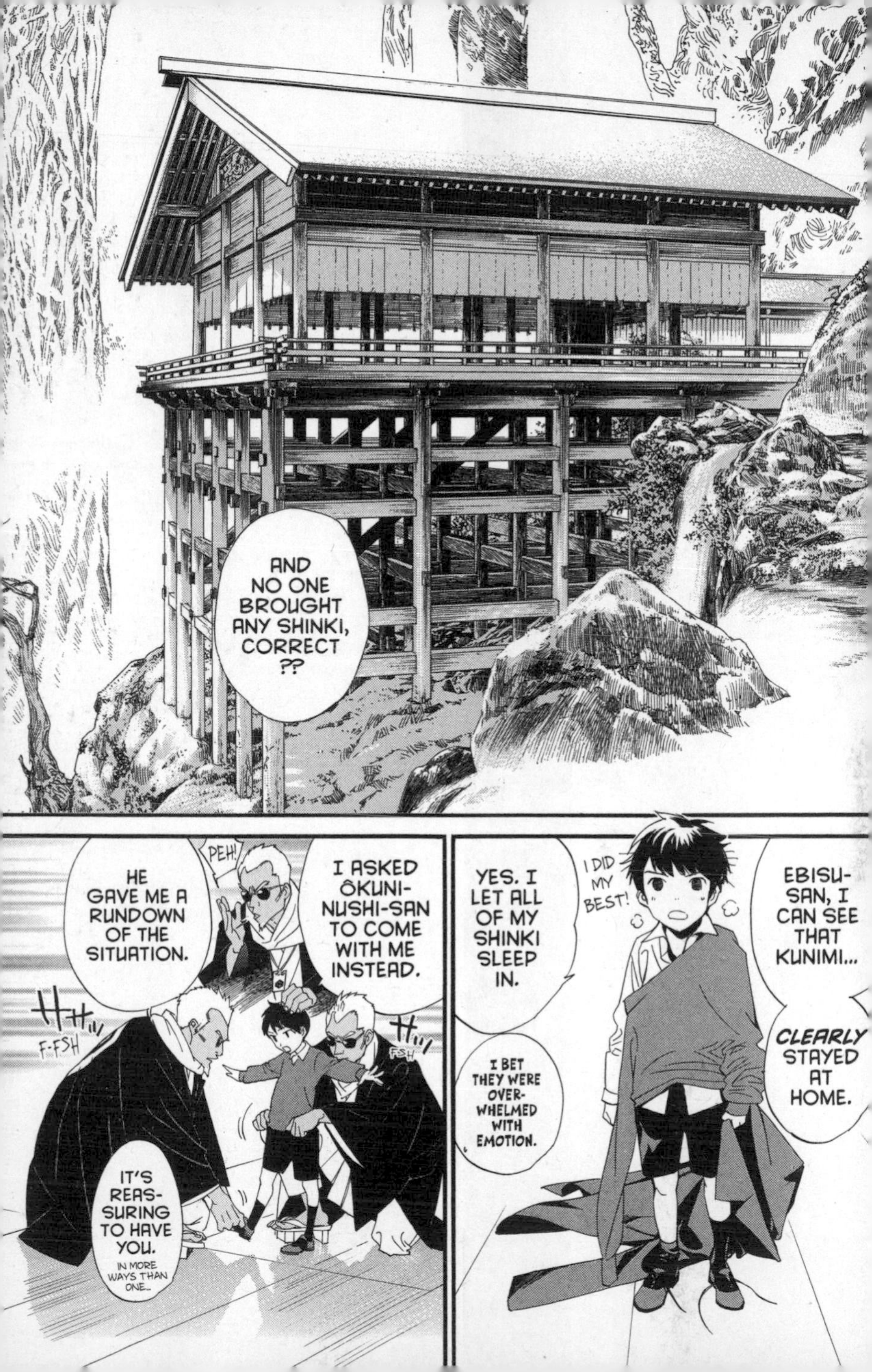
AND NO ONE BROUGHT ANY SHINKI, CORRECT??
EBISU-SAN, I CAN SEE THAT KUNIMI...
I DID MY BEST!
YES. I LET ALL OF MY SHINKI SLEEP IN.
CLEARLY STAYED AT HOME.
I BET THEY WERE OVER-WHELMED WITH EMOTION.
I ASKED ÔKUNI-NUSHI-SAN TO COME WITH ME INSTEAD.
PEH!
HE GAVE ME A RUNDOWN OF THE SITUATION.
FSH
F-FSH
IT'S REAS-SURING TO HAVE YOU.
IN MORE WAYS THAN ONE...

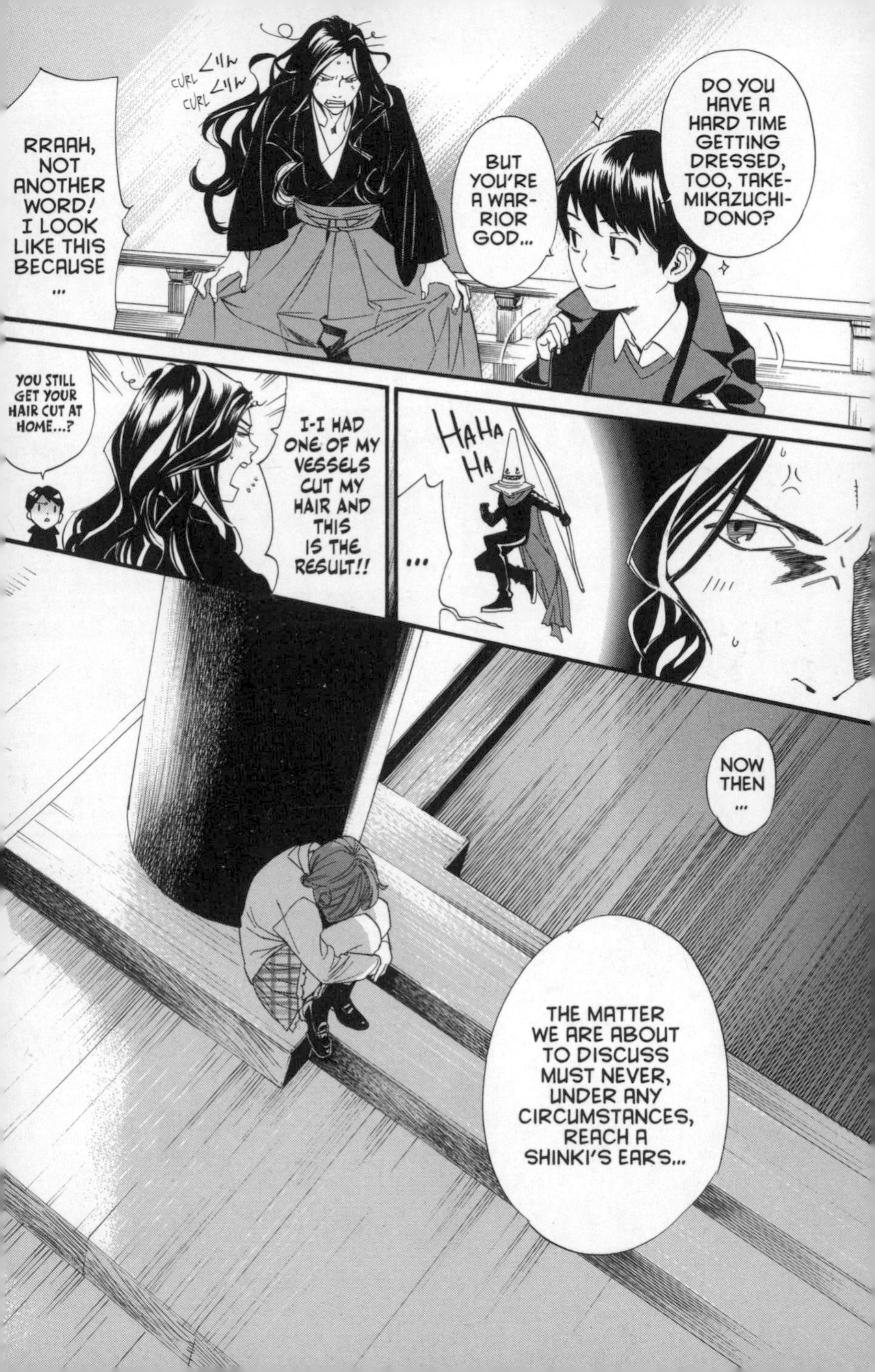
DO YOU HAVE A HARD TIME GETTING DRESSED, TOO, TAKEMIKAZUCHI-DONO?
BUT YOU'RE A WARRIOR GOD...
CURL くりん CURL くりん
RRAAH, NOT ANOTHER WORD! I LOOK LIKE THIS BECAUSE...
HAHA HA
...
I-I HAD ONE OF MY VESSELS CUT MY HAIR AND THIS IS THE RESULT!!
YOU STILL GET YOUR HAIR CUT AT HOME...?
NOW THEN...
THE MATTER WE ARE ABOUT TO DISCUSS MUST NEVER, UNDER ANY CIRCUMSTANCES, REACH A SHINKI'S EARS...

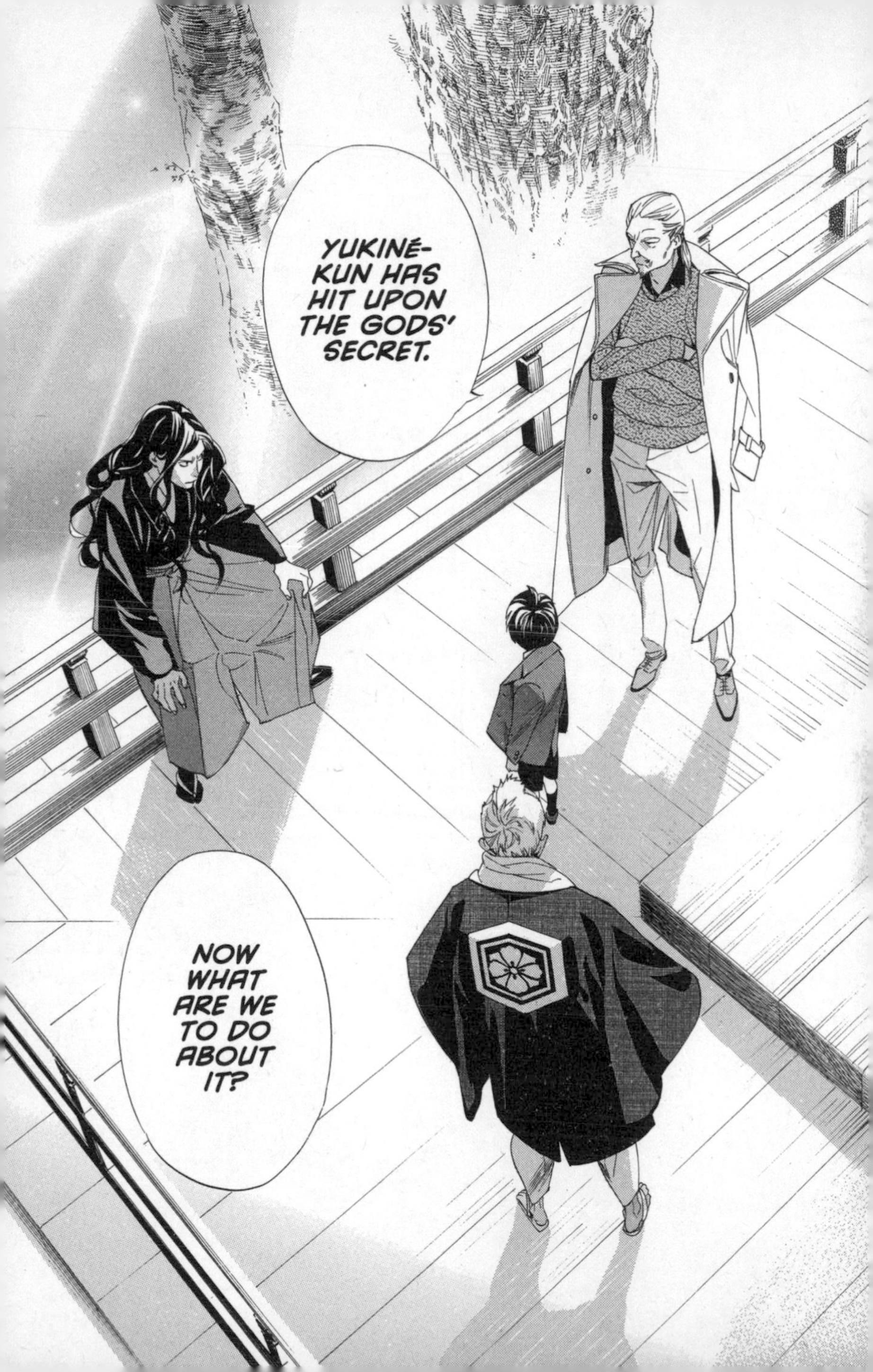
YUKINÉ-KUN HAS HIT UPON THE GODS' SECRET.
NOW WHAT ARE WE TO DO ABOUT IT?

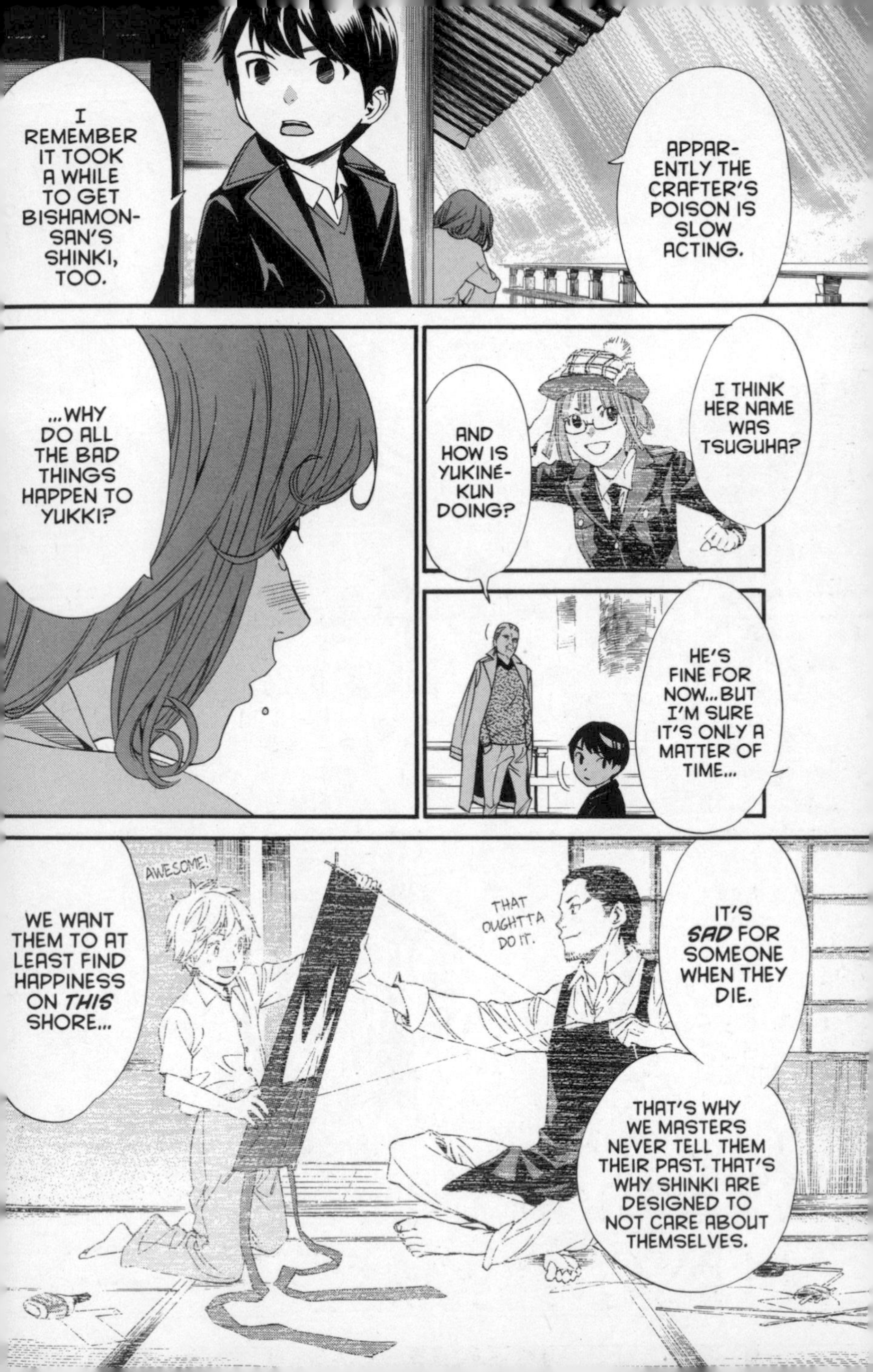

APPAR-ENTLY THE CRAFTER'S POISON IS SLOW ACTING.
I REMEMBER IT TOOK A WHILE TO GET BISHAMON-SAN'S SHINKI, TOO.
I THINK HER NAME WAS TSUGUHA?
AND HOW IS YUKINÉ-KUN DOING?
HE'S FINE FOR NOW... BUT I'M SURE IT'S ONLY A MATTER OF TIME...
...WHY DO ALL THE BAD THINGS HAPPEN TO YUKKI?
IT'S *SAD* FOR SOMEONE WHEN THEY DIE.
THAT OUGHTTA DO IT.
AWESOME!
THAT'S WHY WE MASTERS NEVER TELL THEM THEIR PAST. THAT'S WHY SHINKI ARE DESIGNED TO NOT CARE ABOUT THEMSELVES.
WE WANT THEM TO AT LEAST FIND HAPPINESS ON *THIS* SHORE...

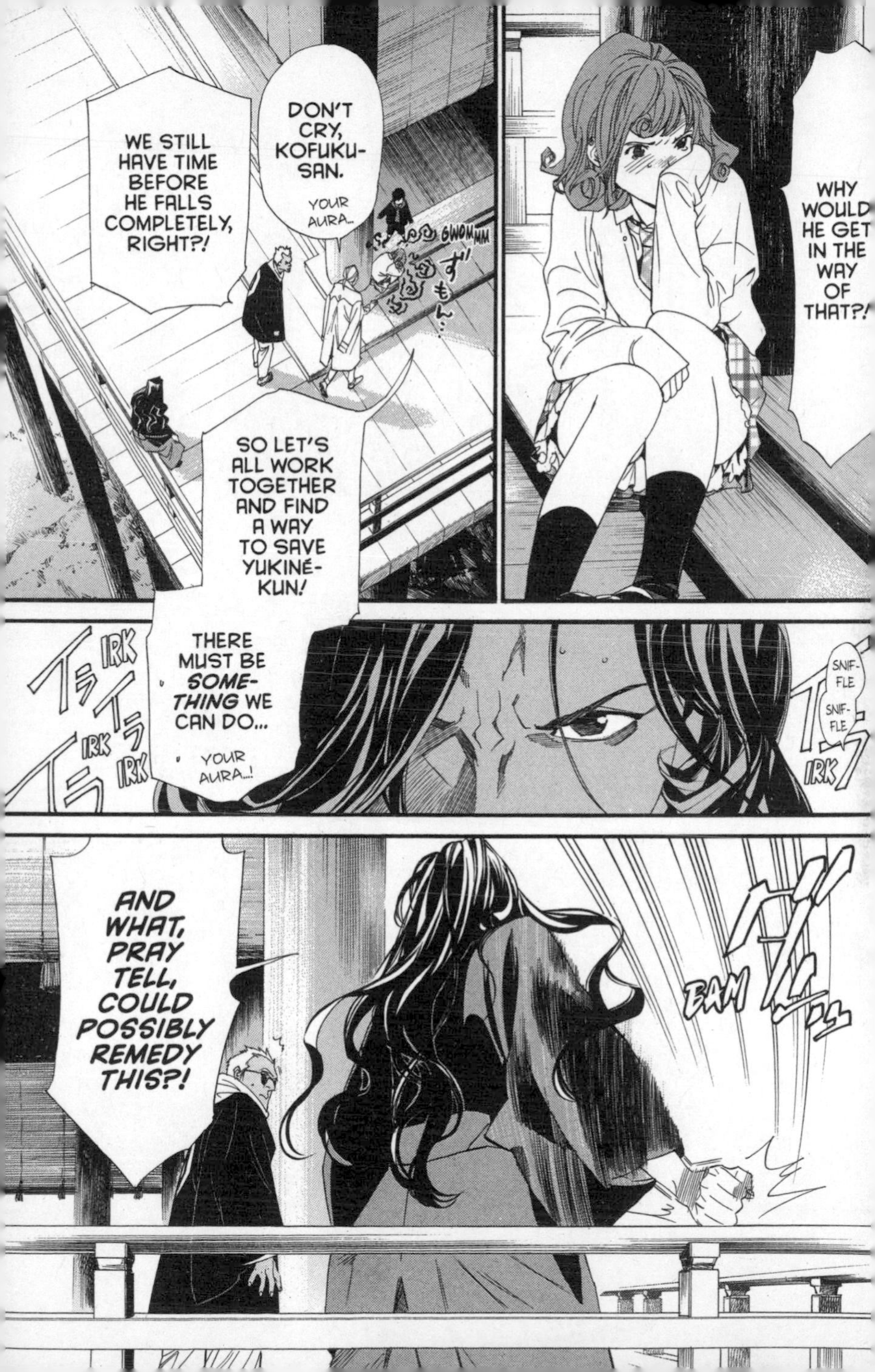

WHY WOULD HE GET IN THE WAY OF THAT?!
DON'T CRY, KOFUKU-SAN.
YOUR AURA...
GWOMMM
ずもん…
WE STILL HAVE TIME BEFORE HE FALLS COMPLETELY, RIGHT?!
SO LET'S ALL WORK TOGETHER AND FIND A WAY TO SAVE YUKINÉ-KUN!
SNIFFLE
SNIFFLE
IRK
THERE MUST BE SOMETHING WE CAN DO...
YOUR AURA...!
IRK
IRK
IRK
BAM
AND WHAT, PRAY TELL, COULD POSSIBLY REMEDY THIS?!

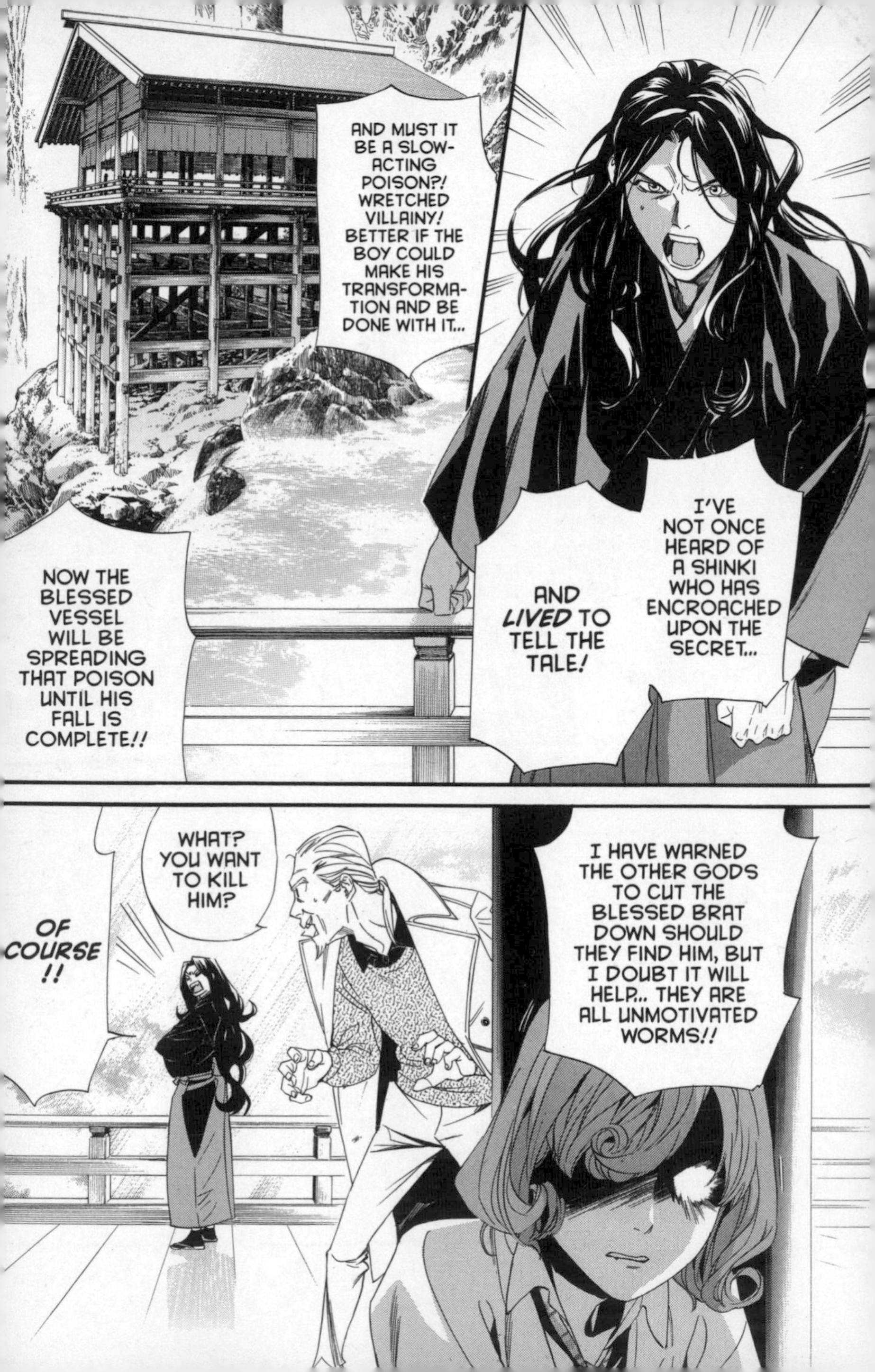
AND MUST IT BE A SLOW-ACTING POISON?! WRETCHED VILLAINY! BETTER IF THE BOY COULD MAKE HIS TRANSFORMATION AND BE DONE WITH IT...
I'VE NOT ONCE HEARD OF A SHINKI WHO HAS ENCROACHED UPON THE SECRET...
AND *LIVED* TO TELL THE TALE!
NOW THE BLESSED VESSEL WILL BE SPREADING THAT POISON UNTIL HIS FALL IS COMPLETE!!
I HAVE WARNED THE OTHER GODS TO CUT THE BLESSED BRAT DOWN SHOULD THEY FIND HIM, BUT I DOUBT IT WILL HELP... THEY ARE ALL UNMOTIVATED WORMS!!
WHAT? YOU WANT TO KILL HIM?
OF COURSE !!

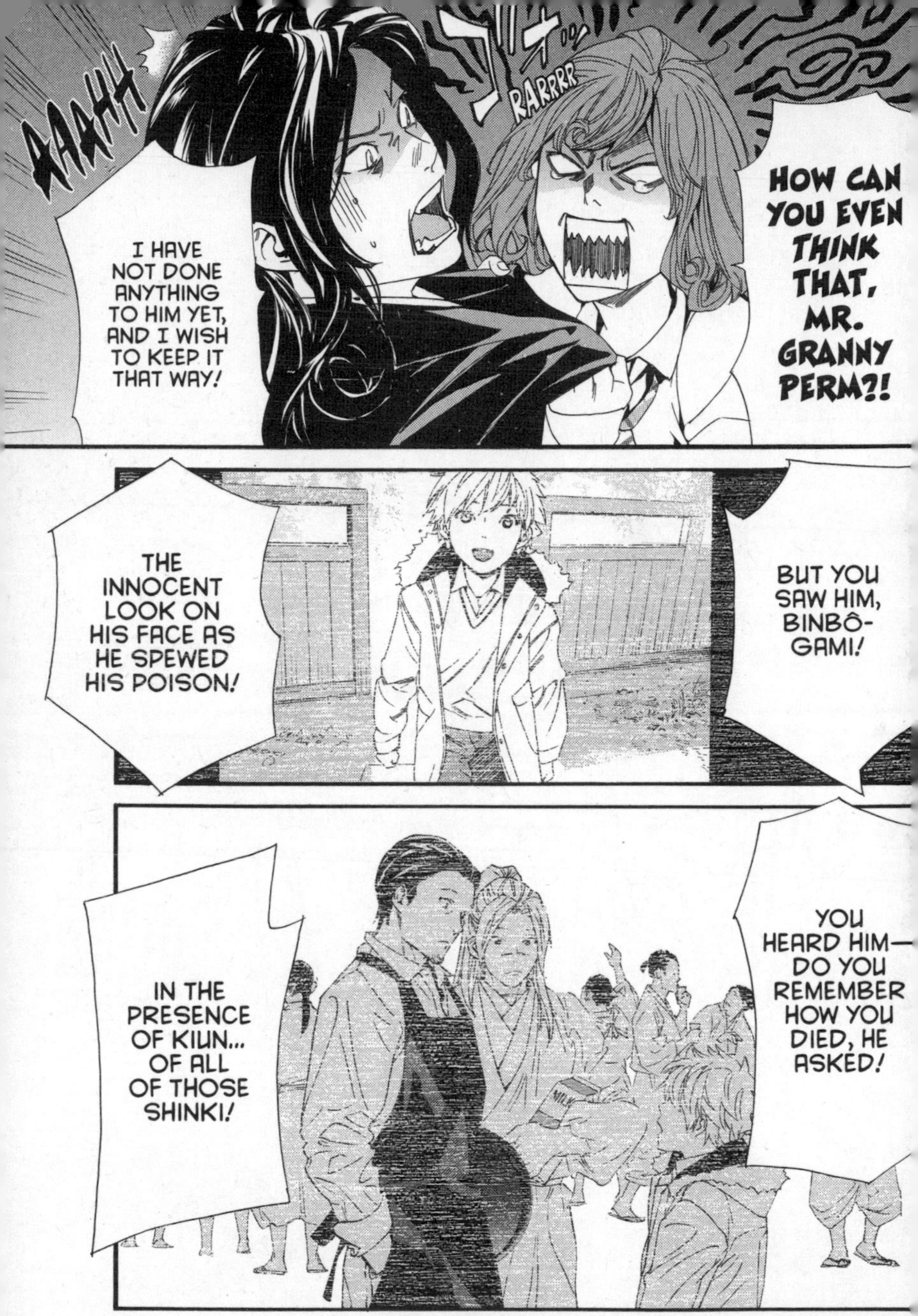
HOW CAN YOU EVEN THINK THAT, MR. GRANNY PERM?!
RARRRR
AAAHH
I HAVE NOT DONE ANYTHING TO HIM YET, AND I WISH TO KEEP IT THAT WAY!
BUT YOU SAW HIM, BINBÔ-GAMI!
THE INNOCENT LOOK ON HIS FACE AS HE SPEWED HIS POISON!
YOU HEARD HIM—DO YOU REMEMBER HOW YOU DIED, HE ASKED!
IN THE PRESENCE OF KIUN... OF ALL OF THOSE SHINKI!

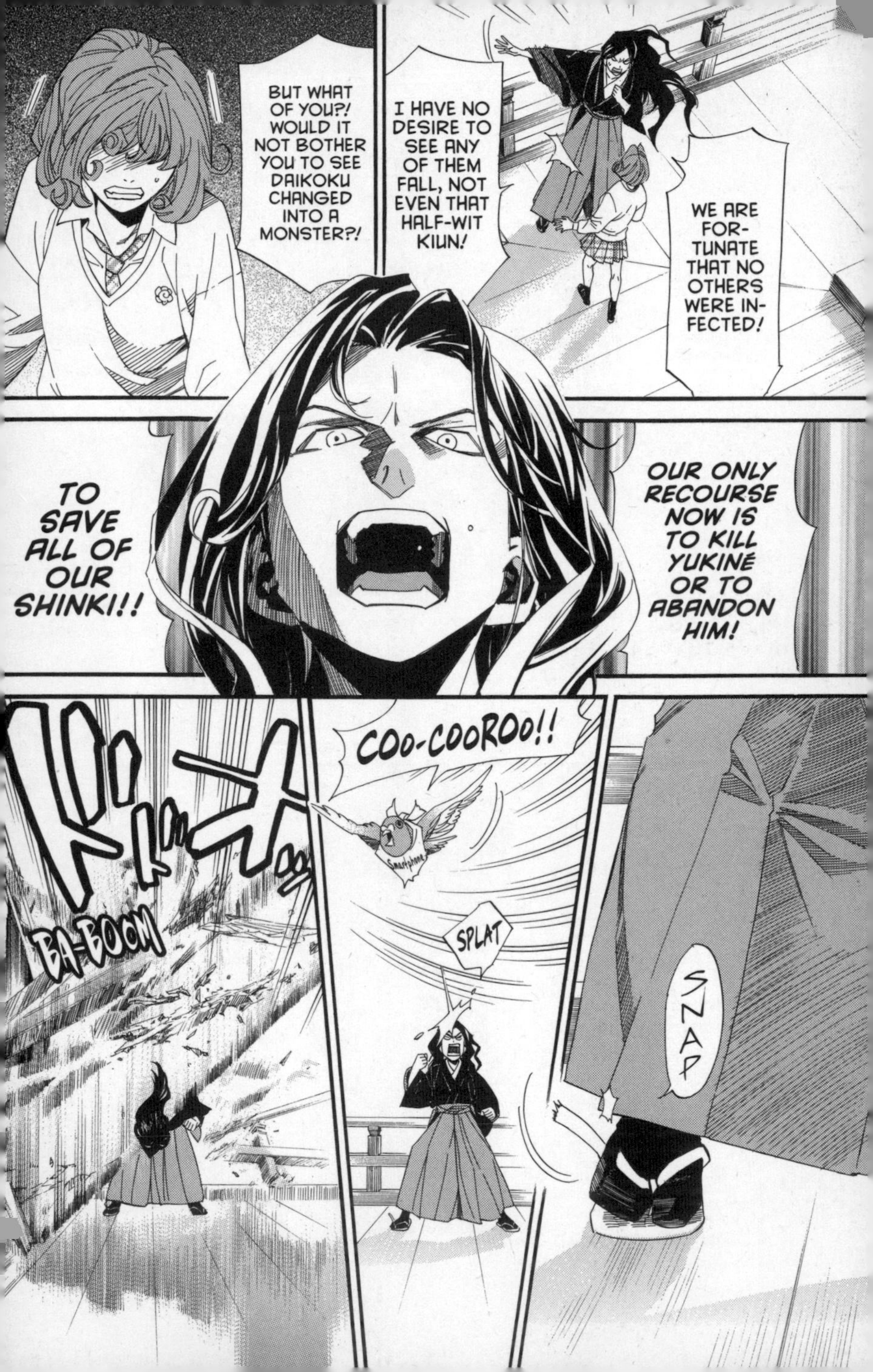
I HAVE NO DESIRE TO SEE ANY OF THEM FALL, NOT EVEN THAT HALF-WIT KIUN!
WE ARE FOR-TUNATE THAT NO OTHERS WERE IN-FECTED!
BUT WHAT OF YOU?! WOULD IT NOT BOTHER YOU TO SEE DAIKOKU CHANGED INTO A MONSTER?!
OUR ONLY RECOURSE NOW IS TO KILL YUKINÉ OR TO ABANDON HIM!
TO SAVE ALL OF OUR SHINKI!!
SNAP
COO-COOROO!!
Smartphone
SPLAT
BA-BOOM

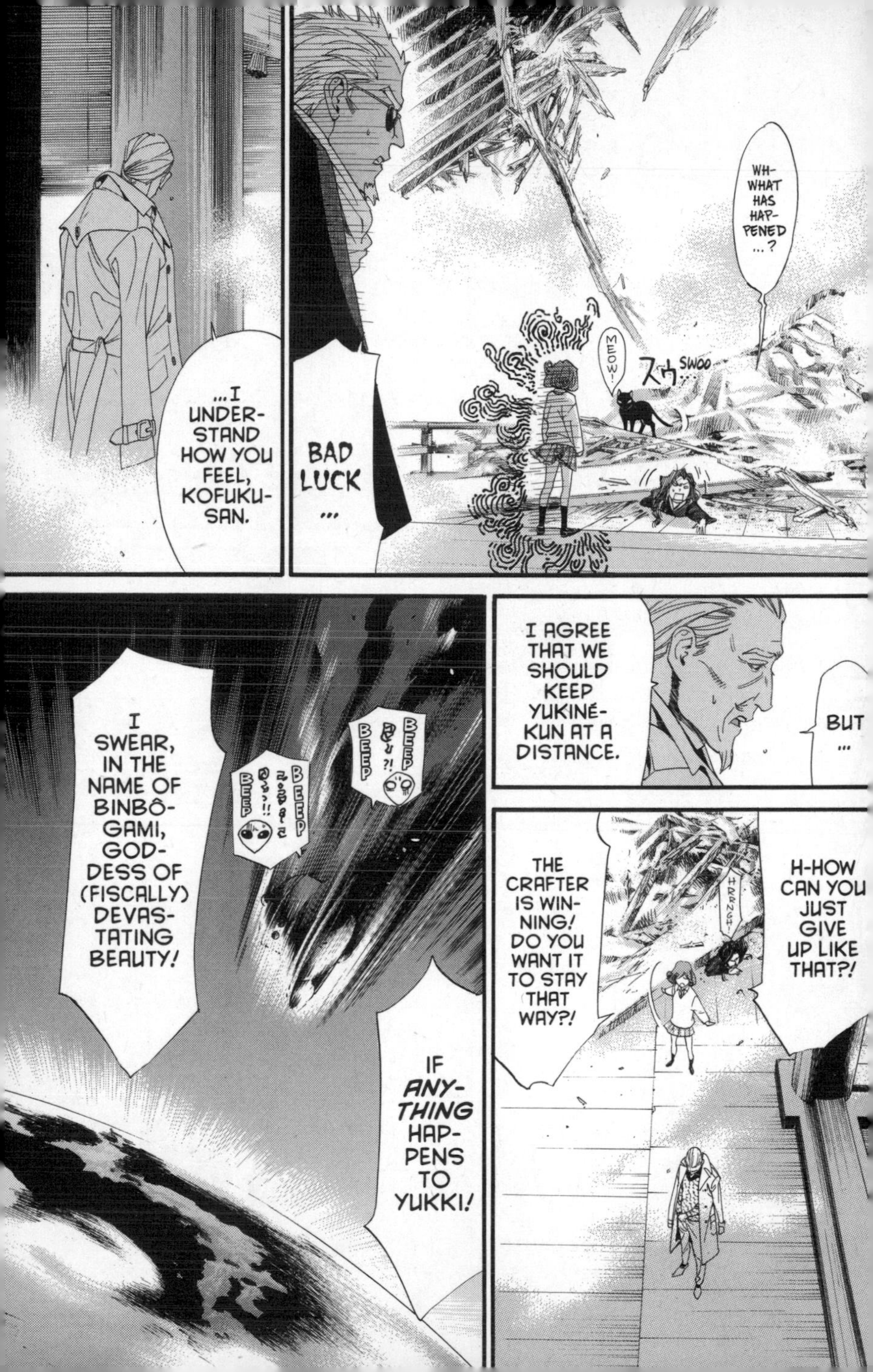
WH- WHAT HAS HAP- PENED ...?
MEOW!
スゥ SWOO
BAD LUCK ...
...I UNDER- STAND HOW YOU FEEL, KOFUKU- SAN.
BUT ...
I AGREE THAT WE SHOULD KEEP YUKINÉ- KUN AT A DISTANCE.
H-HOW CAN YOU JUST GIVE UP LIKE THAT?!
HRRNGH!
THE CRAFTER IS WIN- NING! DO YOU WANT IT TO STAY THAT WAY?!
BEEP BEEP
BEEP BEEP
I SWEAR, IN THE NAME OF BINBÔ- GAMI, GOD- DESS OF (FISCALLY) DEVAS- TATING BEAUTY!
IF ANY- THING HAP- PENS TO YUKKI!

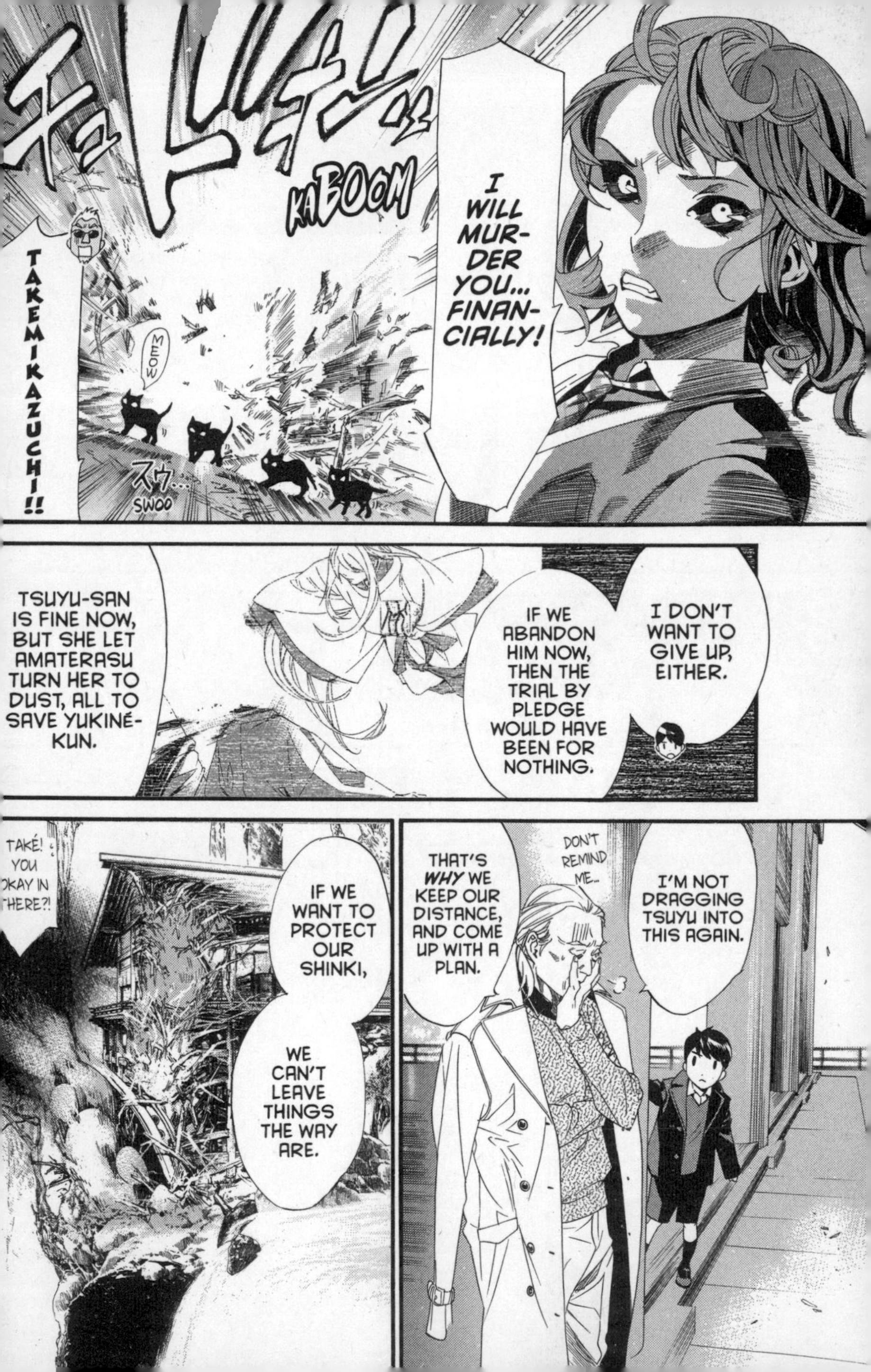
I WILL MURDER YOU... FINANCIALLY!
KABOOM
TAKEMIKAZUCHI!!
MEOW
スゥ…
SWOO
I DON'T WANT TO GIVE UP, EITHER.
IF WE ABANDON HIM NOW, THEN THE TRIAL BY PLEDGE WOULD HAVE BEEN FOR NOTHING.
TSUYU-SAN IS FINE NOW, BUT SHE LET AMATERASU TURN HER TO DUST, ALL TO SAVE YUKINÉ-KUN.
I'M NOT DRAGGING TSUYU INTO THIS AGAIN.
DON'T REMIND ME...
THAT'S *WHY* WE KEEP OUR DISTANCE, AND COME UP WITH A PLAN.
IF WE WANT TO PROTECT OUR SHINKI,
WE CAN'T LEAVE THINGS THE WAY ARE.
TAKÉ! YOU OKAY IN THERE?!

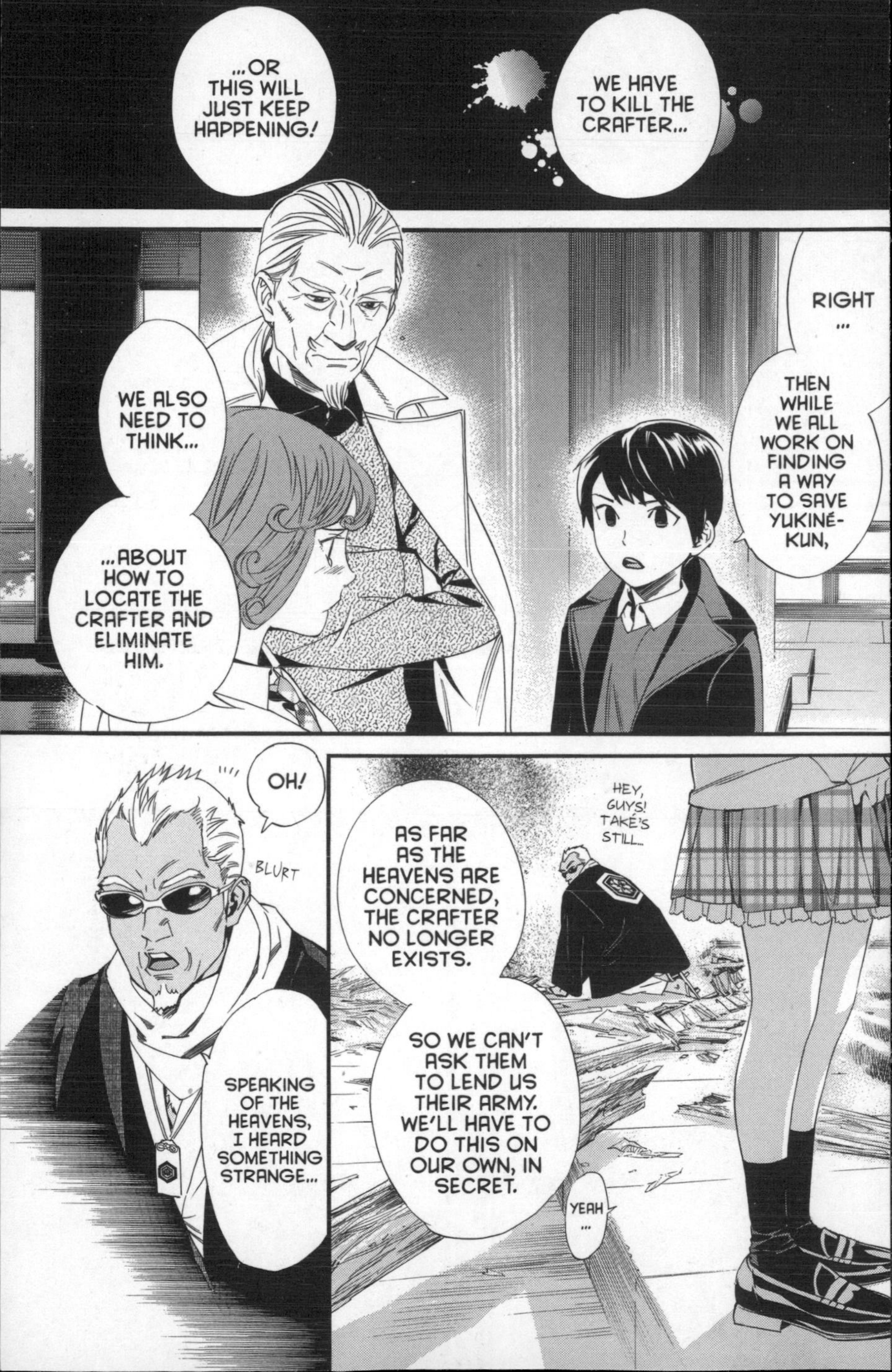

WE HAVE TO KILL THE CRAFTER...
...OR THIS WILL JUST KEEP HAPPENING!
RIGHT...
THEN WHILE WE ALL WORK ON FINDING A WAY TO SAVE YUKINÉ-KUN,
WE ALSO NEED TO THINK...
...ABOUT HOW TO LOCATE THE CRAFTER AND ELIMINATE HIM.
HEY, GUYS! TAKÉ'S STILL...
AS FAR AS THE HEAVENS ARE CONCERNED, THE CRAFTER NO LONGER EXISTS.
SO WE CAN'T ASK THEM TO LEND US THEIR ARMY. WE'LL HAVE TO DO THIS ON OUR OWN, IN SECRET.
YEAH...
OH!
BLURT
SPEAKING OF THE HEAVENS, I HEARD SOMETHING STRANGE...

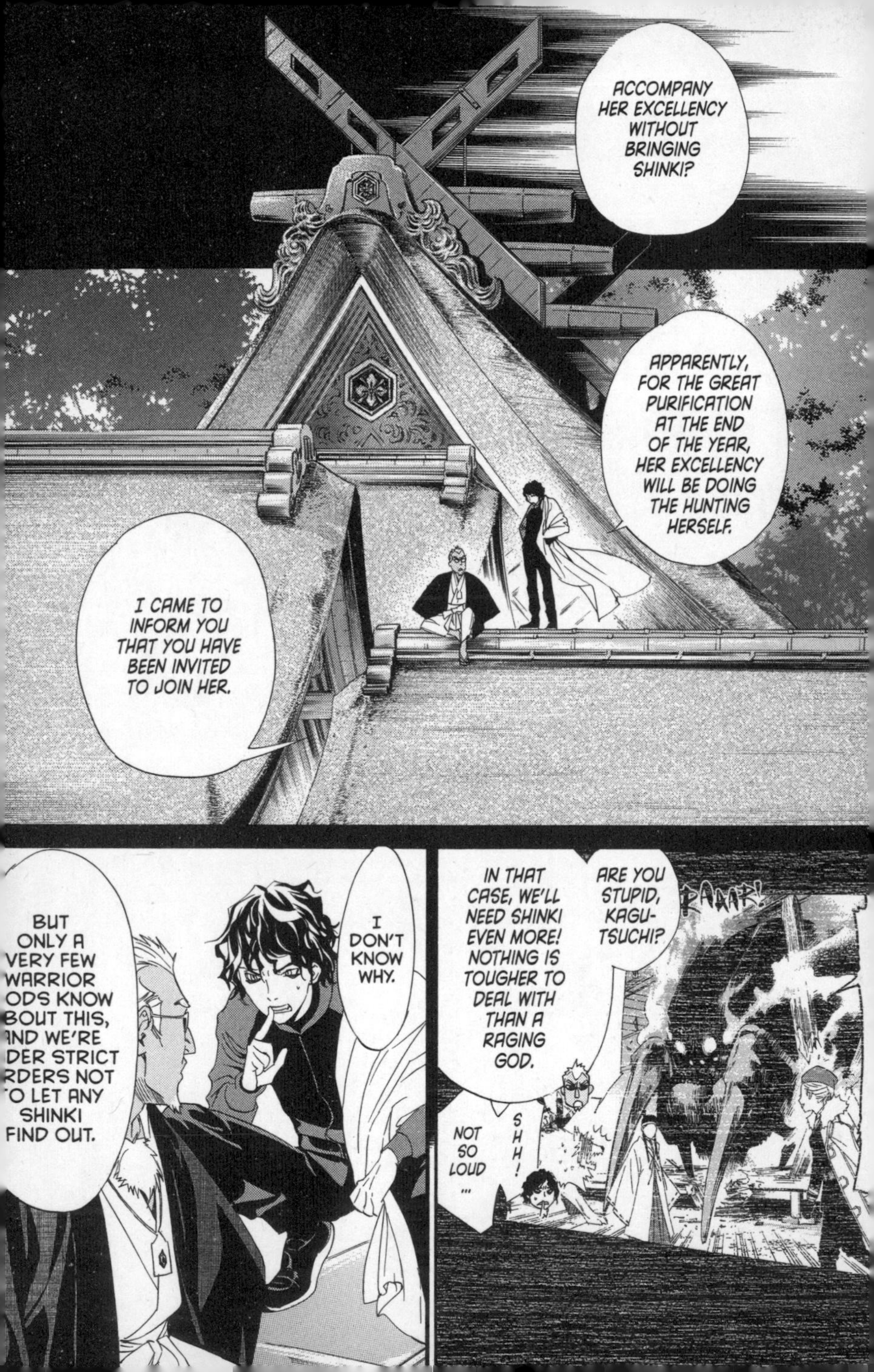
ACCOMPANY HER EXCELLENCY WITHOUT BRINGING SHINKI?
APPARENTLY, FOR THE GREAT PURIFICATION AT THE END OF THE YEAR, HER EXCELLENCY WILL BE DOING THE HUNTING HERSELF.
I CAME TO INFORM YOU THAT YOU HAVE BEEN INVITED TO JOIN HER.
RAAAR!
ARE YOU STUPID, KAGU-TSUCHI?
IN THAT CASE, WE'LL NEED SHINKI EVEN MORE! NOTHING IS TOUGHER TO DEAL WITH THAN A RAGING GOD.
SHH!
NOT SO LOUD...
I DON'T KNOW WHY.
BUT ONLY A VERY FEW WARRIOR ODS KNOW BOUT THIS, ND WE'RE DER STRICT RDERS NOT O LET ANY SHINKI FIND OUT.

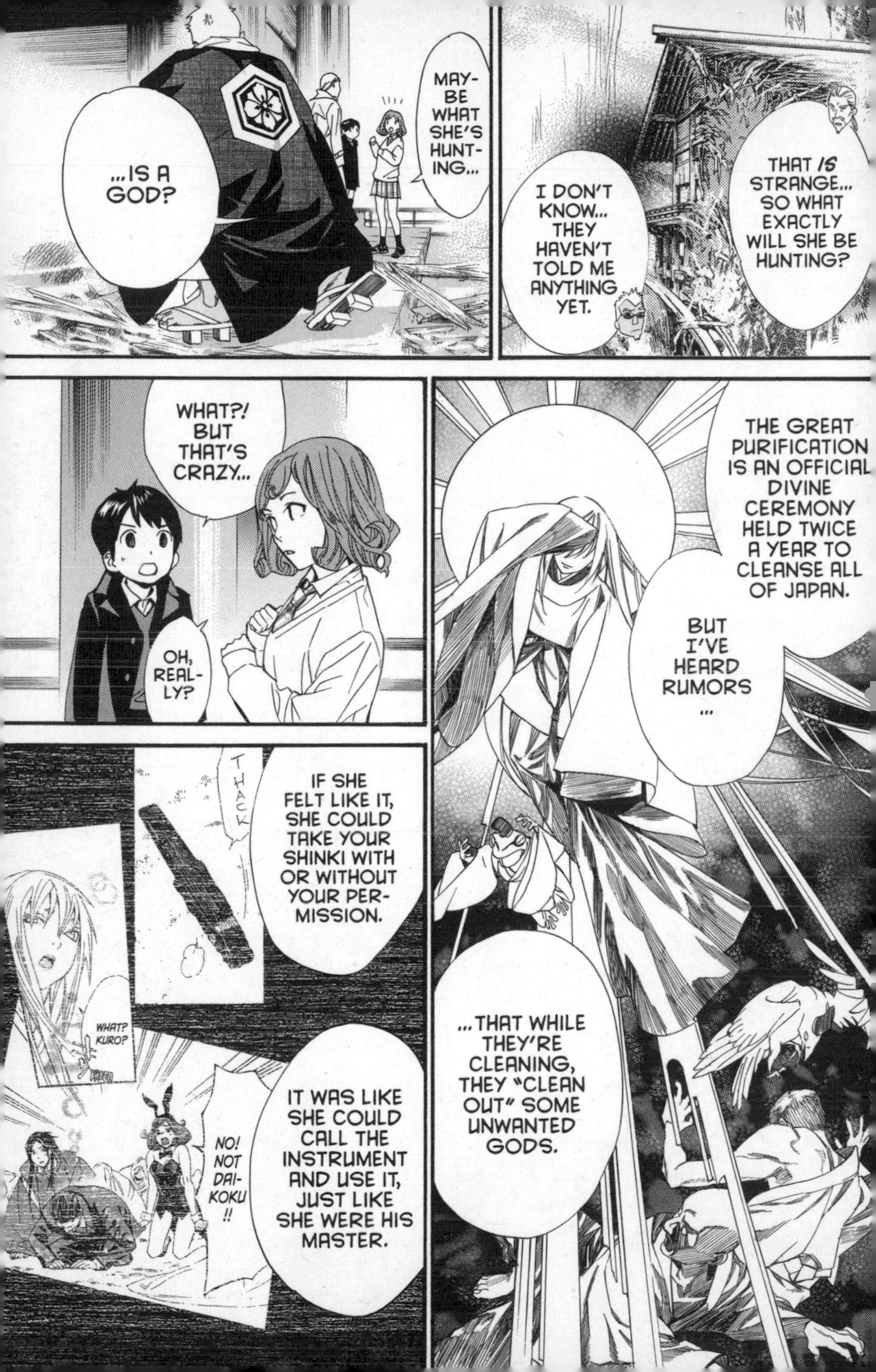
THAT *IS* STRANGE... SO WHAT EXACTLY WILL SHE BE HUNTING?
I DON'T KNOW... THEY HAVEN'T TOLD ME ANYTHING YET.
MAY-BE WHAT SHE'S HUNT-ING...
...IS A GOD?
THE GREAT PURIFICATION IS AN OFFICIAL DIVINE CEREMONY HELD TWICE A YEAR TO CLEANSE ALL OF JAPAN.
BUT I'VE HEARD RUMORS ...
...THAT WHILE THEY'RE CLEANING, THEY "CLEAN OUT" SOME UNWANTED GODS.
WHAT?! BUT THAT'S CRAZY...
OH, REAL-LY?
IF SHE FELT LIKE IT, SHE COULD TAKE YOUR SHINKI WITH OR WITHOUT YOUR PER-MISSION.
THACK
IT WAS LIKE SHE COULD CALL THE INSTRUMENT AND USE IT, JUST LIKE SHE WERE HIS MASTER.
NO! NOT DAI-KOKU !!
WHAT? KURO?

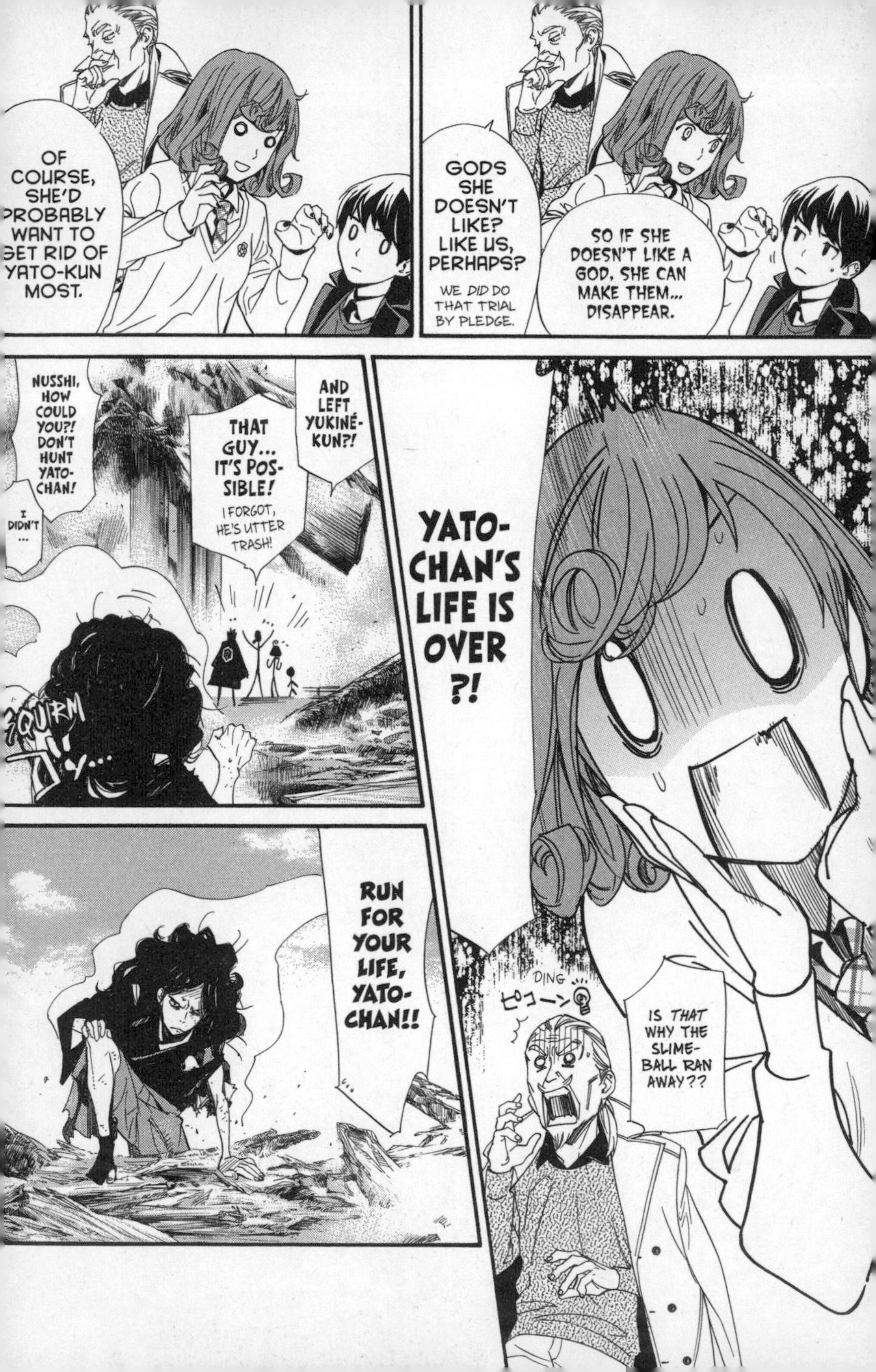
SO IF SHE DOESN'T LIKE A GOD, SHE CAN MAKE THEM... DISAPPEAR.
GODS SHE DOESN'T LIKE? LIKE US, PERHAPS?
WE *DID* DO THAT TRIAL BY PLEDGE.
OF COURSE, SHE'D PROBABLY WANT TO GET RID OF YATO-KUN MOST.
YATO-CHAN'S LIFE IS OVER?!
DING
ピコーン
IS *THAT* WHY THE SLIME-BALL RAN AWAY??
AND LEFT YUKINÉ-KUN?!
THAT GUY... IT'S POS-SIBLE!
I FORGOT, HE'S UTTER TRASH!
NUSSHI, HOW COULD YOU?! DON'T HUNT YATO-CHAN!
I DIDN'T...
SQUIRM
RUN FOR YOUR LIFE, YATO-CHAN!!

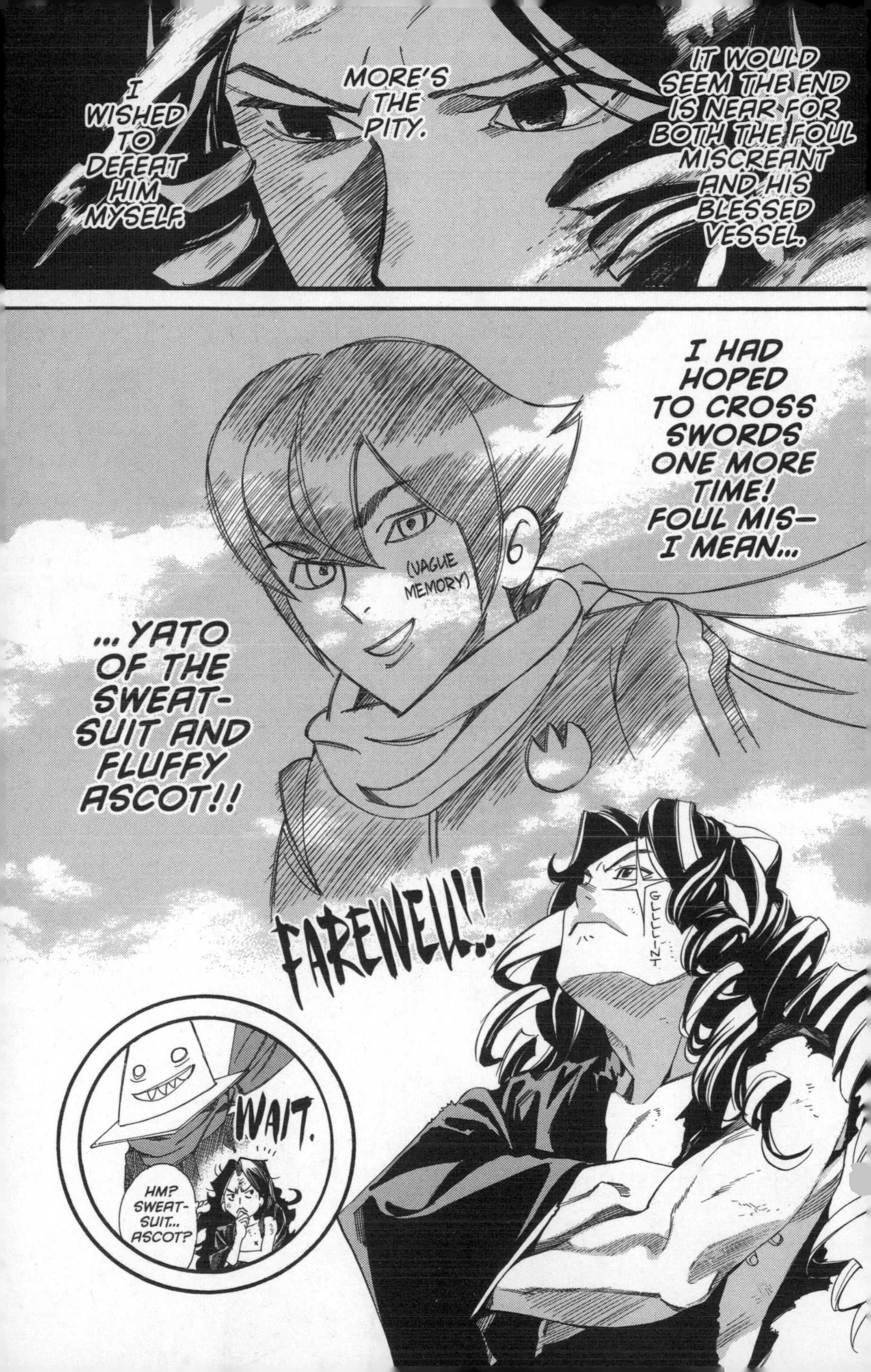
IT WOULD SEEM THE END IS NEAR FOR BOTH THE FOUL MISCREANT AND HIS BLESSED VESSEL.
MORE'S THE PITY.
I WISHED TO DEFEAT HIM MYSELF.
I HAD HOPED TO CROSS SWORDS ONE MORE TIME! FOUL MIS— I MEAN...
(VAGUE MEMORY)
...YATO OF THE SWEAT-SUIT AND FLUFFY ASCOT!!
GLLLINT
FAREWELL!!
WAIT.
HM? SWEAT-SUIT... ASCOT?

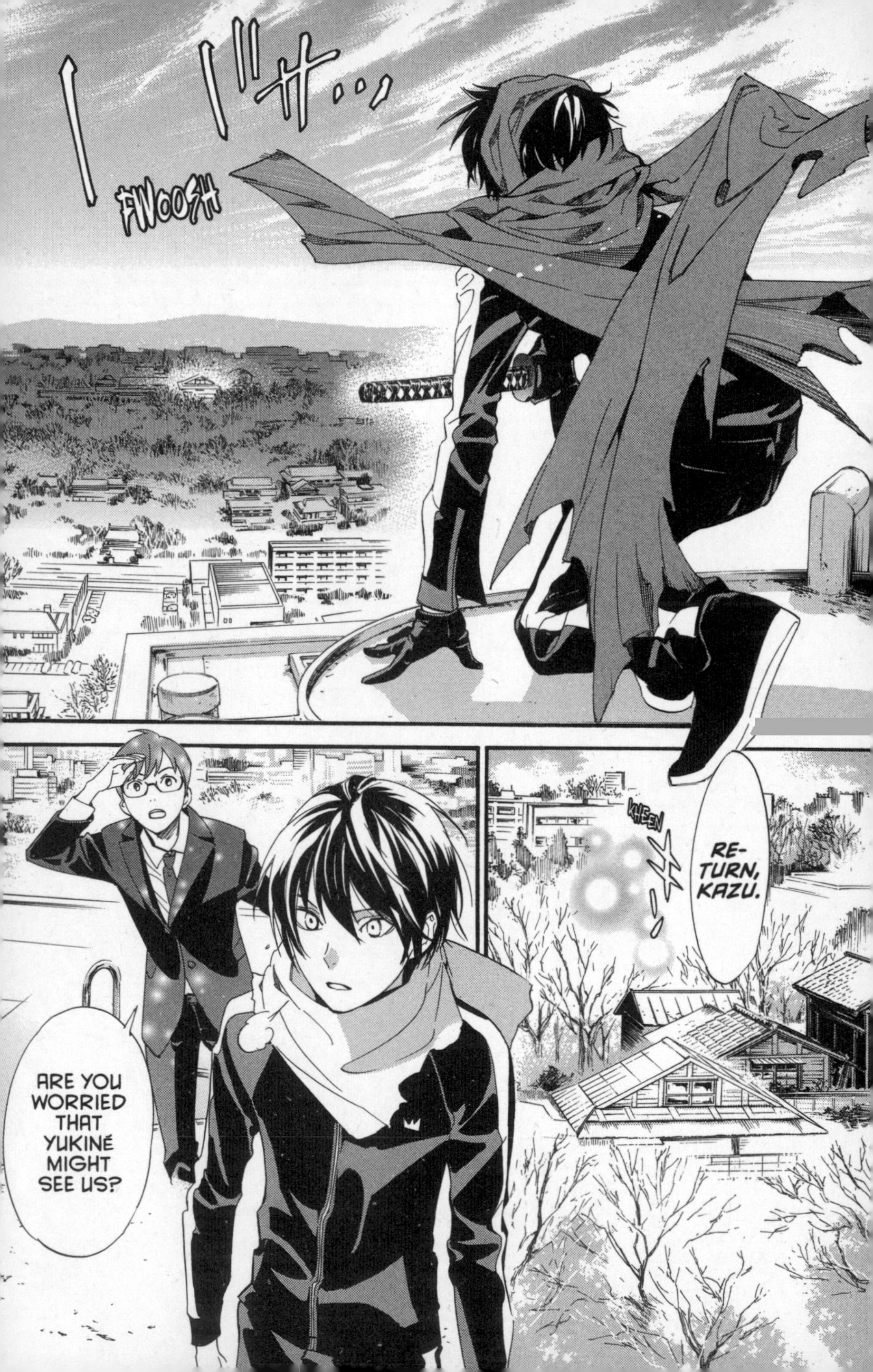
FWOOSH
KHEEN
RE-TURN, KAZU.
ARE YOU WORRIED THAT YUKINÉ MIGHT SEE US?

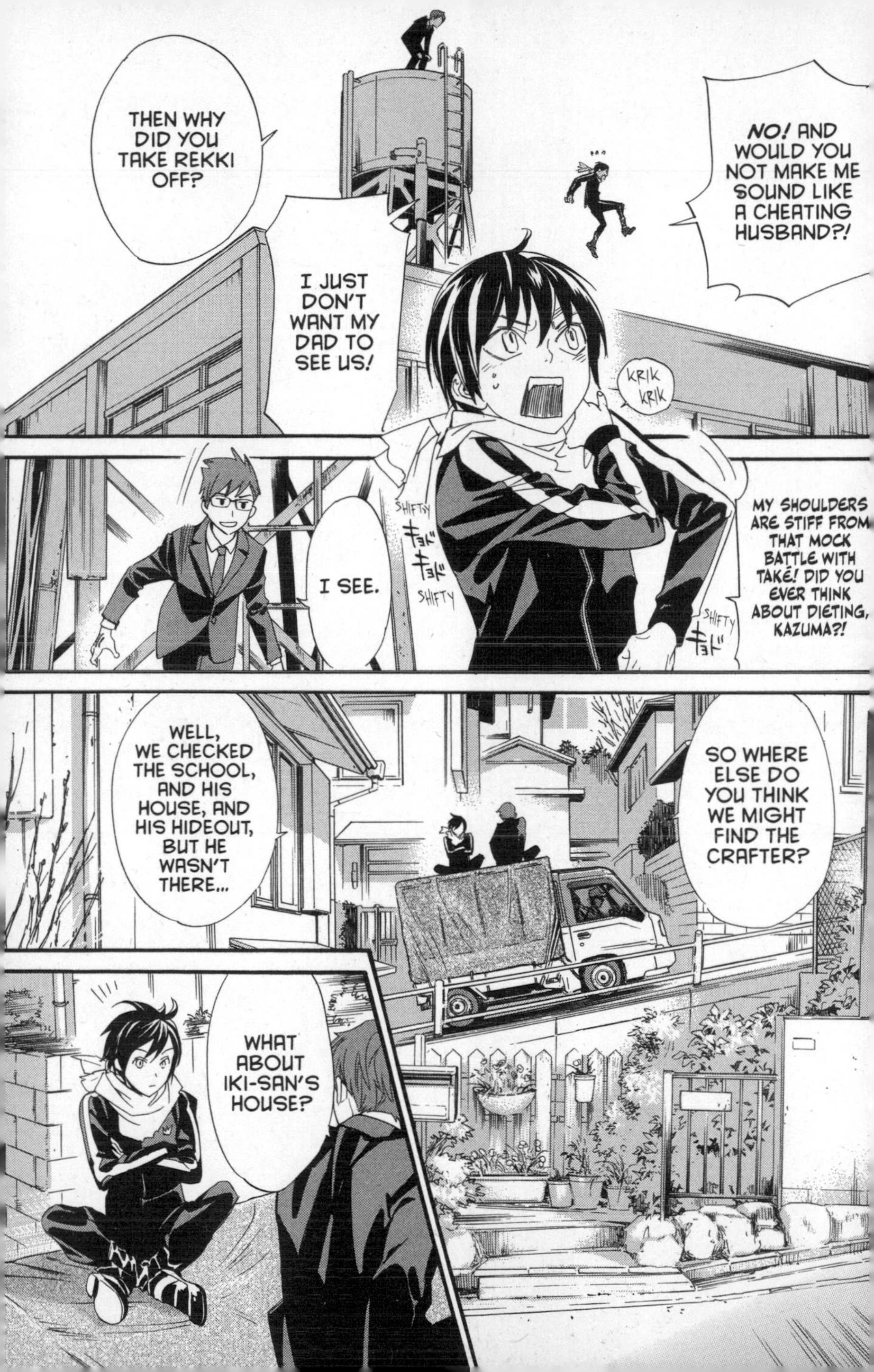
NO! AND WOULD YOU NOT MAKE ME SOUND LIKE A CHEATING HUSBAND?!
THEN WHY DID YOU TAKE REKKI OFF?
I JUST DON'T WANT MY DAD TO SEE US!
KRIK KRIK
MY SHOULDERS ARE STIFF FROM THAT MOCK BATTLE WITH TAKÉ! DID YOU EVER THINK ABOUT DIETING, KAZUMA?!
SHIFTY
SHIFTY
SHIFTY
I SEE.
SO WHERE ELSE DO YOU THINK WE MIGHT FIND THE CRAFTER?
WELL, WE CHECKED THE SCHOOL, AND HIS HOUSE, AND HIS HIDEOUT, BUT HE WASN'T THERE...
WHAT ABOUT IKI-SAN'S HOUSE?

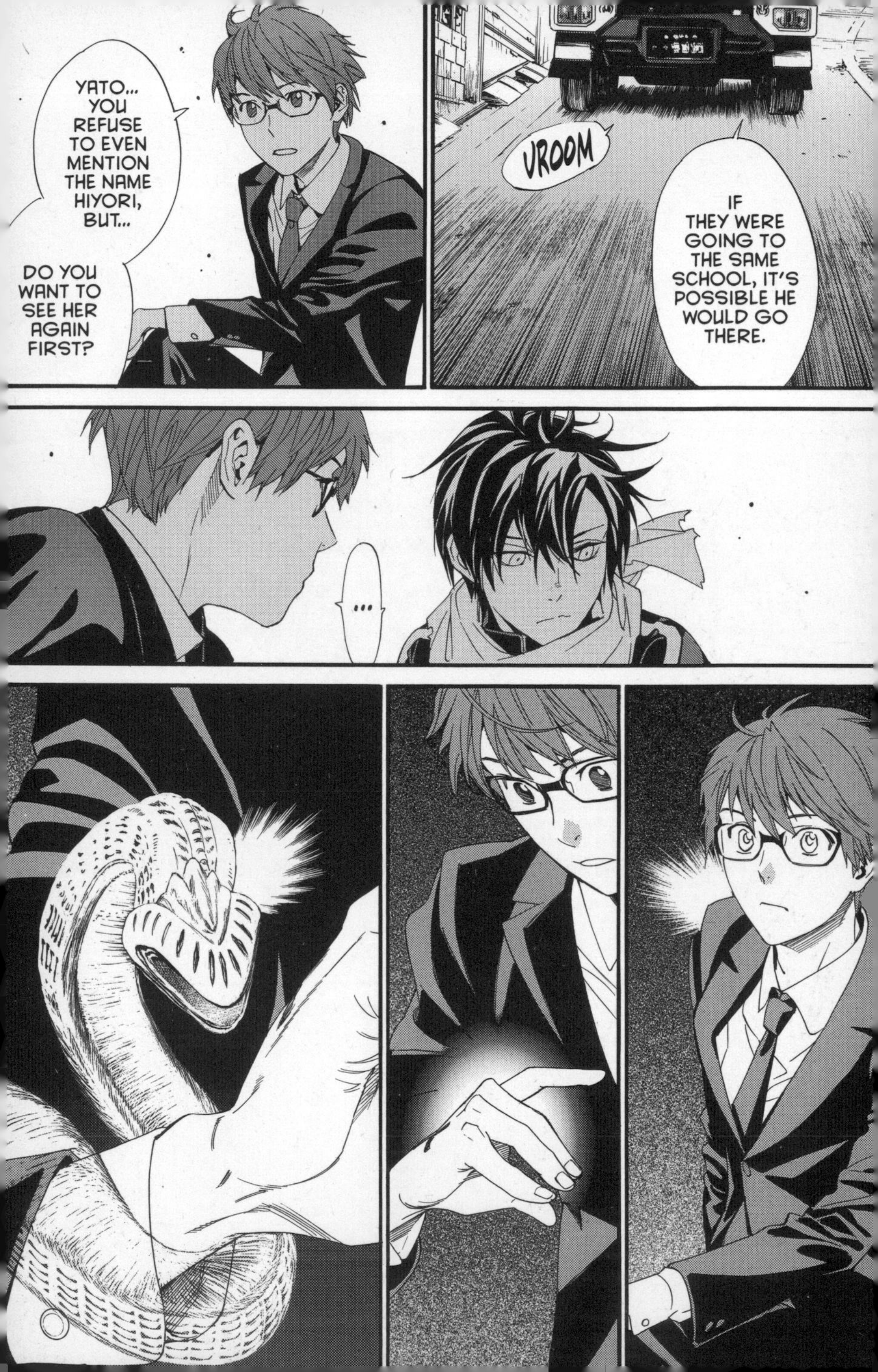
VROOM
IF THEY WERE GOING TO THE SAME SCHOOL, IT'S POSSIBLE HE WOULD GO THERE.
YATO... YOU REFUSE TO EVEN MENTION THE NAME HIYORI, BUT...
DO YOU WANT TO SEE HER AGAIN FIRST?
...

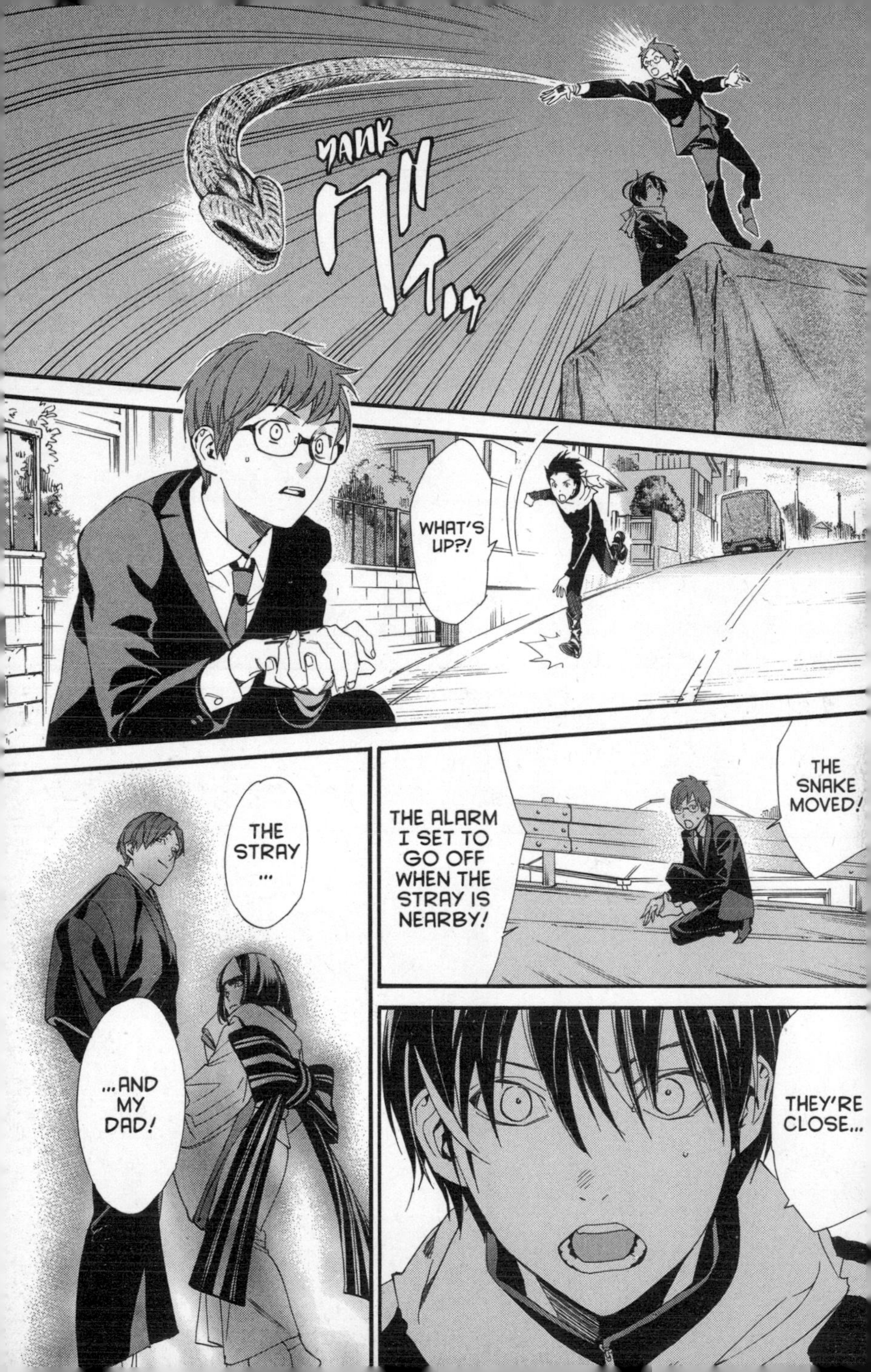
YANK
WHAT'S UP?!
THE SNAKE MOVED!
THE ALARM I SET TO GO OFF WHEN THE STRAY IS NEARBY!
THEY'RE CLOSE...
THE STRAY ...
...AND MY DAD!

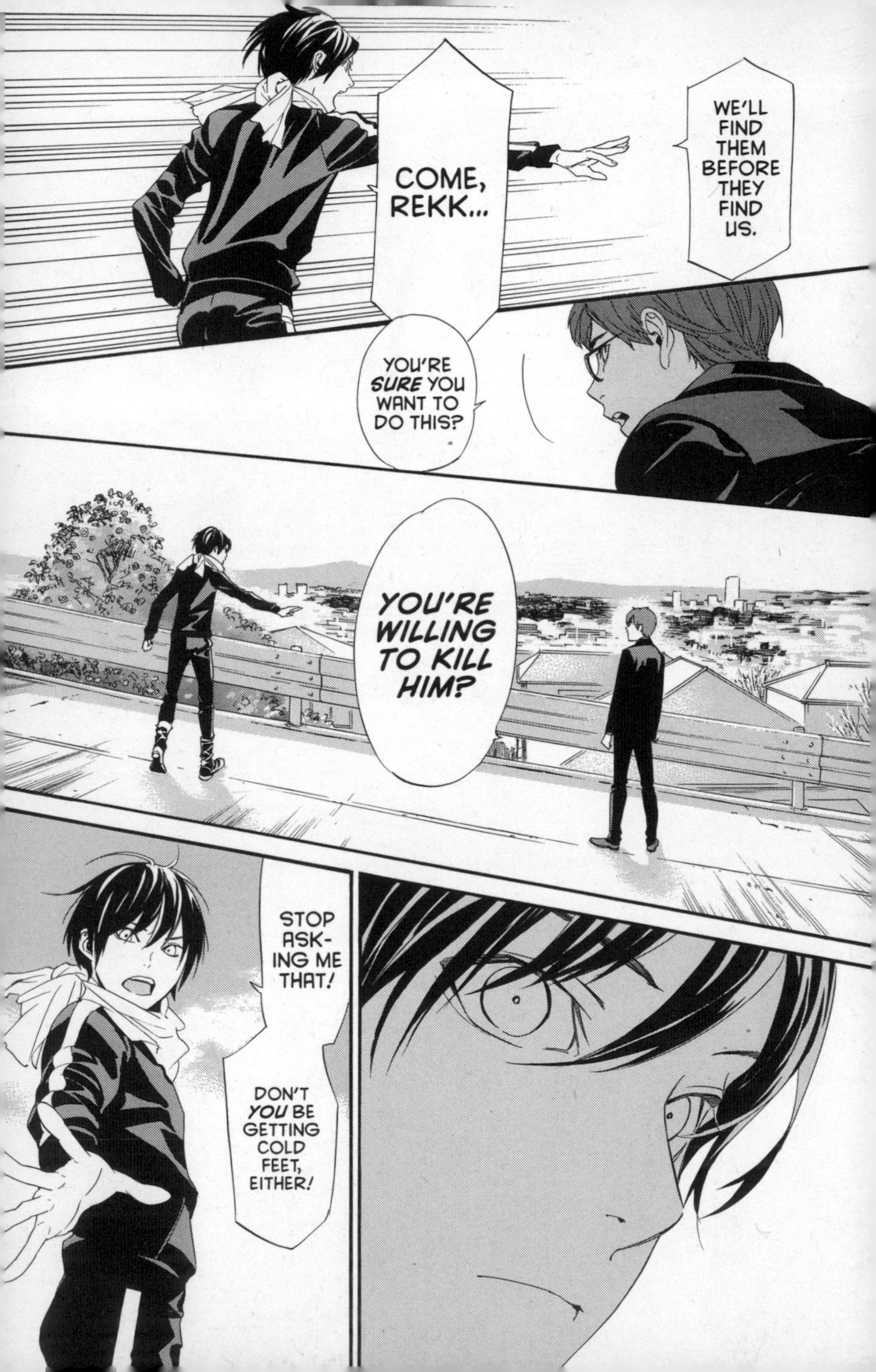
WE'LL FIND THEM BEFORE THEY FIND US.
COME, REKK...
YOU'RE *SURE* YOU WANT TO DO THIS?
YOU'RE WILLING TO KILL HIM?
STOP ASK-ING ME THAT!
DON'T *YOU* BE GETTING COLD FEET, EITHER!

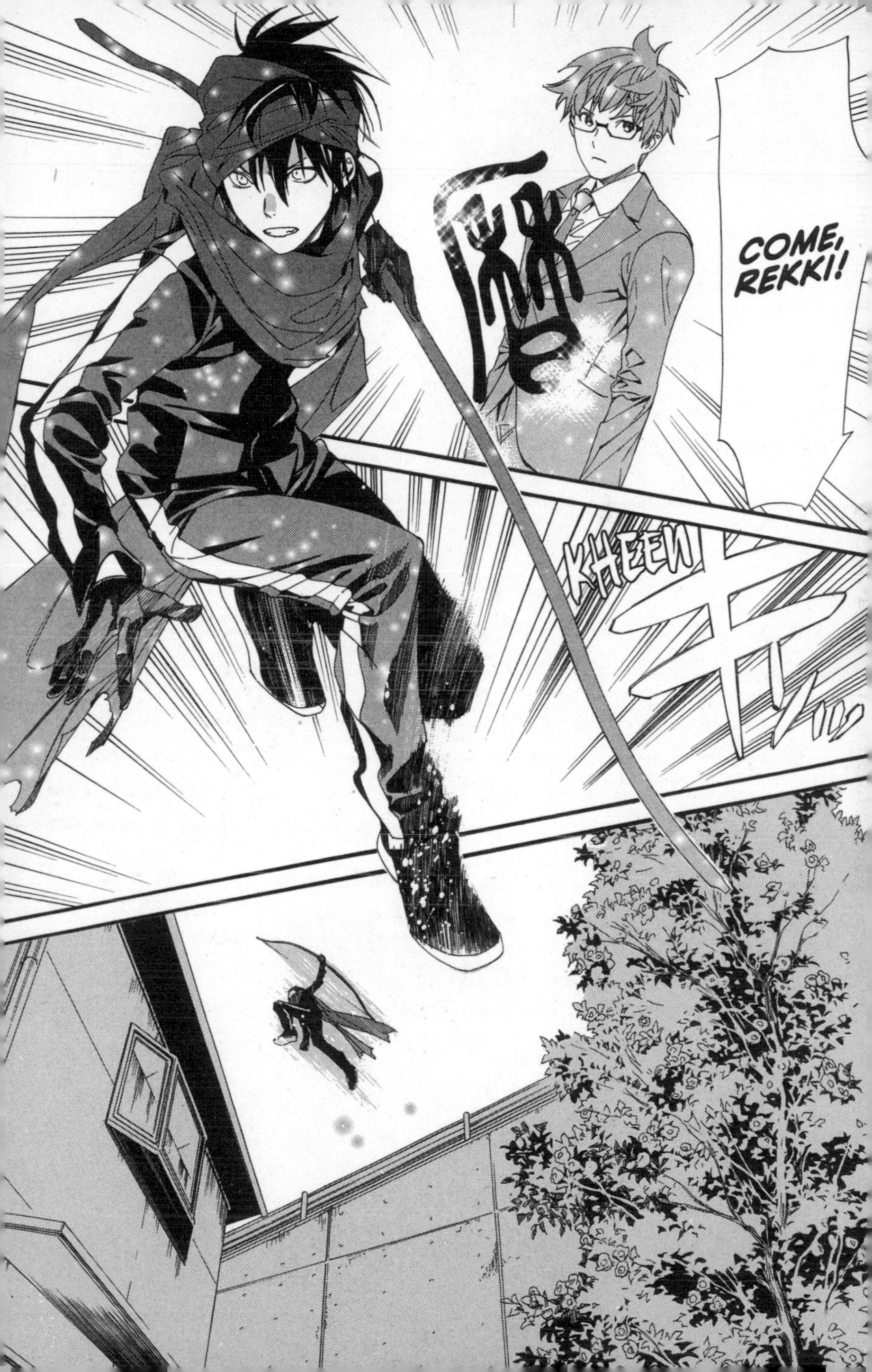
COME, REKKI!
KHEEN

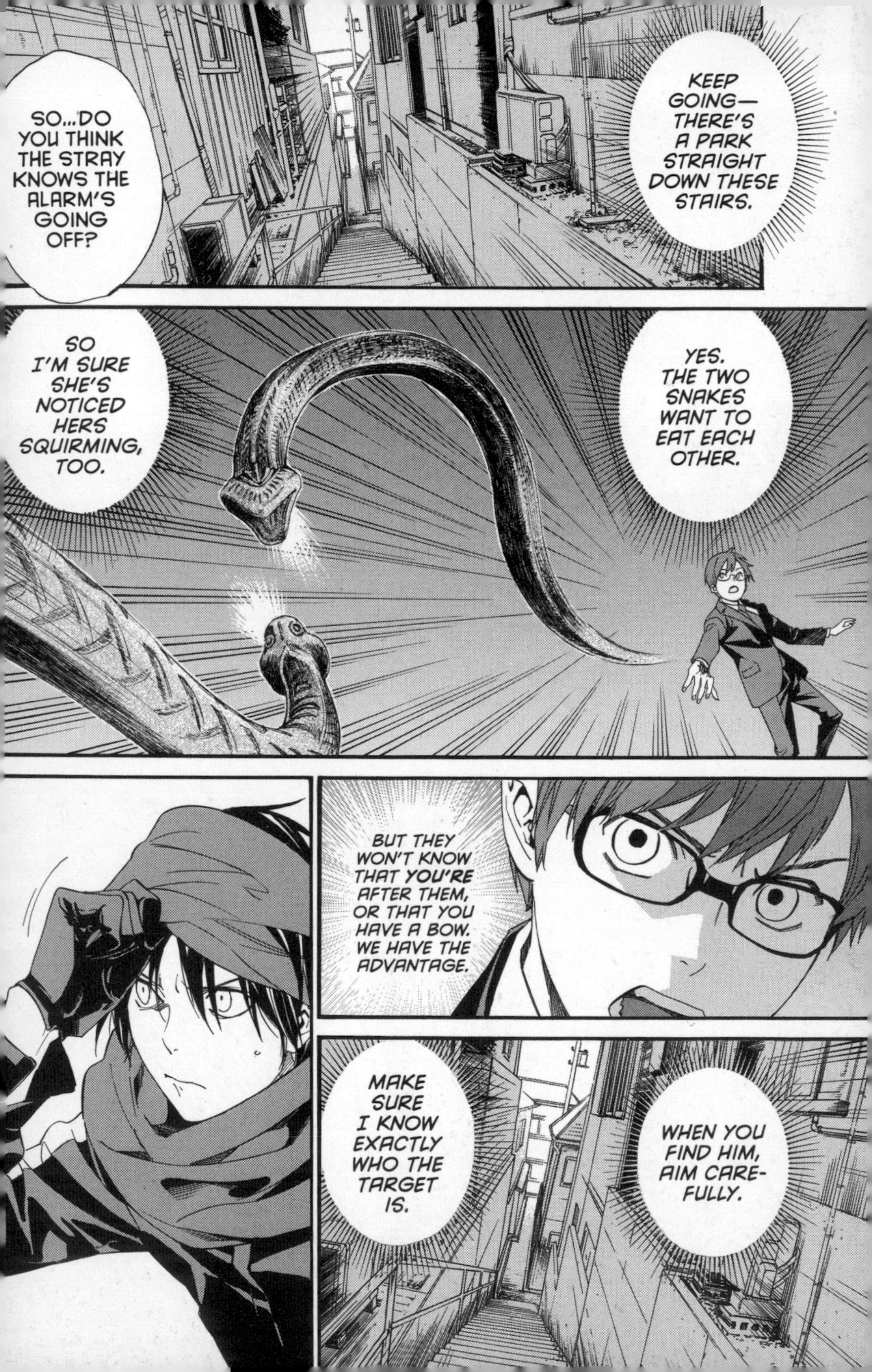
KEEP GOING— THERE'S A PARK STRAIGHT DOWN THESE STAIRS.
SO...DO YOU THINK THE STRAY KNOWS THE ALARM'S GOING OFF?
YES. THE TWO SNAKES WANT TO EAT EACH OTHER.
SO I'M SURE SHE'S NOTICED HERS SQUIRMING, TOO.
BUT THEY WON'T KNOW THAT *YOU'RE* AFTER THEM, OR THAT YOU HAVE A BOW. WE HAVE THE ADVANTAGE.
WHEN YOU FIND HIM, AIM CARE-FULLY.
MAKE SURE I KNOW EXACTLY WHO THE TARGET IS.

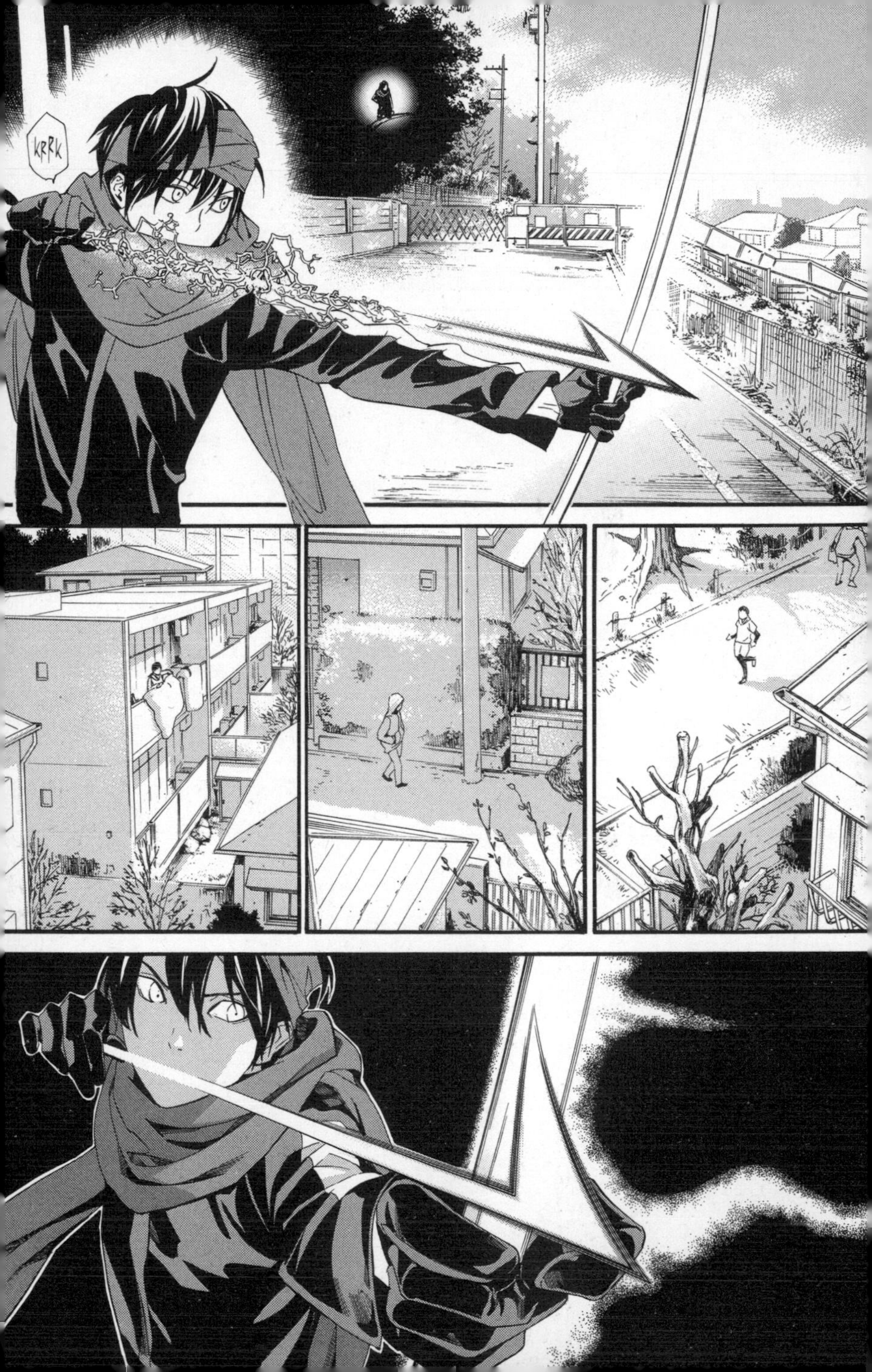
KRRK

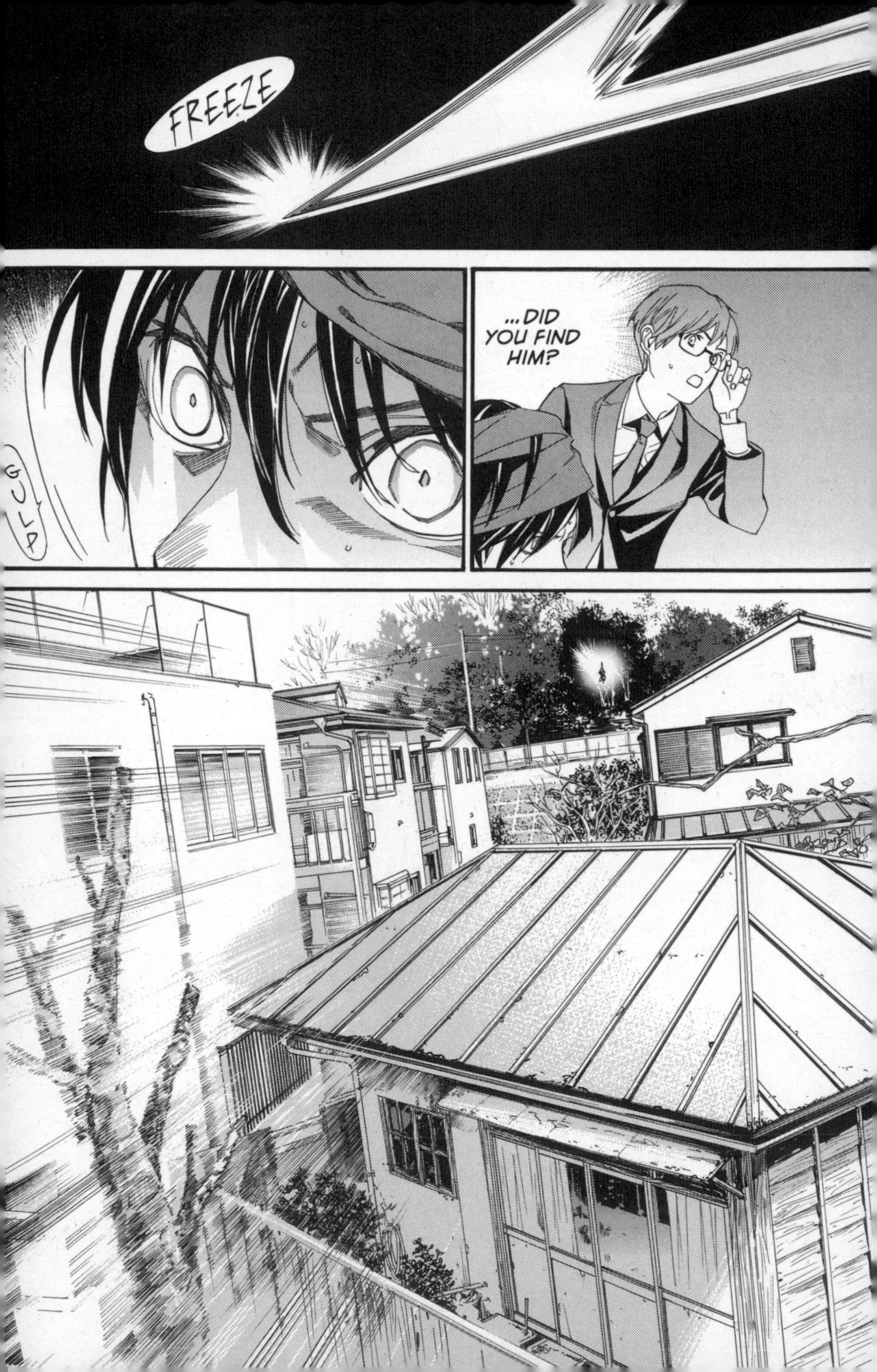
FREEZE
...DID YOU FIND HIM?
GULP

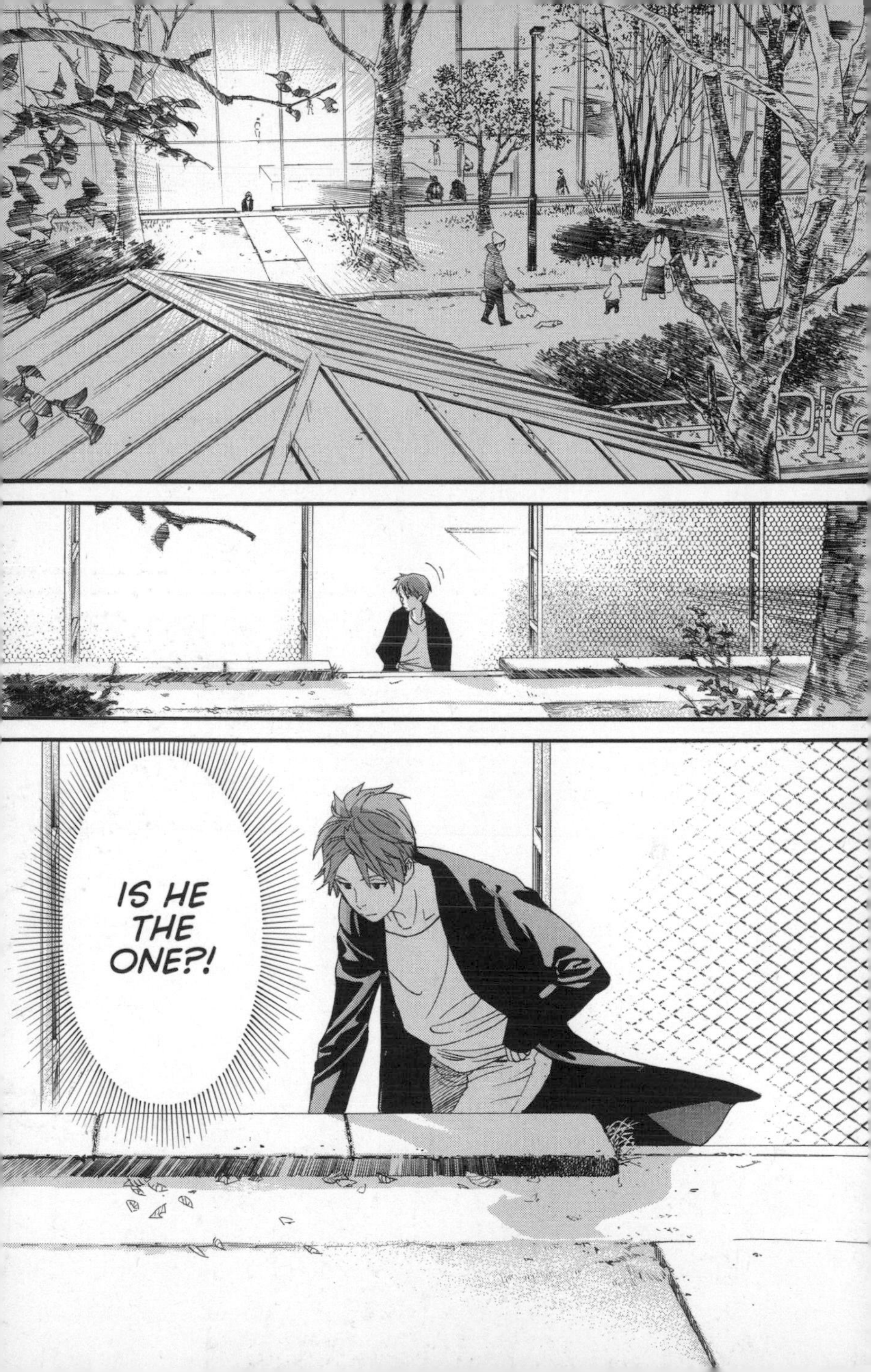
IS HE THE ONE?!

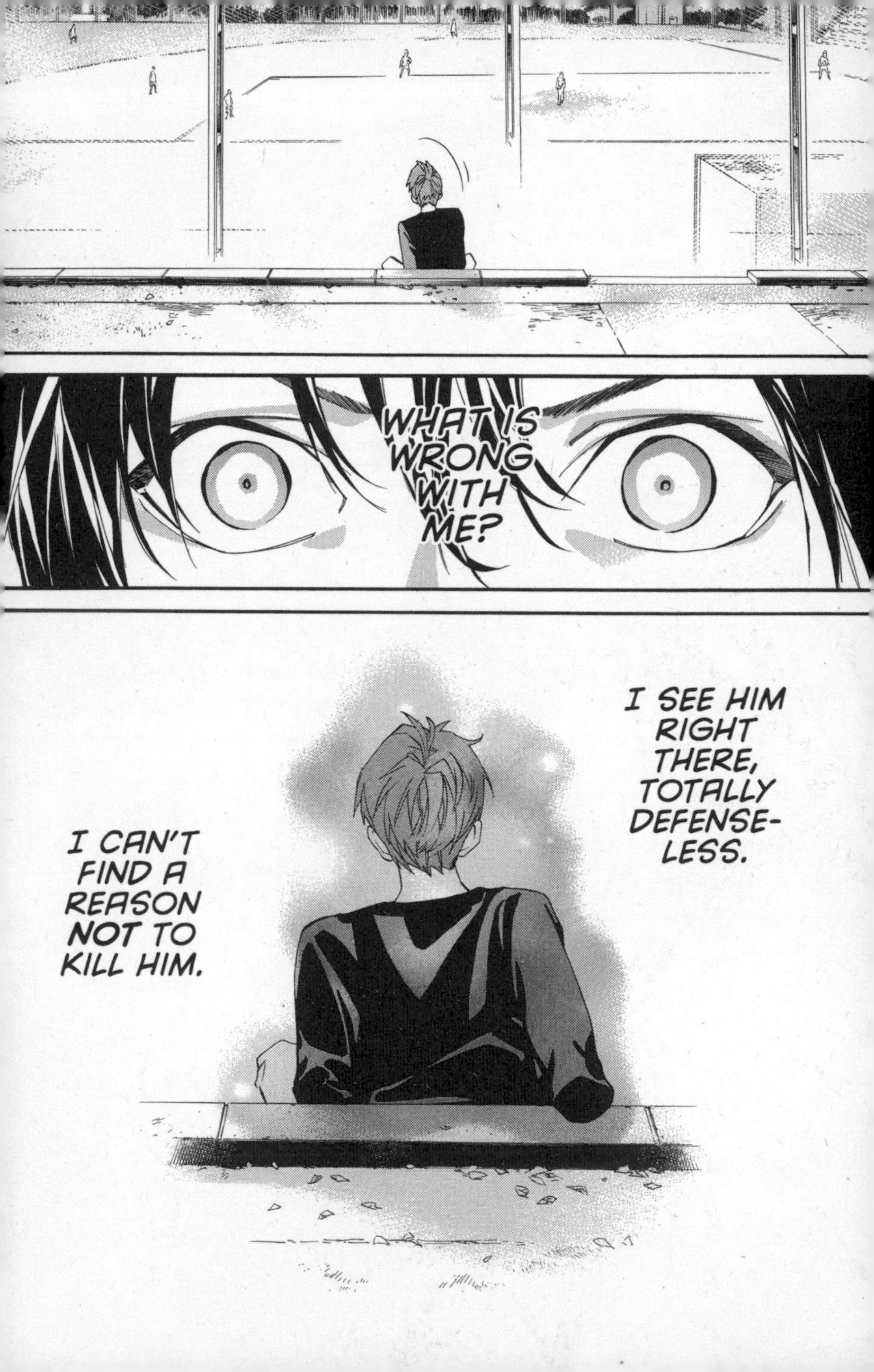
WHAT IS WRONG WITH ME?
I SEE HIM RIGHT THERE, TOTALLY DEFENSE-LESS.
I CAN'T FIND A REASON NOT TO KILL HIM.

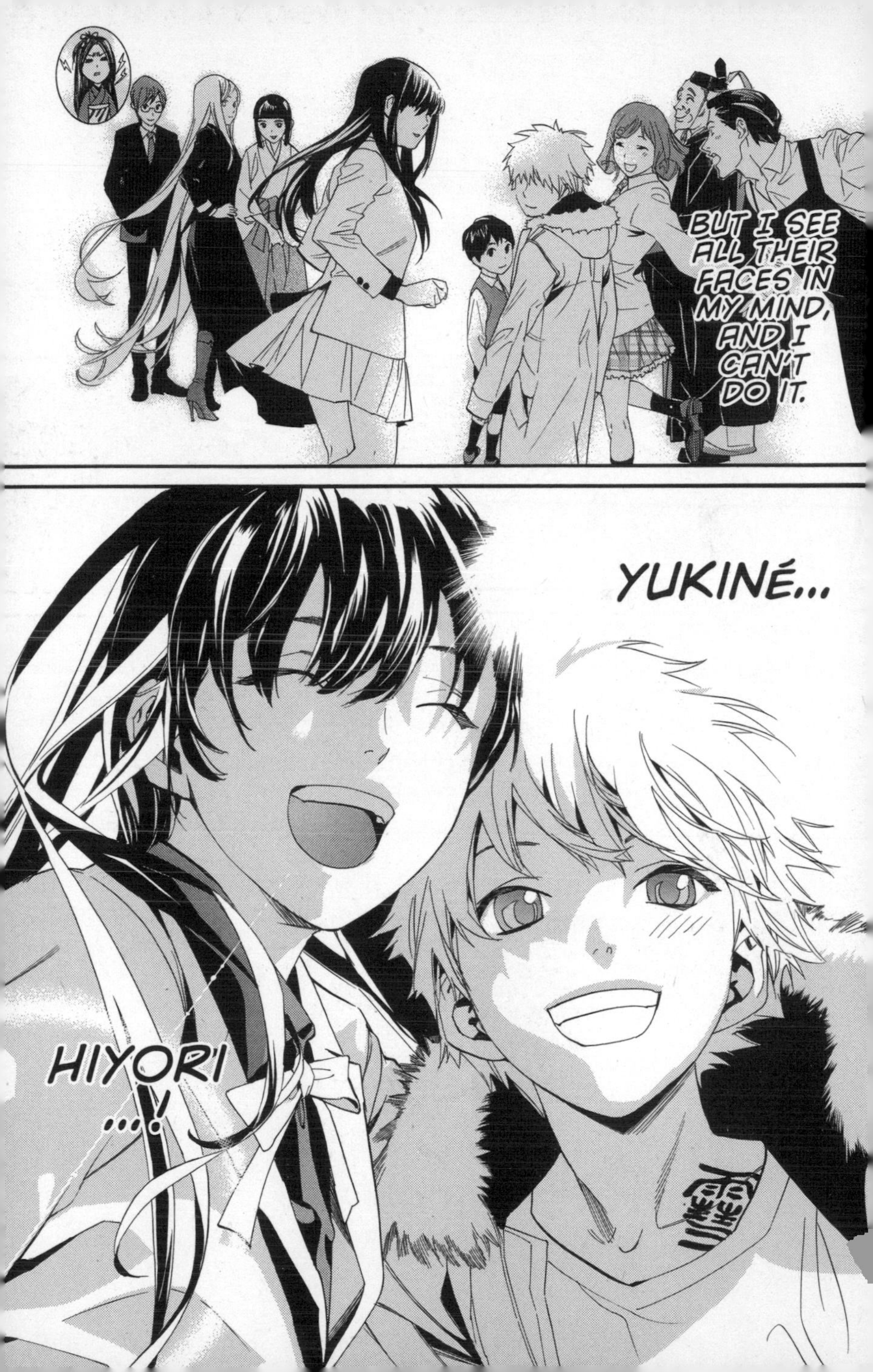
BUT I SEE ALL THEIR FACES IN MY MIND, AND I CAN'T DO IT.
YUKINÉ...
HIYORI ...!

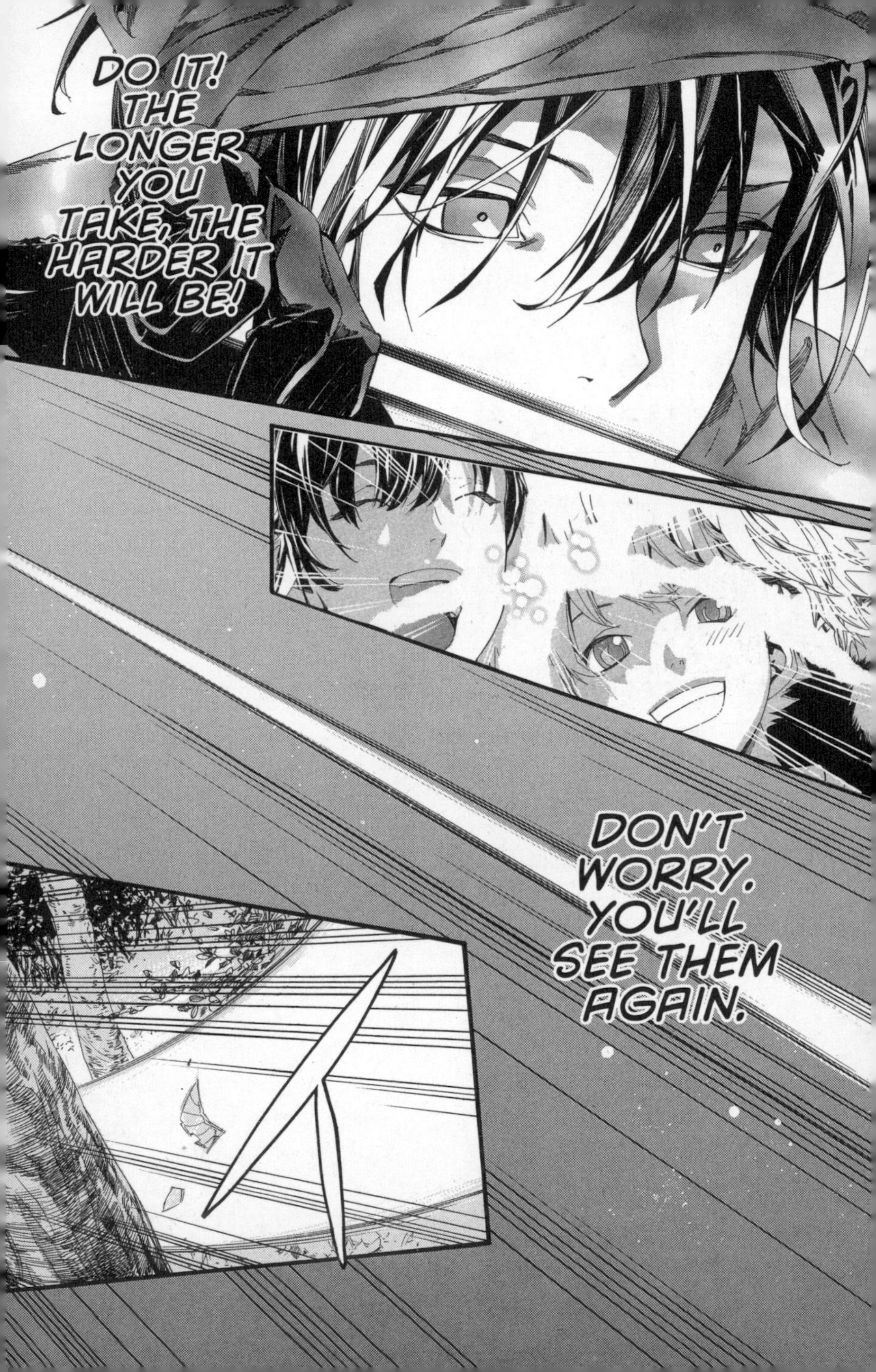
DO IT! THE LONGER YOU TAKE, THE HARDER IT WILL BE!
DON'T WORRY. YOU'LL SEE THEM AGAIN.

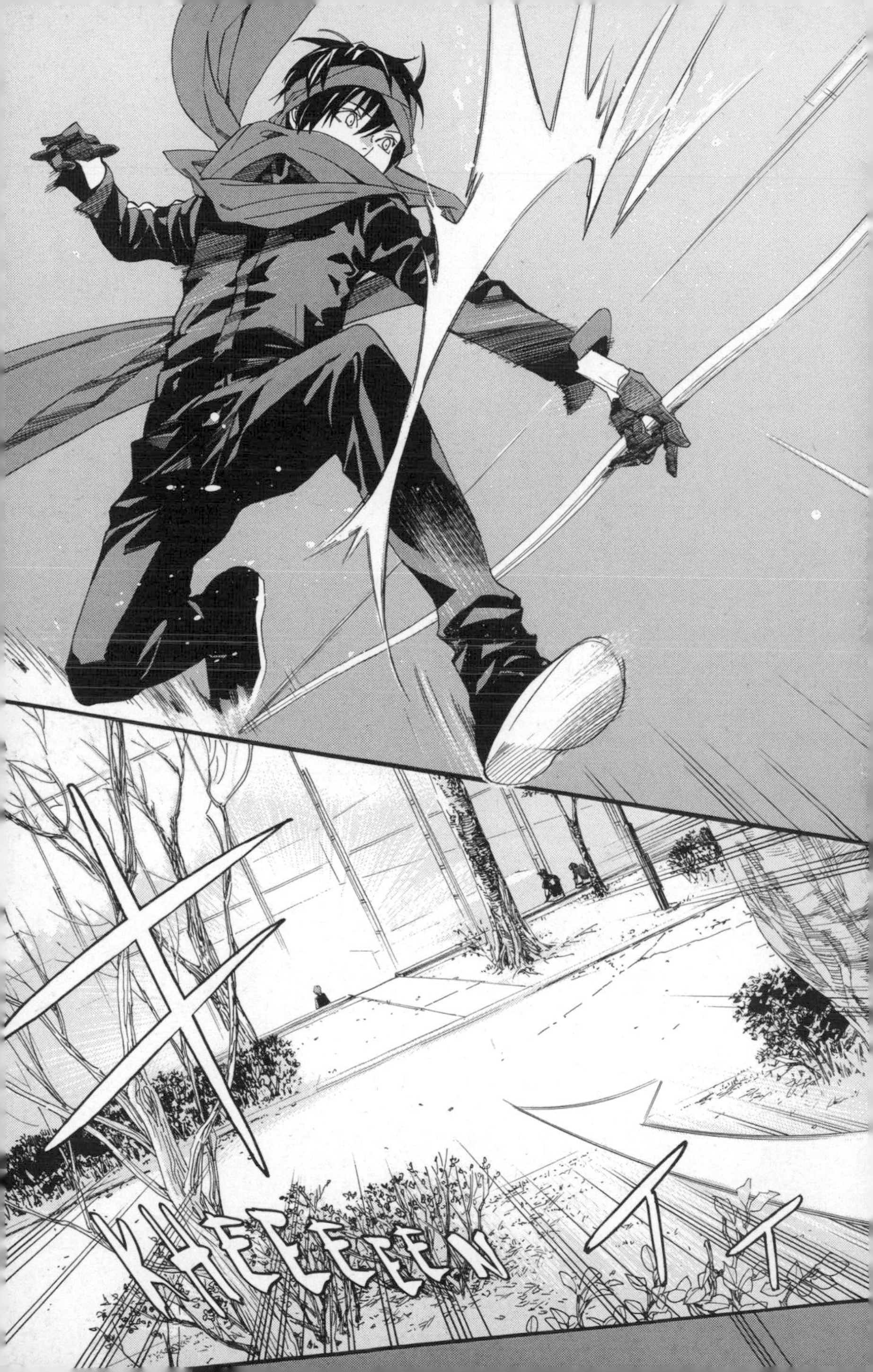
KHEEEEEN

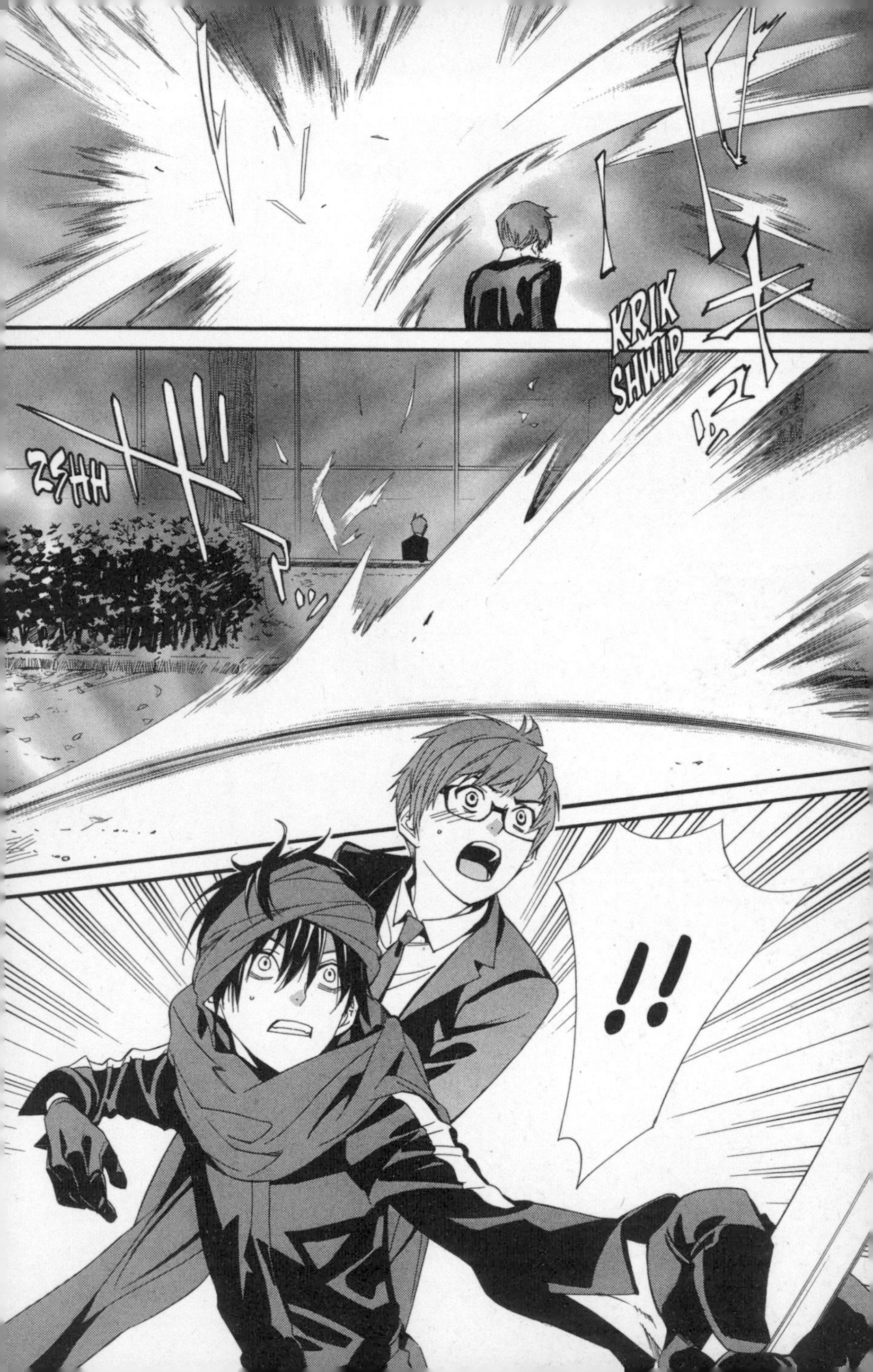
KRIK
SHWIP
ZSHH
!!

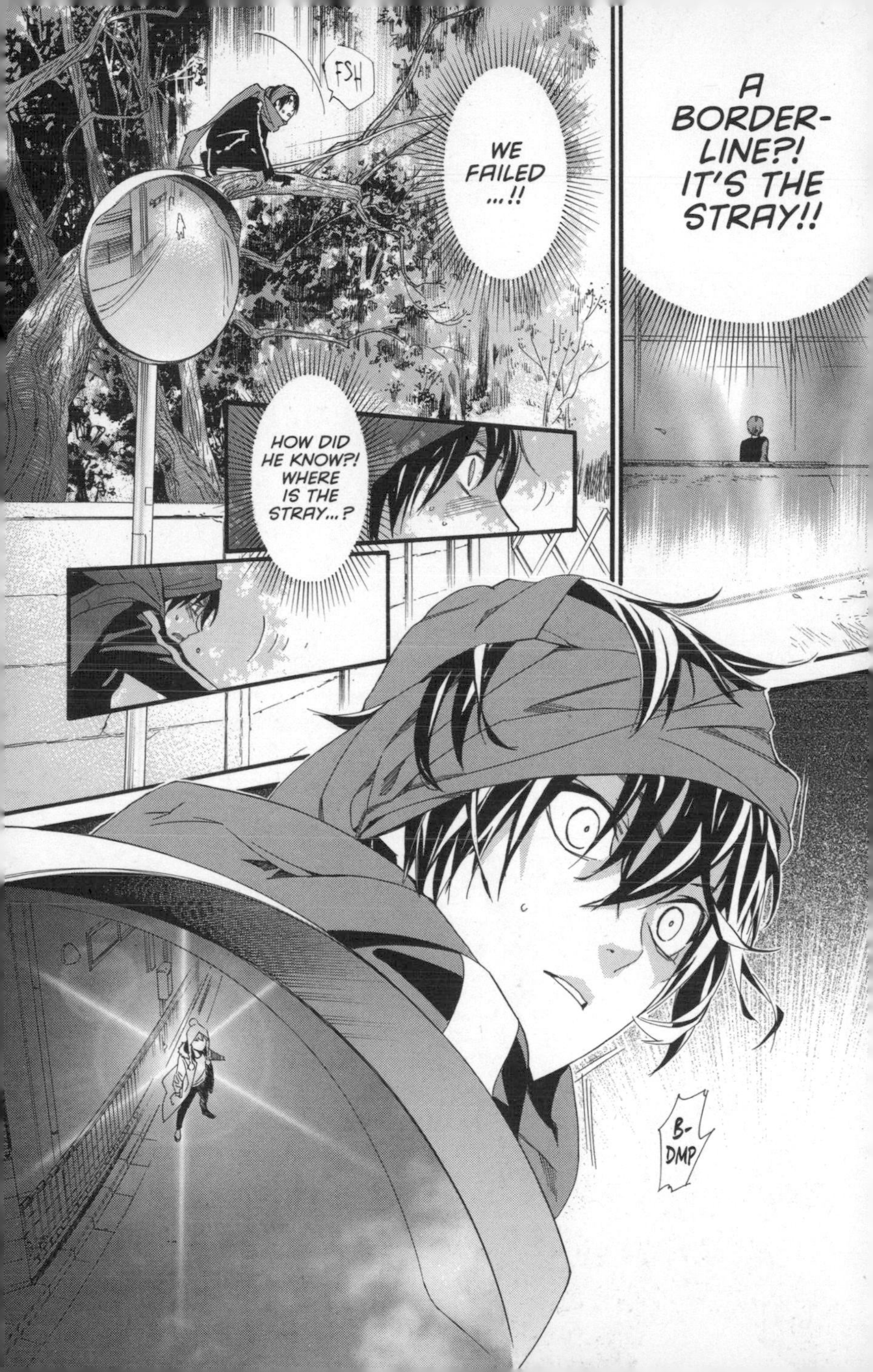
A BORDER-LINE?! IT'S THE STRAY!!
FSH
WE FAILED ...!!
HOW DID HE KNOW?! WHERE IS THE STRAY...?
B-DMP

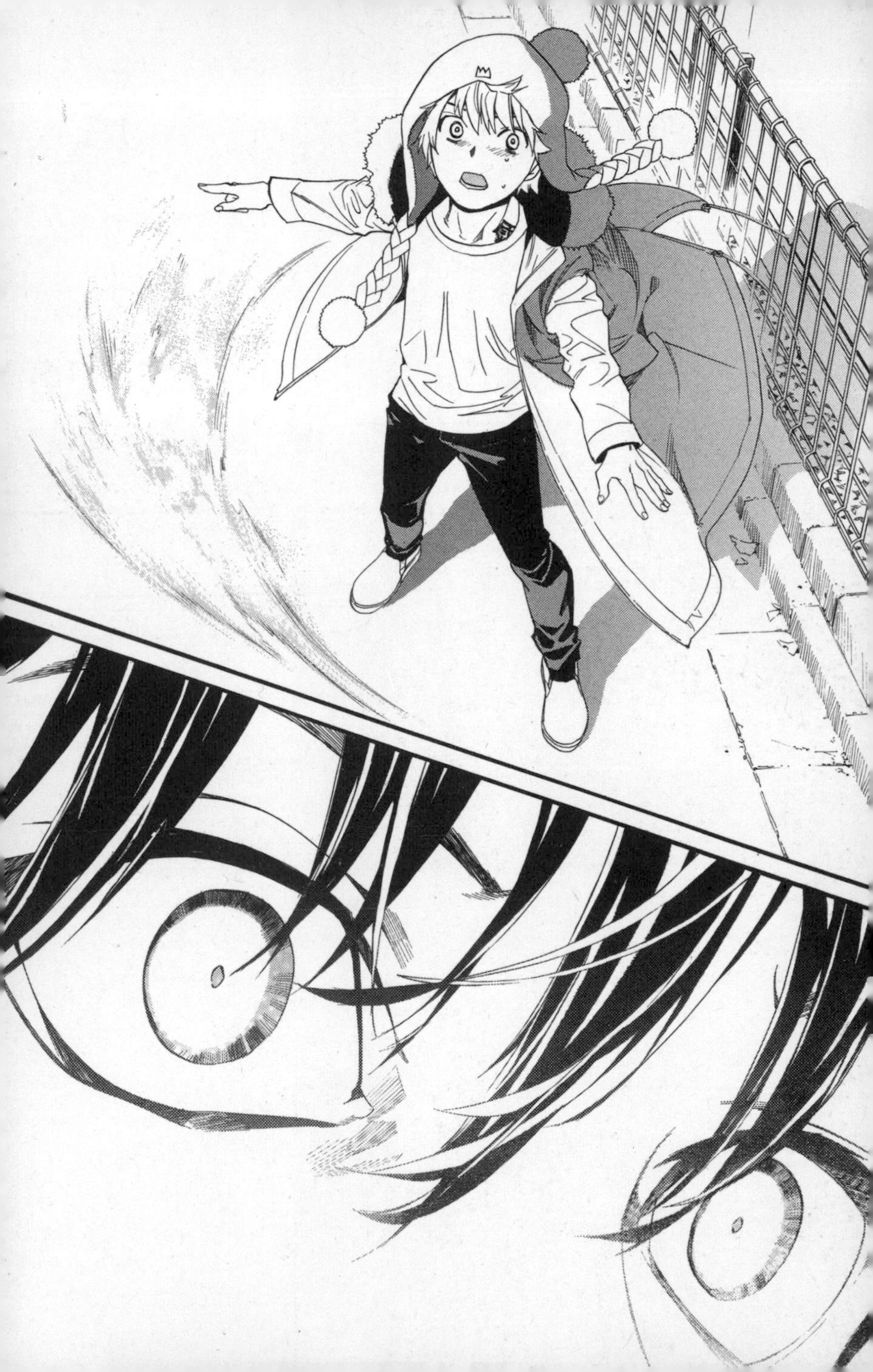

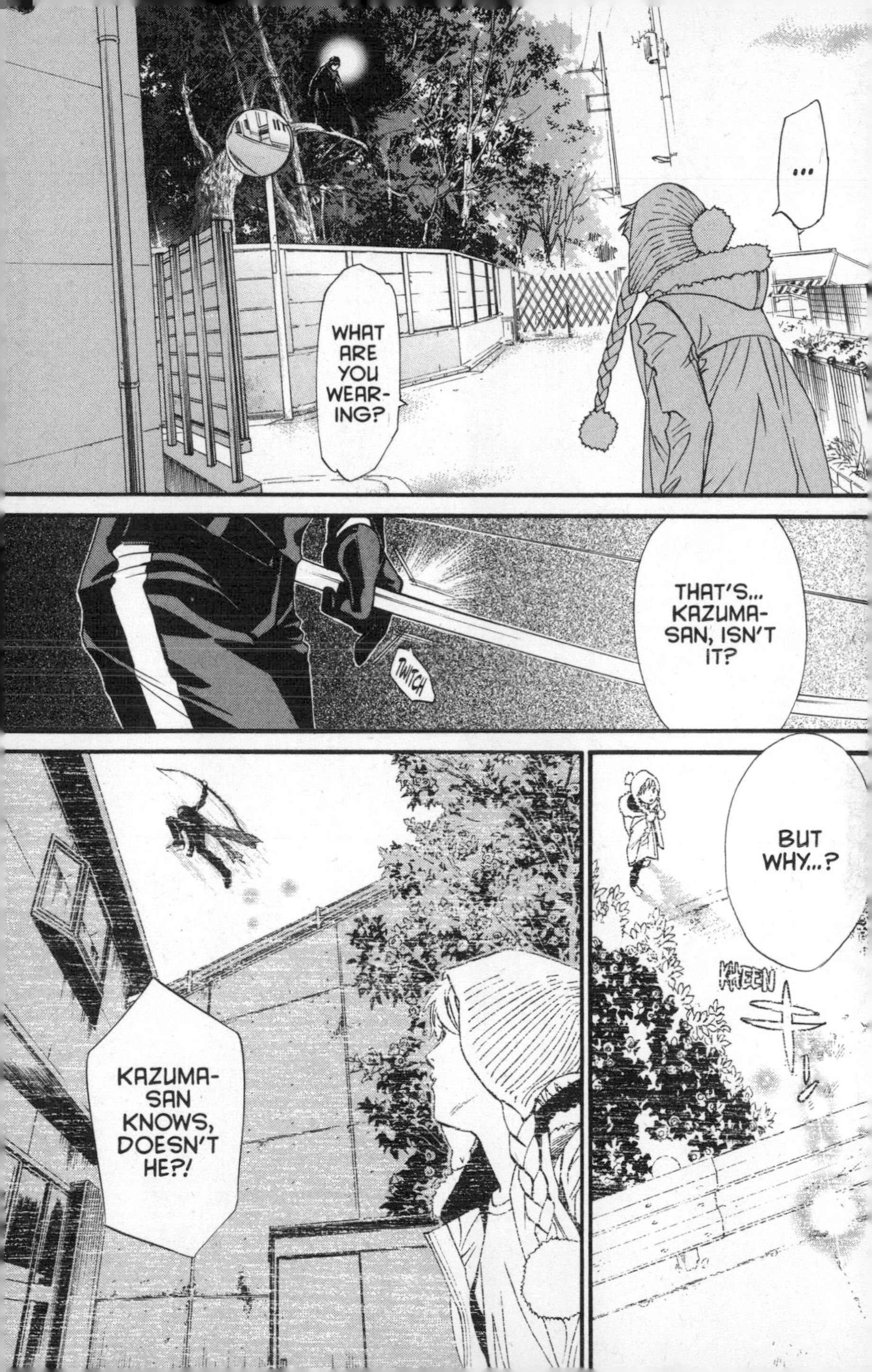
...
WHAT ARE YOU WEARING?
TWITCH
THAT'S... KAZUMA-SAN, ISN'T IT?
BUT WHY...?
KHEEN
KAZUMA-SAN KNOWS, DOESN'T HE?!

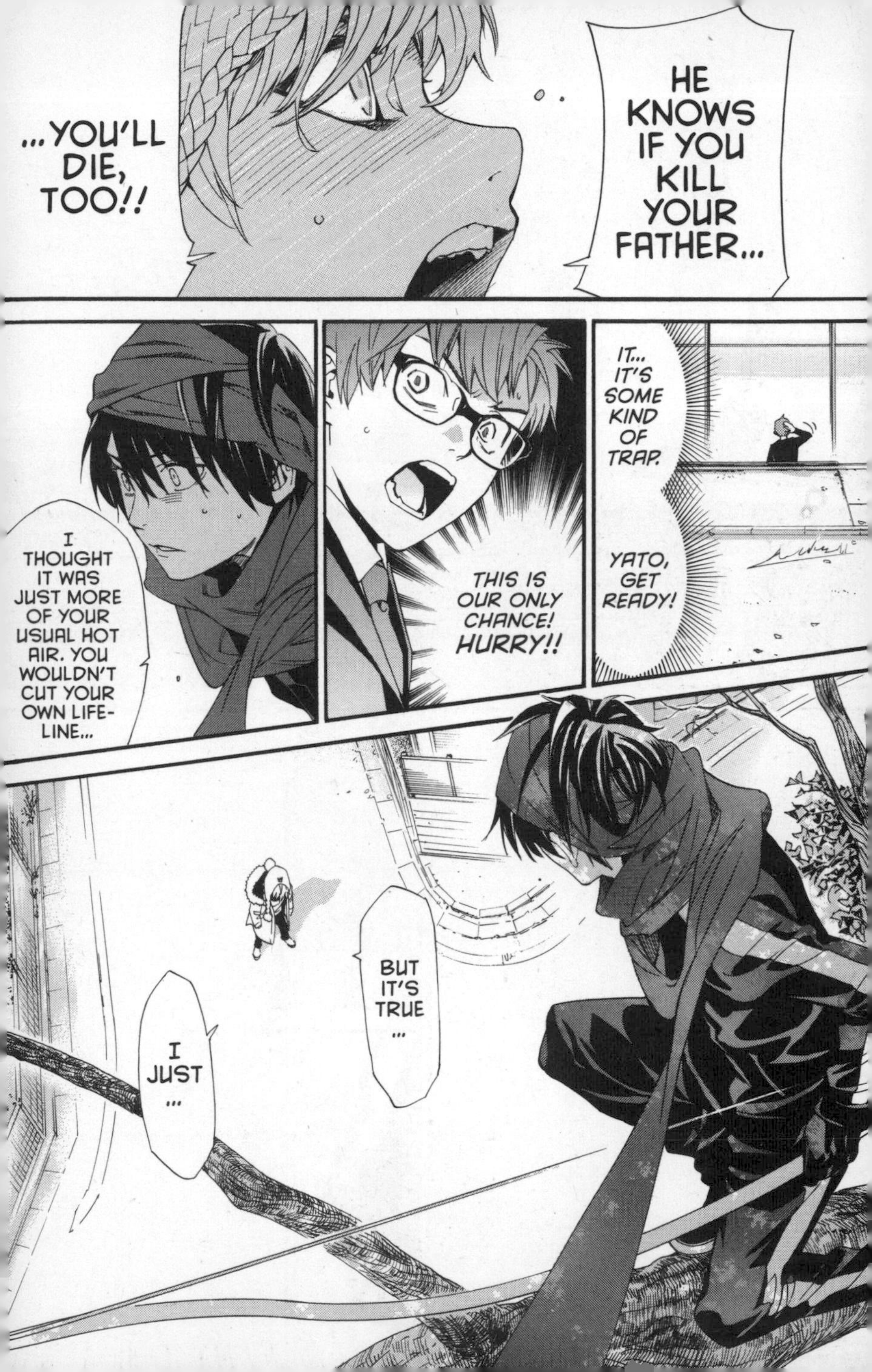
HE KNOWS IF YOU KILL YOUR FATHER...
...YOU'LL DIE, TOO!!
IT... IT'S SOME KIND OF TRAP.
YATO, GET READY!
THIS IS OUR ONLY CHANCE! HURRY!!
I THOUGHT IT WAS JUST MORE OF YOUR USUAL HOT AIR. YOU WOULDN'T CUT YOUR OWN LIFE-LINE...
BUT IT'S TRUE...
I JUST...

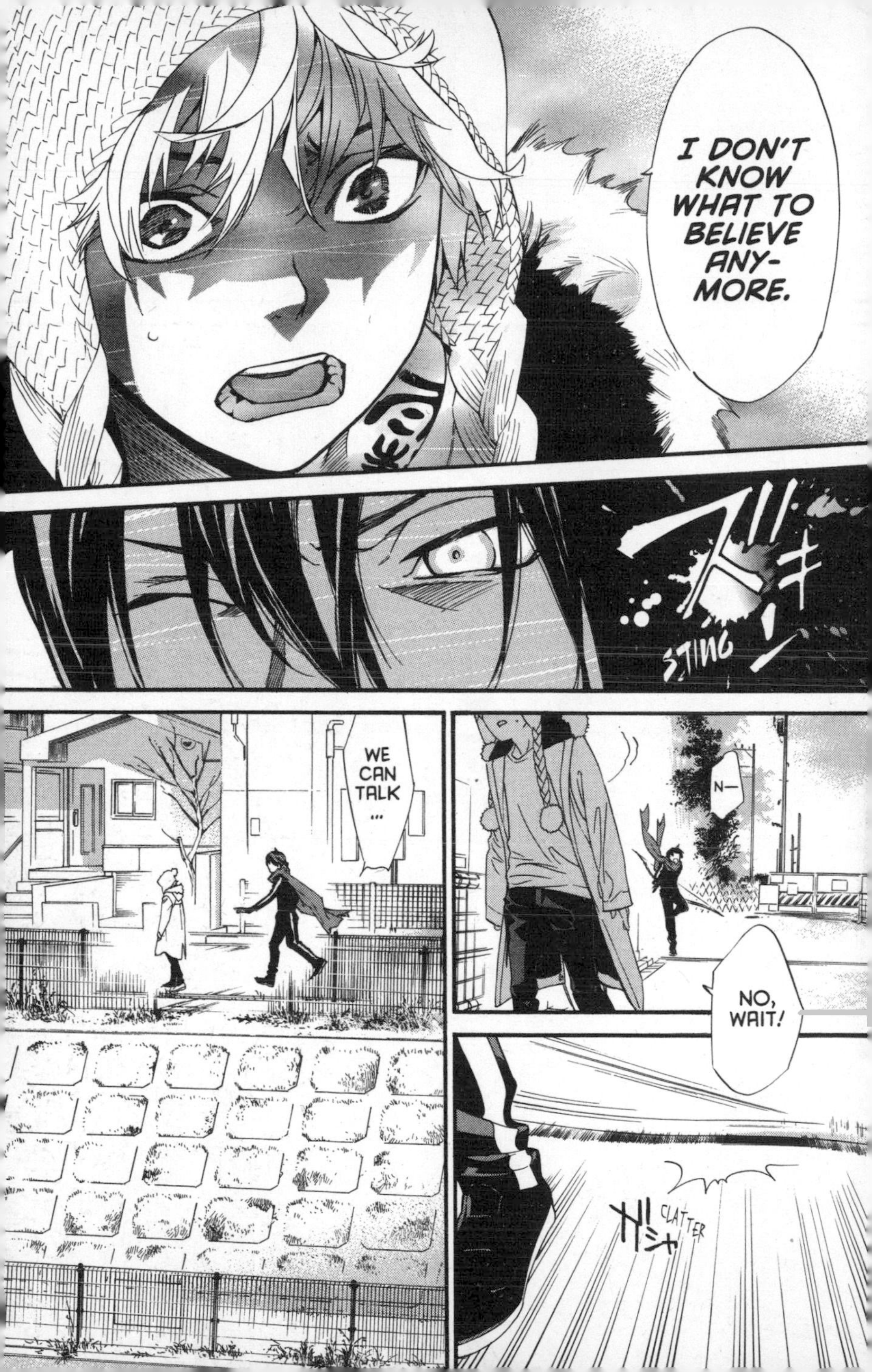
I DON'T KNOW WHAT TO BELIEVE ANY-MORE.
STING
N—
NO, WAIT!
CLATTER
WE CAN TALK ...

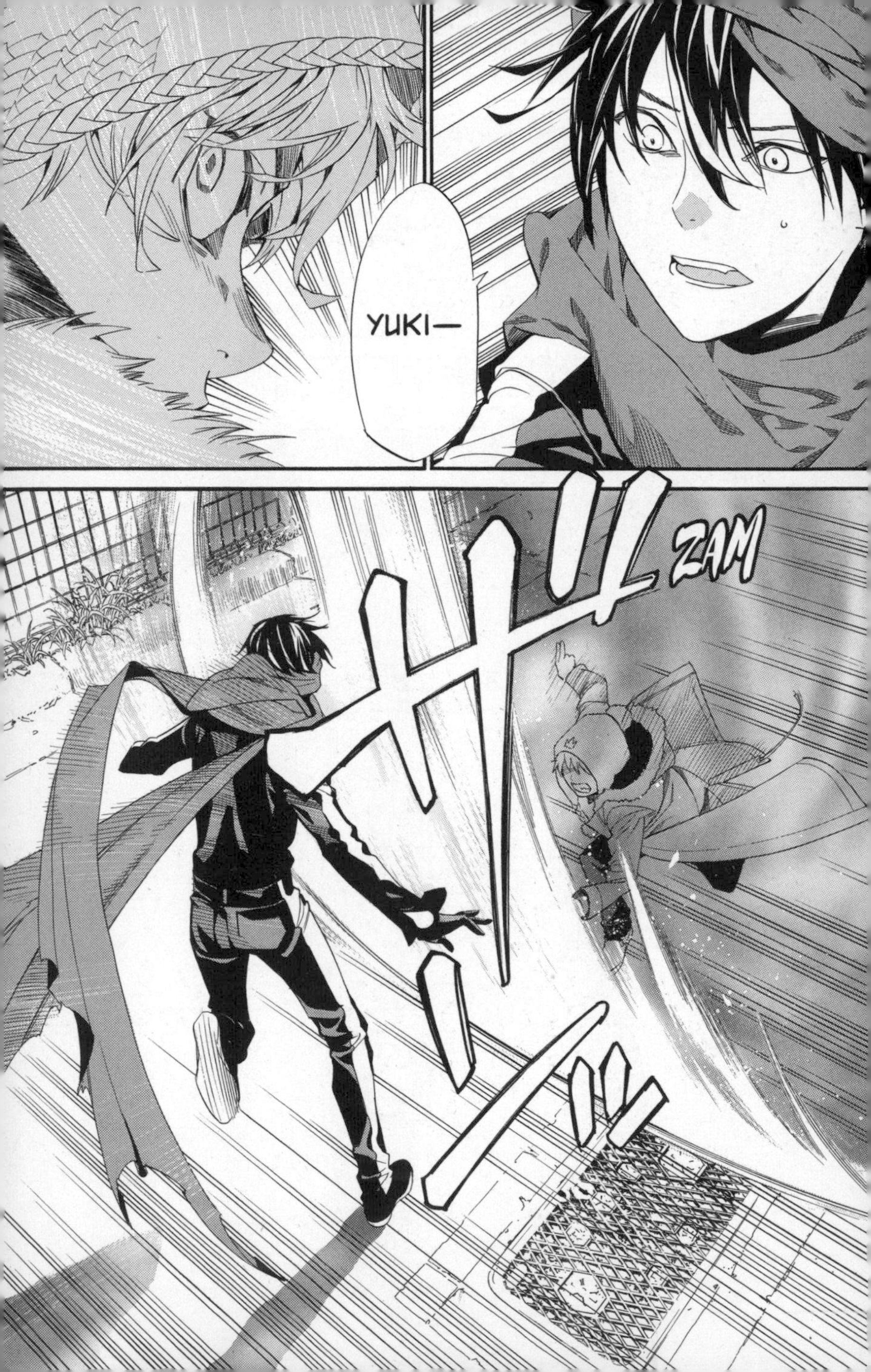
YUKI—
ZAM

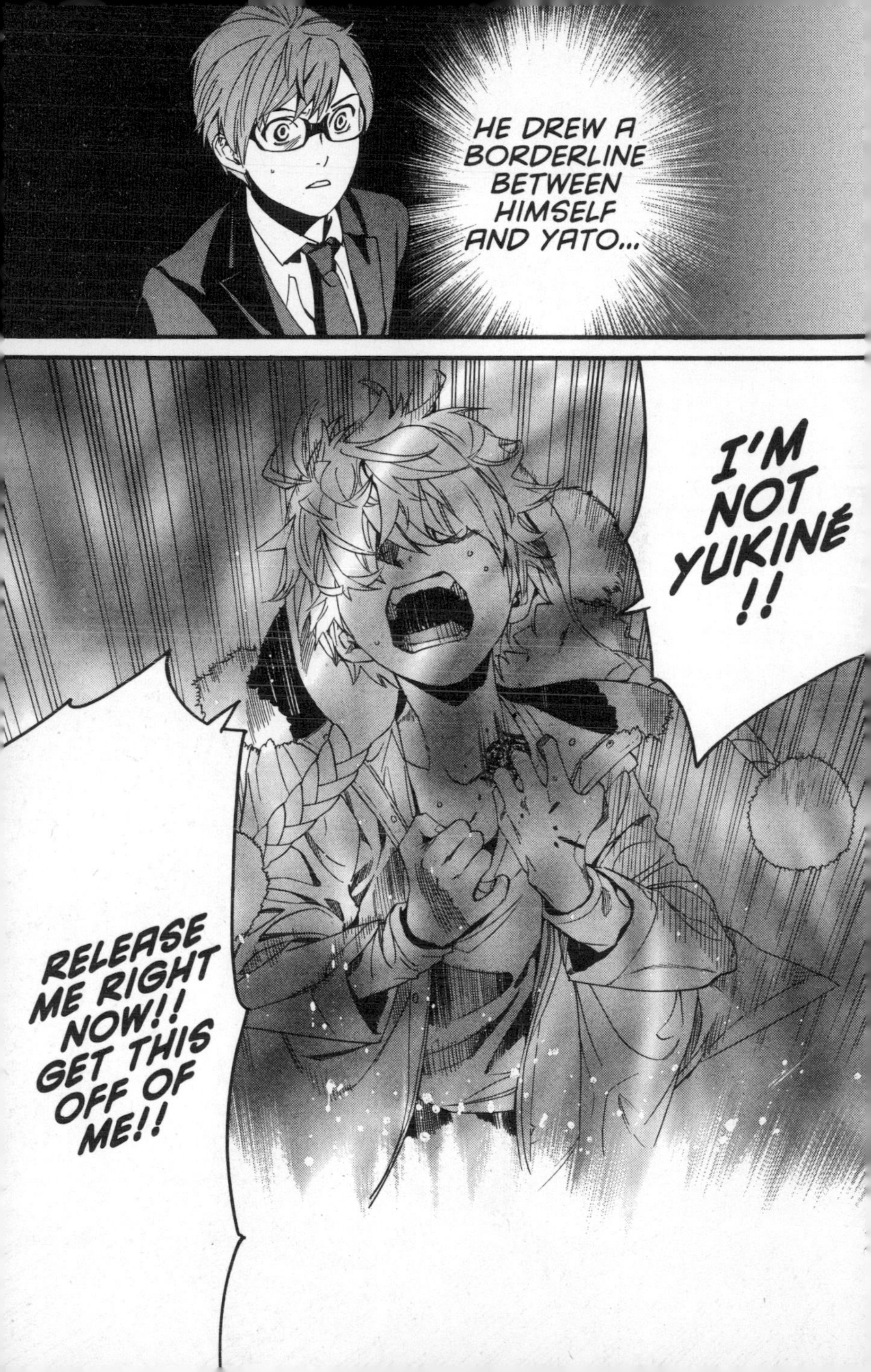
HE DREW A BORDERLINE BETWEEN HIMSELF AND YATO...
I'M NOT YUKINE!!
RELEASE ME RIGHT NOW!! GET THIS OFF OF ME!!

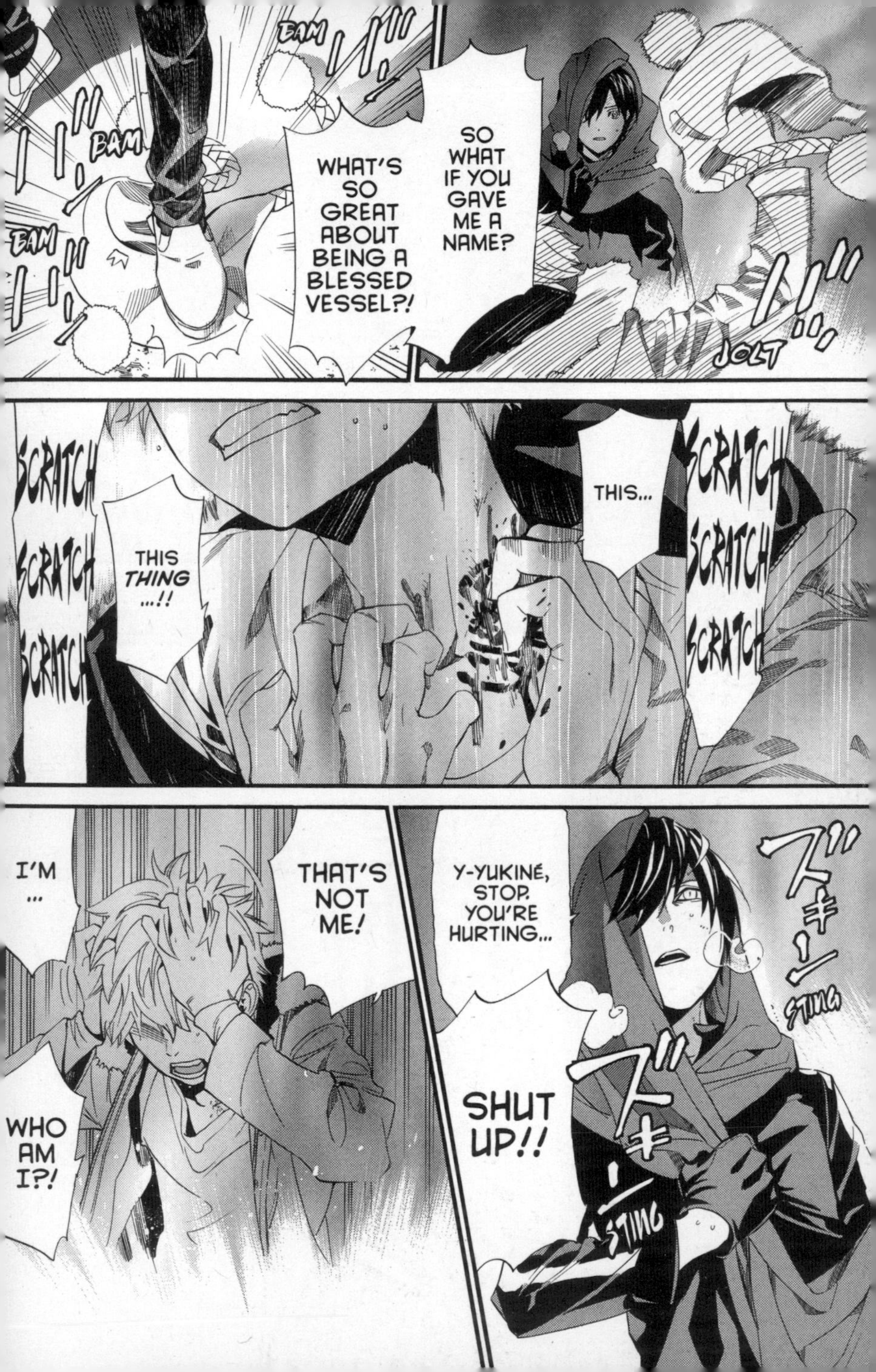
JOLT
SO WHAT IF YOU GAVE ME A NAME?
WHAT'S SO GREAT ABOUT BEING A BLESSED VESSEL?!
BAM
BAM
BAM
SCRATCH SCRATCH SCRATCH
THIS...
THIS *THING* ...!!
SCRATCH SCRATCH SCRATCH
STING
Y-YUKINÉ, STOP. YOU'RE HURTING...
STING
SHUT UP!!
THAT'S NOT ME!
I'M ...
WHO AM I?!

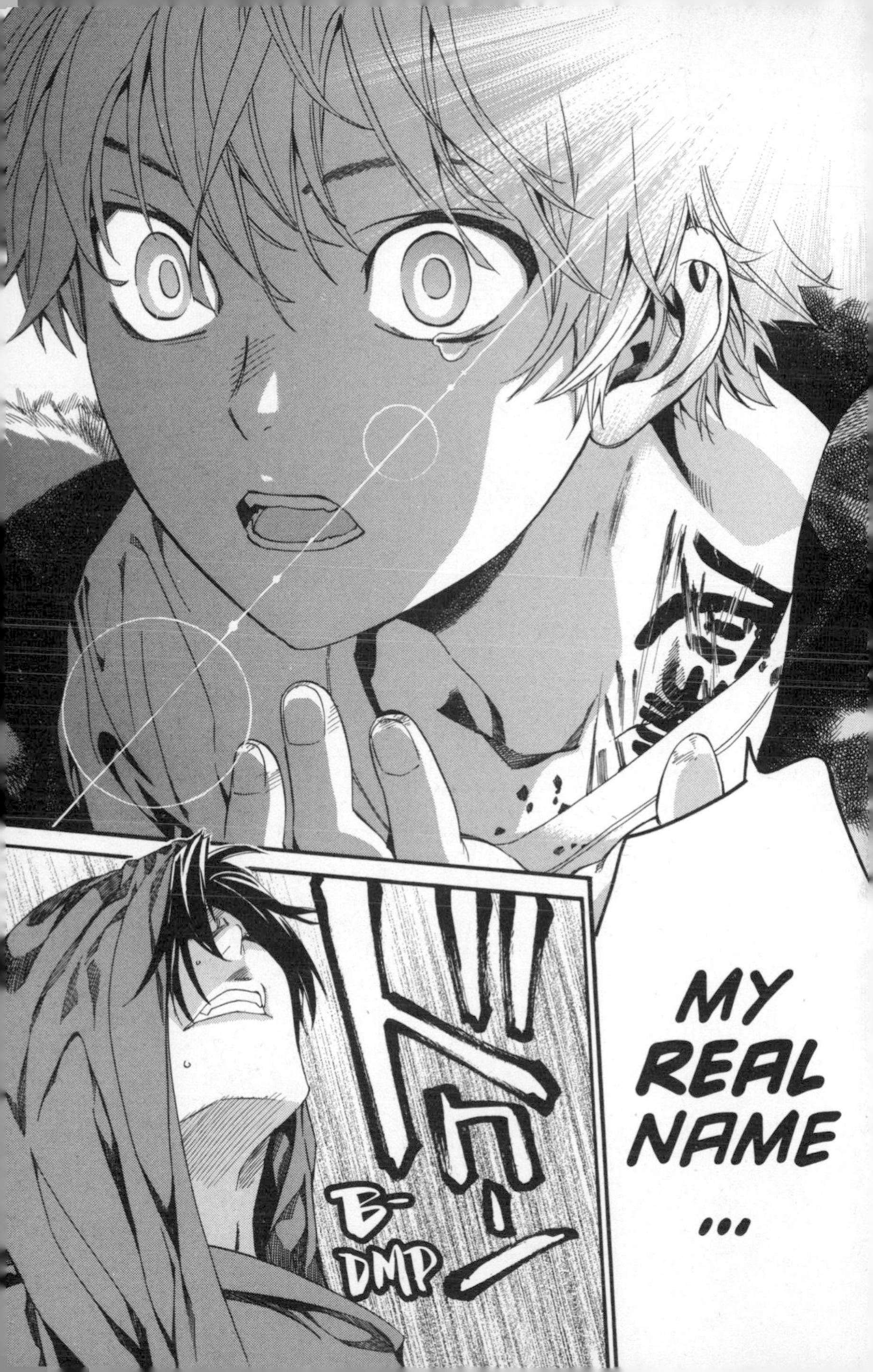
MY REAL NAME ...
B-DMP

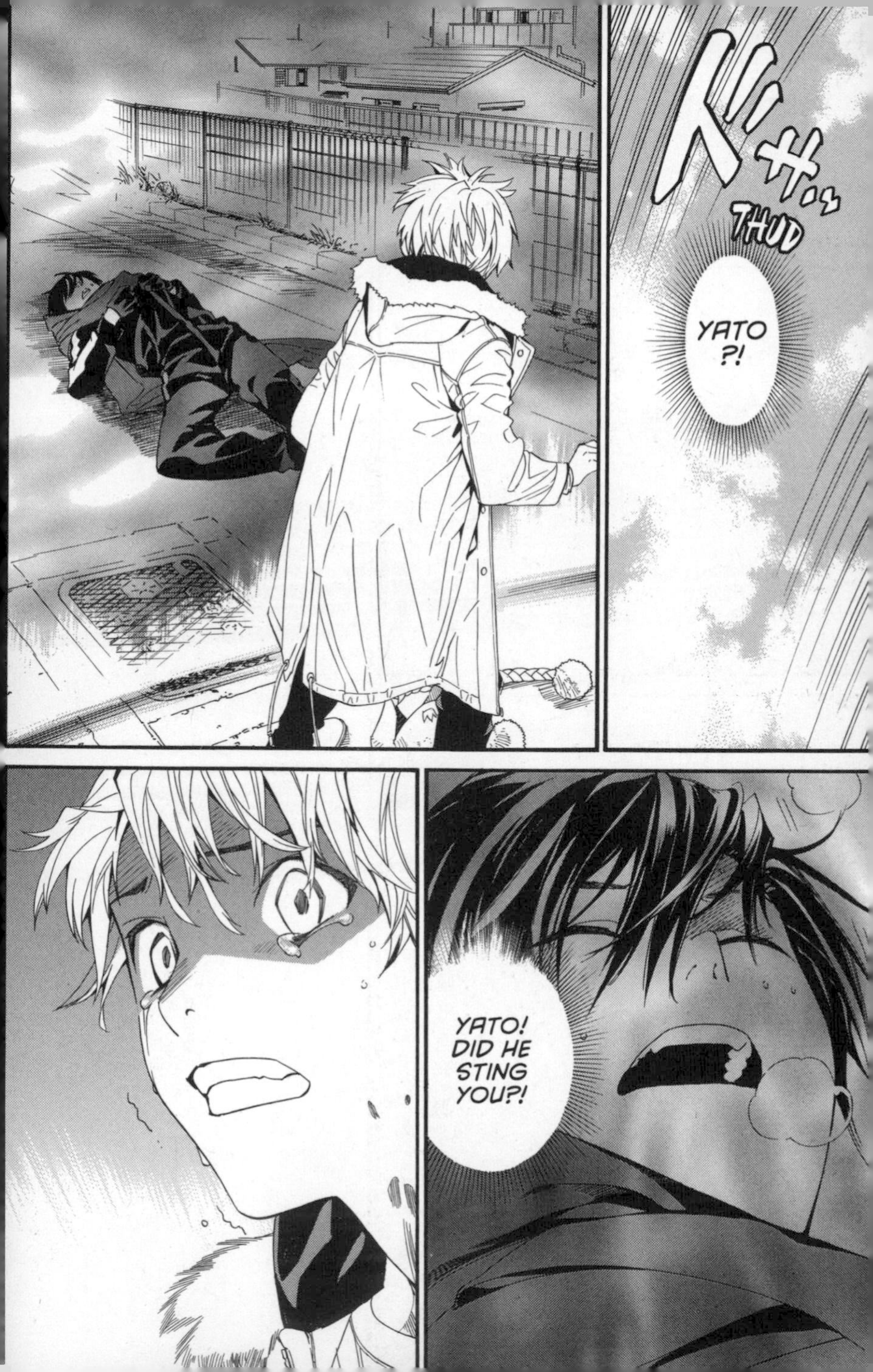
ドサッ
THUD
YATO?!
YATO! DID HE STING YOU?!

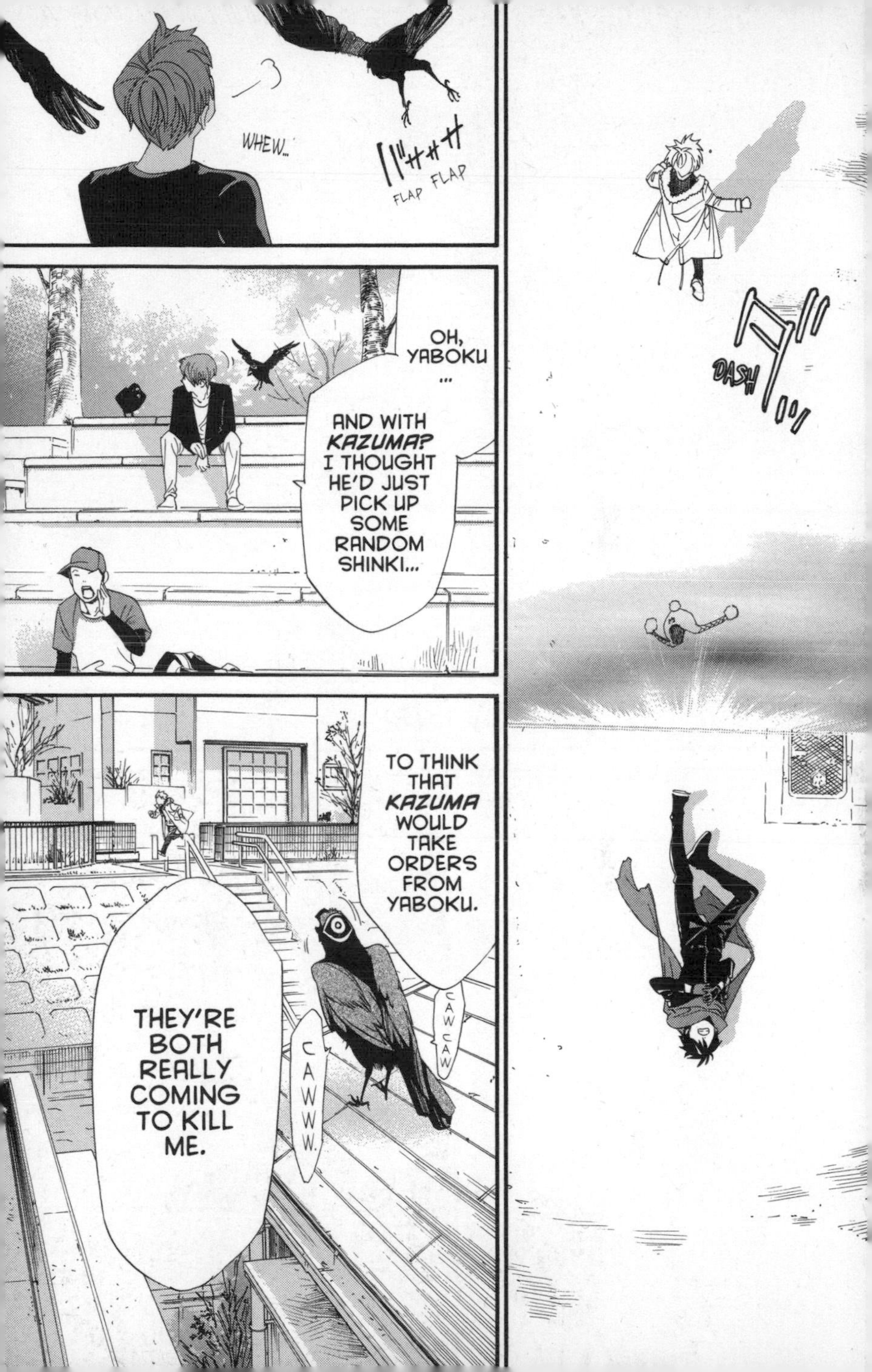
DASH
WHEW...
FLAP FLAP
OH, YABOKU...
AND WITH KAZUMA? I THOUGHT HE'D JUST PICK UP SOME RANDOM SHINKI...
TO THINK THAT KAZUMA WOULD TAKE ORDERS FROM YABOKU.
CAW CAW
CAWWW.
THEY'RE BOTH REALLY COMING TO KILL ME.

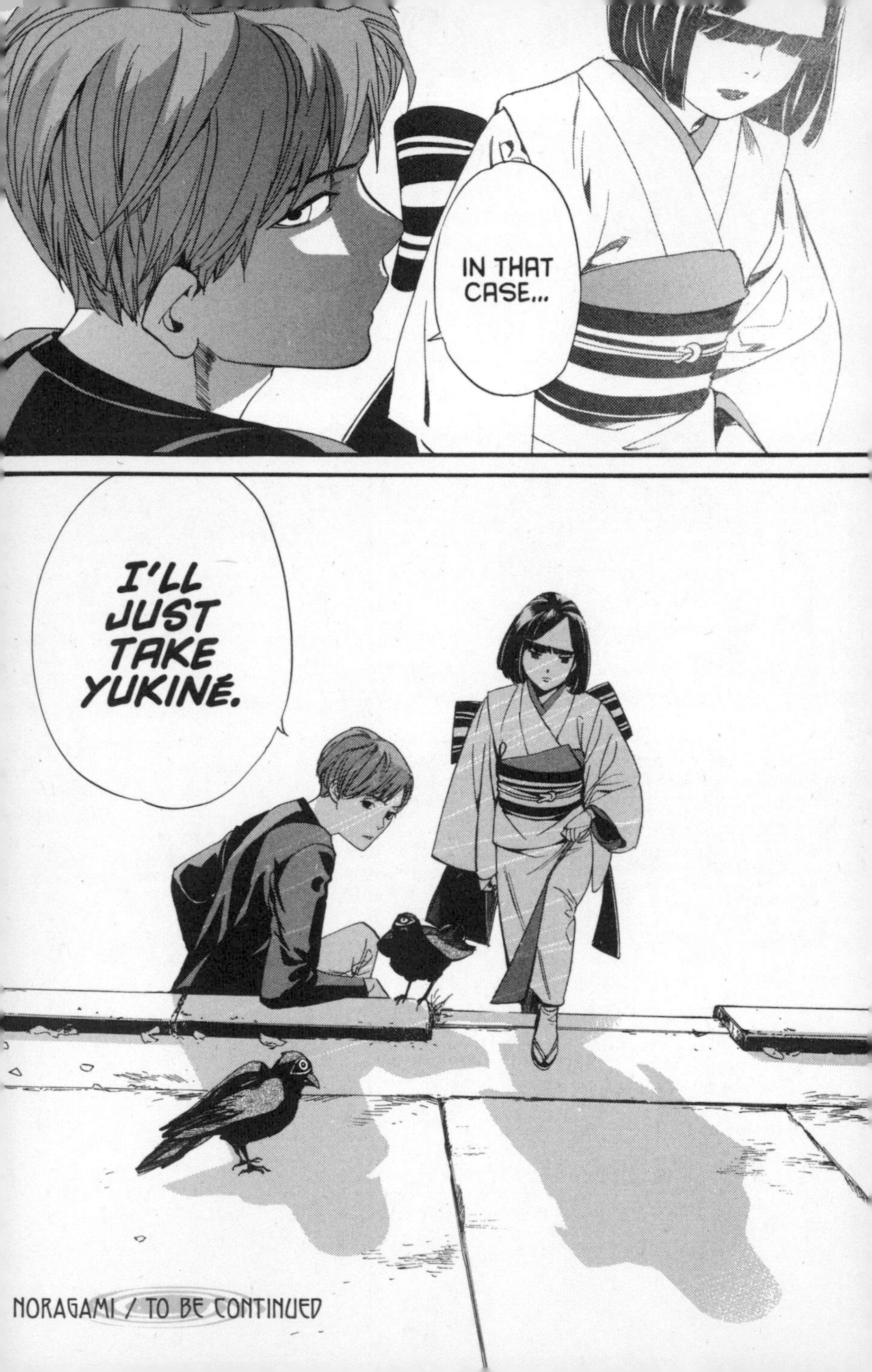
IN THAT CASE...
I'LL JUST TAKE YUKINÉ.
NORAGAMI / TO BE CONTINUED

野

道

神

ATROCIOUS MANGA

~ Také's Diary ~

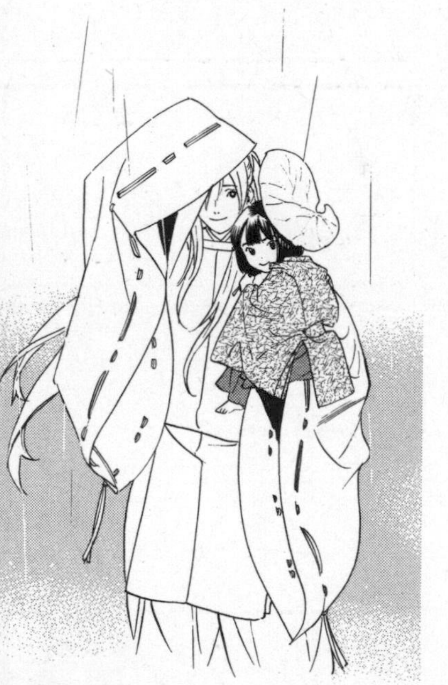

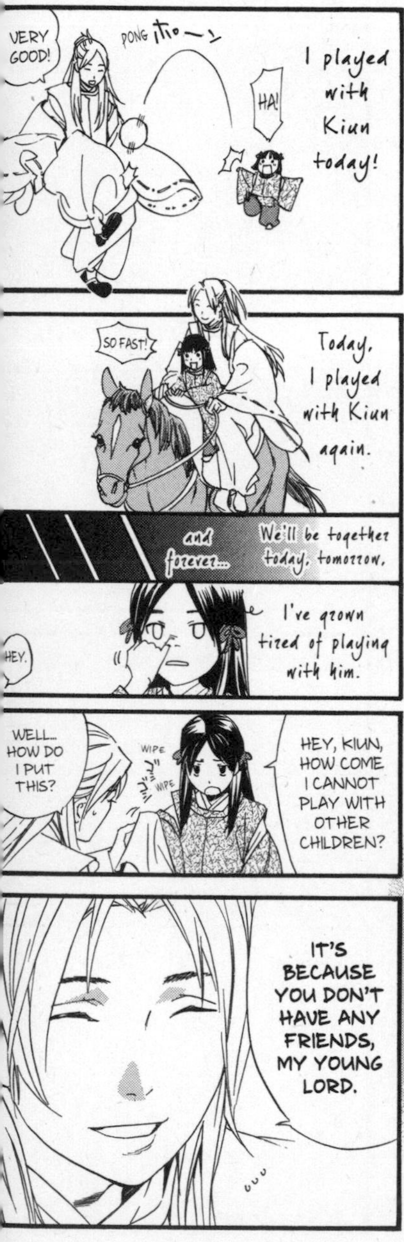
I played with Kiun today!
PONG
HA!
VERY GOOD!
Today, I played with Kiun again.
SO FAST!
We'll be together today, tomorrow,
and forever...
I've grown tired of playing with him.
HEY.
HEY, KIUN, HOW COME I CANNOT PLAY WITH OTHER CHILDREN?
WIPE
WIPE
WELL... HOW DO I PUT THIS?
IT'S BECAUSE YOU DON'T HAVE ANY FRIENDS, MY YOUNG LORD.

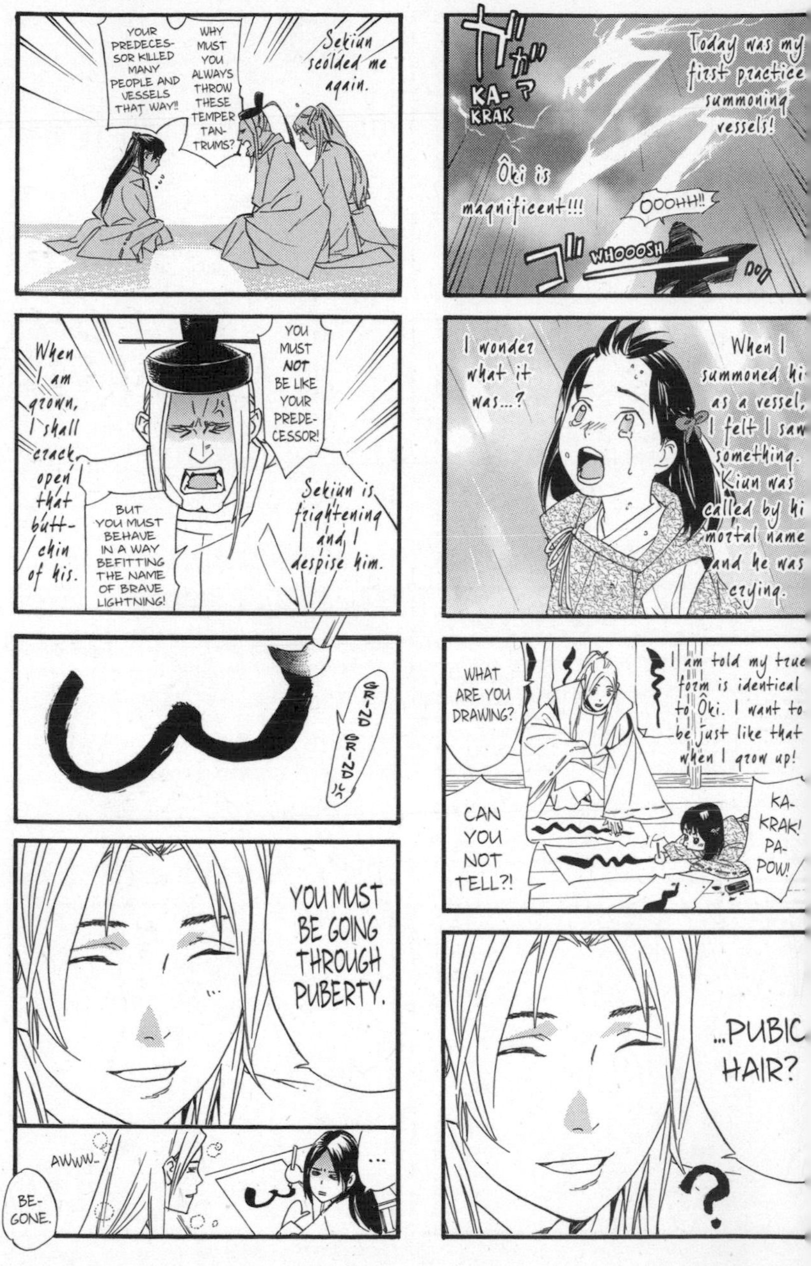

Today was my first practice summoning vessels!
KA-KRAK
Ôki is magnificent!!!
OOOHH!!
WHOOOSH
When I summoned hi as a vessel, I felt I saw something. Kiun was called by hi mortal name and he was crying.
I wonder what it was...?
I am told my true form is identical to Ôki. I want to be just like that when I grow up!
WHAT ARE YOU DRAWING?
KA-KRAK! PA-POW!
CAN YOU NOT TELL?!
...PUBIC HAIR?
Sekiun scolded me again.
WHY MUST YOU ALWAYS THROW THESE TEMPER TANTRUMS?
YOUR PREDECESSOR KILLED MANY PEOPLE AND VESSELS THAT WAY!!
YOU MUST NOT BE LIKE YOUR PREDECESSOR!
When I am grown, I shall crack open that butt-chin of his.
Sekiun is frightening and I despise him.
BUT YOU MUST BEHAVE IN A WAY BEFITTING THE NAME OF BRAVE LIGHTNING!
GRIND GRIND
YOU MUST BE GOING THROUGH PUBERTY.
...
...
AWWW...
BE-GONE.

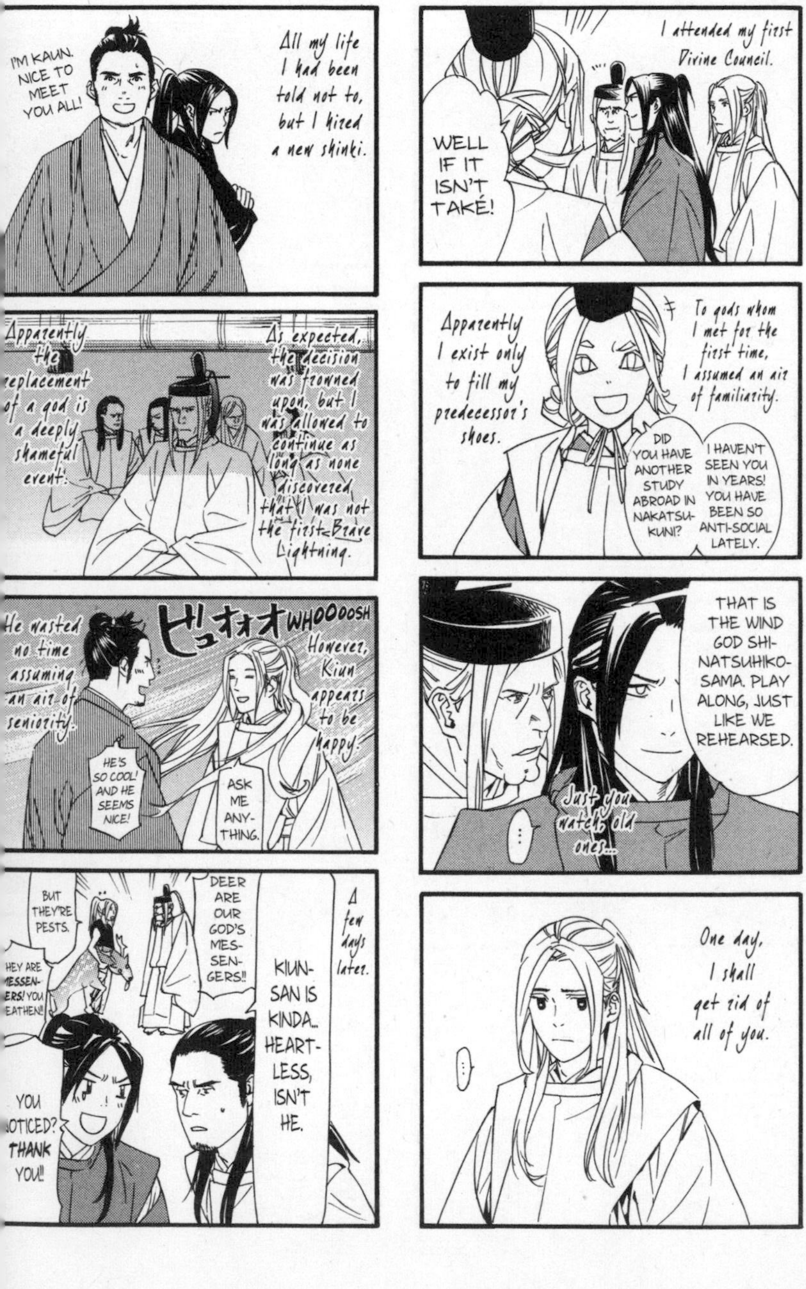
I attended my first Divine Council.
...
WELL IF IT ISN'T TAKÉ!
To gods whom I met for the first time, I assumed an air of familiarity.
Apparently I exist only to fill my predecessor's shoes.
I HAVEN'T SEEN YOU IN YEARS! YOU HAVE BEEN SO ANTI-SOCIAL LATELY.
DID YOU HAVE ANOTHER STUDY ABROAD IN NAKATSU-KUNI!?
THAT IS THE WIND GOD SHI-NATSUHIKO-SAMA. PLAY ALONG, JUST LIKE WE REHEARSED.
Just you watch, old ones...
...
One day, I shall get rid of all of you.
...
All my life I had been told not to, but I hired a new shinki.
I'M KAUN. NICE TO MEET YOU ALL!
As expected, the decision was frowned upon, but I was allowed to continue as long as none discovered that I was not the first Brave Lightning.
Apparently the replacement of a god is a deeply shameful event.
ビュオォオ WHOOOOSH
However, Kiun appears to be happy.
He wasted no time assuming an air of seniority.
ASK ME ANYTHING.
HE'S SO COOL! AND HE SEEMS NICE!
A few days later.
KIUN-SAN IS KINDA... HEARTLESS, ISN'T HE.
DEER ARE OUR GOD'S MESSENGERS!!
BUT THEY'RE PESTS.
HEY ARE MESSENGERS! YOU EATHEN!!
YOU NOTICED? THANK YOU!!

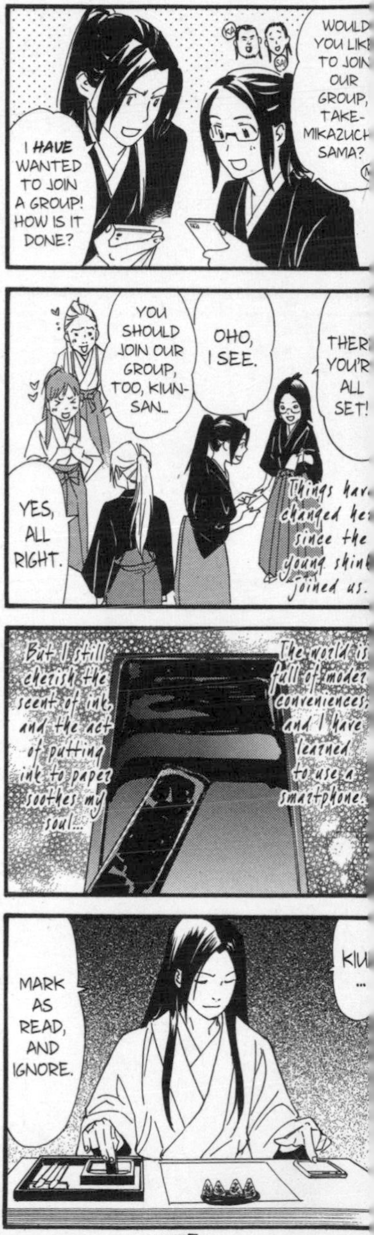
WOULD YOU LIK TO JOIN OUR GROUP, TAKE-MIKAZUCH SAMA?
I HAVE WANTED TO JOIN A GROUP! HOW IS IT DONE?
THER YOU'R ALL SET!
OHO, I SEE.
YOU SHOULD JOIN OUR GROUP, TOO, KIUN-SAN...
YES, ALL RIGHT.
Things hav changed he since the young shink joined us.
The world is full of moder conveniences, and I have learned to use a smartphone.
But I still cherish the scent of ink, and the act of putting ink to paper soothes my soul...
KIU ...
MARK AS READ, AND IGNORE.

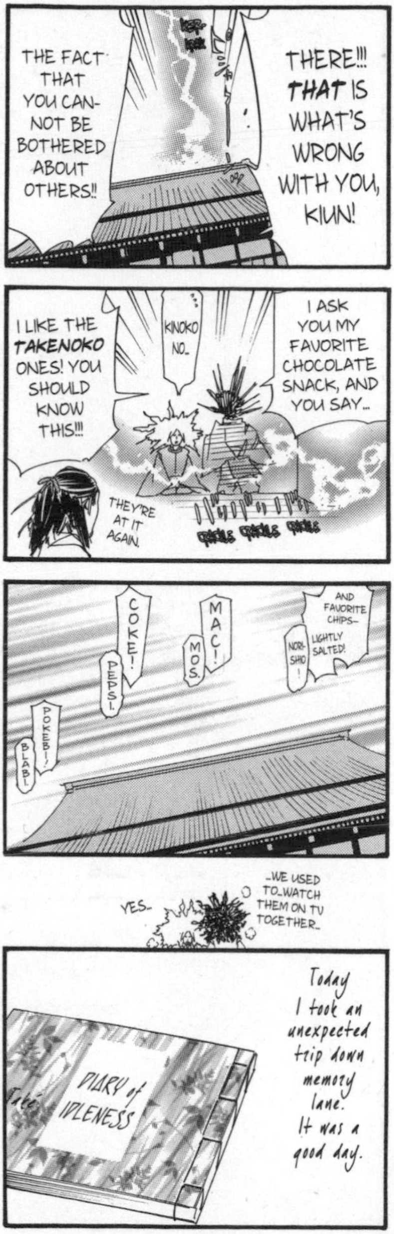
THERE!!! THAT IS WHAT'S WRONG WITH YOU, KIUN!
THE FACT THAT YOU CAN-NOT BE BOTHERED ABOUT OTHERS!!
I ASK YOU MY FAVORITE CHOCOLATE SNACK, AND YOU SAY...
KINOKO NO...
I LIKE THE TAKENOKO ONES! YOU SHOULD KNOW THIS!!!
THEY'RE AT IT AGAIN.
AND FAVORITE CHIPS—
LIGHTLY SALTED!
NORI-SHIO!
MAC!
MOS.
COKE!
PEPSI.
POKEBI!
BLABI.
...WE USED TO...WATCH THEM ON TV TOGETHER...
YES...
Today I took an unexpected trip down memory lane. It was a good day.
DIARY of IDLENESS
Take

THANK YOU TO EVERYONE WHO READ THIS FAR!

TRANSLATION NOTES

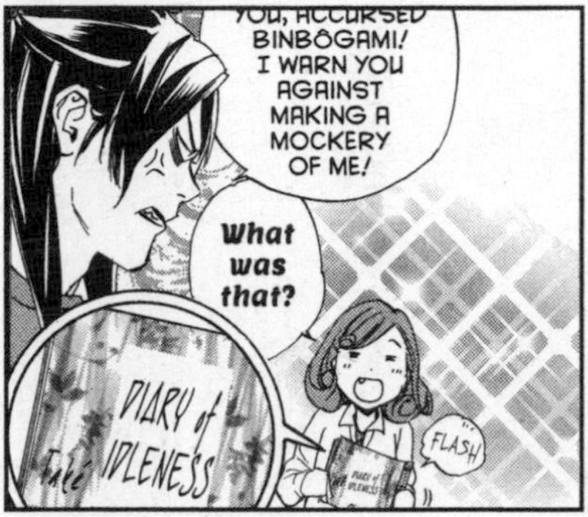
YOU, ACCURSED BINBÔGAMI! I WARN YOU AGAINST MAKING A MOCKERY OF ME!
What was that?
DIARY of IDLENESS
FLASH

Takemikazuchi's diary, page 6

While we only get a peek at Takemikazuchi's heartfelt verse, we can already see that he has used some of the symbols common to ancient Japanese poetry. The Asiatic dayflower is a common blue flower that was often used to dye clothes, but the color comes out easily in water, and so it can represent fickleness. And when a Japanese poet mentions "sleeves wet with dew," the "dew" is usually a metaphor for tears, indicating that the poet has been crying and wiping their eyes with their sleeves.

Inciteful, page 8

The Japanese title of this chapter is "*kotonoha*," which is an old-fashioned way of saying "word" or "words," as in the Word of Yomi. However, in the chapter title, the *kanji* used for *ha* is not the one commonly used (a *kanji* meaning "leaf"), but is one that means "beginning" or "trigger." Thus, the chapter title takes on a second meaning: "the trigger of events."

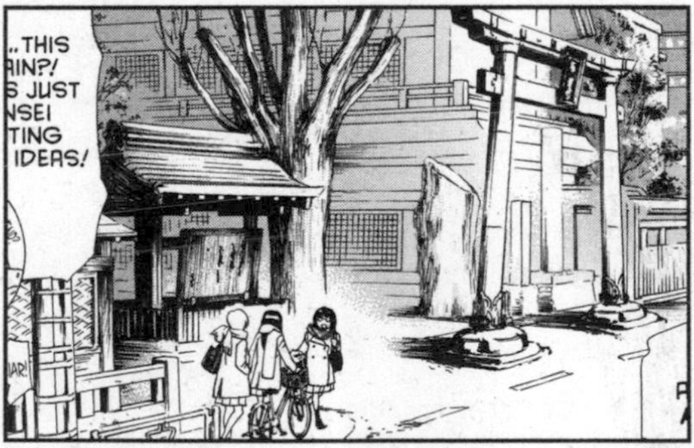
..THIS
IN?!
S JUST
NSEI
TING
IDEAS!

Tenjin Shrine, page 80

Here we see another shrine to Tenjin, where Hiyori faithfully stops to give an offering. This particular shrine is the historic Yushima Tenman-gû in Tokyo.

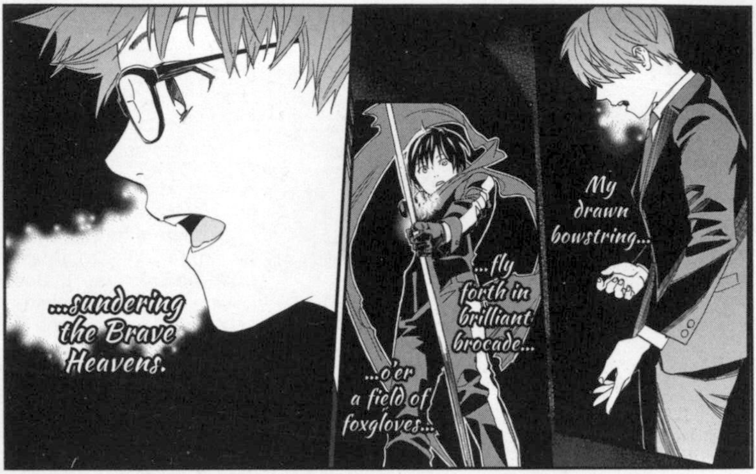
My drawn bowstring...
...fly forth in brilliant brocade...
...o'er a field of foxgloves...
...sundering the Brave Heavens.

My drawn bowstring, page 129

As Kazuma explains, this song is an anagram of the firefighting incantation Yukiné used in volume 11, and indeed the Japanese version of both poems use the exact same set of syllables. It may go without explaining that the same is not true for the English versions—even when Kazuma's poem uses the same word as the firefighting incantation, he uses a different meaning which doesn't have even the same sound as the original, much less a similar spelling. For example, the word *hari* in the original is used to mean "beam" or "rafter," while Kazuma's *hari* means "stretch" or "draw," as in "to draw a bowstring."

It is worth noting, however, that there is still some symbolism to be found in Kazuma's spell. "Brocade" is fabric woven in elaborate patterns, much like the brilliant pattern created by a barrage of fire arrows. Foxglove, or paulownia, is a tree associated with the Hô'ô, or Fenghuang, an immortal bird sometimes called the Chinese Phoenix. The "Brave Heavens (*takeki ame*)" are a direct reference to Takemikazuchi—the Brave Lightning.

Takemikazuchi's broken sandal strap, page 152

It may seem random that Takemikazuchi's shoe strap would break at this very moment, but in fact it is an omen of things to come. The breaking of a thong on a *zôri* or *geta* sandal is a sign of impending bad luck.

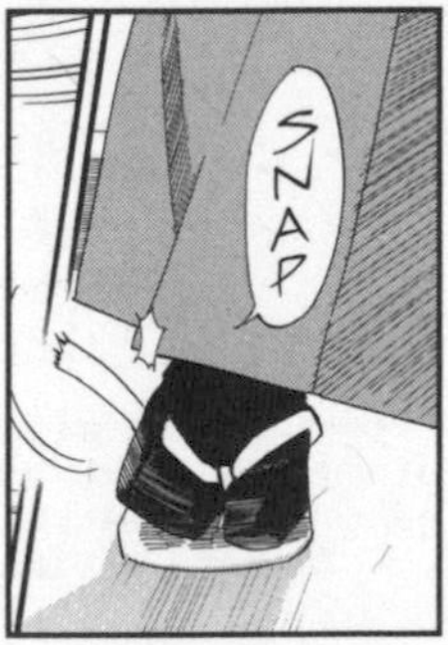
SNAP

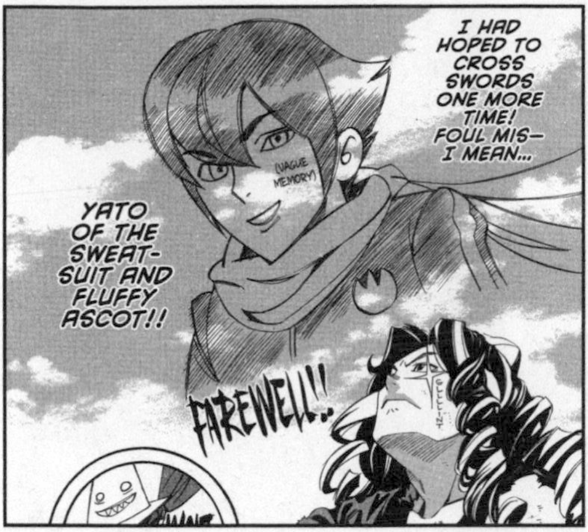
I HAD HOPED TO CROSS SWORDS ONE MORE TIME! FOUL MIS— I MEAN...
(VAGUE MEMORY)
YATO OF THE SWEAT-SUIT AND FLUFFY ASCOT!!
FAREWELL!!

Yato of the Sweatsuit and Fluffy Ascot, page 159

The Yato of Takemikazuchi's memory bears a striking resemblance to the classic manga character Cyborg 009, created by Shotaro Ishinomori. While Cyborg 009 (Joe Shimamura) does wear a scarf that looks something like Yato's ascot, the resemblance stops there.

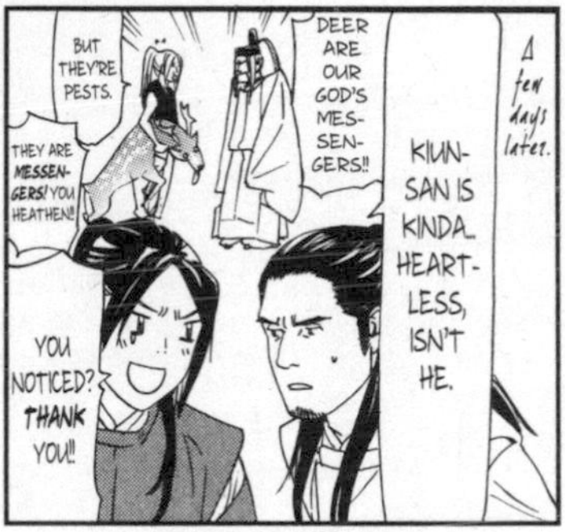
A few days later.
KIUN-SAN IS KINDA HEARTLESS, ISN'T HE.
DEER ARE OUR GOD'S MES-SEN-GERS!!
BUT THEY'RE PESTS.
THEY ARE MESSEN-GERS! YOU HEATHEN!!
YOU NOTICED? THANK YOU!!

Takemikazuchi and deer, page 190

Many years ago, Takemikazuchi-no-Mikoto visited Nara Park from his shrine in Ibaraki. He came riding a white deer, and the deer have been seen as his sacred messengers ever since.

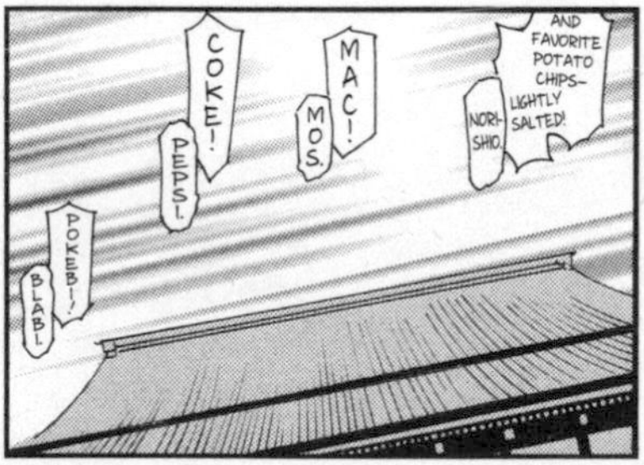
AND FAVORITE POTATO CHIPS— LIGHTLY SALTED!
NORI-SHIO.
MAC!
MOS.
COKE!
PEPSI.
POKEBI!
BLABI.

The Také-Kiun Wars, page 191

While the chocolate snacks have already been explained in a previous note (see vol.17), and the readers are likely aware of the rivalry between Coke and Pepsi, the other debates may be less familiar. *Nori-shio* is "seaweed-salt" flavor. While the McDonald's rivalry with Burger King is fairly well known in the West, in Japan, the Golden Arches' biggest competition is a home-grown fast-food chain called MOS Burger. They are the second biggest fast-food chain in Japan after, of course, McDonald's. Pocket Biscuits and Black Biscuits are only related to food insofar as they are named after biscuits. These are the names of two music groups that were formed in the late '90s, and they had a widely publicized rivalry.

身

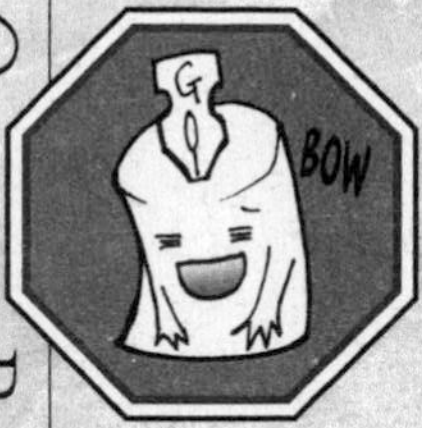
BOW

I actually always avoided drawing long-haired male characters because they gave me a hard time, but the anime inspired me to start putting them in the manga, too, and now I really like them. Having those challenges really can make life more fun in the future.

Adachitoka

‹ KAMOME ›
SHIRAHAMA

Witch Hat Atelier

A magical manga
adventure for
fans of Disney
and Studio
Ghibli!

Witch Hat Atelier © Kamome Shirahama/Kodansha Ltd

The magical adventure that took Japan by storm is finally here, from acclaimed DC and Marvel cover artist Kamome Shirahama!

In a world where everyone takes wonders like magic spells and dragons for granted, Coco is a girl with a simple dream: She wants to be a witch. But everybody knows magicians are born, not made, and Coco was not born with a gift for magic. Resigned to her un-magical life, Coco is about to give up on her dream to become a witch…until the day she meets Qifrey, a mysterious, traveling magician. After secretly seeing Qifrey perform magic in a way she's never seen before, Coco soon learns what everybody "knows" might not be the truth, and discovers that her magical dream may not be as far away as it may seem…

KC
KODANSHA
COMICS

Magus of the Library

Mitsu Izumi

MITSU IZUMI'S STUNNING ARTWORK BRINGS A FANTASTICAL LITERARY ADVENTURE TO LUSH, THRILLING LIFE!

Young Theo adores books, but the prejudice and hatred of his village keeps them ever out of his reach. Then one day, he chances to meet Sedona, a traveling librarian who works for the great library of Aftzaak, City of Books, and his life changes forever...

Acclaimed screenwriter and director Mari Okada (*Maquia, anohana*) teams up with manga artist Nao Emoto (*Forget Me Not*) in this moving, funny, so-true-it's-embarrassing coming-of-age series!

When Kazusa enters high school, she joins the Literature Club, and leaps from reading innocent fiction to diving into the literary classics. But these novels are a bit more... *adult* than she was prepared for. Between euphemisms like fresh dewy grass and pork stew, crushing on the boy next door, and knowing you want to do that *one thing* before you die—discovering your budding sexuality is no easy feat! As if puberty wasn't awkward enough, the club consists of a brooding writer, the prettiest girl in school, an agreeable comrade, and an outspoken prude. Fumbling over their own discomforts, these five teens get thrown into chaos over three little letters: *S...E...X...!*

Anime coming soon!

O Maidens in your Savage Season

Mari Okada   Nao Emoto

KC/ KODANSHA COMICS

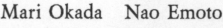

Yuri Is My Job!

JOIN US FOR AFTERNOON TEA WITH EQUAL PARTS YURI, ROM-COM, AND DRAMA!

miman

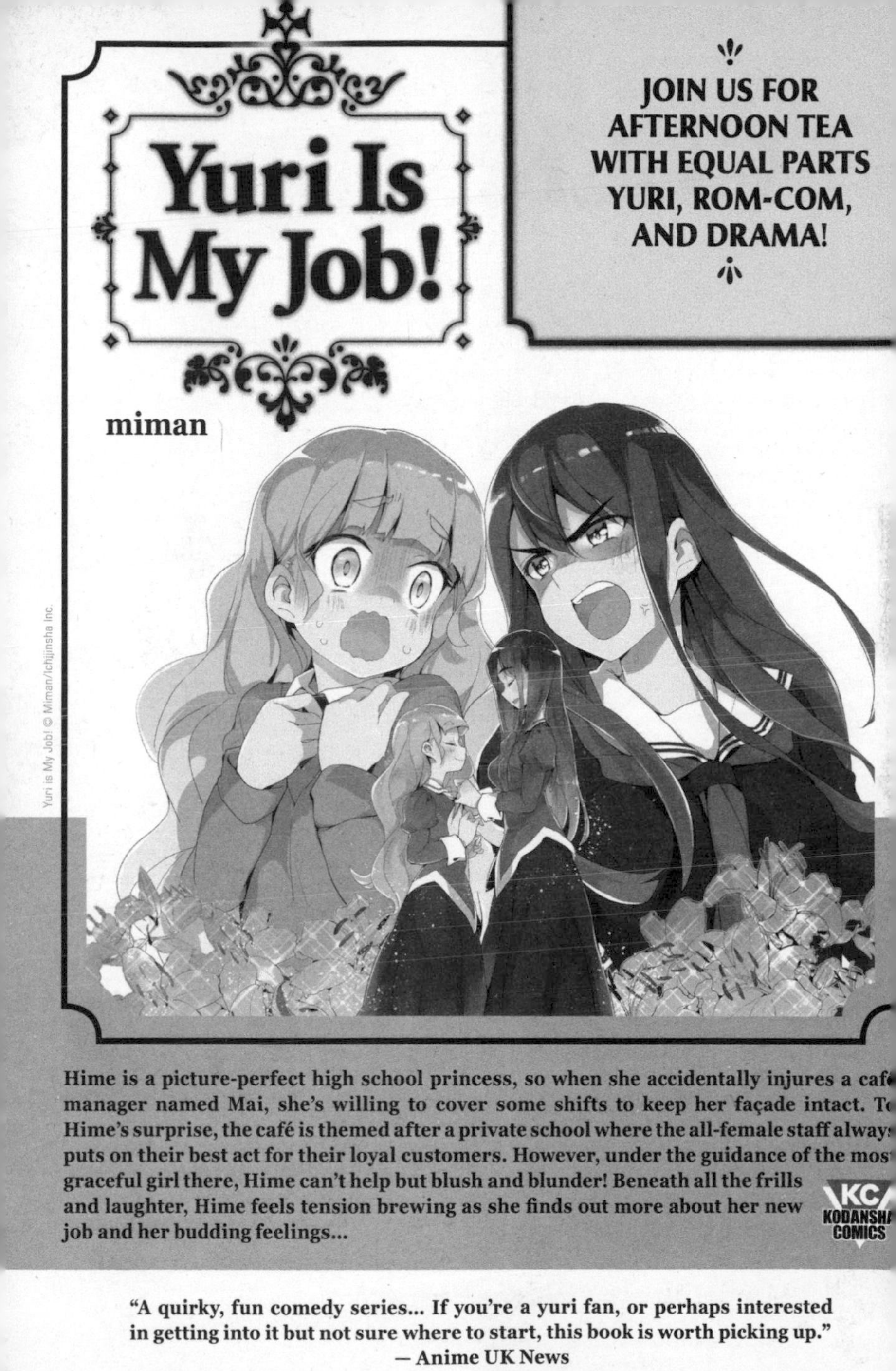

Hime is a picture-perfect high school princess, so when she accidentally injures a café manager named Mai, she's willing to cover some shifts to keep her façade intact. To Hime's surprise, the café is themed after a private school where the all-female staff always puts on their best act for their loyal customers. However, under the guidance of the most graceful girl there, Hime can't help but blush and blunder! Beneath all the frills and laughter, Hime feels tension brewing as she finds out more about her new job and her budding feelings...

KC KODANSHA COMICS

"A quirky, fun comedy series... If you're a yuri fan, or perhaps interested in getting into it but not sure where to start, this book is worth picking up."
— Anime UK News

EDENS ZERO
エデンズゼロ

HIRO MASHIMA IS BACK! JOIN THE CREATOR OF *FAIRY TAIL* AS HE TAKES TO THE STARS FOR ANOTHER THRILLING SAGA!

A high-flying space adventure! All the steadfast friendship and wild fighting you've been waiting for...IN SPACE!

At Granbell Kingdom, an abandoned amusement park, Shiki has lived his entire life among machines. But one day, Rebecca and her cat companion Happy appear at the park's front gates. Little do these newcomers know that this is the first human contact Granbell has had in a hundred years! As Shiki stumbles his way into making new friends, his former neighbors stir at an opportunity for a robo-rebellion... And when his old homeland becomes too dangerous, Shiki must join Rebecca and Happy on their spaceship and escape into the boundless cosmos.

CAN A FARMER SAVE THE WORLD? FIND OUT IN THIS FANTASY MANGA FOR FANS OF *SWORD ART ONLINE* AND *THAT TIME I GOT REINCARNATED AS A SLIME*!

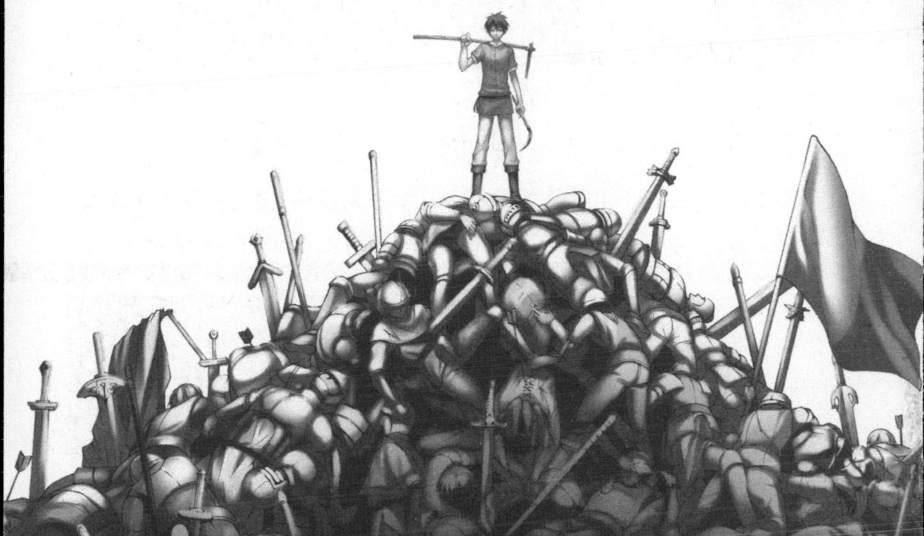

I'M STANDING ON A MILLION LIVES

By
Akinari Nao

Original Story by
Naoki Yamakawa

Yusuke Yotsuya doesn't care about getting into high school—he just wants to get back home to his game and away from other people. But when he suddenly finds himself in a real-life fantasy game alongside his two gorgeous classmates, he discovers a new world of possibility and excitement. Despite a rough start, Yusuke and his friend fight to level up and clear the challenges set before them by a mysterious figure from the future, but before long, they find that they're not just battling for their own lives, but for the lives of millions…

KC KODANSHA COMICS

Futaro Uesugi is a second-year in high school, scraping to get by and pay off his family's debt. The only thing he can do is study, so when Futaro receives a part-time job offer to tutor the five daughters of a wealthy businessman, he can't pass it up. Little does he know, these five beautiful sisters are quintuplets, but the only thing they have in common...is that they're all terrible at studying!

The Quintessential Quintuplets © Negi Haruba/Kodansha, Ltd.

THE QUINTESSENTIAL QUINTUPLETS

negi haruba

ANIME OUT NOW!

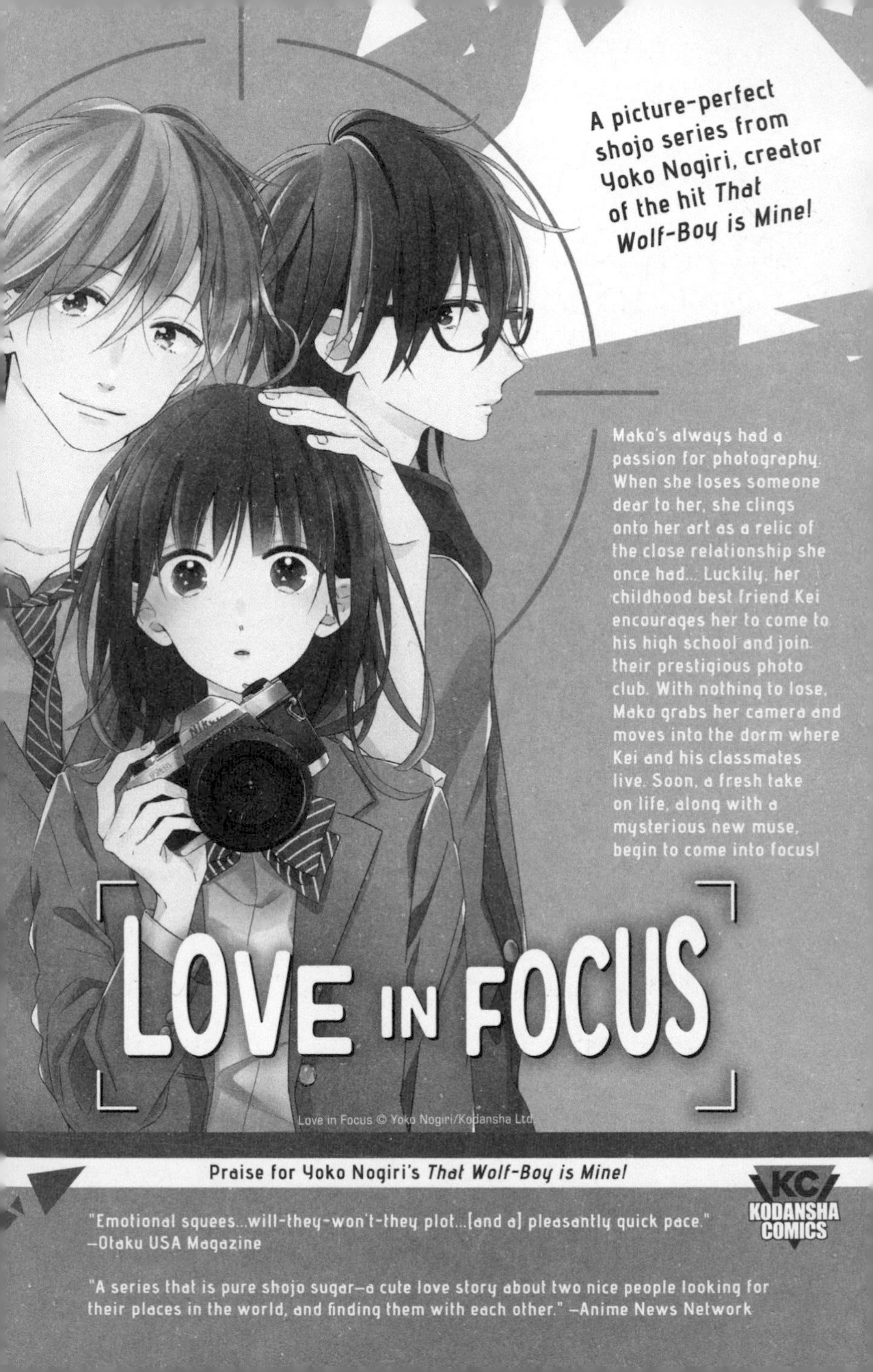
A picture-perfect shojo series from Yoko Nogiri, creator of the hit *That Wolf-Boy is Mine!*
Mako's always had a passion for photography. When she loses someone dear to her, she clings onto her art as a relic of the close relationship she once had... Luckily, her childhood best friend Kei encourages her to come to his high school and join their prestigious photo club. With nothing to lose, Mako grabs her camera and moves into the dorm where Kei and his classmates live. Soon, a fresh take on life, along with a mysterious new muse, begin to come into focus!
LOVE IN FOCUS
Love in Focus © Yoko Nogiri/Kodansha Ltd.
Praise for Yoko Nogiri's *That Wolf-Boy is Mine!*
KC KODANSHA COMICS
"Emotional squees...will-they-won't-they plot...[and a] pleasantly quick pace." –Otaku USA Magazine
"A series that is pure shojo sugar—a cute love story about two nice people looking for their places in the world, and finding them with each other." –Anime News Network

CARDCAPTOR SAKURA
COLLECTOR'S EDITION
C L A M P

Cardcaptor Sakura Collector's Edition © CLAMP • Shigatsu Tsuitachi Co., Ltd. / Kodansha Ltd.

Noragami: Stray God 21 is a work of fiction. Names, characters, places, and incidents are the products of the author's imagination or are used fictitiously. Any resemblance to actual events, locales, or persons, living or dead, is entirely coincidental.

A Kodansha Comics Trade Paperback Original

Published in the United States by Kodansha Comics, an imprint of Kodansha USA Publishing, LLC, New York.

Publication rights for this English edition arranged through Kodansha Ltd., Tokyo.

First published in Japan in 2019 by Kodansha Ltd., Tokyo.

ISBN 978-1-63236-849-2

Printed in the United States of America.

www.kodanshacomics.com

9 8 7 6 5 4 3 2 1
Translation: Alethea Nibley & Athena Nibley
Lettering: Lys Blakeslee
Editing: Haruko Hashimoto
Kodansha Comics edition cover design by Phil Balsman

KC
KODANSHA COMICS

Publisher: Kiichiro Sugawara
Managing editor: Maya Rosewood
Vice president of marketing & publicity: Naho Yamada

Director of publishing services: Ben Applegate
Associate director of operations: Stephen Pakula
Publishing services managing editor: Noelle Webster
Assistant production manager: Emi Lotto, Angela Zurlo